# Fundamentals of Security

Mark A. Rohlehr

Nora Rock

Ehsan Roshanafshar

**CONTRIBUTORS**
Darion Boyington
Jacob Davis-Mendelow
Scott Duncanson
Brine Hamilton
John Hubbell
Adrian Knetsch
Amit Rajput
Brian Robinson

emond • Toronto, Canada • 2018

Copyright © 2018 Emond Montgomery Publications Limited.

NOTICE & DISCLAIMER: All rights reserved. No part of this publication may be reproduced in any form by any means without the written consent of Emond Montgomery Publications. Emond Montgomery Publications and all persons involved in the creation of this publication disclaim any warranty as to the accuracy of this publication and shall not be responsible for any action taken in reliance on the publication, or for any errors or omissions contained in the publication. Nothing in this publication constitutes legal or other professional advice. If such advice is required, the services of the appropriate professional should be obtained.

We have attempted to request permission from, and to acknowledge in the text, all sources of material originally published elsewhere. If we have inadvertently overlooked an acknowledgment or failed to secure a permission, we offer our sincere apologies and undertake to rectify the omission in the next edition.

Emond Montgomery Publications Limited
60 Shaftesbury Avenue
Toronto ON M4T 1A3
http://www.emond.ca/highered

Printed in Canada.

We acknowledge the financial support of the Government of Canada. Canadä

Emond Montgomery Publications has no responsibility for the persistence or accuracy of URLs for external or third-party Internet websites referred to in this publication, and does not guarantee that any content on such websites is, or will remain, accurate or appropriate.

Vice president, publishing: Anthony Rezek
Publisher: Mike Thompson
Director, development and production: Kelly Dickson
Developmental editor: Nora Rock
Production supervisor: Laura Bast
Copy editor: Cindy Fujimoto
Permissions editor and indexer: Karen Hunter
Typesetter: SPi Global
Text designer: Tara Agnerian
Proofreader: Erin Moore
Cover image: Andrey Popov/Shutterstock

**Library and Archives Canada Cataloguing in Publication**

Fundamentals of security / Mark A. Rohlehr, Nora Rock, Ehsan Roshanafshar.

Includes bibliographical references and index.
ISBN 978-1-77255-272-0 (softcover)

1. Private security services—Textbooks.   2. Textbooks.   I. Rohlehr, Mark Anthony, 1956- . Introduction to the security industry.   II. Rock, Nora, 1968- . PSISA.   III. Roshanafshar, Ehsan. Report writing

HV8291.C3F86 2017       363.2'89       C2017-903978-4

This is dedicated to my wonderful wife, Jewel, and to my children, Danielle and Jordan, whose support and encouragement made this all possible. —MR

To my former students, with gratitude. —NR

This book is dedicated to my family, Maryam, Shahrokh, Shirin, Sheida, and my wife Jessica. Without their encouragement and support, this project would not have been possible. —ER

# Brief Contents

Detailed Contents .................................................... vii
Preface ............................................................. xiii
About the Authors ................................................... xvii

## PART I  Foundations of Security

1. Introduction to the Security Industry / *Mark Rohlehr* .................. 3
2. The Private Security and Investigative Services Act / *Nora Rock* ....... 17

## PART II  Core Skills

3. Basic Security Procedures / *Ehsan Roshanafshar* ....................... 39
4. Report Writing and Note Taking / *Ehsan Roshanafshar* .................. 65
5. Health and Safety / *Brine Hamilton* ................................... 85
6. Emergency Response Preparation / *Mark Rohlehr* ........................ 107
7. Canadian Legal System / *Nora Rock* .................................... 123
8. Legal Authorities / *Nora Rock* ........................................ 141
9. Effective Communications / *Scott Duncanson* ........................... 163
10. Sensitivity Training / *Darion Boyington* ............................. 187
11. Use of Force Theory / *Jacob Davis-Mendelow & John Hubbell* ........... 205

## PART III  Additional Skills and Topics

12. Security Issues in the 21st Century / *Amit Rajput* ................... 221
13. Crime Prevention Through Environmental Design / *Mark Rohlehr* ........ 235
14. Evidence and Investigation / *Ehsan Roshanafshar* .................... 251
15. Retail Security / *Brian Robinson* .................................... 261
16. Safes, Vaults, Locks, and Alarms / *Mark Rohlehr* ..................... 277

## APPENDIXES

A. Emergency First Aid ................................................. 295
B. Private Security and Investigative Services Act, 2005 ................ 313
C. Code of Conduct ..................................................... 327
D. Standard Radio 10 Codes ............................................. 329
E. The Security Guard Licensing Process ................................ 333

**Glossary** .......................................................... 337
**Index** ............................................................. 341
**Credits** ........................................................... 349

# Detailed Contents

Brief Contents .................................... v
Preface .......................................... xiii
About the Authors ................................ xvii

## PART I: FOUNDATIONS OF SECURITY

### 1 Introduction to the Security Industry ...... 3

Introduction...................................... 4
Early Security Initiatives......................... 4
    Feudalism and the Middle Ages................. 4
    1400–1750: The Emergence of Security Forces
    in Europe..................................... 6
Development of Security in the United States ...... 6
Development of Security in Canada ................. 7
The Security Profession in Canada Today ........... 8
    The Difference Between Private Security
    and Public Police............................. 8
    The Legal Authority of Security Guards........ 8
    Authority of the Police in Canada ............ 9
    Police Roles and Security Roles............... 9
    Professional Associations for Security Personnel .... 10
    Occupations Within the Security Profession ... 10
Reasons for Growth in the Security Industry ....... 11
    1. Growth in the Private Sector .............. 11
    2. The Technology Boom ....................... 11
    3. Crime Rates and the Perception of Security . 11
    4. Law Enforcement and Judicial System Gaps .. 11
    5. Cultural Changes .......................... 12
    6. "Cocooning" ............................... 12
    7. Threats of Global Terrorism................ 13
Chapter Summary .................................. 13
Key Terms ........................................ 14
References ....................................... 14
Performance Application .......................... 14

### 2 The Private Security and Investigative Services Act ............ 17

Introduction...................................... 18
Structure of the Act.............................. 20
    Overview...................................... 20
    Interpretation and Application ............... 21
    Administration................................ 24
    Prohibitions.................................. 24
    Licensing Requirements and Process............ 24
    Complaints and Investigations ................ 28
    General Duties and Standards of Practice...... 28
    Parts VII and VIII ........................... 29
Regulations and the Code of Conduct .............. 30
    Training and Testing ......................... 31
    The Code of Conduct .......................... 31
Chapter Summary .................................. 33
Key Terms ........................................ 34
Note ............................................. 34
References ....................................... 34
Performance Application .......................... 34

## PART II: CORE SKILLS

### 3 Basic Security Procedures................ 39

Introduction...................................... 40
Observational Skills.............................. 40
    Identification of Individuals ................ 40
    Identification of Objects .................... 41
Patrols .......................................... 41
    Patrol Planning .............................. 41
    Building Patrol Functions..................... 41
    Building Patrol Routes ....................... 42
    Site Coordination of Patrols ................. 42
    Foot Patrols.................................. 42
    Mobile Patrols ............................... 43
Situational Awareness ............................ 43
    The Physical Environment...................... 43
    The Human Environment ........................ 44
    Survival Mental State ........................ 44
    Heightened Recall ............................ 44
    Switching On and Off.......................... 45
Access Control ................................... 45
    The ABCs of Visitor Control................... 45
    Elements of a Good ID System ................. 47
Crowd Control..................................... 50
    Planned Events ............................... 50
    Cooperating with Law Enforcement.............. 51

viii   DETAILED CONTENTS

Vehicle and Traffic Control ........................... 51
   Authority Over Vehicular Traffic..................... 52
   Rules of the Road for Private Property ............. 53
   Active Traffic Management and Hand Signals ......... 53
   Stopping Traffic.................................... 55
   Starting Traffic ................................... 55
   Left Turns.......................................... 56
   Right Turns ........................................ 56
   Parking ............................................ 56
   Emergency Vehicles ................................. 57
   Enforcing Traffic and Parking Rules ................ 57
   Accidents........................................... 57
Shift Handover Procedure............................. 57
Drug and Alcohol Effects and Substance
  Abuse .............................................. 59
   Alcohol............................................. 59
   Drugs............................................... 59
Chapter Summary ..................................... 61
Key Terms ........................................... 62
Note ................................................ 62
References .......................................... 62
Performance Application ............................. 62

## 4  Report Writing and Note Taking........... 65

Introduction......................................... 66
Note Taking ......................................... 66
Purpose of Memo or Notebook ......................... 66
   Aide-Memoire ....................................... 66
   Background for Other Security Personnel
     and/or Police.................................... 67
   Grounds for Action ................................. 67
   Official Document .................................. 67
   Performance Measurement and Employment Record.... 67
Specifications and Safekeeping ...................... 67
Rules for Taking Notes .............................. 68
What to Note ........................................ 69
What's Important?.................................... 69
   WANTED.............................................. 70
   The Five Ws ........................................ 70
Report Writing ...................................... 71
   Reporting Basics.................................... 72
Distinguishing Facts, Inferences, and Opinions ...... 72
   Facts............................................... 72
   Inferences ......................................... 72
   Opinions and Judgments ............................. 73
Types of Factual Reports ............................ 73
   General Occurrence Reports (Initial Reports) ....... 74
   Form Reports ....................................... 74
   Specialized Reports ................................ 74
   Supplemental Reports ............................... 76
Basic Principles of Effective Report Writing ........ 77
Statement Taking..................................... 79
   Victim Statements .................................. 79
   Witness Statements ................................. 79
   Suspect Statements.................................. 79

How to Take a Statement ............................. 79
Chapter Summary ..................................... 81
Key Terms ........................................... 82
Reference ........................................... 82
Performance Application ............................. 82

## 5  Health and Safety ....................... 85

Introduction......................................... 86
The Ontario Occupational Health and Safety Act...... 86
   Introduction ....................................... 86
   Structure of the OHSA .............................. 87
   Health and Safety Representation ................... 88
   Health and Safety Representatives .................. 88
   Joint Health and Safety Committees ................. 88
   Certified Members .................................. 88
   More About the JHSC ................................ 89
   Employer Responsibilities with Regard to the JHSC... 90
   Duties of an Employer .............................. 92
   Duties of a Safety Supervisor ...................... 92
   Duties of a Worker ................................. 92
Workplace Accident Investigation..................... 93
   Reporting Requirements............................... 93
   Purpose of a Workplace Accident Investigation...... 93
   Domestic Violence................................... 94
   Procedures for a Workplace Accident Investigation.. 95
   Investigative Pitfalls ............................. 98
Hazards ............................................. 98
   Hazard Classification .............................. 98
   Hazardous Materials and WHMIS ...................... 99
   Hazardous Energy ................................... 104
   Engineering Controls ............................... 104
   Work Practices ..................................... 104
   Administrative Controls ............................ 104
   Personal Protective Equipment....................... 104
Chapter Summary ..................................... 105
Key Terms ........................................... 106
References .......................................... 106
Performance Application ............................. 106

## 6  Emergency Response Preparation.......... 107

Introduction......................................... 108
Fire Emergencies .................................... 108
   Training Requirements............................... 108
   Evacuation Procedures............................... 109
   Fire Is a Common Emergency—Be Ready ............... 110
Bomb Threat Response Emergencies .................... 110
   Elements of a Bomb Threat Response Plan ........... 111
   Bomb Threat Response Procedure .................... 112
Explosive Devices and Suspicious Objects ............ 115
   Identifying Explosive Devices ...................... 116
Observed/Reported Weapon or Active Shooter Situations ... 116
   Security Response .................................. 117
   Arrival of Law Enforcement ......................... 118

| | |
|---|---|
| Protection of Evidence | 119 |
| Collection and Preservation of Physical Evidence | 119 |
| Chapter Summary | 120 |
| Key Terms | 121 |
| Performance Application | 121 |

# 7 Canadian Legal System ... 123

| | |
|---|---|
| Introduction | 124 |
| The Canadian Legal System | 124 |
| Courts Divided by Area of Law | 125 |
| Appeal Courts | 128 |
| The Law of Evidence in Canada | 129 |
| Evidence Statutes | 129 |
| Other Sources of the Law of Evidence | 131 |
| The Evidence of Security Professionals | 133 |
| Preparing for Court | 134 |
| On the Day of the Hearing | 135 |
| Chapter Summary | 137 |
| Key Terms | 138 |
| Note | 138 |
| References | 138 |
| Performance Application | 138 |

# 8 Legal Authorities ... 141

| | |
|---|---|
| Introduction | 142 |
| Privacy Law in Canada | 142 |
| The PIPED Act | 142 |
| Privacy Safeguards on the Job | 143 |
| Protecting Property | 144 |
| The Trespass to Property Act | 144 |
| Prohibiting Entry Under the TPA | 145 |
| Arrest Rules Under the TPA | 146 |
| Requests to Vacate Premises: Practical Issues | 147 |
| Arrest Without Warrant for a Criminal Offence | 148 |
| Enabling Provisions | 148 |
| Steps to a Citizen's Arrest | 148 |
| Canadian Charter of Rights and Freedoms | 149 |
| Search Authority | 149 |
| Search With Consent | 150 |
| Search Without Consent | 150 |
| Protection of Persons Acting Under Authority | 150 |
| Excessive Force | 150 |
| Self-Defence Against Assault or Threatened Assault | 151 |
| Civil Action and the Security Professional | 151 |
| Public Relations Considerations | 151 |
| Provincial Offences Act | 151 |
| Liquor Licence Act | 153 |
| Definitions | 153 |
| Compliance by Consumers | 154 |
| Compliance by Providers | 154 |
| Enforcing the Rules | 154 |
| Controlling Entry | 154 |
| Removal of Offenders | 155 |

| | |
|---|---|
| Public Intoxication | 155 |
| Civil Liability | 156 |
| Residential Tenancies | 156 |
| Landlords Must Not Interfere with Tenants Without Reason | 157 |
| Evictions | 157 |
| Employment Laws | 157 |
| Conflict of Interest? | 158 |
| The Ontario Labour Relations Act | 158 |
| The Ontario Employment Standards Act | 159 |
| Chapter Summary | 160 |
| Key Terms | 161 |
| References | 161 |
| Performance Application | 161 |

# 9 Effective Communications ... 163

| | |
|---|---|
| Introduction | 164 |
| Image and Communication | 164 |
| Personal Appearance | 164 |
| Attitude | 165 |
| Security Professionals Are Customer Service Representatives | 166 |
| Effective Verbal Communication | 167 |
| Overcoming Communication Barriers with Active Listening | 167 |
| Communication During Conflict | 167 |
| Interviewing | 168 |
| How the Mind Works | 168 |
| Common Problems in Interviews | 169 |
| Voluntariness and Legality of Interviews | 170 |
| Interview Styles | 171 |
| Interview Skills Development | 173 |
| Listening | 173 |
| Deception | 174 |
| Preparing for an Interview | 176 |
| Note Taking in Interviews | 176 |
| The Use of Audio and Video During Interviews | 177 |
| Note Taking in General | 178 |
| Radio Procedures | 179 |
| Parts of a Hand-Held Radio | 179 |
| Radio Storage, Retrieval, and Inspection | 180 |
| Safe Use of Hand-Held Radios | 180 |
| Radio Procedures and Etiquette | 180 |
| Chapter Summary | 183 |
| Key Terms | 184 |
| References | 184 |
| Performance Application | 184 |

# 10 Sensitivity Training ... 187

| | |
|---|---|
| Introduction: Diversity in Canada | 188 |
| Immigration and Multiculturalism | 188 |
| The Canadian Human Rights Act and the Canadian Human Rights Commission | 191 |

The Ontario Human Rights Code and the Ontario Human Rights Commission... 191
Implications of Human Rights Legislation for Security Professionals... 192
Diversity and the Private Security and Investigative Services Act... 194
Diversity and Conflict... 195
Indigenous People in Canada... 197
Racial Profiling... 199
Chapter Summary... 202
Key Terms... 203
References... 203
Performance Application... 203

## 11 Use of Force Theory ... 205

Introduction... 206
Legal Authority and an Employer's Use of Force Policy Choices... 206
Canadian Association of Chiefs of Police (CACP) National Use of Force Framework... 208
　The Continuous Assessment Process... 209
　Taking Control, Assessing a Subject's Behaviour, and Choosing a Response... 209
　Identifying a Person in Distress... 209
　Matching Response to Behaviour... 210
　Soft and Hard Compliance Techniques... 210
　Lethal Force... 211
The Framework in Action... 211
Potential Consequences of the Use of Force... 213
Handling a Subject in Distress... 214
　Responding to Excited Delirium... 214
　Responding to Positional Asphyxia... 214
Chapter Summary... 215
Consequences of the Use of Weapons... 215
Key Terms... 216
References... 216
Performance Application... 216

# PART III: ADDITIONAL SKILLS AND TOPICS

## 12 Security Issues in the 21st Century ... 221

Introduction... 222
Technology on the Job... 222
Liability and Risk Management... 224
Terrorism and Security... 225
Cybersecurity... 226
Training and Education... 228
Security Guard Health... 228
Mental Health First Aid... 229
Uniforms and Professionalism... 231
Chapter Summary... 231

Key Terms... 233
References... 233
Performance Application... 233

## 13 Crime Prevention Through Environmental Design ... 235

Introduction... 236
CPTED Defined... 236
CPTED Concepts... 236
Application of CPTED Principles... 237
The Three Ds... 237
　Designation... 237
　Definition... 237
　Design... 238
The Nine Major CPTED Principles... 238
　1. Provide Clear Border Definition of Controlled Space... 242
　2. Provide Clearly Marked Transitional Zones... 242
　3. Relocation of Gathering Areas... 242
　4. Place Safe Activities in Unsafe Locations... 242
　5. Place Unsafe Activities in Safe Locations... 243
　6. Redesign the Use of Space to Provide Natural Barriers... 243
　7. Improve Space Management... 243
　8. Redesign Space to Increase the Perception of Natural Surveillance... 243
　9. Overcome Distance and Isolation... 244
Example 1: CPTED Applied to Storefronts... 244
　1. Natural Access Control... 244
　2. Natural Surveillance... 244
　3. Territorial Reinforcement... 245
　4. Management... 245
Example 2: CPTED Applied to Shopping Malls... 245
　1. Natural Access Control... 245
　2. Natural Surveillance... 245
　3. Territorial Reinforcements... 245
　4. Management... 246
Example 3: CPTED Applied to a Drive-Through... 246
　1. Natural Surveillance... 246
Example 4: CPTED Applied to Parking Facilities... 246
　1. Natural Access Control... 246
　2. Natural Surveillance... 246
　3. Management... 247
Chapter Summary... 247
Key Terms... 248
Note... 248
References... 248
Further Reading... 248
Performance Application... 248

## 14 Evidence and Investigation ... 251

Introduction... 252
Types of Security Investigations... 252

| | |
|---|---|
| Conducting an Investigation | 252 |
| Vehicle Accident Investigation | 252 |
| Evidence | 253 |
|     Types of Evidence | 253 |
| Expert Testimony | 255 |
| Standards of Proof | 255 |
| Admissibility of Evidence | 255 |
| Collection and Preservation of Physical Evidence | 255 |
| Evidence Control | 256 |
| Securing Evidence | 256 |
| Protecting Evidence | 257 |
| Control and Continuity of Evidence | 258 |
| Record-Keeping | 258 |
| Consequences | 258 |
| Chapter Summary | 258 |
| Key Terms | 259 |
| References | 259 |
| Performance Application | 259 |

## 15 Retail Security ... 261

| | |
|---|---|
| Introduction | 262 |
| Principal Sources of Loss | 262 |
| The Nature of Retail Crime | 263 |
|     National Figures | 264 |
| Categories of Shoplifters | 265 |
| Asset Protection | 265 |
|     Human Surveillance | 265 |
|     Closed-Circuit Television Cameras | 266 |
|     Electronic Article Surveillance | 266 |
|     CheckInk II | 266 |
|     Tamper-Evident Seals | 266 |
|     Signs | 267 |
|     Mirrors | 267 |
|     Merchandise Display | 268 |
|     Packaging | 269 |
|     Store Layout | 269 |
|     Fitting Room Policy | 270 |
|     Refund Procedures | 270 |
| Special Tips and Strategies | 271 |
|     Training Tips | 271 |
|     Undercover Security Tips | 271 |
| Chapter Summary | 273 |
| Key Terms | 274 |
| References | 274 |
| Performance Application | 274 |

## 16 Safes, Vaults, Locks, and Alarms ... 277

| | |
|---|---|
| Introduction | 278 |
| Electronic Access Control | 278 |
|     Types of Access Control Technologies | 278 |
| Biometric Access Control | 281 |
| Cabinets, Safes, and Vaults | 282 |

| | |
|---|---|
|     Safe-Keeping Needs | 283 |
|     Types of Filing Cabinets, Safes, and Vaults | 284 |
|     Security Filing Cabinets | 284 |
|     Safes | 284 |
|     Industry Standards for Security Safes in Canada | 285 |
|     How to Select a Safe | 286 |
| Locks | 286 |
|     Mechanical Locks | 287 |
|     Warded Locks | 287 |
|     Lever Locks | 287 |
|     Modern Pin Tumbler Locks | 287 |
|     Wafer or Disc Tumbler Locks | 287 |
|     Tubular Cylinder Locks | 287 |
|     Lock Evaluation | 288 |
|     Pick-Resistant Features | 288 |
|     Security Applications for Mechanical Locks | 289 |
|     Key Control | 290 |
| Alarms | 291 |
|     Alarm System Capabilities | 291 |
|     Elements of an Alarm | 291 |
|     Alarm System Monitoring | 292 |
| Chapter Summary | 292 |
| Key Terms | 293 |
| References | 293 |
| Performance Application | 293 |

## APPENDIXES

| | | |
|---|---|---|
| **A** | Emergency First Aid | 295 |
| **B** | Private Security and Investigative Services Act, 2005 | 313 |
| **C** | Code of Conduct | 327 |
| **D** | Standard Radio 10 Codes | 329 |
| **E** | The Security Guard Licensing Process | 333 |

| | |
|---|---|
| Glossary | 337 |
| Index | 341 |
| Credits | 349 |

# Preface

The provision of uniformed security services is the cornerstone of the security industry in Canada. Prior to the changes brought about by the Patrick Shand inquest in 2004, security guards in Ontario and across Canada were subject to varying standards of performance, training, and regulatory limitations. Collectively, these inconsistencies were responsible for the varying levels of manpower that security services provided to our communities, and many of the problems that occurred as a result. As students of security, it is essential that you understand the regulatory changes that have been implemented in response to the recommendations resulting from "Shand," and appreciate the significant impact these changes have had on the security industry itself.

The purpose of this book is to provide you with a fundamental and practical understanding of the elements of the security industry that are key to the provision of effective uniformed security services. It reviews the introduction of the *Private Security and Investigative Services Act, 2005* (PSISA) and provides context to the changes that this Act has introduced to the security industry since its implementation in 2007. The text also covers a variety of new or upgraded security service elements that have been developed due to new and emerging technologies, as well as the explosion of social media devices and the integration of web-based services with existing security service platforms.

The original 2005 edition of this book was divided into 7 parts comprising a total of 27 chapters. We attempted to cover as much of the spectrum of security fundamentals as possible in order to provide students with a comprehensive overview of the industry and its practices. (Note that this new edition is not being called a "second edition," due to the numerous changes that have been made to the content, structure, pedagogy, and authorship; it is, in many ways, a new book.) By contrast, while essential security principles and practices have been maintained, this edition focuses more on the core skills required by students interested in joining the security industry as licensed professionals, and incorporates the outcomes established by the Canadian General Standards Board (CGSB) for the training of uniformed security guards in Ontario and across Canada. Readers should note that the sequence and names of the first 11 chapters reflect the Ontario Government's training guidelines for security guards, while the 12th section in those guidelines (Emergency First Aid) is represented here in Appendix A. Furthermore, the end-of-chapter review questions have been designed and written to reflect the types of questions that appear on security guard licensing exams.

Part I of this new edition presents an introduction to the security industry that provides students with a logical and well-defined starting point for their studies. This is further enhanced by a review of the importance and scope of the PSISA and the extent to which its implementation has changed the security landscape in Canada.

Part II is the heart of this edition. Composed of Chapters 3 to 11, this section of the text contains the core skills that are essential to the new security practitioner. Chapters 3 and 4 deal with the topics of basic security procedures and report writing and note taking in detail, and provide excellent examples and references for the student. The importance of these topics to the rest of the training is emphasized in these chapters and referenced throughout the remainder of the text. Chapter 5 deals exclusively with the topic of occupational health and safety as it relates to the duties and responsibilities of proprietary and contract security guards in the workplace, and the delivery of security services covered by their individual mandates. In Chapter 6, "Emergency Response Preparation," the techniques and training required to plan for and respond to identified emergency situations are discussed, and several common emergency response scenarios are examined in detail. These include incidents of fire, planning and response protocols for bomb threats (including the use of IEDs, or improvised explosive devices), building evacuations, active shooter scenarios, and the collection and preservation of physical evidence at an incident scene. Chapters 7 and 8 offer a comprehensive overview of the Canadian legal system and the specific legal authorities under which security guards, private investigators, and other industry professionals provide their services to the public. Elements of these chapters support other areas of training and study for the student of security, such as the *Criminal Code* and Ontario regulations. Chapter 9 covers the essentials of effective communications for the security professional, both orally and in written form, and dovetails nicely with parts of Chapter 4, discussed earlier. The issue of sensitivity training, and its importance within the workplace, is discussed in depth in Chapter 10. Students are provided with an opportunity to discuss typical and newsworthy examples of situations where a lack of proper sensitivity training has exposed security guards and service providers to lawsuits, negative public opinion, and a loss of goodwill among its client base.

Finally, Chapter 11 discusses the critical topic of use of force. As previously mentioned, many of the changes to the security industry are due to the recommendations that were presented by the Shand inquest. Central to these changes was the requirement for the implementation of a consistent, measurable, and well-defined use of force mandate designed for the security industry that was itself aligned with the National Use of Force guidelines, and that defined and recognized the signs and symptoms of excited delirium and positional asphyxia.

Part III offers a range of additional and supporting topics essential to the well-rounded security student. It begins with Chapter 12, which examines various security issues in the 21st century. This chapter provides students with the opportunity to discuss, comment on, and conduct research into the many events and newsworthy occurrences that are covered by the media in Canada and abroad. It provides a view of what is to come in this field, and identifies several trends and potential areas of future service for the security professional. Crime prevention through environmental design (CPTED) forms the core of Chapter 13. Students are introduced to the origin and principles of CPTED, examine the "broken windows" theory, and are provided with an opportunity to review and discuss current examples of CPTED use in local communities and at well-known Canadian landmarks. Chapter 14 deals with the collection of evidence and the role of security guards and private investigators in supporting the police and other agencies in ongoing investigation. Elements of this chapter build on the preservation and management of evidence, and the chain of custody ("continuity of evidence") first introduced in Chapter 6. Finally, Chapters 15 and 16 offer a completely redesigned examination of retail security and the extensive range of physical security products and services offered under the umbrella of "safes, locks, and alarms." In the 12 years between editions, there have been many changes and upgrades to existing security products and the manner in which they are used. In addition, advances in technology, and the inclusion of the smartphone and other social media devices in the security realm, have changed the security landscape forever. Students must be mindful of how essential it is for them to have a thorough understanding of the capabilities and limitations of these devices, and of how these security products can be applied to address a security need.

## Acknowledgments

Unlike the original edition, this text has been prepared with the assistance of several authors. Thanks to their efforts, we have produced what we think is an excellent text for students preparing to enter the security industry. Thanks go to Darion Boyington, Scott Duncanson, Brine Hamilton, John Hubbell, Jacob Davis-Mendelow, Amit Rajput, and Brian Robinson for their contributions to this new edition, and to Adrian Knetsch for updating the section on managing traffic in Chapter 3. Thanks also to Neil Gonsalves for contributing Appendix E on the security guard licensing process, and for his work on creating the teaching supplements for this text.

The authors and the publisher wish to thank the following instructors for providing their helpful feedback during the development of this text: Mike Winacott, Georgian College; Amit Rajput, Conestoga College; Brine Hamilton, Fleming College; Pat LeBlanc, St. Clair College; Kevin Rowcliffe, Loyalist College; and Neil Gonsalves, Durham College.

## For Instructors

For information on obtaining the teaching resources available to instructors who have chosen this book for their courses, visit the For Instructors tab on the book's website: **www.emond.ca/security** or contact your Emond Publishing representative for more information.

# About the Authors

**Mark A. Rohlehr** is an accredited security professional, with experience in both the private and public sectors. His military career includes eight years as a Special Forces officer and Airborne Company Commander. He is the author of several works on security controls and systems, as well as the previous iteration of this text, *Fundamentals of Law and Security Administration*. He is a professor in the School of Law Enforcement at Seneca College, where he has been instrumental in the development and delivery of specialized curricula for private security courses, and post-graduate courses in business continuity and disaster recovery and response for the Advanced Investigations and Police Studies Program.

Mark is also the owner of Corporate Safety and Security Services. Established in 1998, CSSS provides a variety of services including crisis management and corporate security consulting for the entertainment industry, government facilities, airports, educational institutions, nuclear power facilities, and many other clients around the world, including in London, New York, Hong Kong, and Yemen.

**Nora Rock** is an Ontario JD (lawyer) working as the corporate and policy writer for LawPRO, the Lawyers' Professional Indemnity Company. Nora is author/co-author of several texts for high school, community college and university, as well as two novels for young adults.

**Ehsan Roshanafshar** is a certified Private Investigator in the province of Ontario and has been working as the Lead Investigator at Algonquin College since 2010. Ehsan is the program coordinator, developer, and instructor for the Public and Private Investigations program offered by the Police and Public Safety Institute at Algonquin. He has also developed the Ontario Basic Security Guard Training offered through Algonquin's Corporate Training Department to external bodies. Ehsan currently lives in Ottawa, Ontario with his wife, Jessica, and his German Shepherd dog, Gus.

## Contributors

**Darion Boyington** is an instructor in the Justice Studies program at Mohawk College.

**Jacob Davis-Mendelow** is an instructor in the Police Foundations and Protection, Security and Investigation programs at Humber College's School of Social and Community Services.

**Scott Duncanson** is an instructor in the Protection, Security and Investigation program at Conestoga College.

**Brine Hamilton** teaches courses in the Protection, Security and Investigation program at Fleming College and is the Coordinator of Security Operations at Trillium Health Partners.

**John Hubbell** is a professor in the School of Public Safety at Seneca College and the president of Watch Hill Security.

**Amit Rajput** is a professor in the Protection, Security and Investigation program at Conestoga College.

**Brian Robinson** teaches retail loss prevention in the School of Justice and Emergency Services at Durham College.

# PART I

# Foundations of Security

# Introduction to the Security Industry

## 1

## LEARNING OUTCOMES

When you have completed this chapter, you will:

- Have a basic knowledge and understanding of the origins and development of the security industry in general, in North America and, more specifically, in Canada.
- Be able to explain the difference in the role of police officers and the role of security guards.
- Be able to identify the trends that currently influence the profession.
- Be able to explain the legal authority of security guards, with reference to relevant legislation and common law.

| | |
|---|---|
| **Introduction** | 4 |
| **Early Security Initiatives** | 4 |
| Feudalism and the Middle Ages | 4 |
| 1400–1750: The Emergence of Security Forces in Europe | 6 |
| **Development of Security in the United States** | 6 |
| **Development of Security in Canada** | 7 |
| **The Security Profession in Canada Today** | 8 |
| The Difference Between Private Security and Public Police | 8 |
| The Legal Authority of Security Guards | 8 |
| Authority of the Police in Canada | 9 |
| Police Roles and Security Roles | 9 |
| Professional Associations for Security Personnel | 10 |
| Occupations Within the Security Profession | 10 |
| **Reasons for Growth in the Security Industry** | 11 |
| 1. Growth in the Private Sector | 11 |
| 2. The Technology Boom | 11 |
| 3. Crime Rates and the Perception of Security | 11 |
| 4. Law Enforcement and Judicial System Gaps | 11 |
| 5. Cultural Changes | 12 |
| 6. "Cocooning" | 12 |
| 7. Threats of Global Terrorism | 13 |
| **Chapter Summary** | 13 |
| **Key Terms** | 14 |
| **References** | 14 |
| **Performance Application** | 14 |

# Introduction

Security is not a new concept. The role of security guard existed in the earliest human societies, where certain individuals were charged with protecting themselves, others, and property from wild animals and rival tribes. Cave drawings and archaeological digs provide evidence that ancient nomadic peoples developed and enforced social and regulatory codes similar in purpose (though of course, not in complexity) to our modern-day justice system. Certain individuals were designated to maintain order and to enforce rules through tribal customs and practices passed down by word of mouth from generation to generation.

Since the beginning of modern history, the needs of society's property owners, business people, and political rulers have shaped the evolution of security. In medieval England, for example, landowners were required to clear brush, large rocks, and tall grasses that might conceal highway robbers on either side of the king's roads. Land was also cleared around military camps and castles to provide visibility and a clear field of fire to defenders. Around the same time, businesses and landowners began employing night watchmen for protection against thieves. These rudimentary measures find their modern counterparts in today's cleared areas that adjoin fence lines and borders, and in security patrols and surveillance cameras.

The notion of "security" suggests a stable and predictable setting in which people can go about their normal activities while feeling safe from intrusion or harm. Because the level of threat varies widely depending on a person's location or the nature of a person's business, the scope of modern security needs varies from situation to situation, reflecting not only our changing social structure, but also economic conditions, our perception of law and crime, and the influences of technology and social media.

Another development in modern security is increasing clarity with respect to the distinction between public and private security. Originally, "police forces" were more akin to private militias, established and maintained by property owners to enforce their rights against those of ordinary citizens. In modern times, ordinary citizens have their own protection, in the form of public police forces maintained by governments. As public policing has developed, the separate but related domains of law enforcement and private property protection have come into clearer focus, and two of the most important duties of security professionals today are to understand the extent and limits of their own role and to support the related role of the police through effective collaboration when they are called upon.

In the latter part of the 20th century, the evolution of technology and information management, and the influences of different forms of extremism that have found expression in the form of terrorism have had a profound influence on the work of security professionals. Now, in the 21st century, security services must be prepared for future challenges; but it's important to not forget the roots from which the field grew, and to study the evolution of security, which now affords a wide array of professional opportunities.

# Early Security Initiatives

## Feudalism and the Middle Ages

In early England, **feudalism** provided a very high degree of security for both the individual and the group. The Anglo-Saxons brought with them to England a culture of mutual responsibility for civil and military protection of individuals. They also brought the concept of the feudal contract, an arrangement by which an overlord provided arms and guaranteed

**feudalism**
medieval social system based on an exchange of military protection for protection and labour

the safety of **vassals** and their property. In exchange, vassals were required to work the land, give a portion of their crop to the overlord, and answer the call to arms to fight under the banner of the overlord when required.

In a world of constant warfare between men of power, the peasants' best chance at security was through this form of feudal allegiance. Although the gulf between rich and poor was incredibly wide, with little or no opportunity to change one's station in life, the system provided the stability necessary to permit the working of the land. The value of a peasant's allegiance depended on the power and cleverness of the overlord. Group security lay in group solidarity. The more formal systems of security that developed during the Middle Ages were largely refinements of this earlier system.

Post-Norman England, beginning with the rule of King John (1199–1216) saw the introduction of the idea of the rule of law through the negotiation of the Magna Carta ("great charter"). In a nutshell, this idea provided that a neutral system of laws was to have supremacy over the arbitrary edicts of whatever ruler was in power at that particular time. The Magna Carta incorporated a formal declaration of the individual's rights and of responsibilities between the state and its subjects and among the subjects themselves.

Judicial reforms during this era included the emergence of local juries and circuit judges to restrain the power of local sheriffs, and justices of the peace appointed to hear and determine criminal cases. The movement also began the complete separation of courts and the exercise of the rule of law from the whims and power of the king.

Related measures were specifically aimed at the enforcement of public order. The **Statute of Winchester**, enacted in 1285, was the first Police Act. It established local law enforcement and reorganized the old institutions of national police and national defence. The Act described the "duty of watch and ward," which enlisted every man to pursue and bring to justice felons whenever a "hue and cry" was raised. Every district was made responsible for crimes committed within its bounds. The gates of all cities were required to be closed at nightfall, and all strangers were required to give an account of themselves to the magistrates.

To control vice and crime at the local level, boroughs enacted their own ordinances (regulations) because organized agencies for the enforcement of such laws were virtually non-existent. However, these efforts had limited success. Privately established night watches and patrols were often the only protection citizens had against direct assault.

**vassal**
person who exchanged labour and loyalty for protection in feudal society

**Statute of Winchester**
legislation passed in 1285 that established local law enforcement in parishes throughout England

## FOCUS ON TECHNOLOGY

### Primitive Alarm Systems

Since the beginning of time, inventive humans have devised ways to detect intruders or threats and warn their allies of danger. Some simple examples include:

#### *Canary Martyrdom*

Miners traditionally brought domesticated canaries with them underground. The canaries, more sensitive than humans to deadly carbon monoxide fumes, would cease singing, lose consciousness (or die) if fumes reached dangerous levels.

#### *Snap, Crackle, Pop*

When camping alone in the bush, you may be concerned for your personal safety because of the possibility of predatory animals or strangers approaching your campsite while you were asleep. Some natural defences include positioning your campsite with clear sightlines in all directions and spreading a wide circle of dry twigs and leaves around your sleeping area. This will serve as a primitive alarm system: anyone or anything disturbing the dry twigs and leaves will make enough noise to warn you of danger or a possible intruder.

## 1400–1750: The Emergence of Security Forces in Europe

Security was one thing in a largely rural society controlled by kings and feudal barons; it was another thing entirely in a world swept by enormous changes. From about the 15th century, European explorers opened new markets and trade routes, creating an increasingly important merchant class whose activities came to dominate the port cities and trading centres. By 1700, the social patterns of the Middle Ages were breaking down. Urbanization of the population (migration of peasants into cities) and related poverty had led to increased crime that primitive public police forces could not contain effectively.

Different solutions evolved from attempts to deal with the problem. Individual merchants hired men to guard their property. Merchant associations created the merchant police to guard shops and warehouses. **Night watchmen** were employed to make rounds. **Agents** were engaged to recover stolen property, and various church parishes hired **parochial police** to protect their property and parishioners within major city districts.

In 1748, Henry Fielding, who was both a magistrate and an author, proposed a permanent, professional, and adequately paid public security force. He refined a system of foot patrols to make the streets safe, a mounted patrol for the highways, and created his famous "Bow Street Runners"—a group of amateur police volunteers or special investigators. During his jurisdiction, legislation was refined to include common rights to property, and the receipt of stolen goods became an offence.

**night watchmen**
guards hired by merchants in the 1700s to patrol their properties at night and to protect their shops and warehouses from thieves and vandals

**agents**
first private detectives hired by merchants and private owners to recover stolen property

**parochial police**
regional guards hired by clergy in the 18th century to protect church property and parishioners within major city districts or dioceses

# Development of Security in the United States

Across the Atlantic in the United States, public law enforcement was represented by the introduction of town sheriffs and federal marshals. In the early 1800s, sheriffs were elected by a town council and given the authority to maintain the law inside the town limits—they made arrests, investigated crime, and enforced town statutes. They were armed and expected to use deadly force in many circumstances, as most outlaws were armed and dangerous.

The US Marshals Service was introduced in 1789. A marshal's duty was to enforce the rule of the federal courts. Since marshals worked for the federal government, they had jurisdiction everywhere, but only to do specific jobs. One of those jobs was to apprehend fugitives from justice, and a marshal's authority could supersede that of a sheriff where apprehending a wanted fugitive was concerned.

The state of Texas took the concept of the tough, gun-slinging lawman to a new level. Originally formed in 1823, the Texas Rangers is one of the oldest state law enforcement agencies in North America. The typical ranger has been described as "an officer who is able to handle any given situation without definite instructions from his commanding officer, or higher authority" (Cox, 2009). The Rangers are part of the history of the Old West, and part of its mythology.

By 1844, New York had its first police department.

Henry Wells and William Fargo founded a freight company they called Wells Fargo and Company. In the 1850s and 1860s, Wells Fargo boasted a line of 1,500 horses and 150 Concord coaches. When gangs of thieves robbed their stagecoaches and bands of Indigenous people terrorized their passengers, they hired their own detectives and security guards to **ride shotgun** to protect their shipments.

Alan Pinkerton introduced "modern-day" security in Chicago when he opened the country's first private detective agency in the late 1880s. Pinkerton, originally from Scotland, became a deputy in Cook County at the same time that Chicago formed its first police force. He later became a special agent of the US Post Office Department, and finally

**ride shotgun**
job of riding atop Wells Fargo stagecoaches to protect passengers and cargo from robbers during the late 1800s

Chicago's first and only public police detective. It was while in that role that he conceived the idea of a private detective agency, originally constituted to protect railroad companies from train robberies. His agency provided investigators and trained guards for railroad companies and industrial organizations. The Civil War provided Pinkerton with a new opportunity: he was engaged to send agents into the South to spy for the Union. As well, he supplied personal protection for President Lincoln.

In 1859, Perry Brink and his wife Fidelia opened a freight and package forwarding company in Washington. In 1891, Brink's made its first payroll delivery and the Brink's armoured security service was born. By 1900, Brink's was transporting bank shipments, and in 1904, the company put its first gasoline-powered vehicle into service. Between 1918 and 1932, branch banking led to the establishment of Brink's offices and services in another 48 cities. In 2009, Brink's celebrated 150 years in business.

In 1909, William J. Burns, a Secret Service investigator for the president, challenged Pinkerton's service monopoly when he established a rival private detective agency. The American Banking Association hired Burns's agency to become its investigative arm. George Wackenhut, a former FBI agent, formed a security company in 1954. Today, Wackenhut is the second-largest security company in North America, while Pinkerton, Brinks, and Burns have remained big names in the security industry in both the United States and Canada. Until the founding of the Federal Bureau of Investigation in 1932, private companies (primarily Pinkerton and Burns) were the sole non-military providers of security and investigative services for the US federal government.

The demand for private security services in the United States has shown consistent growth over the past 200 years and is expected to continue to do so for the foreseeable future.

As in other industries, mergers have influenced the makeup of the security industry. A Swedish security company, Securitas AB, bought both Pinkerton and Burns International (in 1999 and 2000, respectively) and merged these two well-known companies into its multinational family, making Securitas the largest security company in the world.

# Development of Security in Canada

Pioneering in the Canadian prairies did not parallel the American's wild vigilante brand of law and order. In 1873, to avoid the mounting violence associated with American trade expansion into the Canadian prairies, Prime Minister John A. Macdonald created a paramilitary force of mounted police to stop the pillaging of tribal lands. The mission of the North West Mounted Police (NWMP), now known as the Royal Canadian Mounted Police (RCMP), included orders to gain the respect and confidence of the Indigenous peoples, to collect customs due on traded goods, and to enforce law and order. Within months of the creation of the first police outpost at Fort Macleod, the NWMP suppressed the growing lawlessness on Canada's western frontier.

The next challenge to Canadian security came in the form of railroad development. When the Canadian Pacific Railway (CPR) sought to build a rail line from the Pacific Coast to Eastern Canada, it encountered problems with theft, workers' strikes, and vandalism. In response, CPR began hiring its own security guards.

In 1885, after government surveyors threatened the Métis people with eviction from their lands if they tried to block the railroad's progress along the North Saskatchewan River, Louis Riel led his people in rebellion against the federal government. Outnumbered, the NWMP recruited Canada's first private force of 43 Prince Albert volunteers. When hostilities erupted, 12 of the 99-man volunteer police force were killed. Riel's victory was short-lived, however, when the railway delivered army reinforcements to crush his rebellion.

The use of volunteers to supplement the public police force and the introduction of railway guards marked the birth of private security in Canada. As the United States security market became saturated with security companies, established organizations such as Pinkerton, Brink's, and Burns looked north to sell their security systems and services to Canada's growing manufacturers, banks, institutions, and building developers.

## The Security Profession in Canada Today

As in the United States and in other places around the world, the distinction between public and private security has become sharper over time. Today, there is a clear division of powers as between members of public police services and private security professionals. Both categories of professionals derive their authority and their powers from specific, separate legislative sources, although it is common for police officers and security guards to cooperate effectively in protecting people and property.

### The Difference Between Private Security and Public Police

It will be important for you as a security professional to have a clear sense of the parameters of your work so that you can carry it out effectively without exceeding your mandate. Part of developing that understanding involves appreciating the difference in roles between police officers and private security guards.

Police officers serve the community as a whole and derive their authority from the *Criminal Code* (ss. 495 to 497), among other sources. They are charged with enforcing the law and are granted a wide range of powers, not available to private citizens, for that purpose.

While private security guards have the limited authority to take certain actions to enforce the law, they do not have the same positive duty of enforcement that police officers do, because the duty of private security guards is not to the community as a whole, but rather to private employers or clients.

This means that, in most cases, security guards are private employees with no special status or authority to enforce the law. There is, however, an exception: some private security guards are selected for special appointments that confer law enforcement responsibilities upon them; for example, appointment as "special constables." An example of this is the appointment of certain Toronto Transit Commission (TTC) security employees as special constables for the enforcement of the law on TTC property.

### The Legal Authority of Security Guards

Because they are employed by the private sector, and because their work relates primarily to the protection of property, security professionals are regulated primarily by provincial governments. This is because the division of powers created by the Canadian Constitution provides that the regulation of private property and commerce within a province is the responsibility of provincial governments.

Chapter 2 of this book is devoted to an overview of the main statute that regulates security professionals in Ontario: the *Private Security and Investigative Services Act* (see Appendix B). Many other Canadian provincial and territorial jurisdictions have similar legislation. The work of private security professionals is also shaped by provisions in many other statutes; for example, legislation prohibiting trespassing, legislation that creates quasi-criminal provincial offences (for example, violations of rules for the use of provincial parks), legislation governing alcohol, legislation designed to support the rights of employees, and much more. Some of these statutes are introduced in Chapter 8, which provides a more detailed overview of the legal authority of security professionals.

Finally, a few aspects of the work of security professionals are governed by the *Criminal Code*, a federal statute; but as you will learn, these provisions treat security professionals in almost the same way as all other private citizens are treated, although there are a few differences that reflect the fact that security guards are more likely than the average citizen to observe the commission of criminal offences.

## Authority of the Police in Canada

Because security professionals are expected to cooperate effectively with police, particularly when "handing over" criminal matters to them, it is useful for security professionals to have a basic understanding of the authority and structure of the police forces they may encounter.

In Canada, there are separate police forces governed by four different levels of government: federal, provincial, Indigenous, and regional/municipal. However, not all parts of Canada have all four types. Not all provinces have provincial forces, and only a few areas have regional/municipal police forces. Not all First Nations reserves have their own police forces. In fact, in some parts of Canada, provincial governments contract with the federal force, the RCMP, to enforce all aspects of the law, including provincial law. As a result, it is important for security professionals to learn which forces exist in the communities in which they work, and how those forces define their mandates. This will allow the seamless transfer of criminal matters over to police.

## Police Roles and Security Roles

As we have noted, the roles of police and of security personnel have become well defined. The main role of the police is to enforce the law. This includes:

- crime prevention,
- crime detection,
- apprehension of offenders,
- investigation of offences,
- supporting the enforcement of the law (by providing evidence to the prosecution),
- maintaining public order, and
- protection of the public and their property.

The primary role of private security personnel is not the enforcement of the law for the benefit of the state, but, rather, the protection of private property and of individuals for the benefit of a private employer. The specific duties that make up that role are discussed in detail in later chapters of this text.

There is obvious overlap between these two sets of duties because both police and security personnel perform protective, preventive, and detection functions. Where the overlap ends, however, is with respect to enforcement: while a private security guard may detect a crime, the enforcement of the law must be handed over to the police. While in some cases a security guard may make a citizen's arrest (more on this in Chapter 8, Legal Authorities and Chapter 11, Use of Force Theory), he or she is required to promptly report the situation to the police so that they can take the suspect into custody and proceed with an investigation, if appropriate. It is never appropriate for a private security professional to take action that would amount to the enforcement of the law, especially where this is done in a manner that may confuse the public about the security professional's role. In fact, section 130 of the *Criminal Code* makes it an offence for any person, including a security professional, to impersonate a police officer, and this includes confusing the public into believing that the security guard is a police officer. Included in that offence is the use of a badge or uniform to deceive the public about the nature of the individual's role.

## Professional Associations for Security Personnel

By 1954, security services in Canada had grown significantly. Security professionals banded together to form the Security Officers' Association of Ontario; later, a national association was created in the form of the Canadian Society for Industrial Security Inc. (CSIS).

CSIS is a professional organization that consists of individual and corporate members that represent industry and business in and outside Canada, as well as all levels of government and law enforcement agencies. A national board of directors meets four times a year to discuss policy issues and problems that relate to commercial, industrial, and institutional security. CSIS encourages members to air their concerns as it seeks to set high standards for security education and nationally accredited training programs. The organization also lobbies the federal and provincial governments for legislative changes that will benefit the security industry. One of CSIS's specific goals is to help provinces form security advisory committees that are mandated to set standards for the security industry within their respective regions.

CSIS provides a certification program that leads to a number of different types of professional accreditation for security professionals. The three initial types of certification are Certified Security Officer (CSO), Certified Security Supervisor (CSS), and Certified Security Professional (CSP). In general, certification depends on proof of completion of education and/or training programs that meet learning objectives set out by CSIS.

Certification/accreditation is intended to identify the recipient, within the marketplace, as a person whose training and knowledge in the area meets recognized professional standards. Maintaining CSIS certification requires payment of an annual fee, and recertification if the original certification is allowed to lapse.

Central to CSIS's emphasis on education and communication is its recognition of and support for the national magazine *Canadian Security*. Each edition of the publication has "how-to" articles, information on the increasingly rapid development of sophisticated security technology, and case studies of developments in the industry.

## Occupations Within the Security Profession

Security professionals perform a wide range of roles, and some of them are becoming increasingly specialized. Security training and certification can prepare an individual to serve in many roles:

- private investigator,
- security guard,
- close protection guard/bodyguard,
- door person/bouncer,
- retail loss prevention guard,
- armoured vehicle guard (usually for the transportation of money or valuables),
- security screener (for example, for airplane pre-boarding or entry to secure sites, like courthouses),

- security consultant (for example, a person who makes recommendations to businesses about the choice of security technologies or procedures), or
- installer of security technologies such as alarms, locks, or security lighting.

Depending on the nature of the work performed, security professionals may be hired as "in-house" security (that is, full-time employees of a single employer); may work on temporary contracts with various employers who hire them directly (many private investigators work this way); or may work for agencies that supply security professionals on contract to businesses or to individuals.

# Reasons for Growth in the Security Industry

Several factors are responsible for the current dynamic growth in the security industry. These factors reflect the cultural, industrial, political, social, and financial influences of our time.

## 1. Growth in the Private Sector

The Canadian economy is growing. Retail and manufacturing numbers are up. Building starts are up. Real estate is booming and home ownership has increased substantially in the last 15 years. Small businesses—especially in high-tech fields—continue to be formed. All of these require physical security and contingency planning.

## 2. The Technology Boom

Technology has allowed smaller companies to compete with large, established organizations. With the benefits of computer technology come risks associated with the exposure of sensitive personal and corporate information. In addition, the ability to manipulate and transmit large quantities of sensitive material increases the potential for theft of information and industrial espionage. The need to protect private, corporate, and government information has led to the rapid development of a security sub-industry dedicated to information security. Criminal enterprises associated with information technology such as hacking private databases to release information that will damage an organization's reputation, or a denial-of-access attack (ransomware) that installs a computer virus that "locks out" the owner of the database until a "bitcoin" ransom is paid to the hacker are just two examples of this growing phenomenon.

## 3. Crime Rates and the Perception of Security

Despite conflicting evidence—including statistics suggesting that the contrary is true—there is a prevailing public perception that the crime rate is increasing. This perception is heavily influenced by trends in media reporting and, regardless of accuracy, it tends to provoke fear. As we suggested earlier in this chapter, "security" requires not only actual safety, but also the perception of safety. This perceived gap in security has a negative impact on both quality of life and productivity and leads to an increased demand for security services.

## 4. Law Enforcement and Judicial System Gaps

Because funding for public policing is subject to political control, the level and quality of policing varies. Constant cuts to policing budgets have left some communities and

> ## Security Spotlight
>
> ### A Growing Industry
>
> Security is a large and growing industry in North America. It exceeds 1 percent of the American GDP. In a 2002 paper for the Canadian Department of Justice, Trevor Sanders analyzed Statistics Canada data and came to the preliminary conclusion that
>
>> employment in the field of Investigation and Security Services has increased by more than 60 percent during the 11-year period from 1991 to 2001. This figure is contrasted with an increase of less than 1 percent in the number of public police officers over the same time period.
>>
>> And the profession continues to grow: according to a CBC news report, there were approximately 70,000 active police officers—and 140,000 security guards—licensed in Canada as of 2013.
>
> Sources: CBC News, 2013; Sanders, 2002.

businesses feeling insecure about the ability of public law enforcement to maintain an expected level of service with decreased resources. This insecurity has led to increased demands for private security.

When offenders are given light sentences for hard crimes and criminal cases are dropped due to legal technicalities, overcrowded courts, or lack of investigative resources, the public doesn't feel safe. Criminal court caseloads are backlogged to such an extent that in 2016, after serving four years awaiting trial in Ontario, an individual charged with murder was released from jail and all charges were dropped. The perceived burdens on the justice system stimulate demand for increased private security.

## 5. Cultural Changes

Increased diversity in the Canadian population and the incorporation of foreign cultures and business practices into the broader Canadian culture can lead to conflicts between individuals and neighbourhoods. These conflicts sometimes manifest in criminal activity. Clashes between culturally identified gangs (for example, Asian gangs such as 14K Triad, Wo Shing Wo, and Luen Group) can lead to flare-ups of violence, especially in urban centres. Increased security can help business owners in these neighbourhoods feel safer.

## 6. "Cocooning"

With the advent of new entertainment and information technologies, agile workplaces, and the "work-from-home" business model, many individuals have embraced valuable technologies (IT and entertainment systems, etc.) that make their homes more attractive to break-ins. Specialized security services can provide protection for the owners of these new consumer and home business goods.

> ### Security Spotlight
>
> **Canada's First Private, Armed Tactical Response Unit**
>
> After the events of September 11, 2001, the Canadian Nuclear Safety Commission (CNSC) hired personnel from Globe Risk Holdings Inc. to provide immediate and effective armed security intervention at the Bruce nuclear facilities. Globe Risk was the first private security company in Canada to develop and train several armed tactical response teams in accordance with the CNSC mandate. Supplemented by tactical support from the Ontario Provincial Police (OPP), Globe Risk filled the gap until Bruce Power could train and implement its own rapid deployment teams.

## 7. Threats of Global Terrorism

The attacks on the United States on September 11, 2001 and the more recent attacks in Paris (on the offices of Charlie Hebdo on January 7, 2015 and the concert hall, soccer stadium, bar, and restaurant attacks on November 13, 2015), Brussels (on March 22, 2016), and Nice (on July 14, 2016) have made people and businesses feel more vulnerable to violence from international sources. More recently, on Monday, May 22nd 2017, Salman Abedi, a 22-year-old British man of Libyan descent detonated a bomb at an Ariana Grande concert in Manchester, England killing 22 and injuring 59, most of them teenage girls. Days later, three radicalized Britons were shot by police after driving a stolen van into pedestrians on the London Bridge and abandoning the vehicle to carry out knife attacks on persons in the Borough Market while wearing mock suicide vests in an attempt to maximize the terror event. People increasingly look to security services to conduct threat assessments, minimize risks, and guide them in preparing and implementing more effective security strategies.

> ## CHAPTER SUMMARY
>
> Since the first humans lived in caves, there has been a role for security. Security became more formalized in the feudal era, when a lord's protection was offered in return for tenants' work. Through the 17th and 18th centuries, escalating urbanization and trade growth led to demand for security innovations that included merchant police, night watchmen, agents to recover stolen goods, and parochial police to protect parish property.
>
> The 19th century brought the birth of the modern security industry in North America, and led to an increasingly clear distinction between the roles of police officers who are charged with enforcing the law, and security personnel hired by private employers to protect property and individuals. This chapter introduced the difference between police officers and private security guards and described the legal authority that supports the work of security guards, which includes provincial private security legislation, *Criminal Code* provisions that deal with self-defence and citizens' arrest, and a wide range of provincial/territorial statutes that contain provisions relevant to security work.
>
> This chapter also introduced the duties and roles of private security professionals, as well as the specific occupations in which they are employed. It concluded with an overview of the trends that shape the industry today, such as cultural and political challenges and rapid technological growth. These factors only serve to highlight the increasing demand for new and specialized security services both in Canada and around the world.

## KEY TERMS

agents, 6
feudalism, 4
night watchmen, 6
parochial police, 6
ride shotgun, 6
*Statute of Winchester*, 5
vassal, 5

## REFERENCES

*Canadian Security*. Magazine. Retrieved from https://www.canadiansecuritymag.com

CBC News. (2013, January 16). Surge in private security raises concerns over rights. Retrieved from http://www.cbc.ca/news/canada/surge-in-private-security-raises-concerns-over-rights-1.1335730

Cox, Mike. (2009). *A Brief History of the Texas Rangers*. Retrieved from http://www.texasranger.org/history/BriefHistory1.htm

*Criminal Code*, RSC 1985, c C-46.

*Private Security and Investigative Services Act, 2005*, SO 2005, c 34.

Sanders, Trevor. (2002). Department of Justice. *Rise of the rent-a-cop: Private security in Canada, 1991–2001*. Abstract. Retrieved from http://www.utpjournals.press/doi/abs/10.3138/cjccj.47.1.175

## PERFORMANCE APPLICATION
### Multiple Choice

1. How did the feudal socio-economic system meet the security needs of both lords and vassals?
    a. the political feuds took the place of armed warfare
    b. in return for the vassals' agricultural labour, lords offered protection in the form of security technologies and an organized army/security detail
    c. under the feudal system, there was no private property and therefore no need for security
    d. vassals performed security functions in exchange for a tithe (transfer payment) from medieval lords
    e. all of the above

2. Which of the following were important security challenges in the United States during the 1800s?
    a. train robberies and thefts from freight coaches
    b. secure locks and safes had not yet been invented, so all property had to be guarded by personnel, 24/7
    c. extreme corruption in the police service of the time meant that property needed to be protected from both criminals and the state
    d. continual warfare meant that most of the young male populace were out of the country for months at a time, leaving property unguarded
    e. none of the above

3. Canada's *Criminal Code* regulates private security professionals primarily as
    a. peace officers
    b. special constables
    c. members of the general public
    d. provincial law enforcement officers
    e. all of the above

4. The primary role of private security personnel is to:
    a. detect the commission of criminal offences on private property
    b. enforce the *Provincial Offences Act*
    c. maintain social order and control
    d. protect private property and private individuals
    e. provide assistance to the police

5. Which of the following are factors that have stimulated growth in security in the last several decades?
    a. private sector growth
    b. technological advances
    c. crime rates and the perception of security
    d. law enforcement and judicial system gaps
    e. all of the above

6. In-house security personnel:
    a. are not required to be formally licensed
    b. are directly employed by the organizations whose properties they are employed to protect
    c. work in indoor facilities only and are not trained to do vehicle patrol
    d. work for contract security guard service companies
    e. work only in locations closed to the public

7. In Canada, public police forces include:
   a. the Royal Canadian Mounted Police, provincial police forces, regional or municipal police forces, and Indigenous police forces on reserves
   b. the Royal Canadian Mounted Police and provincial police forces
   c. peace officers, army reservists, and security professionals
   d. the RCMP, the OPP, and municipal by-law enforcement officers
   e. law enforcement, security guards, and private investigators

8. Section 130 of the *Criminal Code* makes it an offence for any person to:
   a. work as a security professional without being licensed
   b. moonlight as a security guard while employed as a police officer
   c. falsely represent him or herself as being a police officer
   d. wear a security uniform while off-duty
   e. all of the above

## Short Answer

1. Research and list five security companies in your local area. What kinds of services do they provide? What kinds of clients do they serve?

2. What do you anticipate will be the primary challenges facing security in the 21st century? How are these challenges different from those of the previous two centuries?

3. Prepare a one-page profile of a criminal organization or gang that operates in this province. Include appropriate statistics, at least one photo, and a short narrative that can be delivered in three minutes or less in class, as instructed.

# The Private Security and Investigative Services Act

## 2

| | |
|---|---|
| **Introduction** | 18 |
| **Structure of the Act** | 20 |
| Overview | 20 |
| Interpretation and Application | 21 |
| Administration | 24 |
| Prohibitions | 24 |
| Licensing Requirements and Process | 24 |
| Complaints and Investigations | 28 |
| General Duties and Standards of Practice | 28 |
| Parts VII and VIII | 29 |
| **Regulations and the Code of Conduct** | 30 |
| Training and Testing | 31 |
| The Code of Conduct | 31 |
| **Chapter Summary** | 33 |
| **Key Terms** | 34 |
| **Note** | 34 |
| **References** | 34 |
| **Performance Application** | 34 |

## LEARNING OUTCOMES

When you have completed this chapter, you will:

- Be familiar with and understand the *Private Security and Investigative Services Act* of Ontario.
- Understand the licensing requirements for Ontario security guards.
- Know the rules with respect to uniforms, titles, and duties prescribed under the Act.
- Understand and be able to apply the Code of Conduct contained in a regulation made under the Act.

## Introduction

As you learned in Chapter 1, the role of private security is likely as old as the concept of exclusive property ownership. The public *regulation* of private security, however, is relatively recent.

Because early private security guards were employed by private businesses, the terms of their employment and the rules of their work were governed by private contracts made between the guards and their employers, and the employers got to make whatever rules suited their needs.

This same arrangement governs all types of work in developing societies, until the time comes that a government determines that there is a reason to intervene, and makes rules that override or supplement the terms that employers and employees make among themselves. In general, government intervention into private sector employment happens for one of two reasons: the protection of workers' rights or the protection of the public in cases where there is a perception that the public may be at risk due to the work being done by a private employee.

An example of a workers' rights intervention is the introduction, by a government, of a piece of legislation that sets standards for employment, for example, how long employees can be required to work without getting a break for a meal. In Ontario, that legislation is called the *Employment Standards Act*. The *Employment Standards Act* applies to most workers in Ontario, including private security guards and certain private investigators (those who have an employer).

An example of a public protection intervention is the *Regulated Health Professions Act*, a statute that imposes various requirements (training, licensing, etc.) on individuals who work in health care; for example, chiropractors and optometrists. This legislation is designed to ensure that when a member of the public visits, for example, a chiropractor, the patient can trust that the chiropractor has met certain standards appropriate to the profession and so will be able to provide health care in a safe way.

Private security services also have the potential to pose a threat to the public, because members of the public have been taught to obey the directives of peace officers, and to the public, security guards appear to serve some of the same functions as peace officers. Confusion about whether an individual is or is not a public law enforcement officer can give that individual inappropriate power over the public. Even where members of the public can tell that a worker is private, not public security, the profession carries with it an implication that the guard has been hired to impose consequences for inappropriate behaviour. A guard might be expected to quickly summon police in the event of a trespass incident, or even to make a citizen's arrest. These expectations mean that members of the public are likely to obey security personnel and so, if a security guard were motivated to use his or her uniform to manipulate peoples' behaviour or limit their freedom inappropriately, there might be a risk to the public.

In recognition of this risk, Ontario passed its first modern-era public security legislation in 1966. That statute was called the *Private Investigators and Security Guards Act* (PISGA).

The PISGA, when it was introduced, applied to only about 4,000 individuals in the province, partly because the profession was much smaller then but also because "in-house" private security guards and private investigators—that is, those who were employed by a single employer—were exempt from the application of the legislation and so did not need to be licensed.

The PISGA was also fairly rudimentary legislation in that the path to getting licensed was very basic—there was no standardized training, and the background check required for a licence was a search for federal convictions, outstanding criminal charges, and warrants. There was no requirement, for example, to search for criminal convictions for which the worker had been pardoned, or for convictions under provincial or territorial statutes. Licences expired automatically and had to be applied for through the agency for which the security guard worked, meaning that if he or she changed companies, he or she would need a new licence. There was no tribunal established for hearing appeals of licensing decisions. There was also no process for investigating public complaints about a security professional.

By the beginning of the 21st century, there was a growing consensus that the legislation needed a very significant revision. The private security profession had evolved significantly: the kinds of security personnel working in the province had become much more diverse and, in some cases, the kinds of risks that security professionals were guarding against had become very specialized. A basic background check no longer seemed like enough assurance, for the public, that the individuals protecting sensitive assets such as nuclear plants, large arenas, transportation, and information networks had the background and training needed to keep people safe.

And so government policy personnel began a process of consultation with stakeholders to find out what kinds of issues needed to be covered in a new legislative scheme. The private security sector was consulted, as well as those in public policing and many other sectors of the economy that use security services, such as retail, travel, banking, insurance, health care, colleges and universities, and unions.

In 2005, public hearings on new draft legislation for the private security industry began, and in December 2005 the new legislation, the *Private Security and Investigative Services Act*, 2005 (PSISA), was created. It was proclaimed in force in 2006. (See Appendix B.)

Other Canadian jurisdictions, including British Columbia, Alberta, Manitoba, Quebec, and Nova Scotia, were going through the same process around the same time. For an overview of private security industry legislation across the country, see Figure 2.1.

**Figure 2.1**  Overview of Private Security Legislation Across Canada

| Province/Territory | Act |
| --- | --- |
| AB | Security Services and Investigators Act, SA 2008, c S-4.7<br>http://www.canlii.org/en/ab/laws/stat/sa-2008-c-s-4.7 |
| BC | Security Services Act, SBC 2007, c 30<br>http://www.canlii.org/en/bc/laws/stat/sbc-2007-c-30 |
| MB | The Private Investigators and Security Guards Act, CCSM c P132<br>http://www.canlii.org/en/mb/laws/stat/ccsm-c-p132 |
| NB | Private Investigators and Security Services Act, RSNB 2011, c 209<br>https://www.canlii.org/en/nb/laws/stat/rsnb-2011-c-209/latest/rsnb-2011-c-209.html |
| NL | Private Investigators and Security Services Act, RSNL 1990, c P-24<br>http://www.canlii.org/en/nl/laws/stat/rsnl-1990-c-p-24 |
| NS | Private Investigators and Security Guards Act, RSNS 1989, c 356<br>http://www.canlii.org/en/ns/laws/stat/rsns-1989-c-356<br>Security and Investigative Services Act, SNS 2010, c 9 (not yet in force)<br>https://www.canlii.org/en/ns/laws/stat/sns-2010-c-9/latest/sns-2010-c-9.html |
| ON | Private Security and Investigative Services Act, 2005, SO 2005, c 34<br>http://www.canlii.org/en/on/laws/stat/so-2005-c-34 |
| PE | Private Investigators and Security Guards Act, RSPEI 1988, c P-20<br>http://www.canlii.org/en/pe/laws/stat/rspei-1988-c-p-20 |
| QC | Private Security Act, CQLR c S-3.5<br>http://www.canlii.org/en/qc/laws/stat/rsq-c-s-3.5 |
| SK | Private Investigators and Security Guards Act, 1997, SS 1997, c P-26.01<br>http://www.canlii.org/en/sk/laws/stat/ss-1997-c-p-26.01 |
| YT | Private Investigators and Security Guards Act, RSY 2002, c 175<br>http://www.canlii.org/en/yk/laws/stat/rsy-2002-c-175/latest/rsy-2002-c-175.html |

## Structure of the Act

The PSISA follows a familiar structure that is common to many Canadian **statutes**. It opens with definitions of important terms used in the Act and a statement of whom the legislation applies to, and it closes with a provision that empowers the government to make **regulations** under legislation (more on this below). In between are separate sections that deal with the general business of the statute.

**statute**
a piece of legislation passed by a government (either federal or provincial/territorial)

**regulation**
a rule that supports and is subordinate to legislation, and that often deals with practical aspects of administration of a statutory scheme

## Overview

Those who wish to read the PSISA online can find it, along with historical (previous) versions of it, at http://www.ontario.ca/laws (often called "e-Laws") and at CanLII (The Canadian Legal Information Institute), at http://www.canlii.org. The e-Laws website provides a detailed table of contents for longer statutes, including this one. A review of the table of contents for the PSISA reveals a structure that includes multiple "parts," some with sub-parts, with "sections" (also described as "provisions") contained within the parts or sub-parts. The basic structure is as follows:

| Title |
| --- |
| Citation |
| Part I: Interpretation and Application |
| Part II: Administration |
| Part III: Prohibitions |
| Part IV: Licensing |
| Part V: Complaints and Investigations |
| Part VI: General Duties and Standards of Practice |
| Part VII: General |
| Part VIII: Regulations |

Some statutes have a "full" title that is rarely used and a short title. The PSISA has only one title: *Private Security and Investigative Services Act, 2005*. The date is actually part of the title, so those who cite the legislation in formal reports and texts would be expected to include it.

A statute's **citation** contains publication, date, and jurisdictional information about a statute that assists researchers in locating it. The citation for the PSISA is "S.O. 2005, Chapter 34" (or SO 2005, c-34). "S.O." (or "SO") stands for "statutes of Ontario"—a clue that this is provincial law, not federal law, and specifically law made by the Ontario legislature.

**citation**
the code that incorporates the elements of a statute (or case's) bibliographical "address" so that researchers can find it

The year is the year in which the statute was passed into law, but not necessarily the year that the statute came into force (began to govern peoples' behaviour). Many statutory schemes cannot be instantly implemented because an administrative framework (like a department and/or a tribunal to manage the enforcement of the statute) must be put into place first. In the case of the PSISA, the bill introducing the legislation was passed into law in December 2005, but the legislation came into force in June of 2006. Finally, "Chapter 34" or "c 34" tells us that the PSISA was the 34th Ontario statute proclaimed in the year 2005.

## Interpretation and Application

Part I of the statute provides the reader with tools that support understanding of the provisions that follow. Nearly all statutes contain an "interpretation" section, which consists of a list of definitions for terms that are used in the statute. The definitions given for words in a statutory interpretation section may be different from other definitions (for example, dictionary definitions) for the relevant terms. By providing precise definitions for terms used, the legislators can control how and to whom the statute applies without having to repeat certain details throughout the provisions.

For example, many Canadian laws apply differently to adults and to minors. However, what constitutes a minor can vary widely; for the purpose of voting, a minor may be a person aged 17 or under, while for the purpose of obtaining a fishing licence or even a marriage licence, a minor may be aged 15 or under. An establishment that serves alcohol may be prohibited from "serving alcohol to minors," which actually means people under the age of 19. So instead of repeating the age criteria each time a provision makes a distinction between an adult and a minor, the statutes governing these issues set out, in their interpretation section, a definition of "minor" that applies for the purpose of that statute.

The following terms are defined in section 1 the PSISA: business entity, employee, licensee, Minister, prescribed, provincial offence, Registrar, and Tribunal. The content of those definitions, where relevant, will be discussed in this chapter.

Part I also contains a provision, section 2, that explains the application of the statute; in other words, to whom, and under what circumstances, the provisions included in part I apply. This single provision incorporates nine subsections (ss. 2(1) through 2(9)), multiple *levels* of sub-sub-sections (for example, s. 2(7)(b)(ii)) and is more than 600 words long. This demonstrates that an important condition to understanding the PSISA is having an understanding of to whom it does—and doesn't—apply.

The complexity of the application section reflects two things: first, that there is great diversity in the working arrangements and job titles of people who offer private security and/or investigative services; and second, that the details of these arrangements and roles were an important consideration to lawmakers when deciding who needed to be regulated and why. As a security practitioner, you are required to pay close attention to section 2 so that you can determine key issues such as whether or not you need to be licensed in order to do your job.

Section 2 opens with the following general statement:

> 2(1) This Act applies to private investigators within the meaning of subsection (2) and to security guards within the meaning of subsection (4).

We learn from this that the Act covers at least some private investigators, but that we will need to read subsection 2(2) to find out which ones, and that it also covers at least some security guards, but that we will need to read subsection 2(4) to find out which. So first we turn to subsection 2(2) and learn that:

> (2) A private investigator is a person who performs work, for remuneration, that consists primarily of conducting investigations in order to provide information.

And reading further, we see that subsection 2(3) offers helpful examples of the kind of information mentioned at the end of subsection 2(2):

> (3) Examples of the types of information referred to in subsection (2) include information on,
> (a) the character or actions of a person;
> (b) the business or occupation of a person; and
> (c) the whereabouts of persons or property.

Now that we know what a private investigator is, what is a security guard?

> (4) A security guard is a person who performs work, for remuneration, that consists primarily of guarding or patrolling for the purpose of protecting persons or property.

And for greater clarity:

> (5) Examples of the types of work referred to in subsection (4) include,
> (a) acting as a bouncer;
> (b) acting as a bodyguard; and
> (c) performing services to prevent the loss of property through theft or sabotage in an industrial, commercial, residential or retail environment.

With these definitions in mind, we may wonder, are there any individuals who work in the private investigation and private security industries who are NOT covered by the act? We can find the answer to that question in subsections 2(6) and 2(7):

> (6) A person who performs work, for remuneration, that consists primarily of acting for or aiding others in soliciting or procuring the services of a private investigator or security guard shall be deemed to be in the business of selling private investigator or security guard services.

A reader may be left wondering, what does this have to do with anything? (The answer comes in part II of the statute, which creates rules for people who are in this business.)

But we can assume, at least for now, that the provisions of the Act do NOT apply to people described in subsection 2(7):

> (7) This Act does not apply to,
> (a) barristers or solicitors engaged in the practice of their profession;
> (b) persons who perform work, for remuneration, that consists primarily of searching for and providing information on, [the definition of "work for remuneration" is given in subsection 2(8)]
>   (i) the financial credit rating of persons,
>   (ii) the qualifications and suitability of applicants for insurance and indemnity bonds, or
>   (iii) the qualifications and suitability of persons as employees or prospective employees;
> (c) a person who is acting as a peace officer; [what is meant by "peace officer" for the purpose of this application section is explained in subsection 2(9)]
> (d) insurance adjusters licensed under the *Insurance Act* while acting in that capacity, and their employees while acting in the usual and regular scope of their employment;
> (e) insurance companies licensed under the *Insurance Act* and their employees while acting in the usual and regular scope of their employment;

(f) persons residing outside Ontario who are licensed employees of a private investigation agency licensed or registered in a jurisdiction outside Ontario, but elsewhere in Canada who,

    (i) on behalf of a person situated outside Ontario, make an investigation or inquiry partly outside Ontario and partly within Ontario, and

    (ii) come into Ontario solely for the purpose of such investigation or inquiry;

(g) persons who receive remuneration for work that consists primarily of providing advice with respect to security requirements but who are not soliciting or procuring the services of private investigators or security guards for the purposes of subsection (6);

(h) persons who receive remuneration for work that consists primarily of providing an armoured vehicle service;

(i) locksmiths; and

(j) any class of persons exempted by the regulations. [An example of persons exempted in this way are bodyguards who work in the film and TV industry; they are exempted by Ontario Regulation 435/07.]

In a nutshell then, a person is not an Ontario private investigator or a security guard when he or she is providing services, including investigation or security-type services, in the context of his or her work as a lawyer; a person who does certain kinds of background checks (typically for credit advancement or recruiting); an insurance adjuster or insurance company employee; an out-of province private investigator or security guard (because that person will be regulated by their own home jurisdiction); a security consultant; an armoured car service provider; or a locksmith.

## Security Spotlight

### Is a Door Person at a Pub a Private Security Guard?

Many establishments that serve alcohol post staff at the door to check identification. For one-time or larger events (for example, a temporary beer garden at a summer festival), these guards are often hired on contract from an agency, and are clearly covered by the Act. But smaller establishments may ask an employee who may have other roles within the business to stand at the door to check ID or limit entry at busy times. Are these "door people" private security guards?

The question came up in 2012, after the Ontario Provincial Police issued tickets to a number of establishments in the Peterborough area, including a pub called Spanky's, for employing what the OPP characterized as unlicensed security guards (Wedley, 2012).

The owners of Spanky's vowed to challenge the ticket in court. They planned to argue that unlike large nightclubs that have dedicated security teams, they were a small pub with a total of 20 to 30 staff, mostly college and university students who often worked on a part-time or temporary basis. They also argued that the students would likely decline the job if it meant having to take a 40-hour course and write an exam, a process that would cost each of them approximately $300.

The case was ultimately dismissed because the prosecution failed to appear for the hearing. Spanky's management speculated that the prosecution had determined that their chances of a conviction were weak, and that the Crown hoped to avoid setting a legal precedent that might prevent the laying of such charges in the future.

## Administration

The administration provisions of the PSISA, set out in part II, describe the "system" created by the government for the administration of the Act. Section 3 creates the role of Registrar of Private Investigators and Security Guards—the person who will oversee the administration—and provides for the appointment of deputies if the Registrar cannot act.

The administration section also lists the six kinds of licences available under the Act. A party (person or business) can be licensed as a private investigator, a security guard, a combined private investigator and security guard, a seller of private investigator services, a seller of security guard services, or a seller of both private investigation and security guard services.

The PSISA also provides that other kinds of parties—employers who employ private investigators or security guards but are not in the business of selling the services of those guards—must be registered under the legislation as belonging to this category of employers.

The PISGA—the legislation in place prior to the PSISA—made an important distinction between private investigators and security guards based on their working arrangements. Under the PISGA, investigators and guards who were employed by a security agency that sent them out to work in other workplaces (companies that were clients of the agency) were required to be licensed, while security professionals who were the employees of the companies to which they provided services were not. Because this distinction was not especially meaningful in the context of the reasons for the regulation of the industry, it was eliminated when the PSISA was introduced. Now, all security guards who meet the section 2 application-of-the-statute criteria must be licensed, regardless of whether they are hired "in-house" by a direct employer or hired out on contract by an agency.

## Prohibitions

After describing the kinds of licences available under the regulatory scheme and before explaining how to obtain a licence, the legislation sets the issue of licensing aside for the moment and moves on to address "prohibitions." This structure is less awkward than it seems, because the first prohibition mentioned is a prohibition on providing private security services without a licence. In other words, the legislation "makes a case" for licensing before explaining how to obtain a licence.

Section 6 explains that security guards must both have the appropriate kind of licence for the work they do and either own or work for a business that has an appropriate licence for that kind of business.

Businesses, in turn, must, as per section 7, either be licensed (as a seller of security services), or registered (as an employer of licensed security professionals).

Following the prohibitions on providing security services without a licence, the legislation moves on to two more miscellaneous "prohibitions." These provide that security professionals as defined by the legislation cannot act as account collectors, bailiffs, or eviction officers (s. 9(1)); and that they cannot hold themselves out as available to be hired to locate witnesses who are a part of a witness protection program.

## Licensing Requirements and Process

Part IV of the PSISA sets out the requirements for obtaining a licence, and they are relatively straightforward:

> 10(1) No person is eligible to hold a licence under this Act unless,
> (a) the person possesses a clean criminal record; and

(b) in the case of an individual,
    (i) the person is 18 years old or older,
    (ii) the person is entitled to work in Canada, and
    (iii) the person has successfully completed all prescribed training and testing.

Subsections 10(2)–(4) set out the rules for what happens when a person "no longer meets the requirement for a licence" (for example, is convicted of a criminal offence). In these cases, the person must surrender the licence to the Registrar, who will remove the person from the list of licensees. If the individual wishes to challenge his or her removal from the register, he or she can request that the Registrar reconsider.

Leading up to the passage of the legislation, there was some debate about whether applicants for licensing ought to be automatically excluded if they had **provincial offences** convictions. This was ultimately rejected. For the purpose of licensing, a clean criminal record is defined by subsection 10(5):

> (5) For the purposes of subsection (1), a person possesses a "clean criminal record" if,
>     (a) the person has not been convicted of a prescribed offence under the *Criminal Code* (Canada), the *Controlled Drugs and Substances Act* (Canada) or any other Act of Canada; or
>     (b) the person has been convicted of such an offence and a pardon under the *Criminal Records Act* (Canada) has been issued or granted.

**provincial offence**
an offence established under a provincial statute that is administered by a provincial offences court (for example, an offence under the PSISA itself, or under a provincial highway traffic statute)

It should be noted that in recent years, the rules with respect to pardons (which are actually called "**record suspensions**" under the *Criminal Records Act*) have become more restrictive; for example, some offences (notably sexual offences involving minors) are no longer pardonable, and the amount of time that must pass before a pardon can be granted for other offences has been extended. Since approximately 10 percent of Canadians have a criminal record, the requirement that security professionals have a clean record combined with stricter parole rules mean that there are greater barriers to licensing today than in the past.

**record suspension**
the official name under the *Criminal Records Act* for what used to be called a "pardon"

There are also some situations in which, even where an applicant has been pardoned (granted a record suspension), he or she will still not be deemed to have a clean criminal record for the purposes of licensing. A list of those offences can be found in Ontario Regulation 37/08, Eligibility to Hold a Licence—Clean Criminal Record, a regulation made under the PSISA. The list includes more than 80 *Criminal Code* offences, including murder, serious assaults, sexual offences involving children, offences against police officers, forgery, and arson; and two offences—trafficking and importing/exporting—under the *Controlled Drugs and Substances Act*.

Although section 10(5) excludes provincial offences convictions as an automatic bar to being licensed, an applicant is required to disclose provincial offences convictions and convictions from other jurisdictions as part of his or her application. The full list of what must be disclosed can be found in subsection 11(1)(c), in the form of the content of a "declaration" that must accompany an application for licensing:

> 11(1) . . .
>     (c) provide a declaration that lists,
>         (i) all of the person's convictions for and findings of guilt for offences under a law of Canada up to the date of the declaration for which a pardon under the *Criminal Records Act* (Canada) has not been issued or granted,
>         (ii) all of the person's convictions for and findings of guilt for a provincial offence or an offence under a law of any other province or territory of Canada,

(iii) all fines levied against the person for a provincial offence that remain unpaid on the date of the declaration,

(iv) all of the person's convictions for criminal offences under the laws of other jurisdictions for which a pardon has not been issued or granted,

(v) all charges for allegedly committing an offence against a law of Canada that have been laid against the person and that have not been resolved on the date of the declaration, and

(vi) all charges for allegedly committing a criminal offence against the laws of another jurisdiction that have been laid against the person and that have not been resolved on the date of the declaration.

The applicant is also required to consent to having the Registrar access records with respect to these offences.

While not an automatic barrier to licensing, these quasi-criminal or extra-jurisdictional (outside Canada) offences can be taken into consideration by the Registrar under section 13, which gives the Registrar the right to decline to issue a licence to an applicant. Even where the applicant meets the basic criteria set out in section 10, the Registrar has **discretion** to decline or refuse to renew a licence if he or she believes that the applicant is unfit to serve as a private investigator or security guard. When exercising this discretion, the Registrar is to be guided by subsection 13(2), which reads:

> **discretion**
> a decision-maker is said to have discretion when he or she is left free to apply his or her professional judgment in deciding an issue, rather than being strictly bound to rule in a particular way when particular facts are proven

(2) The Registrar may decline to issue or renew a licence if the Registrar is of the opinion that one of the following applies, and if the Registrar is of the opinion that the matter is relevant to the applicant's fitness to hold a licence:

1. The applicant or an interested person in respect of the applicant is carrying on activities,

   i. that are in contravention of this Act or the regulations, or

   ii. that will be in contravention of this Act or the regulations if the applicant is issued a licence or a licence is renewed.

2. The past conduct of the applicant or of an interested person in respect of the applicant affords reasonable grounds to believe that the applicant will not carry on business in accordance with the law and with integrity and honesty.

3. The applicant, an employee or agent of the applicant makes a false statement or provides a false statement in an application for a licence or for a renewal of the licence.

4. The applicant is a business entity and,

   i. having regard to its financial position or the financial position of an interested person, the applicant cannot reasonably be expected to be financially responsible in the conduct of its business,

   ii. having regard to the financial position of its officers, directors or partners or of an interested person, the applicant cannot reasonably be expected to be financially responsible in the conduct of its business,

   iii. the past conduct of its officers, directors or partners or of an interested person affords reasonable grounds for belief that its business will not be carried on in accordance with the law and with integrity and honesty, or

   iv. an officer, director or partner of the business entity makes a false statement or provides a false statement in an application for a licence or for renewal of a licence.

5. The applicant,

   i. has been convicted of or found guilty of an offence under a law of Canada for which a pardon under the *Criminal Records Act* (Canada) has not been issued or granted,

   ii. has been convicted of or found guilty of a provincial offence or an offence under a law of any other province or territory of Canada,

iii. is liable to pay a fine for a provincial offence that has not been paid,

iv. has been convicted of a criminal offence under the law of another jurisdiction for which a pardon has not been issued or granted.

6. A ground exists that is prescribed as a ground for which an application for the issuance or renewal of a licence may be refused.

7. It is in the public interest to refuse to issue or renew the licence.

Section 13 was incorporated into the statute to balance the aims of protecting society from those who lack the integrity to serve as security professionals with the aim of ensuring that restrictions on licensing are truly warranted and that applicants are not excluded from the profession because of mistakes made in the past that do not reflect poorly on the applicant's general judgment and good character.

A provision in the British Columbia legislation (the British Columbia *Security Services Act*) that is analogous to Ontario's section 13 was considered in a case called *Kostyra v. Victoria Police Department*. The *Kostyra* case was a human rights complaint brought before British Columbia's Human Rights Tribunal. Ms. Kostyra, a security professional, had had a run-in with the City of Victoria police. While Ms. Kostyra was on driving patrol in the city (she worked for a large apartment building), the police observed what they felt was suspicious behaviour on her part: she stopped to talk to a homeless man, then sped away when a police cruiser approached her car, and she took photos of the police cruiser. Police obtained her cellphone number from her employer and called her while she was in her car. They characterized her manner on the phone as belligerent and aggressive. Upon performing a criminal records search, they discovered that she had had 29 prior interactions with police, and had been charged with a number of offences in Alberta, including assaulting a police officer, driving under the influence, and possession of a controlled substance. These offences dated to a time when Ms. Kostyra was battling an addiction, and had been eventually dismissed; however, she had not reported the offences, which she was required to do regardless of their status, when applying for the most recent renewal of her security licence.

The Victoria police reported their experience with Ms. Kostyra to the BC Deputy Registrar in charge of security professionals, and the Deputy Registrar wrote to Ms. Kostyra, declining to renew her licence. In declining to renew, the Deputy Registrar explained that "defiant conduct towards the police while holding a valid security worker licence is of grave concern" (*Kostyra*, para. 56).

Ms. Kostyra lost her job as a result, and made a complaint to the Human Rights Tribunal alleging that the actions of police had been motivated by discrimination on grounds of sex, gender, disability, and ethnicity (Ms. Kostyra was an Indigenous woman; the nature of her disability was unclear). The complaint was ultimately dismissed because it was determined that before contacting her, the police had no way of knowing that she was Indigenous or disabled, and there was no evidence that she was targeted for being female. She had been approached by police for behaving in a paranoid and evasive fashion.

This case illustrates that even though the applicant met the basic requirements for licensing—she had taken the course and the exam and, since her Edmonton criminal charges were dismissed, she had a clean criminal record—the Registrar was willing to exercise its discretion to decline her renewal on the grounds that her behaviour made her unfit to serve. That unfitness was established on two bases: her dishonesty in failing to disclose the Edmonton charges on her renewal application and her belligerent conduct toward the police.

Where the Registrar has concerns about a security professional that do not warrant the rejection of a licensing application, the Registrar can instead impose conditions on the licence: section 14. The Registrar can also revoke a licence (s. 15) at any time for breach of those conditions, or for any reason that could have prompted a refusal to issue or renew under section 13. When revoking a licence, the Registrar will generally suspend it immediately (ss. 15(2) and (3)) so that it is not in force.

Where the Registrar refuses to issue or renew a licence, or revokes it, the Registrar will give notice to the applicant, who can then request a hearing to show cause why he or she should be given a licence (or have conditions removed). The applicant can bring a lawyer to the hearing. If after the hearing the licence is still denied, the applicant can initiate an **appeal**. That appeal will be heard by the Licence Appeal Tribunal.

**appeal**
a new hearing (oral or in writing) to review an administrative or judicial (court) decision

## Complaints and Investigations

One of the most highly publicized features of the PSISA, when it was introduced, was the procedure established for handling complaints and investigations. Part V of the legislation sets out this procedure.

Any person can make a complaint against a security guard or private investigator, or employer, that is licensed under the PSISA:

> 19(1) The Registrar may receive a complaint from any person alleging that a licensee has breached the code of conduct established under the regulations or alleging that a licensee has failed to comply with this Act or the regulations or has breached a condition of a licence.

The complaint is to be made in writing, and the Registrar may (but need not) give notice of the complaint to the licence holder.

If the Registrar determines that the complaint is "frivolous, vexatious or not made in good faith" (subs. 19(4)), it can decline to deal with the complaint and will give notice of that decision to the complainant: subsection 19(5)).

If the Registrar does not reject the complaint and it deals with an alleged breach of the Code of Conduct (established by a regulation made under the Act; more below under "Regulations and the Code of Conduct"), the complaint is then referred to a process called "facilitation." Facilitation generally consists of one or more meetings that include a "facilitator" appointed under the Act, the licensee (security professional), and the person who made the complaint. At the conclusion of the facilitation, the facilitator reports the result to the Registrar. The result can include a recommendation that the guard take part in "remedial instruction" to reduce the chance that he or she will be the subject of future complaints.

Where the complaint is more serious, the Registrar may order an investigation (dealt with under ss. 20 to 25) and/or an "inspection," which includes limited warrantless searches, and is covered by sections 26 to 29. The Registrar can also initiate investigations or inspections where there has not been a complaint; for example, where the Registrar, on its own, has become concerned about the conduct of a licensee.

Investigations are conducted by investigators appointed for the purpose under the Act, and can include peace officers. The legislation allows for investigators to obtain warrants by applying to a justice of the peace, and the powers granted under those warrants are wide-ranging. Warrants can allow entry onto private premises, searches, seizures, and testing. Where force is necessary to execute a warrant, investigators are generally expected to obtain police assistance. Where an inspection instead of an investigation is ordered, and no search warrant is obtained, the inspector can still arrest a person found to be in contravention of the Act, as long as the terms for warrantless arrests are complied with (see s. 29.1).

## General Duties and Standards of Practice

Part VI of the PSISA sets out the general duties created for licensees under the Act. Some of the duties apply to individual security professionals, and others to security companies (for example, the requirement under section 30 to obtain insurance).

The basic duties of a security guard or a private investigator are:

- to be licensed (s. 31);
- to ensure that the Registrar has up-to-date contact details for the professional (s. 32);
- to carry one's licence on one's person while working (for guards,[1] s. 35(1)(a));
- to, on request, identify himself or herself as a licensed security guard (for guards, s. 35(1)(b));
- to, on request, show his or her licence (for guards, s. 35(1)(c)); and
- not to wear or carry "other symbols of authority," for example, a badge (for guards, s. 35(4)).

Private investigators, and security guards working as bodyguards (s. 35(3)), are not required to work in uniform. Security guards who are not working as bodyguards must wear a uniform that complies with Ontario Regulation 362/07, Uniforms. The uniform regulation is primarily concerned with ensuring two things:

1. Both the guard and his or her employer can be identified from looking at the uniform; for this purpose, the name of the employer and guard's name OR licence number must be on the guard's shirt;
2. The guard cannot be mistaken for a peace officer. For this purpose, the uniform is not to be easily confused with a police uniform; for example, shirts cannot be navy blue or black and cannot incorporate rank chevrons, and pants cannot have the characteristic police stripe down the side.

These uniform requirements are supplemented by a general prohibition in the legislation:

> 39 No person who holds a licence under this Act shall hold himself, herself or itself out as providing services or performing duties connected with police.

These requirements are designed to make it unlikely that a member of the public who encounters a security guard will make an inaccurate assumption about the powers that the guard has, and thereby be coerced into deference and obedience that he or she would not show to someone who is not a peace officer.

## Parts VII and VIII

Parts VII and VIII of the PSISA deal with various administrative issues, such as the power to make regulations (s. 54), the form of service where service of documents is required under the Act (s. 41), managing misleading advertising (s. 42), and liability of the Registrar for acts of negligence (s. 48).

More relevant to individual security professionals licensed under the Act is section 43, the general offence provision, which provides:

> 43(1) A person is guilty of an offence if he, she or it,
> (a) knowingly furnishes false information in any application under this Act or in any statement or return required under this Act or the regulations;
> (b) fails to comply with any order or other requirement made under this Act or the regulations;
> (c) fails to comply with a condition of a licence; or
> (d) contravenes or fails to comply with any provision of this Act or the regulations.

A review of this provision makes it clear that a wide range of actions can lead to a charge being laid under the PSISA. When that happens, the security professional will typically be issued a ticket, and ordered to appear in Provincial Offences Court. The penalties that can be imposed are significant:

> 45(1) Every individual convicted of an offence under this Act is liable to a fine of not more than $25,000, imprisonment for a term of not more than one year, or both.

Of course, the amount of the fine, and the likelihood of imprisonment, will vary widely depending on the nature of the offence; and much lower sentences are possible.

## Regulations and the Code of Conduct

When a government passes a statute, especially one that creates an administrative framework, there is generally included in that statute a provision providing for the making of regulations.

Regulations are rules made "under" a statute (subordinate to it). They are drafted by government personnel and need not be voted through the legislature the way statutes are, and they can be amended (changed) or repealed (withdrawn) without a vote. While a statute is typically concerned with general principles, regulations often deal with the technical or operational details of how a legislative scheme will work in practice. They often contain, for example, tables and charts.

There are 13 regulations made under the PSISA:

|  |  |
|---|---|
| O. Reg. 26/10 | Training and Testing |
| O. Reg. 37/08 | Eligibility to Hold a Licence—Clean Criminal Record |
| O. Reg. 462/07 | Insurance |
| O. Reg. 435/07 | Exemptions from the Act |
| O. Reg. 434/07 | Recordkeeping Requirements for Licensed Business Entities |
| O. Reg. 368/07 | Registration Requirements for Business Entities |
| O. Reg. 367/07 | Term of Licences |
| O. Reg. 366/07 | Equipment |
| O. Reg. 365/07 | Use of Animals |
| O. Reg. 364/07 | Vehicles |
| O. Reg. 363/07 | Code of Conduct |
| O. Reg. 362/07 | Uniforms |
| O. Reg. 361/07 | Information to Be Provided to the Registrar |

We have already mentioned three of these regulations in this chapter. The exemption regulation (O. Reg. 435/07) excludes certain security professionals (such as bodyguards who work in the film industry) from the application of the Act. We also mentioned Ontario Regulation 37/08, which expands on the definition of "clean criminal record" to explain that an applicant will not be considered to have a clean record if he or she has been convicted of, but pardoned, of certain serious offences. Finally, we touched on Ontario Regulation 362/07, Uniforms.

A discussion of the regulations that apply mainly to business licensees and employers (O. Regs 368/07, 434/07, and 462/07) is beyond the scope of this text, and the rules that deal with equipment (mostly weapons), service animals, and vehicles will be discussed in the context of those topics elsewhere in this book. That leaves two regulations for discussion here: Training and Testing, and Code of Conduct.

## Training and Testing

The training and testing regulation, Ontario Regulation 26/10, provides that in order to obtain a new licence to work as a security guard or private investigator in Ontario, a person must complete a prescribed training program that complies with the "Training Syllabus for Private Investigators" that was developed by the Ministry and published in January 2015. A syllabus is an outline of the content that must be covered in a training course. The Training Syllabus is publicly available online at http://www.mcscs.jus.gov.on.ca/english/PSIS/Training/PrivateInvestigatorSyllabus/PSIS_PI_syllabus.html; but because it is an outline and not the full content of the program, it is not sufficient just to read it—the applicant must actually take the 40-hour course of study from a provider that is permitted to deliver it. Those providers are defined at section 2(3) of the regulation:

> 2(3) The training programs required by subsections (1) and (2) must be provided by,
> (a) a public university;
> (b) a college established under the *Ontario Colleges of Applied Arts and Technology Act, 2002*;
> (c) a private career college registered under the *Private Career Colleges Act, 2005* as part of a program approved under that Act;
> (d) a licensed business entity; or
> (e) a registered business entity that employs the applicant or that has made a conditional offer of employment to the applicant.

Besides taking the course, applicants must have completed the St. John Ambulance first aid program: subsection 2(1)(a.1).

After taking the course and obtaining the St. John Ambulance Emergency First Aid Certificate (or its equivalent), applicants must sit for, and pass, a test. (See Appendix A.)

There are some exceptions to the training and testing requirement for guards who were licensed in other jurisdictions (and trained there), and for guards who were licensed before these rules came into force. These are set out in sections 4 through 6 of the regulation.

## The Code of Conduct

A fundamental feature of most schemes of professional regulation is a code of conduct. Some of these codes are highly detailed and some are more general, but they all serve the same purpose: to establish a basic standard of behaviour that professionals must meet.

Codes of conduct are often made public in statutes or regulations because it is considered appropriate that people outside the profession should be able to review them so that they can know what to expect from the professionals with whom they interact.

Understanding and complying with the Code of Conduct (O. Reg. 363/07) is an essential obligation for security professionals. While you may have additional rules that apply to your work (for example, rules established by your specific employer), those rules should not be inconsistent with and never replace the Code of Conduct. Being a professional is something more than simply being a worker; as a professional, even when you are not yet working for any particular employer, you are still a security guard or a private investigator. Most professionals view membership in their chosen profession as part of their human identity, and take pride in complying with the standards of that profession regardless of where they happen to be working at any given moment. In other words, a job is a job, but a profession is something you take with you wherever you go. Living up to your code of conduct is a way to prove that you are worthy of the title of "professional."

The Code of Conduct for security guards and private investigators licensed under the PSISA in Ontario Regulation 363/07 is quite a simple document. We have reproduced it in its entirety in this text as Appendix C; but here are the provisions at the heart of the code, which can be found at section 2(1):

> 2(1) Every individual licensee, while working as a private investigator or security guard, shall,
> (a) act with honesty and integrity;
> (b) respect and use all property and equipment in accordance with the conditions of his or her licence;
> (c) comply with all federal, provincial and municipal laws;
> (d) treat all persons equally, without discrimination based on a person's race, ancestry, place of origin, colour, ethnic origin, citizenship, creed, sex, sexual orientation, age, marital status, family status or disability;
> (e) refrain from using profane, abusive or insulting language or actions or actions that are otherwise uncivil to any member of the public;
> (f) refrain from exercising unnecessary force;
> (g) refrain from behaviour that is either prohibited or not authorized by law;
> (h) respect the privacy of others by treating all information received while working as a private investigator or security guard as confidential, except where disclosure is required as part of such work or by law; and
> (i) co-operate with police where it is required by law.
> (2) No individual licensee shall,
> (a) be unfit for duty, while working, through consumption of alcohol or drugs;
> (b) conspire with another person or aid or abet another licensee in a breach of this code of conduct;
> (c) wilfully or negligently make a false statement or complaint against another licensee; or
> (d) misrepresent to any person the type, class or conditions of his or her licence.

As you can see, many of the specific requirements boil down to two things: (1) treating the public (and colleagues) with appropriate respect and fairness, and (2) obeying the law. In a sense, the Code of Conduct requires that security professionals model the precise behaviours that they are aiming to enforce in others. As many security professionals instinctively know, setting the tone for behaviour—especially in a rowdy or high-conflict situation—is useful as a means of influencing others. Even in calmer situations, security professionals make their work easier by earning the respect of the public. Doing that requires unimpeachable standards of personal behaviour.

At least three of the requirements of the Code of Conduct are actually more complicated than they initially appear. The requirement to refrain from discrimination requires sensitivity to differences, patience with individuals who may have special needs or different values, and an awareness of one's own biases. Actively monitoring one's own behaviour for discrimination and striving to overcome those tendencies requires thought and effort, and security professionals are encouraged to take advantage of any training that may be made available to them in this regard. Chapter 10 of this book deals with sensitivity training, and offers useful information to support non-discrimination.

Likewise, the protection of privacy requires an awareness that, as a security professional, you may have access to information about individuals that must be protected. It is essential to avoid disclosing any personal information gained in the course of your duties to any other party, except as permitted by law.

Finally, the Code of Conduct requires you to "refrain from exercising unnecessary force." The use of force is a very complex topic for security professionals, and an entire chapter of this book is devoted to it.

## CHAPTER SUMMARY

Most security guards and private investigators who work in Ontario are required to be licensed under the *Private Security and Investigative Services Act, 2005*, a statute of the Ontario government. This chapter provided an overview of the Act. The PSISA explains that security professionals and certain businesses that employ them must be licensed, and that obtaining a licence depends on meeting certain minimum requirements, including having a clean criminal record and undergoing training and testing. The PSISA also sets out the basic duties of a security professional, and certain prohibitions on what those professionals can do. It establishes a process for handling complaints, including via facilitation, investigation, and inspection. Finally, the legislation is supported by several regulations, one of which contains the Code of Conduct with which all security professionals must comply.

## KEY TERMS

appeal, 28
citation, 20
discretion, 26
provincial offence, 25
record suspension, 25
regulation, 20
statute, 20

## NOTE

1. Comparable requirements for private investigators are set out in section 34 of the PSISA.

## REFERENCES

*Code of Conduct*, O Reg. 363/07.

*Controlled Drugs and Substances Act*, SC 1996, c 19.

*Criminal Code*, RSC 1985, c C-46.

*Criminal Records Act*, RSC 1985, c C-47.

*Eligibility to Hold a Licence—Clean Criminal Record*, O Reg. 37/08.

*Employment Standards Act, 2000*, SO 2000, c 41.

*Exemptions from the Act*, O Reg. 435/07.

*Insurance*, O Reg. 462/07.

*Kostyra v. Victoria Police Department*, 2015 BCHRT 124 (CanLII).

Ontario Ministry of Community Safety & Correctional Services, Private Security Investigative Services. (2015). *Training Syllabus for Private Investigators*. Retrieved from http://www.mcscs.jus.gov.on.ca/sites/default/files/content/mcscs/docs/ec164552.pdf

*Private Security and Investigative Services Act, 2005*, SO 2005, c 34 [PSISA].

*Recordkeeping Requirements for Licensed Business Entities*, O Reg. 434/07.

*Registration Requirements for Business Entities*, O Reg. 368/07.

*Regulated Health Professions Act, 1991*, SO 1991, c 18.

*Security Services Act*, SBC 2007, c 30.

*Training and Testing*, O Reg. 26/10.

*Uniforms*, O Reg. 362/07.

Wedley, Brendan. (2012, December 29). Spanky's fighting charge over doormen licensing. *Peterborough Examiner*. Retrieved from http://www.thepeterboroughexaminer.com/2012/12/29/spankys-fighting-charge-over-doormen-licensing

## PERFORMANCE APPLICATION
### Multiple Choice

1. The requirements for licensing of security professionals in Canadian jurisdictions can be found in:
   a. the *Criminal Code*
   b. federal legislation
   c. provincial or territorial legislation
   d. municipal by-laws
   e. Provincial Offences Acts

2. The PSISA does NOT apply to:
   a. security guards who work only for their employers
   b. private investigators
   c. security guards employed by agencies that sell their services to other businesses
   d. insurance adjusters
   e. any of the above

3. An applicant for a licence under the PSISA meets the requirement of having a clean criminal record even if he or she has:
   a. been convicted of an offence under the *Criminal Code* for which he or she has not been pardoned
   b. been convicted of an offence under the Ontario *Highway Traffic Act*
   c. been convicted of the offence of trafficking under the *Controlled Drugs and Substances Act*
   d. been convicted of assaulting a police officer under the *Criminal Code* but has received a record suspension (pardon)
   e. any of the above

4. Which of the following is permissible as part of a security guard uniform?
   a. black pants
   b. a navy blue shirt
   c. chevrons denoting rank
   d. a metal badge that reads "Officer Khan" (or any name)
   e. a red stripe down the side of the uniform pants

5. Being impaired by alcohol at work is a violation of:
   a. the *Controlled Drugs and Substances Act*
   b. the *Liquor Control Act*
   c. the PSISA Code of Conduct
   d. the *Criminal Code*
   e. all of the above

6. A contract security guard who is working for the provider of an outdoor music festival should behave as though he or she is representing:
   a. him or herself
   b. the provider of the music festival
   c. the agency that has hired him or her out
   d. the security industry as a whole
   e. him or herself, his or her employer agency, the music festival provider, and the security industry as a whole

7. Where a security guard has a clean criminal record as defined by the PSISA and meets all the other essential requirements (age, ability to work in Canada, training and testing, etc.) he or she:
   a. is automatically entitled to a licence
   b. will be granted a licence once he or she shows proof of employment in the profession
   c. will be granted a licence after a hearing
   d. can still be deemed unfit to serve by the Registrar and denied a licence
   e. will be licensed in all provinces and territories of Canada

8. A security guard on patrol duty must produce and show his or her licence:
   a. if he or she has it readily available
   b. to any peace officer
   c. to any person who requests to see it
   d. to the Registrar
   e. to a party who produces a valid warrant

## Short Answer

Review the Security Spotlight feature on page 23. Do you believe that employees who work as door people at pubs should be required to be licensed as security guards under the PSISA? Why or why not?

# PART II

# Core Skills

# Basic Security Procedures

3

| | |
|---|---|
| Introduction | 40 |
| Observational Skills | 40 |
| Patrols | 41 |
| Situational Awareness | 43 |
| Access Control | 45 |
| Crowd Control | 50 |
| Vehicle and Traffic Control | 51 |
| Shift Handover Procedure | 58 |
| Drug and Alcohol Effects and Substance Abuse | 59 |
| Chapter Summary | 61 |
| Key Terms | 62 |
| Note | 62 |
| References | 62 |
| Performance Application | 62 |

## LEARNING OUTCOMES

When you have completed this chapter, you will be able to:

- Describe basic security procedures, including patrol procedures, observational skills, shift hand-over procedures, access control, and crowd control.
- Explain the principles of vehicle and traffic control.
- Understand the importance of creating a security plan for gatherings.
- Explain basic procedures for cooperating with police personnel.

# Introduction

In recent years, there has been an increasing demand for security guards in the private sector. This has happened partly because companies and people feel safer with a show of uniformed personnel despite the fact that sophisticated technology may also be in place, and partly because an important aspect of the role of security guards is to help people more than it is to regulate them. Hospitals and health care facilities, for instance, now provide their own security services, and security guards are often called upon to track down patients who have wandered from their rooms or help restrain patients who have become uncontrollable and violent.

Mainly, however, security guards serve the following functions:

- protecting premises and property against natural and man-made threats, and helping to prevent workplace accidents by identifying, reporting, or eliminating hazards;
- controlling access to property (including by vehicles) and maintaining or restoring control over crowds;
- preventing, detecting, and responding appropriately to criminal or otherwise prohibited activities on private property;
- cooperating effectively with law enforcement personnel and the justice system in the event of the commission of crime on the property being guarded; and
- providing leadership and guidance in the event of an emergency on the premises.

Guards may perform their duties on foot, on bicycles, or in patrol cars.
This chapter will describe the basic procedures underlying these core duties.

# Observational Skills

Although you might imagine that the daily patrol function of security guards is routine, once you understand this function, you will come to see that patrol duty is far from dull. As security professionals, we are the "eyes and ears" of the client. We "observe and report" and it is very important for any security professional to develop strong **observational skills** to be able to execute their duties. Humans have five senses, and some may even argue for a sixth. These senses make up one of the most sophisticated alarm and early warning systems on the planet. Security professionals may use all of their senses at any time when they are on patrol.

Security personnel must be keenly observant of their surroundings and especially observant of other people and potential hazards and deficiencies. Unless something is heard, seen, smelled, felt, or tasted, it cannot be remembered. The ability to describe a person or object accurately is of utmost importance and plays a vital role in the protection of self, property, and others.

**observational skills**
the ability to critically observe one's surroundings with a heightened awareness so that details of and changes in the physical environment can be readily detected

## Identification of Individuals

At first sight, we usually notice someone's gender, build, and age. After closer observation, we notice facial features, clothing, and demeanour.

We may look for clues to a person's age. Facial features may give some clues to age, but it is a combination of looks with actions and mannerisms that gives us a better indication. Generally, the older the person, the more difficult it is to assess their age accurately.

A difference of 20 years in a young adult is quite noticeable and in young children, a difference of six months or a year is clearly distinguishable.

Another basic detail is skin colour and ethnic background. An individual's complexion may change on a daily basis. For instance, a Caucasian person who has been carrying out strenuous physical activity may appear to have a darker or red complexion, whereas that same individual at rest may appear to have a lighter skin tone.

## Identification of Objects

A full description of an object should include information about its composition, style, colour, manufacture, model, age, and size. Any serial numbers or unique markings should be noted.

When obtaining a description of a physical object, particular attention should be paid to marks, scratches, and damage of any type. A useful means to distinguish an item (for example, a bicycle) from other similar items is to observe the characteristics that it has developed through use.

# Patrols

For a company to provide a complete security service, it must have an effective and dynamic patrol program. This can be achieved only if personnel understand how a patrol program works.

A patrol program has five essential objectives:

- To gain an intimate knowledge of the site.
- To establish a visible presence to deter potential offenders within the complex.
- To build confidence in security on the part of employees, management, residents, and/or tenants.
- To detect crimes, safety hazards, and emergencies.
- To detect, investigate, and report on any and all situations that affect the normal routine of the site.

## Patrol Planning

Patrols must be organized in a logical fashion to maximize coverage and limit gaps in surveillance. Buildings or outdoor areas should be systematically patrolled floor-by-floor and area-by-area. Outside zones should be divided into "blocks" and covered individually.

It is important for guards to pause often; ideally, once every two minutes for a minimum of 15 seconds. These pauses allow the guard to switch from walking mode into observing mode, so that he or she can better focus on the surroundings.

## Building Patrol Functions

During a building patrol, a security guard inspects, records, and reports on the following:

- Improperly secured doors, windows, gates, offices, equipment, computers, files, personal items, materials, or documents.
- Signs of fire, flooding, spills, leaks, structural failure, or other safety hazards.
- Signs of theft or break-in.

- Signs of a threat from properties adjacent to the site.
- Presence of employees or other personnel within the complex who have not signed in at security.
- Any situation of an unusual nature.

The topic of workplace health and safety—an important consideration for security personnel—is the subject of Chapter 5 of this text.

## Building Patrol Routes

During normal business hours, a useful formula for patrols involves having each guard complete four separate patrol routes at least twice during his or her shift. During **silent hours**, guards should increase patrols to at least three times each during the shift. While on **high-risk patrol** in dangerous areas, coverage should be increased further. Patrols are most likely to deter unwanted activity when they are highly visible to potential wrongdoers.

To confuse anyone who may be monitoring security routines, guards must be careful to randomly select the order of their patrol routes so that anyone monitoring them is never sure where a guard will be at any given time. If there is an increased threat against one of the buildings or if there is any cause for suspicion, the security supervisor will include this building in the silent hours patrol route.

## Site Coordination of Patrols

The normal chain of command is that security guards report to and are directed by the security supervisor. The **control room** is usually the command centre for security response on a site. All security systems can be monitored and activated from the control room, and the various modes of communication are also provided from there. Communication between security personnel and supervisors is often done by radio; radio use, etiquette, and language will be discussed in detail in Chapter 9.

There are two types of patrols—foot patrols and mobile patrols. The benefits and disadvantages of each type are described below.

## Foot Patrols

Unless responding to a specific incident, foot patrols are always preferable to mobile patrols. Security guards on foot can interact more easily with their environment and the people on the site more freely. By being more accessible, security guards gather more information about the property and the people they are responsible for protecting. Foot patrols are the normal

**silent hours**
time outside of normal business hours

**high-risk patrol**
patrol that takes place in an area known for dangerous activity or in an area that may be dangerous due to a particular situation, such as a labour dispute

**control room**
a central and secure location where dispatch officers are located. This location can be used as a hub for all secondary operations such as report writing, conducting interviews, statement taking, shift briefing, etc.

### WHAT WOULD YOU DO?

You are a security guard assigned to work from 1500 to 2300 hours at an office complex. This office building has 15 floors and you are scheduled to work with two other security guards. One guard must remain at the main entrance for access control.

- How would you schedule, plan, and coordinate each patrol?
- How many patrols will you be conducting?
- What were you told at 1500 hours and what will you tell the person relieving you at 2300 hours?

method of patrolling within most sites, unless the security supervisor takes over a specific mobile patrol.

Building patrols are designed to act as a deterrent against any form of security incident, breach, or problem. By conducting routine building patrols, security staff provide a highly visible security presence in the workplace.

Routine building patrols achieve four main objectives. They

- deter employees who feel inclined to conduct criminal acts;
- prevent incidents from occurring through early detection and monitoring of deteriorating situations in the workplace;
- promote the service aspect of security, fostering a sense of safety in the workplace or facility; and
- develop a rapport between security personnel and employees, giving employees the confidence to report items that are out of place or situations that cause concern.

A disadvantage of foot patrols is that they take longer to complete, and response time to an incident is increased if security personnel are distant from the incident site (often an indication that there are too few security guards for the site).

## Mobile Patrols

When a security vehicle is available, mobile patrols allow security staff to cover more ground in a short time. However, there is a price to pay for faster coverage—patrol guards lose the benefit of using all their senses. This can be mitigated to some extent by getting guards to an area quickly and then having them conduct an area inspection.

An advantage of mobile patrols is that patrol vehicles are usually equipped with personal protective equipment, emergency gear, and full voice communication capability, including cellular.

In some cases, security guards may use equipment such as bicycles or golf carts in order to facilitate more comprehensive security coverage over a large area. A good use of this would be during patrols of a multilevel parking garage, where a properly equipped guard's ability to quickly respond to a remote section of the facility may be essential.

# Situational Awareness

**Situational awareness** describes a state of mind that every patrol professional must develop with respect to the specific patrol function being performed. A well-developed sense of situational awareness keeps the patrol function dynamic and provides a high level of safety. Training in situational awareness helps security personnel detect even the subtlest change in both the physical and human environments.

**situational awareness**
the ability to draw accurate, real-time inferences from observations; for example, the ability to determine whether the presence of a particular individual poses a risk to others

## The Physical Environment

If, over the course of several patrols, security guards focus on their surroundings, they will develop a mental picture of a particular location. Then, on subsequent patrols, they will notice any changes that affect that mental picture of the **physical environment**. Sometimes simple changes will trigger an alert—a truck that has been moved or a garbage bin that's been emptied. Trained security professionals will notice the change, consider it, and then mentally file it away for later reference. They are able to train their minds to do this

**physical environment**
surroundings or particular locations at the worksite

automatically. It's useful, in understanding this skill, to compare a security professional's mind to that of an airline pilot.

When a plane is on autopilot, a pilot doesn't have to think; but the trade-off is that he or she loses the ability to react immediately. When the pilot takes the controls off autopilot and takes over the aircraft manually, he or she is in greater control. It's as if the controls become extensions of the pilot's hands, feet, and mind. The pilot and the plane function as one to become an integrated machine performing at its peak. So, when security guards are more aware of what they notice, consider, and mentally file away on patrol, they will be more aware of or in control of their surroundings and any changes that may affect security.

## The Human Environment

Worksites are often large facilities with many departments and functions. There may be hundreds of employees with different backgrounds, interests, and concerns. While patrolling, security personnel should include this **human environment** in their mental picture of each location. By talking to employees and observing their routines, security staff can become fully aware of what a "normal" day is, making it easier to spot differences.

**human environment**
personnel at the worksite

## Survival Mental State

Unlike a police officer who has been told what to expect when called to an alarm, a security guard usually has no idea what to expect. Police can rely on a firearm, baton, and backup from other police; security guards cannot carry a gun in self-defence, may not be wearing a bulletproof vest, and may not have a partner in a squad car. All they can rely on when they arrive at the site of the alarm is themselves and their situational awareness skills. Before getting out of the patrol car, they should be anticipating all the possibilities that may confront them and should have a plan of action to handle them. This level of preparedness is sometimes described as a "survival" mental state.

## Heightened Recall

There is another advantage to adopting a state of situational awareness. Not only do security professionals train themselves to detect early warnings of impending events, in subsequent investigations they can also access sharper recall from their mental "files" to report more accurate details about locations and people. They will likely find themselves able to recite licence plate numbers and describe faces with remarkable clarity after only a glimpse. Answers to questions such as "Was a valve open or shut?" or "Was that door open or closed?" will come in a flash and they will be accurate.

### ON THE JOB

**What to Look For**

In observing the human environment, consider these questions:

- Is an employee distraught or acting peculiar?
- Is an entire department nervous, angry, or distressed?
- Is an employee in an area where he/she should not be?
- Is an employee missing from his/her post?

## Switching On and Off

No human being can be in a state of alert at all times. Neither can they sustain situational awareness forever. The demand on the conscious and unconscious mind is simply too great. As a result, security guards must get into the habit of mentally "turning on" when setting out on a patrol and, during the course of the patrol, maintaining that level of concentration even when chatting casually with employees. On returning to the control room, however, they need to "turn off" and rest. Let the security system's automated surveillance pick up the slack. This does not mean that they can become oblivious to their duties, but their level of concentration can be substantially reduced. Security guards should practice moving quickly from a state of increased awareness to a normal state, and back.

# Access Control

Security professionals may be tasked with controlling and monitoring the entrance to a secured location or area to detect, deny, or deter unauthorized access. Here are some reasons why **access control** may be required:

- To control the flow of traffic.
- To document who gained accessed.
- To prevent unauthorized access.
- To stop unauthorized taking of valuables.

**access control**
procedures designed to limit entry to premises to individuals authorized to enter, and to ensure that visitors comply with rules such as rules prohibiting bringing in alcohol or weapons

For the purpose of controlling the access to a specific location some sites use security personnel to physically verify authorization, whereas some use other methods, such as card access entries. Many businesses leave the matter of access control to a receptionist or a security guard stationed at the entrance of the facility. But in plants with over 50 employees per shift or in high-turnover businesses, this type of access control is simply not sufficiently secure.

Where security concerns warrant such measures, employers may be justified in having their receptionist or security guard request to check an unknown visitor's photo ID or driver's licence before allowing the person access to secure employee areas, however intrusive this action may seem to be. Most large employers, in order to protect their personnel, place of business, and their assets, will issue some form of positive photo identification. This allows them to exclude all but authorized personnel, as well as control their movement once they are inside the facility.

## The ABCs of Visitor Control

The following guidelines are appropriate for most reception area security personnel and receptionists:

1. Greet all visitors. A friendly "good morning" or "good afternoon" relaxes the visitor and makes it easier to ask questions later.
2. Question all visitors. Depending on the company's security needs, certain questions will be appropriate. Security guards and receptionists should be encouraged not to hesitate to ask for appropriate information if it is necessary for a security purpose. For example:
   - What is your name?
   - Who are you here to see?
   - Do you have an appointment?

- What company do you represent?
- May I see some identification?

3. Announce all visitors to the person being visited. In many cases, the person receiving the visitor will want to come down to reception to escort the visitor to the meeting room. If this is the company's policy, ensure that it is followed.
4. Confirm that the visitor has parked in the appropriate area and has a parking permit if required.
5. Ensure that the visitor wears an identification badge. Some companies issue repair people and temporary personnel with their own identification badges instead of a visitor badge.
6. Collect all badges when visitors depart. Record all uncollected and/or lost badges.
7. Record all visits in a visitor log. The log should record the following:
    - visitor's name,
    - date,
    - visitor's signature,
    - arrival time,
    - name of employee being visited,
    - departure time,
    - purpose of visit,
    - department/area visited,
    - security personnel signature/initials confirming that the visitor's ID was checked,
    - visitor's company phone number, and
    - vehicle licence number.
8. Ask any visitor claiming to be a federal or provincial law enforcement officer for identification. Government and law enforcement agents always have photo ID. Take the time to examine the ID carefully. Record the badge or ID number.
9. Ask any person leaving the premises with company property (such as office equipment) to show a property pass dated and signed by authorized personnel, along with a list showing the contents that are being removed.
10. If a visitor seems nervous or hostile or if he or she is sweating or pacing, looks unkempt, distraught, or disoriented, do not allow that person access to the premises. If you are the receptionist, call a security guard immediately. Better safe than sorry!

## *Visitor Passes*

As with employee ID cards, visitor passes should be unique to the facility and tamper-proof. Passes should be laminated, recognizable from a distance, and prominently displayed on a clip or chain. In some facilities, visitors are required to exchange a piece of personal identification before a pass is issued. When passes are returned, they should be kept in a secure place.

Passes should contain the company name and logo and an expiry period. Some passes may be issued for a designated area to be visited, such as the warehouse. The authorized area may be indicated with a letter or colour coded on the pass.

> ## ON THE JOB
>
> ### What About Your Own ID?
>
> - Carry your ID card/cards at all times.
> - Display your ID card/cards in the required location on your uniform as per site instructions.
> - Replace worn, outdated, and damaged ID cards as soon as possible.
> - Request a replacement card if you have altered your appearance significantly—for example, if you are no longer wearing eye glasses (using contacts/had eye surgery), have removed or grown a beard or moustache, or changed your hair colour.
> - Secure your ID card when it is not in use.
> - Leave your ID cards in a locked container in the security office when you go on vacation.
> - Report any lost or stolen ID cards to the shift supervisor immediately.

## Elements of a Good ID System

The type of identification system chosen typically depends on the sensitivity of the facility. A good security ID policy should include provisions that cover the following:

- When, where, how, and to whom passes should be displayed.
- What is to be done in case of loss of the pass.
- Procedures for retrieving badges from departing employees.
- A system for periodic cancellation and reissue of all passes in response to security concerns.

### *Vulnerabilities*

Unfortunately, ID cards are open to abuse. They can be bought or stolen, forged, and produced internally without authorization.

1. **Bought or Stolen ID:** Purse snatchers and pickpockets have been known to sell employee ID cards to other criminals.
2. **Forged ID:** Employee ID cards and visitor passes can be forged using computers and colour printers in an effort to gain access to restricted areas for criminal activity.
3. **Unauthorized ID:** An employee with access to ID production equipment and blank card stock can produce an unauthorized ID card, badge, or pass, and use it to gain access to restricted areas. These cards and passes can also be given to an accomplice for future activity.

### *Standards for ID Cards*

Here are some general criteria for ID card effectiveness:

- Cards and badges should be tamper-resistant and difficult to alter or reproduce. For example, they may be printed or embossed on a distinctive stock that incorporates designs that are difficult to reproduce.

- They should contain a clear and recent photograph of the employee, preferably in colour. The photograph should be at least 6.5 cm square and should be updated every two or three years, or when there is any significant change in facial appearance, such as the removal or growth of a beard or moustache.
- ID cards should incorporate vital statistics such as the employee's name, number, date of birth, height, weight, hair and eye colour, gender, signature, and, where required, a fingerprint.
- They should be wallet-sized, computer-generated on special paper, and laminated.
- In facilities where there are areas with different access restrictions, cards and badges should be colour-coded to reflect specific access privileges.
- ID cards should be unique to the facility, containing the company name and logo and a serial number.
- Cards should have a date of issue and expiry and bear an authorizing signature, preferably in a different colour from other types of ID card (for example, plant staff card colour will differ that of janitorial staff).

## TYPES OF IDENTITY CARDS AND THEIR USES

Identification cards can generally be grouped into four categories or types: simple laminated cards, light-sensitive badges, time-sensitive badges, and high-security, computer-generated cards and badges.

### Simple Laminated Card

This form of ID card is widely used for small businesses, schools, health clubs, and the retail industry. Made of paper or cardboard, this form of ID card is printed on coloured paper or "stock," using an approved layout that contains the employee's basic information. The employee and the department head usually sign it. A photograph is usually taken separately, cut to size, and attached to the card before it is sealed in the laminate pouch.

### Light-Sensitive Badges

Light-sensitive badges are created with a chemically treated insert or patch that reacts to sunlight. When exposed to sunlight, the patch changes colour, and the word "VOID" appears in a pattern across the patch. This renders the card useless for future use. Used mainly as a form of visitor ID, this badge is normally issued with instructions to return it to security before the visitor's departure from the facility.

### Time-Sensitive Badges

Time-sensitive badges are also used primarily for visitor access. This badge or pass consists of two portions. The base is pre-printed and can be filled out with the visitor's information by the security guard. A small patch is applied to a chemically treated "red" section of the badge. A chemical reaction takes place over a specific period of time when the "Front/Visitor" portion of the pass is applied to the "red" or expired portion.

Depending on the period of time granted for access, time-sensitive badges may be used

- by new employees, while an official employee ID is being prepared; and
- by contractors, when multiple entries are required over a specific period of time.

Time-sensitive badges can be designed so that different patches take longer to change colour to indicate when they are void—one day, two days, or seven days.

### High-Security, Computer-Generated Cards and Badges

When designing a secure employee ID card, there are three primary considerations to keep in mind: security, functionality, and appearance.

*Card Security*

If security concerns are relatively low, a digitally printed card with a clear or holographic "topcoat" may provide plenty of protection. Clear topcoats and laminates made of durable polymers provide an extra line of defence against forgery or alteration of cards. Topcoats feature edge-to-edge protection across a card surface, while laminates provide greater thickness for extended durability. If a strong line of defence against forgery and alteration is required, there are several advanced card security technologies available:

- *Laser engraving* technology embeds data into ID cards to guard against forgery. A laser beam permanently engraves (or burns) data into the inner core of the card. The information cannot be mechanically or chemically removed without damaging the surface of the card, providing an extremely effective, tamper-evident barrier. Laser-engraved data can also be printed to "disturb" the outer surface of a card, creating a tactile effect. This high-resolution technology supports "microprinting," or printing of extremely small characters invisible to the naked eye, as an added measure against counterfeiting.
- *Ghost printing* technology is used to create a substantial level of tamper-resistance by adding a lighter reproduction of an image on an identity document, typically in the same area of the document as personalized data. The second image appears as a light background to text data, significantly increasing the difficulty of altering the photo image or the data. Any attempt at photo substitution would require altering the printed data as well as the ghost image. Ghost images can be printed in full colour or one colour in a wide range of inks, including laser and UV.
- *Computer-generated image modification* uses digital printing technology to pre-print or variable-print advanced computer-generated graphic elements on identity documents. With a special reader or viewer, certain elements become visible—elements that disappear when the document is reproduced with a copier or scanner.
- The latest entry into badge protection is *holography*. The introduction of holography into badge control systems reduces the chance of counterfeit ID cards being produced. Holograms, together with other technological advances, have produced an identification card system that is almost forgery-proof.

### Functionality

To secure ID cards beyond visual verification, smart card chips, magnetic strips, bar codes, or proximity capabilities (radio frequency) can be added.

"Smart" cards offer the highest level of security for storing machine-readable data on a card. Information on these chips can be protected with passwords and PINs, or integrated with biometric technology that requires matching cardholder profiles to gain access to information on the chip. Smart cards can store vital cardholder data that can be accessed offline and offer you a secure method for conducting online transactions with government agencies.

### Appearance and Branding

Some card providers offer the option of printing full-colour images, text, and other graphics on identification cards. These options support company branding initiatives.

## Temporary ID Cards

The following guidelines for the issuance of temporary ID cards are appropriate in most facilities:

- Ensure that all required forms are filled out when issuing the card.
- Get a signature before issue.
- Confirm identification of a temporary employee from an approved Canadian photo ID.
- Advise temporary employees to wear their ID card visibly at all times while on site.
- Advise temporary employees of any areas to which their cards do not allow them access.
- Make temporary employees wait for their escort (if required). Do not send them or allow them to find their escort on their own.
- Ensure that all cards are returned as required.
- Follow up on all outstanding cards immediately.
- Protect and secure blank cards.

# Crowd Control

From time to time, a security professional may encounter a large group of people inside or outside a building during a planned event/drill or an emergency situation/crisis. Planned events may include concerts and large meetings; drills may include fire alarm drills or emergency exercises; and emergency situations and crises may include protests, actual fires, or natural disasters.

Where a crowd gathers unexpectedly due to a crisis, security professionals must remain calm and execute the prepared emergency plan. Where a crowd appears to be protesting, it is important that security guards carefully monitor the situation. In the absence of provocation, crowds tend to be peaceful. However, whenever large numbers of people gather, there are increased chances that accidents (for example, tripping, jostling, etc.) will occur. If emotions are running high at a protest, for example, violence and property damage become risks. Security personnel should be careful not to overreact to a crowd in a way that might increase these risks, and should avoid overly aggressive attempts to disperse the crowd, which can increase the risk of both violence and accidents. Instead, security personnel should radio for backup from colleagues, closely monitor the crowd, and be prepared to call law enforcement if violence does occur.

## Planned Events

For each planned event hosted by the security guard's employer or client, there should be a corresponding security plan. Senior security personnel may be given a role in creating these plans. A security plan should include details on a wide range of issues, including vehicular and on-foot access management; access for disabled individuals; directing individuals to appropriate locations; signage; sufficiency of emergency exits, warning systems, and lighting; washroom access and sufficiency; waste collection; management of potential hazards (like electrical cords that could be tripped over); and a plan for communication in the event of an emergency.

There should also be a plan for allowing prompt access to the property by first responders, should they need to be called. For very large gatherings, for gatherings that involve strenuous physical activity (like a charity run), or for gatherings where environmental conditions may be challenging (for example, an outdoor event in summer heat), and to set up a first-aid station or tent.

As a starting point, prior to any planned event, security personnel must have the answers to the following questions:

- What is the nature of the event?
- Who is the target audience?
- Has this event ever been held at the same location in the past?
- What is the maximum capacity of the location?
- How many tickets have been sold?
- How many people have confirmed attendance?
- Are there any sensitive areas within or near the location?
- What are the house rules?
- Is there a special post order for this particular event?

- Is there an emergency plan in effect?
- Who are the key persons to communicate with?
- Is there sufficient medical emergency personnel/equipment on site?
- Are aisles and steps well-lit?
- Who will direct patrons to the appropriate location/seat?
- Who will provide appropriate service to handicapped and disabled persons?
- When will the doors open?
- Is it safe to wait outside?
- What is the weather condition?
- How many entry/exit points will be utilized?
- How familiar are the security personnel with the facility and the post orders?

## Cooperating with Law Enforcement

Hosting a large event increases the potential for requiring backup assistance from law enforcement. All security personnel should be appropriately trained in cooperating with law enforcement, and there should be a set of procedures in place for these interactions.

Procedures for working with law enforcement should include the following:

- Criteria and guidelines for determining when law enforcement personnel should be called to attend.
- Guidelines about who is responsible for calling police, and who should call if that person is not available.
- Guidelines for preparing for the arrival of law enforcement. These should include:
  - ensuring that prompt access is provided and directions to the scene are given;
  - asking witnesses to remain and keeping them calm and comfortable;
  - establishing a secure perimeter to protect evidence.
- Guidelines for cooperation with police personnel. Ideally, interaction with police should be managed by a supervisor.
- Guidelines about how to cooperate with police. Security personnel:
  - must pay attention to instructions from police, but let supervisor decide who will brief police; and
  - must follow instructions about when and how information will be handed over in order to protect the confidentiality of information.
- Guidelines about reporting on interactions with law enforcement.

# Vehicle and Traffic Control

Facilities patrolled by security guards are often on private property. This means that provincial traffic legislation is not enforceable on these sites. However, security guards acting according to the instructions of their employer or client are entitled to set limits on the use of the employer's or client's property, and that includes controlling traffic and parking.

## Authority Over Vehicular Traffic

Drivers are typically admitted to private roadways by the property owner's authorization. This authorization can either be express or implied. An example of **express authorization** is when entry is allowed after swiping a card at an entry gate. **Implied authorization** occurs where, for example, there is a sign denoting the boundaries of private property, but no barrier restricting the flow of traffic from a public roadway onto a private one.

Authorized users of a private roadway (for example, employees, contractors, and suppliers) are often invited to do so on condition that they comply with all parking and traffic rules in force on the site. As an agent of the owner, a security guard has legal authority to control vehicular access to private property. Owners and agents (security guards) have the authority, under municipal by-laws or municipal codes, to have a by-law officer tag a car that is illegally parked on private property. They can have the car towed off the property and taken to a private pound. The owner of the vehicle must then pay for the ticket, towing, and storage charges. In addition, under the *Trespass to Property Act* (TPA), section 5(1) requires the security guard to give a verbal or written warning.

In addition, section 9(1) of the TPA gives a security guard the power to arrest without warrant when he or she believes, on reasonable and probable grounds, that an individual has violated section 2(1) of the TPA which states:

> **Trespass an offence**
>
> 2(1) Every person who is not acting under a right or authority conferred by law and who,
>
> (a) without the express permission of the occupier, the proof of which rests on the defendant,
>
> (i) enters on premises when entry is prohibited under this Act, or
>
> (ii) engages in an activity on premises when the activity is prohibited under this Act; or
>
> (b) does not leave the premises immediately after he or she is directed to do so by the occupier of the premises or a person authorized by the occupier,
>
> is guilty of an offence and on conviction is liable to a fine of not more than $10,000.

In addition, section 11 of the TPA clearly outlines who is liable for a fine when individuals operate a motor vehicle or a motorized snow vehicle:

> **Motor vehicles and motorized snow vehicles**
>
> 11. Where an offence under this Act is committed by means of a motor vehicle, as defined in the *Highway Traffic Act*, or by means of a motorized snow vehicle, as defined in the *Motorized Snow Vehicles Act*, the driver of the motor vehicle or motorized snow vehicle is liable to the fine provided under this Act and, where the driver is not the owner, the owner of the motor vehicle or motorized snow vehicle is liable to the fine provided under this Act unless the driver is convicted of the offence or, at the time the offence was committed, the motor vehicle or motorized snow vehicle was in the possession of a person other than the owner without the owner's consent.

The above section points out that:

1. the driver may be charged;
2. if the driver is not the owner then the owner may be charged;
3. if the driver (who is not the owner) is convicted then the owner is not charged; and
4. if the driver took the motor vehicle or motorized snow vehicle without consent (or it was stolen), then the driver—not the owner—may be charged.

---

**express authorization**
admission to private roadways by invitation of the property owner

**implied authorization**
admission to private roadways is not prohibited by the property owner

# Rules of the Road for Private Property

In general, the easiest way to manage traffic on private property is to adopt the same rules of the road that apply to public property, because these rules are familiar to drivers. It also makes sense for private property owners to adopt and use, where necessary, traffic signs, road configurations, and road markings consistent with those in public use.

# Active Traffic Management and Hand Signals

In some cases where there is heavy traffic caused by, for example, a special event or work being carried out by construction or transportation vehicles, security personnel may be called on to actively direct traffic.

## *Apparel, Equipment, and Safety*

When directing traffic, security personnel should wear appropriate clothing and carry appropriate equipment. In daylight and/or clear weather, this means wearing or carrying:

- high-visibility clothing (HVC) or a fluorescent vest that fits over a regular uniform;
- steel-toed footwear;
- a hardhat;
- a whistle; and
- a notebook.

In addition to the above-noted clothing and equipment, in darkness or foul weather, security guards should wear or carry:

- clothing or a vest with large reflective (able to reflect light from headlights) stripes or markings;
- where appropriate, reflective wristbands and/or ankle cuffs; and
- a flashlight (check batteries on a regular basis and carry extras).

Equipment that may be used in support of traffic control includes:

- flags to increase the visibility of hand signals;
- flashlights and/or traffic wands for increasing the visibility of hand signals at night;
- barricades with fluorescent and/or lighted reflective markings; and
- radio equipment for communication with other traffic control personnel.

Equipment that is designed to control traffic without a human operator—for example, traffic lights—may be used in very high-traffic areas. Where employed, this equipment should meet standards similar to those used in public roadway applications. Ontario standards for traffic control equipment and the meanings of signals are described in RRO 1990, Regulation 626, *Traffic Control Signal Systems* made under the *Highway Traffic Act*. Similar standards exist under other provincial traffic control legislation.

Many traffic control garments are designed to incorporate both fluorescent colours and reflective materials. The *Occupational Health and Safety Act* and Regulation 362-07 of the *Private Security and Investigative Services Act, 2005* contain standards with respect to some items of traffic control apparel—for example, high-visibility clothing (HVC) and reflective vests. Apparel purchased for wear by security personnel should meet or exceed government standards for visibility.

Also, where the employer or client anticipates that nighttime traffic direction will be needed, roadways and intersections should be equipped with good-quality lighting.

Security personnel directing traffic should be instructed to stand only where they can be clearly seen from all directions and where they have a safe escape route. Ideally, a person directing traffic should stand not in the roadway, but on a median or raised platform that is clearly not part of the right-of-way. Where it is necessary to stand in the roadway, security personnel normally position themselves in the middle of an intersection, so that their position is not blocked from view by traffic from any direction.

Finally, where security personnel will be required to work near or direct the movements of construction equipment or vehicles, they should receive training with respect to safe work practices for work near the relevant equipment or vehicles.

### *Traffic-Management Signals*

Effective and safe traffic control depends on good communication. Signals, whether hand signals or audible signals (whistle), must be precise and clearly and easily understood. When directing traffic, security personnel should be conscious at all times of the degree to which they are visible from the direction of traffic, avoiding, where possible, having their back to traffic. They should not make any unnecessary movements that could be mistaken for hand signals, and when making traffic signals, they should strive for precision and authority in their body language. *Making eye contact* with both motorists and pedestrians when giving signals is essential.

Where an employee is required to direct the flow of traffic, he or she should use standard traffic-management hand signals as shown in Figures 3.1 through 3.3.

**Figure 3.1** Hand Signals for Traffic Control: Stopping Traffic

*Source*: Manitoba Justice, 2005.

## Stopping Traffic

1. Choose the vehicle you want to stop.
2. Look directly at the driver and point at them with your arm fully extended.
3. Make sure the driver has noticed your gesture, and then raise your hand so that your palm is facing the driver. Bend your arm slightly at the elbow.
4. Hold this position until the vehicle has stopped.
5. Keep your arm in position and turn your head to the opposite direction.
6. Repeat steps 1 to 4.
7. Do not lower your arms until all traffic has completely stopped.

## Starting Traffic

1. Make sure the intersection is clear and safe.
2. Place yourself with your side toward to the vehicles you want to move.
3. Look directly at the lead driver and point at them with your arm fully extended.
4. Make sure the driver has noticed your gesture. Turn your palm up, bend your arm at the elbow, and swing your hand up from the elbow and past your chin making a semi-circle. This looks like the common signal used for "Come here."
5. Repeat the gesture until the traffic begins to move.
6. When the traffic begins to move, drop your hand to the side.
7. Repeat steps 3 to 5 with your other arm for traffic coming from the opposite direction.

**Figure 3.2** Hand Signals for Traffic Control: Starting Traffic

*Source*: Manitoba Justice, 2005.

**Figure 3.3**  Hand Signals for Traffic Control: Left Turns

*Source*: Manitoba Justice, 2005.

## Left Turns

These turns are very dangerous, as vehicles will be turning into oncoming traffic. You must make a decision about when to allow left turns depending on how heavy the traffic is and how many people need to make the turn. Use caution.

1. Stop the traffic coming from the opposite direction. Hold the stop signal.
2. Make sure the intersection is clear of vehicles and pedestrians.
3. With your opposite arm fully extended, point at the driver who wants to turn.
4. Make sure the driver has noticed you. Make a downward swinging motion in the direction you want the driver to go.

## Right Turns

Drivers will need little direction when making right turns, as they will not be turning directly into oncoming traffic. If traffic is heavy, you may need to stop drivers turning right to let traffic pass from the other direction. Also if there are many vehicles turning right, you may need to hold back pedestrians, so that the traffic can flow smoothly. If you need to signal a right turn, make sure the driver has noticed you and then make a downward swinging motion to the driver's right.

## Parking

Where necessary, a private facility may need to develop and enforce rules for parking. These rules are usually communicated to drivers either by signs or pavement markings.

## Signs

Parking signs should be clear, simple in content, placed for good visibility, and, to the extent possible, similar to public parking signs. Parking signs at a private facility may be used to indicate reserved parking spaces, handicapped parking spaces, no-parking zones, and seasonal no-parking zones (for example, snow removal zones).

## Pavement Markings

Pavement markings are typically used to delineate parking spaces (including reserved and handicapped spaces). Properly marked parking areas ensure that vehicles will park in such a way as to permit safe entry and exit from the parking area.

# Emergency Vehicles

Emergency vehicles are typically exempt, at least while on emergency duty, from normal traffic signals (as per s. 144(20) of the *Highway Traffic Act*) and parking prohibitions. In an emergency, security guards may be called upon to direct traffic in support of access by emergency vehicles. In general, to allow entry for emergency vehicles, other traffic is directed to pull over as quickly as safety permits to the far right-hand side of the roadway.

# Enforcing Traffic and Parking Rules

As mentioned in Vehicle and Traffic Control above, private facilities are exempt from the application of provincial traffic legislation, which includes the Ontario *Highway Traffic Act*, and therefore the penalties under that legislation are not enforceable on private property. However, under the common law, private property owners have a right to control drivers' entry onto and activities on their property.

In general, private facility owners enforce parking by issuing verbal or written warnings to people who violate traffic and parking rules. Repeat offenders may have their entry and/or driving privileges suspended. In some cases, employers may use other sanctions against employees who violate traffic rules—for example, serious offenders may lose certain employment privileges or be subject to disciplinary procedures and notices. In support of these sanctions, some private facilities issue traffic or parking tags or tickets, similar in design to public tickets. Where there is a ticketing policy in place, all security guards should receive training in how to fill out a ticket and learn how the system is administered.

In case of a serious violation—for example, where a driver's actions threaten the safety of others or create damage to private property—facility owners may seek to have the offender charged under the *Trespass to Property Act* or the *Criminal Code*.

# Accidents

When a traffic accident occurs, security personnel should adopt the same priorities as with any security incident; namely, they should first assist those who are injured, before moving on to other concerns, such as preserving the crime scene as well as encouraging all involved parties to move to an area of safety. Please note that any security guard will always carry his or her licence and will produce his or her licence when asked for identification by any member of the public.

When there are injured parties or damage to property is in excess of $2,000, the police shall be called.[1] Further, the police are to be notified if the security guard suspects a person to be under the influence of alcohol or drugs.

**Figure 3.4** Sketch of an Intersection for an Accident Report

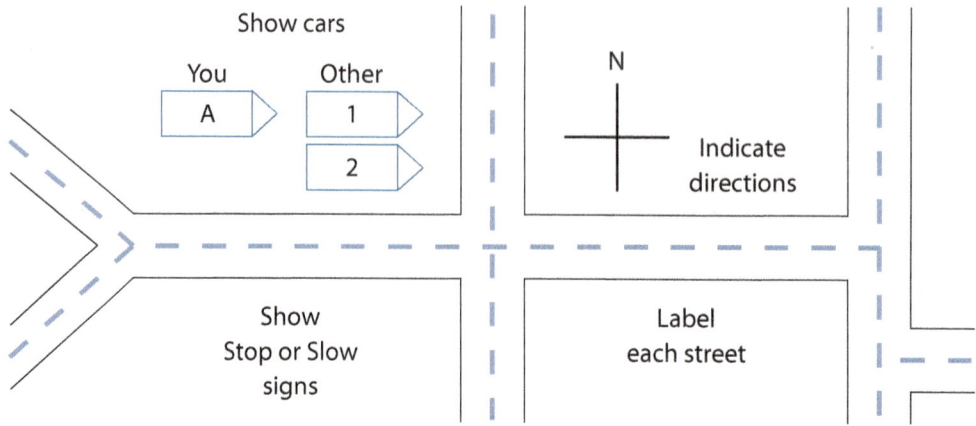

Regardless of whether police are involved in the investigation of the accident, security personnel should quickly identify witnesses who might be useful in documenting the occurrence. When possible, witnesses should be interviewed at the scene of the accident, before memory of the details fades. When making notes of the accident—indeed, in ANY investigation—the security guard will ask himself or herself the following questions: Who? What? When? Where? Why? and How? A security guard should also, as soon as possible, prepare a sketch or sketches that describe the accident (see Figure 3.4), because, in many cases, vehicles will need to be moved to restore traffic flow.

# Shift Handover Procedure

All security personnel should follow the guidelines below.

1. **At the Start of Your Shift**
   - Conduct a briefing with your co-workers, supervisor on duty, or client.
   - Be sure to know the route and areas that are to be patrolled during your shift.
   - Know the parameters and boundaries.
   - Check all equipment at the start of your shift and if you notice a malfunction, notify a supervisor immediately.

2. **During Your Shift**
   - Document the start, end, route, and location of each patrol.
   - Conduct random patrols and not structured (every 30 minutes/same route/same location).
   - Be vigilant and look for any deficiencies.
   - Document any abnormalities and, if required, contact a supervisor.

3. **At the End of Your Shift**
   - Conduct another briefing with your co-workers, supervisor on duty, or client.
   - Pass on any information to the appropriate person.
   - Report and document all of your findings in an incident report if necessary.
   - Return any equipment you used and ensure that the equipment is in working condition. If equipment is damaged during your shift, notify your supervisor immediately.

# Drug and Alcohol Effects and Substance Abuse

As a security professional, you are bound to interact and deal with individuals under the influence of drug(s) or alcohol. Knowing the characteristics of a person under the influence plays a vital role in being able to effectively reach a resolution. In this section we will review the common signs and symptoms of alcohol intoxication and the effects of some of the most common drugs and controlled substances. (See Appendix A.)

## Alcohol

When consuming alcohol, everyone experiences different signs and symptoms because there is a direct relationship between the individual's weight, alcohol tolerance, the amount ingested, and the time period of drinking. When dealing with an individual under the influence of alcohol, all attempts should be made to identify the four factors mentioned above.

### Mobility

Consumption of alcohol negatively affects coordination, which causes the individual to sway and struggle for balance. This often results in the person falling down.

### Smell of Alcohol

Some alcoholic beverages, such as beer and wine, have a distinct smell and you may be able to smell them on the person's breath while speaking to them.

### Vision

As with mobility, alcohol negatively affects the consumer's vision and that is why it is very dangerous to operate a vehicle while under the influence of alcohol. The person's vision will be blurred and he or she will not be able to focus.

### Behaviour

A person under the influence of alcohol tends to behave on impulse with an extreme lack of logic. They experience extreme emotions and are quite often disrespectful toward others.

## Drugs

According to Narconon (2017), there are many signs, both physical and behavioural, that indicate drug use. Each drug has its own unique manifestations, but there are some general indications that a person is using drugs:

- sudden changes in behaviour;
- mood swings: irritable and grumpy and then suddenly happy and bright;
- withdrawal from family members;
- carelessness in personal grooming;
- loss of interest in hobbies, sports, and other favourite activities;
- changes in sleeping pattern: up at night and asleep during the day;
- red or glassy eyes; and
- sniffly or runny nose.

## Methamphetamine

The user will appear to be "wired": sleepless for days and weeks at a time, and suffering from total loss of appetite, extreme weight loss, dilated pupils, excitation, talkativeness, a deluded sense of power, paranoia, depression, loss of control, nervousness, unusual sweating, shaking, anxiety, hallucinations, aggression, violence, dizziness, mood changes, blurred vision, mental confusion, and/or agitation.

## Ecstasy

Ecstasy causes changes in mental and physical stimulation, altered perception of sound, light, and touch; stimulation of physical energy with related decrease in appetite and increase in body temperature; an increase in emotional response and sensual reactions; teeth clenching; muscle cramping; nausea; chills; and sweating. The body may overheat, which can lead to fatalities.

## Cocaine

This drug results in impaired thinking, confusion, anxiety, depression, a short temper, panic attacks, suspiciousness, dilated pupils, sleeplessness, loss of appetite, decreased sexual drive, restlessness, irritability, talkativeness, scratching, hallucinations, and paranoia.

## LSD (Acid)

Lysergic acid diethylamide causes dilated pupils, skin discoloration, loss of coordination, a false sense of power, euphoria, distortion of time and space, hallucinations, confusion, paranoia, nausea, vomiting, loss of control, anxiety, panic, helplessness, and self-destructive behaviour.

## Inhalant

Short-term use of inhalants will result in euphoria, giggling, silliness, and dizziness, followed by headaches and fainting or unconsciousness. Long-term use effects: memory loss, emotional instability, impairment of reasoning, slurred speech, clumsiness, a staggering gait, eye fluttering, tremors, hearing loss, loss of sense of smell, and escalating stages of brain atrophy. Sometimes these serious long-term effects are reversible with body detoxification and nutritional therapy; sometimes the brain damage is irreversible or only partially reversible.

## Heroin

The results of heroin use are chemically enforced euphoria and a dreamlike state similar to sleep in which the person can drift off for minutes or hours at a time. For long-time abusers, heroin may act like a stimulant, and users can perform a normal daily routine. Others may find themselves completely powerless to do anything.

## Marijuana

Marijuana use results in compulsive eating, bloodshot and squinty red eyes (there may be trouble keeping them open); a dry mouth; excessive and uncontrollable laughter; forgetfulness and short-term memory loss; extreme lethargy; delayed motor skills; occasional paranoia; hallucinations; laziness and lack of motivation, stupidity; a sickly sweet smell on the body, hair, and clothes; and strong mood changes and behaviours when the person is "high."

## CHAPTER SUMMARY

In this chapter, we discussed the main roles and duties of security personnel. The importance of observational skills was explained, and the concept of situational awareness and its benefits for security guards was introduced.

We also identified different types of patrols and their applications.

Also addressed here is the importance of controlling access by both staff and visitors to a secured area; we discussed both procedures and the use of appropriate access technologies. As with access control, controlling the flow of traffic on a property is also very important, and the topic of vehicular traffic control was introduced.

When events and gatherings are hosted on the employer or client's property, appropriate plans should be made for the provision of crowd management and control. The elements of a crowd control plan were described. Because the risk of criminal or other incidents increases during major gatherings, we also explained appropriate procedures for cooperation with law enforcement personnel.

Finally, the common signs and symptoms of drug and alcohol use were discussed, so that security guards encountering intoxicated individuals are better prepared to provide support and control when dealing with these individuals.

## KEY TERMS

access control, 45
control room, 42
express authorization, 52
high-risk patrol, 42
human environment, 44
implied authorization, 52
observational skills, 40
physical environment, 43
silent hours, 42
situational awareness, 43

## NOTE

1. See section 199(1) of the *Highway Traffic Act* and O Reg 596, General, section 11 under the *Highway Traffic Act*.

## REFERENCES

*Criminal Code*, RSC 1985, c C-46.

*Highway Traffic Act*, RSO 1990, c H.8.

Manitoba Justice. (2005). *Manitoba Security Guard Training Program Participant's Manual*. Retrieved from https://www.gov.mb.ca/justice/safe/private/pubs/securityguard_manual.pdf

Narconon. 2017. *Signs and Symptoms of Drug Use*. Retrieved from http://www.narconon.ca/drug-abuse/signs-symptoms-of-drug-abuse.html

*Occupational Health and Safety Act*, RSO 1990, c O.1.

*Private Security and Investigative Services Act, 2005*, SO 2005, c 34.

*Traffic Control Signal Systems*, RRO 1990, Reg 626.

*Trespass to Property Act*, RSO 1990, c T.21 [TPA].

*Uniforms*, O Reg 362-07.

## PERFORMANCE APPLICATION

### Multiple Choice

1. Which is the correct assumption and approach when encountering an unexpected crowd on the premises?
   a. recognize that most large crowds are peaceful and take no special action
   b. recognize that all large crowds pose an immediate danger and call police
   c. recognize that all large crowds pose an immediate danger and take aggressive steps to gain control of the situation and disperse the crowd
   d. recognize that large crowds are generally peaceful but do pose potential danger, and monitor the crowd continuously and carefully
   e. approach the crowd and attempt to establish friendly relations with the apparent leader

2. Patrols are most likely to deter unlawful behaviour when they are highly:
   a. disorganized
   b. aggressive
   c. visible
   d. repetitive
   e. secretive

3. Visitors to a facility may be required to sign in and out in a book known as a:
   a. post order
   b. building manifest
   c. hot list
   d. occurrence report
   e. sign-in log or visitor log

4. Alcohol consumption has different effects on individuals because of the effect of:
   a. body weight
   b. age
   c. amount ingested
   d. a and c
   e. alcohol consumption has the same effect on all users

5. A security guard arriving on duty should request the following from the guard he or she is relieving:
   a. a briefing about the events of the prior shift, including any special or unusual instructions for the upcoming shift
   b. three copies of the shift report
   c. that the departing guard submit to a search to ensure that he or she is not removing company property
   d. his or her access pass
   e. that the departing guard perform one last patrol while the incoming guard familiarizes himself or herself with the prior shift report

6. The most important goal of traffic management on private property is:
   a. protecting the safety of people, premises, and property
   b. ensuring compliance by all vehicles with the *Highway Traffic Act*
   c. prioritizing access for employees
   d. reducing driving speeds
   e. ensuring compliance with the *Canadian Charter of Rights and Freedoms*

7. Situational awareness means:
   a. being aware of one's biases and prejudices when going into a situation
   b. maintaining a constant awareness of one's location and surroundings
   c. knowing the location of all escape routes
   d. already knowing all the important facts about a situation before going into it
   e. being able to "read" the intentions and motivations of others

8. The ability of a security professional to promptly and accurately detect changes in his or her physical surroundings on patrol:
   a. comes naturally after a few shifts on the job
   b. requires conscious attention and regular practice
   c. is less important than completing patrols quickly and consistently
   d. is more important during working or open hours than during silent hours
   e. is improved by the consumption of caffeine

9. A security professional derives authority to control traffic on private property from:
   a. the police
   b. the owner's property rights under the common law
   c. the *Highway Traffic Act*
   d. the *Criminal Code*
   e. his or her employment contract

## Short Answer

You are a security professional working at an art gallery. You have been assigned as security's point of contact for the upcoming concert being held in the main hall at your site. Consider the points below and prepare a crowd control plan:

- 500 tickets have been sold,
- the average age of fans ranges from 20 to 30 years of age,
- the hall's maximum capacity is 500,
- there are four emergency exits and two emergency stairwells in the building,
- the parking lot holds 600 vehicles, and
- you are the one in charge.

# Report Writing and Note Taking

## 4

| | |
|---|---|
| Introduction | 66 |
| Note Taking | 66 |
| Purpose of Memo or Notebook | 66 |
| Specifications and Safekeeping | 67 |
| Rules for Taking Notes | 68 |
| What to Note | 69 |
| What's Important? | 69 |
| Report Writing | 71 |
| Distinguishing Facts, Inferences, and Opinions | 72 |
| Types of Factual Reports | 73 |
| Basic Principles of Effective Report Writing | 77 |
| Statement Taking | 79 |
| How to Take a Statement | 79 |
| Chapter Summary | 81 |
| Key Terms | 82 |
| Reference | 82 |
| Performance Application | 82 |

## LEARNING OUTCOMES

When you have completed this chapter, you will be able to:

- Explain the purposes of note taking and report writing by security personnel.
- Describe and distinguish different types of reports.
- Understand the legal implications of on-the-job reports.
- Describe the appropriate content of reports.

# Introduction

In this chapter we will examine the importance of record-keeping, note taking, and report writing. Appropriate methods for taking statements and the legalities surrounding admissibility of such evidence in a court proceeding will be discussed.

In the security industry, security professionals are the eyes and the ears of the client. As previously covered in Chapter 3, security professionals are trained to be observant and to identify deficiencies and security risks. Security guards must relay their findings to the client so that they can be dealt with, and comprehensive documentation is required to enable this information to be relayed accurately and in a timely manner.

People who think of security as an action-based job are often surprised by the amount of paperwork required. Working in security means documenting a wide range of occurrences, both routine and non-routine. Because of this, security professionals must develop strong communication skills, both verbal and written. They must be able to speak clearly and with enough detail for their instructions to be understood completely. They must be able to jot down notes and write reports that not only contain all information necessary to support informed decision-making, but that are also neat and easy to read.

Many security companies have transitioned into electronic record-keeping. Entering information gathered by security professionals into databases permits the information to be stored and organized efficiently, so that incident details can be retrieved quickly—for example, by using a keyword search. Note, however, that the use of electronic record storage demands that proper measures are taken to ensure the security of confidential information.

For the purpose of security operations, we will be discussing note taking and its importance when it is done at the time an incident occurs, and also report writing, which is the final document that is provided to the client for action (if required). The combination of adequate notes and a comprehensive report will paint a clear picture of what transpired and allow the client to take any necessary preventive measures to avoid reoccurrences.

# Note Taking

It is essential that detailed notes are made about observations either at the time or immediately afterward to later assist in information recall. Notes enable security professionals to write a comprehensive report and to refresh memories at a later date. Notes may often be found to contain clues and evidence that were not recognized as such at the time of the incident.

# Purpose of Memo or Notebook

A notebook is intended to serve as a chronological record of a security guard's activities while on duty. It represents his or her findings, observations made, and actions taken during each duty period. Sample entries in a security guard's notebook are shown in Figure 4.1 on page 68. The evidential integrity of the notebook requires that all matters—whether trivial or important—are recorded with the same level of accuracy and detail. A notebook is a security professional's lifeline. It serves the following purposes.

### Aide-Memoire

Because the significance of details may not become apparent until after an occurrence, appropriate notebook entries provide an essential written reference for later consultation—for example, when preparing for a court appearance months or even years after an incident took place.

## Background for Other Security Personnel and/or Police
Accurate and complete notebook entries allow other security personnel and/or police to pick up the investigation where the security guard left off without re-interviewing witnesses.

## Grounds for Action
Notebook entries can serve as support for a security guard's decisions. For example, certain actions, such as making an arrest, require that the guard had reasonable grounds to believe that an offence had been committed before the action was taken. Because actions, such as an arrest, will be scrutinized later, accurate notes help establish the appropriate grounds for the actions taken.

## Official Document
A security professional's notebook often becomes an exhibit—an official document—in any court case arising out of a security incident, and as such, may be examined by lawyers, judges, and a jury. With permission, notes can also be used to refresh your memory when testifying in court. It is almost certain that the court will inquire about when the notes were made and, unless the notes were made at the time or immediately after the incident, the court will usually not give consent for them to be examined. If permission is granted and notes are produced in court, the notebook will become part of the evidence. The notebook may then be examined by any of the parties involved.

## Performance Measurement and Employment Record
A security professional's notes are a measurement of his or her work performance, competency, efficiency, and character. The methods used to write and keep notes can lead to recommendations for promotion and specialized duties.

Notes also become a record of the guard's days off, sick days, overtime, and special duties, and can verify his or her salary and vacation time.

# Specifications and Safekeeping
Notebooks are generally issued by the employer. The typical notebook is hardbound and pocket-sized, with lined pages. Notebook pages are numbered to ensure continuity. Under no circumstances should pages be removed; doing so jeopardizes the integrity of the entire notebook.

Notebooks are considered the property of the organization, not the user. Notebooks are returned to storage at the end of a shift, and filled notebooks are placed in long-term storage for a minimum of seven years. Security guards are responsible for protecting their notebooks during a shift, which means keeping them in their possession for the entire shift. A security professional should have only one notebook in use at a time. Requests to review another guard's notebook are generally processed through the supervisor.

### ON THE JOB
It is important to remember that your notebook should never be used to record personal information. The information in your notebook may be used as evidence in a court case.

**Figure 4.1**  Entries in a Security Guard's Notebook

| | | |
|---|---|---:|
| | *Wednesday, September 13, 2017* | **1** |
| 0700 | Start shift. Walk around. Weather clear, cool. | |
| 0730 | Good visibility, roads dry. Call to attend warehouse B; motion detector triggered. | |
| 0736 | Arrive scene & observe minor disarray, trashcan upturned, spillage of discarded coffee cups, paw prints, apparently raccoon tracks on linoleum. Scuffling sounds heard behind styrofoam sheets against east wall. | |
| 0743 | Raccoon located behind styrofoam sheet and chased out of warehouse. Inspection of premises revealed no other animals or humans present. Garbage cleared. | |
| 0752 | Return to control room, alarm reset. | |
| 0756 | False alarm report completed. | |

At the end of a shift, the supervisor reviews all notebooks. Any comments are made in red ink. Requests for corrections and additions are communicated promptly to the notebook's user, and the notebook is signed by the supervisor after his or her review.

Security personnel must be mindful of the fact that their notes, reports, and statements may contain private and confidential information. It is the security professional's responsibility to ensure the security of such sensitive information. This also applies to any electronic record-keeping or transmission of information.

If it becomes necessary to transmit information electronically to other individuals, the sensitivity of the information will need to be taken into account before choosing a method of transmission. For example, it may NOT be appropriate to transmit these records via email unless special precautions are taken, such as using encryption, or creating password-protected files, or some other security measure. In some settings, security professionals may be instructed to upload files into a secure database designed for the purpose, or onto cloud-based storage systems, placing them in folders to which only authorized individuals have access.

## Rules for Taking Notes

The standard notebook rules that should be abided by are as follows:

- The notebook should be a bound book with each page numbered.
- All entries should be made in chronological order, with the date and time recorded. The 24-hour clock should be used for recording time.

- Entries should be made as soon as possible after events are observed. All entries must be made in ink (preferably, black ink).
- Entries should be neat, legible, and concise.
- Note-takers should avoid the use of jargon and slang.
- There must be no erasures.
- Where an error is made, the incorrect word or words should be crossed out with a single line and the note taker should initial the changes.
- No pages must be removed.
- No words should be written between the lines.
- There should be no spaces left. Any space at the end of a line or page should be crossed through with a single line and initialed.

# What to Note

Security guards must report both routine and non-routine incidents.

Routine incidents reported may include:

- patrol observations (including "all clear"/"all's well" observations);
- observations with respect to the state/condition of objects/equipment;
- observations with respect to things to watch out for—for example, potential hazards that may be developing (ice on walkways, etc.);
- observations with respect to human activities/normal traffic;
- false alarms and how they were handled; and
- anything else that security personnel have been instructed to observe.

Non-routine incidents may include:

- fires;
- bomb incidents;
- violence/assaults;
- thefts and intrusions;
- floods, lightning strikes, and other weather events;
- equipment malfunctions;
- trespass incidents;
- medical emergencies and workplace accidents;
- vandalism;
- protests/demonstrations/labour relations incidents; and
- information technology (IT) incidents.

# What's Important?

In recording the details of an incident, it's important to learn how to prioritize information and express it in a complete and organized way. Determining what information is most relevant is a skill that can be learned, just like any other. A tool that may help security professionals develop this skill is self-questioning—asking questions of themselves and answering them in their notes.

## WANTED

For example, if an object needs to be described, security professionals can determine what information is required by remembering the acronym "WANTED":

| W | What are you describing? |
|---|---|
| A | Appearance (colour, size, material) |
| N | Number (how many articles, pieces, serial number) |
| T | Type (make and model) |
| E | Extraordinary (are there any additional features that make it identifiable?) |
| D | Dollars (apparent value or worth) |

## The Five Ws

Another common strategy for organizing information is to ask the "five W" questions: Who, What, Where, When, and Why, as well as How.

### 1. Who?

When describing a victim, suspect, or witness, and depending on the nature of the incident, a security guard might note:

- gender;
- age (ask for a birthdate; consider whether the age given seems plausible based on observation);
- height;
- weight;
- build;
- hair colour, texture, and style;
- facial hair;
- skin colour (be specific—is the person's skin fair, light, brown, black, olive?) Are there scars or marks? Birthmarks? Tattoos?
- eye colour and whether glasses are worn;
- teeth (protruding, false, irregular, decayed);
- speech (refined, vulgar, foreign, lisp, rapid);
- physical deformities;
- mannerisms/peculiarities;
- a full description of clothing;
- a full description of articles carried (purse, briefcase, cellphone, packages, etc.).

### 2. What?

Record details of injuries or damage observed. Describe vehicles involved, if any. Make notes about any physical evidence secured, where and how it was marked, where it will be stored, and in whose possession it was placed.

### 3. Where?

In describing locations, provide a complete street address. Then, describe the specific location of the incident by reference to non-movable landmarks—for example, "4 metres to the west of the main entrance gate." Be very specific. Note also the location of any evidence

> ## ON THE JOB
>
> ### Describing Vehicles
>
> When describing a vehicle, the following information should be recorded:
>
> 1. licence plate number, colour, province/state, year, and validation number;
> 2. year of manufacture and make;
> 3. body type and colour;
> 4. numbers: vehicle identification number (VIN) and engine number;
> 5. accessories: radio, CD player, navigation system, leather or fabric interior, etc.;
> 6. contents of car (trunk and passenger areas);
> 7. type of transmission, number of cylinders, size of engine;
> 8. odometer reading;
> 9. unusual details: damage, rust, dirt, stains, noise, smoke, dragging/dangling parts, stickers, and decorations; and
> 10. other basic information: owner's name, address, phone number, and driver's licence number.

collected—for example, "from the passenger-side floor of the silver Honda Accord, plate number ASKW 305."

## 4. When?

The time of an incident should be as accurate as possible. If unknown, it may be estimated—for example, between 1330 and 1430 hours. Use the 24-hour clock to ensure that the time of day is never ambiguous.

The date recorded should include day, month, and year, and the day of the week. Note the weather conditions as well. Information such as light conditions, visibility, and the position of the sun and the presence of moonlight may be useful in screening witness testimony for investigations or may be useful in court later.

## 5. Why?

Include information regarding any actions or omissions that contributed to the incident. For example, were possessions left unattended or were keys left in a vehicle? Did a suspect use break-in tools? How do you know?

## 6. How?

When describing what has occurred, explain the events in chronological order. Note which information came from your own observations, and which information came from another person's description of the events.

# Report Writing

In dealing with security incidents, security guards must report the facts about what has happened. Reports are useful not only to the employer/client in reviewing what has happened, but they may also be used in a criminal case for prosecuting offenders or in a civil lawsuit. In order to be useful, security reports must be clear and understandable to a wide range of different types of readers.

## Reporting Basics

To create a successful report, a security guard must have:

1. Complete knowledge of the facts surrounding every occurrence.
2. The intelligence to interpret the facts.
3. The discipline to identify facts from hearsay or outright falsehood for the reader.
4. The ability to express these facts in the report.

Security guards must record in their notebook all the information necessary to compile a complete report. To ensure that they have all possible information, every complaint received must be noted, regardless of its apparent importance or insignificance. Trivial matters may later become significant details in a police investigation. Most security organizations have report forms that cover practically every aspect of any occurrence.

# Distinguishing Facts, Inferences, and Opinions

While report writing often requires the security guard to make inferences from facts, excessive speculation and/or reliance on hearsay evidence may limit the usefulness of reports. Security guards must learn how to tell the difference between fact, inference, and opinion. They must also learn how to indicate secondary material, by making it clear, when using information from other sources, that the security guard is reporting what the person said, not vouching for the truth of the statement.

## Facts

Facts are information that security guards know for certain and that can be substantiated. Proof may consist of physical evidence, or of direct observation evidence—either the security guard's or that of a reliable witness.

A purely factual description of a break-and-enter scene might read something like this:

> The rear door was open. The lock was broken. A crowbar lay on the floor, and there was a set of footprints with toes pointing toward the interior of the building. The victim reported that various items were missing from different rooms.

Facts answer six questions—Who? What? Where? When? Why? and How?

## Inferences

Inferences are deductions or hypotheses of what probably happened based on the facts gathered by the security guard at the crime scene. Formulating a hypothesis is not the reader's function; it is the reporter's responsibility. And here, the reporter is the security guard, performing his or her duty.

To develop a hypothesis, security professionals must make statements about the unknown based on what they do know: in other words, inferences based on the facts or physical evidence, interviews, and investigative results. A security guard can be trained to observe and to think through each occurrence and, in doing so, write an impartial and logical account of what probably transpired.

Most of the time inferences will be correct. But security professionals must also recognize that they may be wrong. This is why it is crucial that they recognize that they are making an inference and not recording a fact. To make the difference clear to the reader, the writer must "tag" each inference as an inference to prevent misleading the reader.

To make an inference clear to the reader or to "tag" it, a security guard would write the following in an occurrence report (but not in a memo or notebook, where facts only are recorded):

*Based on the evidence gathered at the scene of the crime, including the fingerprints on the gun and the matching bullets, it appears that the victim was attacked by the accused.*

Note the tags: "based on the evidence" and "it appears." Presenting an inference allows a security professional to examine new information that might come forward as the investigation continues.

## Opinions and Judgments

In addition to the facts, which must be included, and inferences, which may be included, a security professional has to know how to recognize opinions and judgments, which should never be included in written reports.

Opinions are personal beliefs or so-called gut-feeling reactions with no substantial evidential basis. This lack of solid factual support distinguishes opinions from inferences.

Judgments also have no place in security or police work. By judgments, we mean expressions of approval or disapproval. These judgments may occur in a blatant statement or more covertly in the slanting of information. For instance, a security guard who was aware that a witness's statement was false might write: "Witness is a liar." Such a declaration involves two assumptions: first, the witness knew the truth, and second, the witness deliberately misstated it. Neither assumption may be correct. Consequently, guards must refrain from using such open expressions of approval or disapproval. After all, to call a witness a liar is to imply that the witness consistently and deliberately gives false information.

Security professionals must also guard against using influential words that indicate approval or disapproval that may, as a consequence, affect the reader's perception of the report. For instance, writing the opinion "the accused was personable and unlikely to commit such a horrible crime" would reflect unprofessional and inappropriate judgment.

Descriptors that have a negative connotation, for example, "squeegee kid" or "bag lady," are to be avoided, because they imply judgment.

Even apparently harmless adverbs may reflect a judgment. Suppose a security guard wrote, "The complainant lamely stated, 'I thought I had locked the door.'" The adverb "lamely" implies that the guard questions the validity of the statement or finds it inadequate; either way, it reflects disapproval. The guard unintentionally influenced the reader's perception of the incident.

# Types of Factual Reports

There are four types of factual reports: general occurrence reports (initial reports), form reports, specialized reports, and supplemental reports. The type of report to be used is based on the type of investigation to be carried out.

## General Occurrence Reports (Initial Reports)

The **general occurrence report** covers the preliminary investigation of an incident and is prepared by the security guard who was the first to encounter the incident. Examples include arrest reports and security reports. A general occurrence report contains all or most of the following information:

- type of crime or incident (classified);
- date, time, and location;
- names, addresses, postal code, telephone numbers of all involved;
- details of conversations with persons involved (witnesses, suspects, complainants, and victims);
- detailed descriptions of persons, vehicles, property, and locations; and
- statements of all facts relevant to the case and inferences related to the facts (that is, the security professional's hypothesis).

### Advantages of the General Occurrence Report

The report is prepared in a narrative format, and it is freeform, continuous, and does not follow a prescribed pattern or outline. The focus is on a written account of the incident in chronological order.

### Disadvantages of the General Occurrence Report

The report is often too long and confusing, difficult to read, and time consuming to write.

## Form Reports

The **form report** is designed to cover essential data relating to specific crimes or events. It is used where standardization of essential information is necessary, and it consists mainly of blank spaces and/or check boxes. Traffic reports (see Figure 4.2), missing-person reports, stolen bicycle or vehicle reports, and security violation reports are examples of the form report.

### Advantages of the Form Report

Form reports are quick and easy to fill in. They also reduce the danger of overlooking essential data.

### Disadvantages of the Form Report

The form is restrictive. No two cases are the same. As a result, variations in detail or complexity cannot be expressed fully.

## Specialized Reports

**Specialized reports** are used for complex and detailed investigations and other non-routine matters. The format is generally flexible and centres on the story. Examples of specialized reports include court (Crown) briefs, private investigation reports, and security surveys.

### Advantages of Specialized Reports

A specialized report can fit any type of case. It is flexible and allows for a more detailed document with full and complete information.

---

**general occurrence report**
a report describing the preliminary investigation of an incident by the security professional who was the first to encounter it

**form report**
a report template that includes blank spaces and/or check boxes and that provides for the standardized entry of essential data relating to specific incidents

**specialized report**
a report used for complex and detailed investigations or for non-routine matters

## Disadvantages of Specialized Reports

Like the general occurrence report, it can be too long and confusing for the reader. The narrative form also makes it difficult and time consuming to pull out statistics.

**Figure 4.2** Traffic Report

| Insurer | Agent or Broker | Claim No. |
|---|---|---|

**POLICY HOLDER**

| Name of Insured | Policy Number |
|---|---|
| Residence Phone ( ) | Business Phone ( ) |
| Home address | Postal Code |
| Business address | Postal Code |

**VEHICLE**

| Registered owner | Address |
|---|---|
| Actual owner | Address |

| Make of vehicle | Year | Model | Serial No. | Plate No. & Province |
|---|---|---|---|---|
| Mileage | Describe damage | | | $ Estimate of damage |

**DRIVER**

| Name of driver | Age | State any physical disabilities | How long driving? |
|---|---|---|---|
| Home address | | Business address | |
| Residence phone ( ) | Business phone ( ) | Driver's licence no. | |
| Previous accidents or convictions | | Date of accident: day/mt/yr | |
| Time ☐ A.M ☐ P.M. | Lighting conditions ☐ Daylight ☐ Dusk ☐ Dark | Location of accident | |
| Purpose vehicle used for at time of accident | | Weather conditions | Road conditions |
| Your speed | Direction | Other vehicle's speed | Direction |
| Police investigation by | | Charges | |
| Had you taken any alcohol or drugs prior to the accident | | Who was responsible? (State reason) | |

**Figure 4.2** Continued

| DAMAGE TO PROPERTY OF OTHERS |||||
|---|---|---|---|
| Name | Phone No. | Name | Phone No. |
| Address || Address ||
| Year and make of vehicle | Licence No. | Year and make of vehicle | Licence No. |
| Name of insurer | Policy No. | Name of insurer | Policy No. |
| Description of damage || Description of damage ||
| Where vehicle can be inspected || Where vehicle can be inspected ||
| Name of driver | Phone No. | Name of driver | Phone No. |
| Address || Address ||

| DETAILS OF PERSONS INJURED ||||||
|---|---|---|---|---|---|
| Name | Age | Address | Phone No. | Nature of injuries | Hospital |
|  |  |  |  |  |  |
|  |  |  |  |  |  |

| DETAILS OF WITNESSES ||||
|---|---|---|---|
|  | Witness No. 1 | Witness No. 2 | Witness No. 3 |
| Name |  |  |  |
| Address |  |  |  |
| In which Vehicle? | ☐ In your car? ☐ Car No. 1 ☐ Car No. 2 ☐ Other | ☐ In your car? ☐ Car No. 1 ☐ Car No. 2 ☐ Other | ☐ In your car? ☐ Car No. 1 ☐ Car No. 2 ☐ Other |

## Supplemental Reports

**supplemental report**
a report added at a later time to a general occurrence report by, for example, other personnel assisting in the investigation

**Supplemental reports** are a continuation or addition to the general occurrence report and the specialized report. A supplemental report may be submitted by:

- the person originally assigned to the case;
- personnel assisting in the investigation; and
- specialists, such as identification officers and youth bureau investigators.

**Figure 4.2** Continued

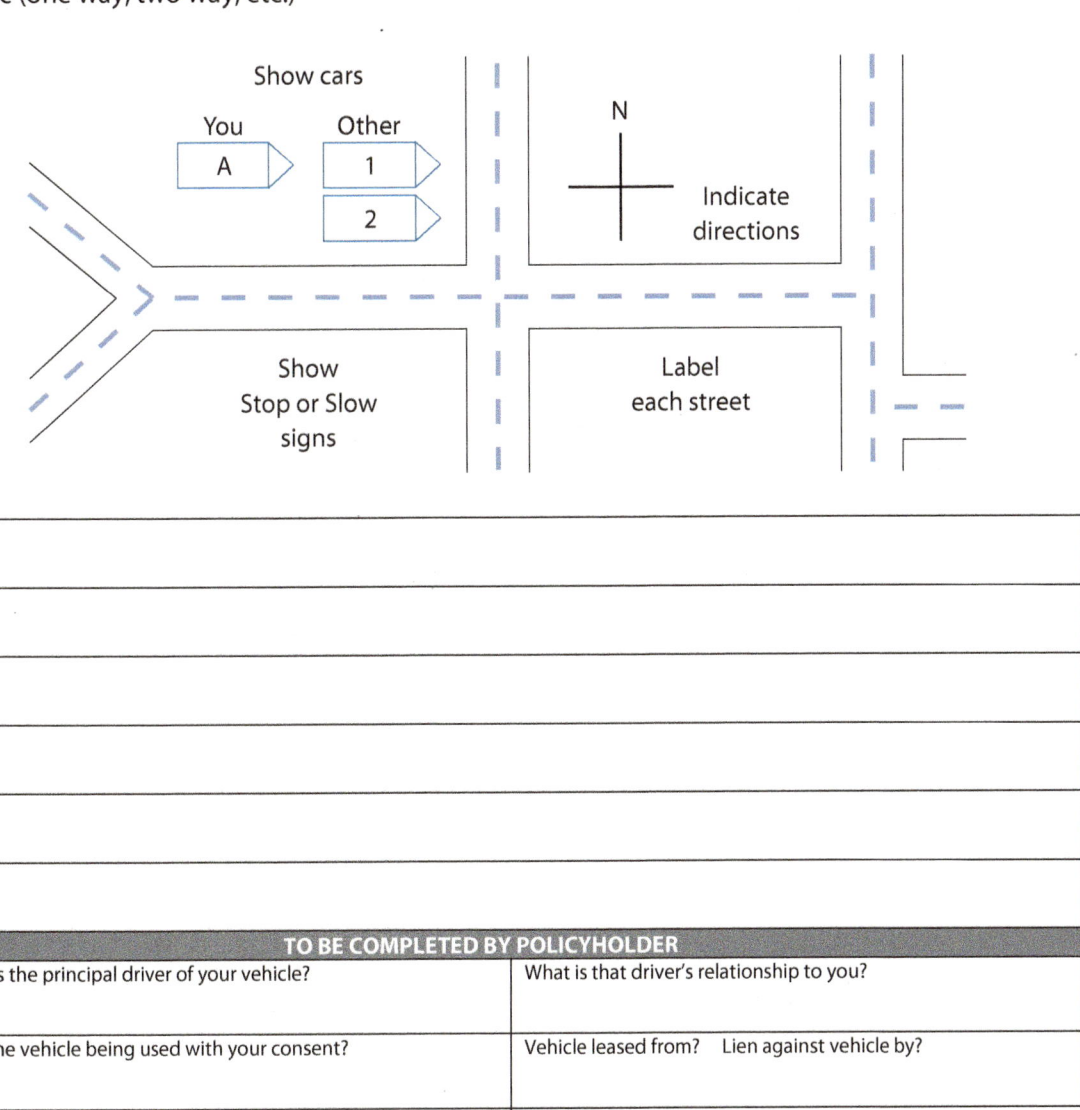

# Basic Principles of Effective Report Writing

A security report is any documentation that is recorded on a departmental form or other approved medium (for example, a computer disk) and maintained as a permanent record. The goal of report writing is to recreate an occurrence or observation in its entirety and to eliminate confusion and loss of relevant information. Despite wide-ranging differences between the types of reports, the following general principles can be applied to write an effective report:

- Assume the reader has absolutely no knowledge of the occurrence, the people involved, or the location of the incident. Inform the reader of all details, whether major or minor.

- Assume that there will be no opportunity to communicate verbally to the reader in order to clarify information. This will prevent vagueness and complacency in relating details.
- When describing an event or observation, avoid using general terms such as assault, theft, robbed, or damaged. Instead, describe the event fully so that the reader can create a mental image and conclude that an assault took place.

    *Bill clenched his right fist and walked toward Helen. He raised his fist and struck Helen's chin.*

- Avoid paraphrasing. Paraphrasing means condensing an observation to a minimal explanation. It lacks specific details and causes the reader to ask questions about the incident. An example of paraphrasing is, "Ralph saw Bill hit Helen." From this sort of statement, the reader would have several outstanding questions: Where was Ralph when he made the observations? Where was Bill? How exactly did Bill hit Helen? What were the relationships between these three people?
- All conversations, statements, and responses made by victims, suspects, or accused persons, and all witness statements (this includes any investigating, assisting, and specialized security personnel) should be recorded verbatim.
- Physical evidence must be described in detail. Draw on your five senses and encourage witnesses to draw on theirs to recreate an image of the scene. Include the location in which the evidence was found and who had the chain of possession over the item.
- Use simple words to eliminate the need to explain further in explanatory phrases.
- Avoid grammatical and spelling errors.
- Avoid verbal diarrhea. Say it once in as few words as possible.
- Keep sentence length to no more than 15 to 18 words.
- Consider reader fatigue. Leave margins, use headings, and use a paragraph form, otherwise, readers will lose interest and will have trouble maintaining concentration.
- Before starting to write, collect the facts and assess and interpret their significance to the incident.
- Always use first person (the "I" voice) in the report.
- Note the condition and characteristics of the witnesses, suspects, and the accused. For example, are they intoxicated? Agitated? Do they have vision limitations? Write down everything that is relevant to the credibility of a witness.
- Include conclusions or inferences and recommendations in the report.
- Always reread the report for any mistakes in spelling or grammar and any omissions.

### ON THE JOB

Remember the five Cs of good report writing: Clear, Concise, Complete, Correct, Chronological order.

# Statement Taking

Taking statements from witnesses is an important part of any field investigation, because the responding security guard is gathering information from bystanders, anyone impacted by the incident, and/or person(s) responsible. While investigations will be discussed in greater detail in Chapter 14, the following is a basic guide to the types of statements that may be recorded by security personnel.

## Victim Statements

Security professionals need to be mindful of the fact that victims have experienced a trauma and might not be emotionally stable immediately after the incident. In such instances, it might be wise to postpone the taking of a **victim statement** to a later time when the victim has had time to recover. A victim's condition must be our number one concern.

## Witness Statements

In cases where someone saw the incident occur, it is crucial to obtain a **witness statement** because witnesses could be the only persons who know what happened and their statements might play a vital role in identifying those responsible and in establishing what has happened.

## Suspect Statements

When the person who appears to be responsible for an incident is present, there could be an opportunity for the responding security guard to engage with and speak with the individual. While the taking of **suspect statements** is primarily the responsibility of police, a suspect might be talkative while waiting for police to arrive.

As you will learn later in this book, if an individual has been arrested, including by a security guard, a "caution" must be administered to inform the person of their legal rights. While statements made prior to arrest can be recorded in the security professional's notes, the caution should be administered prior to an attempt to interview the person or take a formal statement. This is done to preserve the right to have an individual's admission of involvement, if any, included in the evidence at a subsequent trial.

**victim statement**
a written account or the transcript of a verbal account of an incident in the victim's words and from the victim's perspective

**witness statement**
a written account or the transcript of a verbal account of an incident in the words of and from the perspective of an individual who observed the incident

**suspect statement**
a written account or the transcript of a verbal account of an incident in the words of and from the perspective of an individual who has been identified as the suspect in the incident

# How to Take a Statement

Taking a statement is much like telling a story and it is crucial to accurately describe the environment and parameters of the incident. To ensure that the evidential value of a statement remains intact, a security professional must ensure that the witness is identified accurately and his or her identity is recorded on the statement form along with all contact information. In addition, the person who is taking the statement must be identified in the event that that person is required to give testimony in court about the circumstances under which the statement was taken.

In some instances, a witness may not be able to write the statement and the person taking the statement may be required to transcribe what the witness says. In a case such as this, it is important for the security professional to indicate in a short paragraph that he or she was asked to write the statement on the witness's behalf. The witness will then read, sign, and verify that the transcription is accurate to the best of his or her recollection.

A thorough statement should include the following:

- full name of the person making the statement;
- contact information of the person making the statement;
- date, time, and location of the statement;
- identity and credentials of the security professional taking the statement;
- word-for-word transcription of the witness's recollection of what transpired;
- details of the impact the incident had on the witness;
- closing paragraph in which the witness asserts that the contents are a true reflection of the facts to the best of the witness's knowledge, and an assertion that he or she has read the statement and was given an opportunity to correct it; and
- witness's signature and date of signature.

As when writing a report, when taking a statement a security professional must make sure that the following six questions are answered:

1. *Who* was involved?
2. *What* happened?
3. *When* did it happen?
4. *Where* did it happen?
5. *Why* did it happen?
6. *How* did it happen?

## Security Spotlight

### ADVOKATE to Assess the Reliability of Witness Statements

It is important that the statements and reports created by security professionals contain only facts and not opinions. Security guards should not comment in their notes about whether or not they believe witnesses to be reliable or credible. However, having an understanding of the factors that increase the reliability of statements can help security professionals remember which questions to ask of a witness. A 1977 decision of the UK House of Lords (a high-level court), *R v Turnbull*, led to the development of a useful acronym: "ADVOKATE." **ADVOKATE** is used to remember factors that affect statement reliability. Here are the ADVOKATE factors:

**ADVOKATE**
an acronym for a protocol for assessing the accuracy of an eye witness's statement

| | |
|---|---|
| A | Amount of time: How long was the person in view? |
| D | Distance: How far away was the person? |
| V | Visibility: What was the visibility like? |
| O | Obstruction: Did anything obstruct the view? |
| K | Known or seen before: Had the person been known or seen before? |
| A | Any reason to remember: What made the person or incident memorable to the witness? |
| T | Time-lapse: How long has passed since the sighting? |
| E | Errors in the description: Any changes in the description of the person? |

When taking statements, try to keep the ADVOKATE factors in view so that you can either ask appropriate questions of the statement-maker, or add relevant details to your notebook (for example, notes about weather or lighting that might have affected visibility).

## CHAPTER SUMMARY

In this chapter we described the purpose of note taking and its importance to later report writing and court proceedings. We explained how to maintain a notebook and what content to include in (and exclude from) notes.

Notes might be used later as the basis of an incident report, or another kind of report. Several types of reports were described in this chapter. Because they will do it every day of their professional life, writing proper and complete reports is one of the most important communication skills developed by security professionals. It is, therefore, in their best interests to learn, practise, and perfect this skill to the best of their ability.

We also discussed different types of statements and how to take comprehensive and accurate statements from victims, witnesses, and suspects.

Today, many security companies no longer keep hard copies of reports, notes, and statements; they have transitioned into electronic record-keeping. This method of record-keeping allows for more effective and efficient organization and maintenance of information. Although today's methods are very effective and user-friendly, proper measures must be taken to ensure the security of all confidential information.

## KEY TERMS

ADVOKATE, 80
form report, 74
general occurrence report, 74
specialized report, 74
supplemental report, 76
suspect statements, 79
victim statement, 79
witness statement, 79

## REFERENCE

*R v Turnbull*, (1977) QB 224 (CA).

## PERFORMANCE APPLICATION

### Multiple Choice

1. When preparing an occurrence report, a security professional should:
   a. copy word-for-word from notes in his or her notebook
   b. consider whether any content in the notebook reflects poorly on the employer and should be left out
   c. use the contents of the notebook as a memory aid and a source of precise details recorded at the time of the incident
   d. destroy the relevant notebook pages as soon as the occurrence report is completed
   e. avoid reference to the notes so that he or she will not be accused of copying from them

2. _____ are things security guards know for certain and that they can substantiate.
   a. Inferences
   b. Facts
   c. Assumptions
   d. Opinions
   e. all of the above

3. The best place for safekeeping of a notebook during a security guard's shift is
   a. in the guard's physical possession
   b. in the trunk of a patrol car
   c. in a storage cabinet in a staff-only location such as a furnace room
   d. in a filing cabinet in the Control room
   e. any of the above

4. Accurate and complete record-keeping is an essential aspect of a security professional's work because
   a. it is a skill of particular focus in performance reviews
   b. many security guards lack skill in explaining events verbally with clarity
   c. it helps to overcome language barriers in diverse work environments
   d. it serves as a permanent record of events that have occurred and serves to communicate information about the occurrence to others
   e. the attention level involved in writing records helps keep security professionals alert, particularly during night shifts

5. When preparing a report or taking a statement, it is important to include details about
   a. who was involved
   b. what happened
   c. where the incident took place
   d. when the incident took place (time and date)
   e. all of the above

6. Occurrence reports should be submitted to a supervisor:
   a. as a follow-up to a conflict with the supervisor
   b. at the end of every shift
   c. at least once per hour
   d. occurrence reports should never be submitted to one's direct supervisor
   e. whenever an incident of significance occurs

7. The narrative portion of an occurrence report should always be written
   a. in chronological order
   b. in point form
   c. in 100 words or less
   d. in black ink
   e. without reference to names of individuals to protect their privacy

8. Which of these is NOT a standard note-taking rule?
   a. notes should be in ink
   b. errors should be thoroughly erased
   c. notes should be concise
   d. notes should be free of opinions, judgments, and speculation
   e. note takers should avoid the use of jargon or slang

## Write a Report

Write a detailed report, using the information provided below. Be sure to organize the information appropriately and clearly, and include all essential details about what occurred.

- Black Honda Civic had scratches and red paint transfers on the driver side front bumper
- Incident occurred at 2030 hours
- Red Toyota Corolla was parked on the shoulder of the highway
- Incident happened 75 km west of Ottawa on a private service road maintained by security professional's employer
- White Chevy Cruze was flipped over onto its roof in the left lane of the highway and there was blood on the hood
- Red Toyota Corolla only had scratches and black paint transfer on its passenger rear bumper
- Dead moose located 20 metres from the location of the flipped-over vehicle
- Chevy Cruze was not hit by another vehicle
- It was foggy and −5 degrees

# Health and Safety

## 5

| | |
|---|---:|
| Introduction | 86 |
| The Ontario Occupational Health and Safety Act | 86 |
| Workplace Accident Investigation | 93 |
| Hazards | 98 |
| Chapter Summary | 105 |
| Key Terms | 106 |
| References | 106 |
| Performance Application | 106 |

## LEARNING OUTCOMES

When you have completed this chapter, you will:

- Have an understanding of the goals and basic structure of the *Occupational Health and Safety Act* and the various roles of people in the workplace with respect to supporting the principles of the Act.

- Have a basic knowledge of the principles of workplace accident investigation.

- Be aware of the role of legislation and regulations, particularly the Workplace Hazardous Materials Information System, in promoting a safe workplace.

## Introduction

Work can be a dangerous place. While most people can readily identify the hazards associated with certain high-risk occupations such as construction or mining, all work carries with it certain risks.

Workplace health and safety is a highly complex and diverse workplace issue. There are several pieces of legislation in place in Ontario alone (in general, workplace safety is a provincial responsibility) to govern the promotion and enforcement of safety in the workplace. The Ontario *Occupational Health and Safety Act* (OHSA) creates what it describes as an internal responsibility system (IRS), which is a partnership of all workplace parties (including management, supervisors, employees/workers, and unions) for the promotion of workplace safety.

Security personnel, because of their role in providing workplace surveillance and responding to workplace emergencies, are often the first to discover workplace hazards or to respond to workplace accidents. As such, the issue of workplace health and safety is especially pertinent to the security department, and all good security personnel must embrace the enforcement of workplace safety as a core duty.

This chapter will introduce the legislation governing workplace health and safety, and, in particular, the OHSA. It will outline the basic roles of workplace parties and the essential procedures relating to the investigation of workplace accidents. Understanding the range of hazards in the workplace is an important part of a security guard's responsibilities. This chapter will also cover the identification of hazards in general, and also the classification of hazardous materials under the **Workplace Hazardous Materials Information System (WHMIS)**.

**Workplace Hazardous Materials Information System (WHMIS)**
a regulatory scheme that classifies hazards and communicates information about them and about means of reducing risk

## The Ontario Occupational Health and Safety Act

First introduced on October 1, 1979, the OHSA has been revised many times and is published in tandem with the Workplace Hazardous Materials Information System (WHMIS) regulations. The latest full-scale revision occurred in 1990.

### Introduction

Workplace hazards are a reality of the work environment. An essential aspect of safety is the cooperation between employers and employees, meaning both parties are responsible for a safe work environment. All workers have three basic rights:

- the right to be aware of workplace hazards;
- the right to refuse unsafe work; and
- the right to participate in occupational health and safety decisions.

Within this framework, the safety of the workplace is overseen by employers and workers through a joint health and safety committee, safety representatives as needed, and Ministry of Labour inspections.

Under the OHSA, corporations face potential fines of $500,000 per offence for violations of the rules. Individuals face potential fines of $25,000 or 12 months in jail. The courts have proved willing to levy substantial fines against employers, regardless of company size, for violations of health and safety statutes.

For small and medium-sized businesses on limited budgets and with few personnel—which describes many contract security services—trying to adhere to complex health and safety laws as well as many other laws is daunting in light of the severity of fines. This is why security guards need to stay abreast of the basic rights and responsibilities of owners, employers, directors, managers, supervisors, and workers by checking regularly on the Canadian Federation of Independent Business (CFIB) website for OHSA bulletin updates at http://www.cfib-fcei.ca/english/business-support/ontario/214-health-safety.html.

Regardless of size, every corporation can take steps to avoid OHSA violations through effective **due diligence**: showing that every precaution has been taken in the circumstances. Six essential elements of a safety due diligence program are as follows:

1. workplace hazard analysis/audit;
2. corporate safety policy and implementation program;
3. specific critical task policies and procedures;
4. training procedures for workers, supervisors, managers, officers, and directors;
5. enforcement of health and safety procedures; and
6. ensuring supervisor competence.

**due diligence**
taking every reasonable precaution to avoid an undesirable consequence

It is important to note that Ontario's OHSA does not apply to employees of the federal government, banks, communication companies, or transportation companies; they are covered under part II of the *Canada Labour Code*.

Today, in Ontario, both large and small companies recognize the need for safety coordinators, but most companies cannot afford to pay for one. As a result, a volunteer usually assumes the responsibility, but if there is no volunteer, administering safety duties often falls to the company's security guard or manager. For this reason, understanding occupational health and safety is an essential part of security training.

## Structure of the OHSA

Some of the most important sections of the OHSA from the perspective of security guards are

- the rights and responsibilities of the worker,
- the responsibilities of the employer,
- the provisions about violence and harassment, and
- policies and regulations that govern the workplace.

### Security Spotlight

#### Structure of the OHSA

- Part I (ss. 2–4) describes the application of the Act and the agencies responsible for decision making.
- Part II (ss. 4.1–22.1) covers administration.
- Part II.1 (ss. 22.2–22.9) creates the Prevention Council and the role of Chief Prevention Officer.
- Part III (ss. 23–32) outlines responsibilities and duties.
- Part III.0.1 (ss. 32.0.1–32.0.8) covers violence and harassment.
- Part III.1 (ss. 32.1–32.4) describes codes of practice.
- Part IV (ss. 33–42) covers toxic substances.
- Part V (ss. 43–49) covers work refusals.
- Part VI (s. 50) prohibits reprisals by employers.
- Part VII (ss. 51–53) contains special notices.
- Part VIII (ss. 54–65) covers enforcement.
- Part IX (ss. 66–69) outlines offences and penalties.
- Part X (ss. 70–71) covers regulations.

The Act comprises 13 parts. Although it is not necessary to know these parts in detail, it is important to have an understanding of what they cover in case the need to research an issue in further detail arises.

## Health and Safety Representation

Depending on the size of the organization, the OHSA requires the nomination of either a health and safety representative or a joint health and safety committee (JHSC) made up of members representing both management and workers. Only very small organizations are exempt from the need for representation. Figure 5.1 explains the requirements.

## Health and Safety Representatives

In small workplaces, a health and safety representative, chosen by the workers, is required instead of a committee. The representative's duties include, but are not limited to, inspecting the workplace, obtaining health and safety information from the employer, and being involved in testing equipment and products.

## Joint Health and Safety Committees

A JHSC comprises people who represent the employees and the employer. Together, they are committed to improving health and safety conditions in the workplace. Their duties include, but are not limited to, identifying hazardous and dangerous situations, recommending improvements for the improved health and safety of workers, and obtaining information about existing hazards in the workplace.

## Certified Members

All workplaces with 50 or more workers must choose four members to sit on the JHSC: two representing the employer and two representing workers. At least two of the four members must be certified, which means that they have received occupational health and safety training as prescribed by the Act. In many cases, security personnel are chosen to represent management on the committee and receive certification training. The duties of certified members include, but are not limited to, inspecting the workplace, participating in investigations of serious or fatal injury, requesting an investigation of dangerous

**Figure 5.1** Breakdown of Health and Safety Representation by Company Size

| Number of employees | Health and safety representative | Joint health and safety committee |
|---|---|---|
| 0–5 | Not required | Not required |
| 6–19 | One, selected by the workers | Not required |
| 20–49 | Not required | Two members (minimum): one represents workers, one represents management |
| 50–plus | Not required | Four members (minimum): two represent workers, two represent management. Two members must be certified. |

circumstances in the workplace, and recommending a work stoppage where dangerous circumstances are confirmed.

## More About the JHSC

### Term

It is recommended, in the interest of building expertise at the JHSC level, that JHSC members serve terms of at least one year. All vacancies on a JHSC must be filled as soon as possible to maintain compliance with the legislation.

### Security Department Participation

It is very common for a security director/manager to serve as an employer member of a JHSC. It's also possible for a security guard to serve as a worker member.

### Confidentiality

In the course of conducting committee business, confidential company and personnel information may become known to committee members. It is a legal responsibility that members keep such information confidential. For example, in the new provisions about violence and harassment, the legislation provides, at s. 32.0.5(4) that "[n]o employer or supervisor shall disclose more personal information in the circumstances described in subsection (3) than is reasonably necessary to protect the worker from physical injury."

### Duties

The Canadian Centre for Occupational Health and Safety (OHS) lists specific JHSC duties and responsibilities as:

- complying with OHS legislation;
- holding meetings and keeping minutes;
- obtaining information;
- identifying hazardous situations;
- participating in development and implementation of programs to protect the employees' safety and health;
- dealing with employee complaints and suggestions concerning safety and health;
- participating in all safety and health inquiries and investigations;
- consulting with professional and technical experts;
- participating in resolving workplace refusals and work stoppages;
- making recommendations to management for accident prevention and safety program activities;
- ensuring the maintenance and monitoring of injury and work hazard records;
- following up hazard reports and recommending action;
- monitoring effectiveness of safety programs and procedures;
- being consulted on the inventory of hazardous materials and hazardous physical substances;
- setting up and promoting the development and review of instruction and employee training;

- being consulted on safety and industrial hygiene testing; and
- being consulted about assessment and control programs for designated substances.

### *Functions and Powers of Worker Members*

Worker members of the committee have certain legislated roles that are applied to them. For example, the JHSC may:

- designate one worker member to conduct workplace inspections at least once a month;
- ask a worker to accompany a Ministry of Labour inspector during physical conditions inspections;
- designate one or more worker members to investigate critical injuries and/or fatalities;
- designate worker members to be present at the beginning of industrial hygiene testing; and
- assign a worker member to represent a worker in a refusal-to-work situation.

## Employer Responsibilities with Regard to the JHSC

Employers are required by the Act to provide whatever assistance and cooperation are necessary to the committee in carrying out its role. Their main responsibilities are

- to establish a committee;
- to post the names and work locations of the committee;
- to give committee members time for preparation, attendance, and to carry out their duties;
- to pay committee members for carrying out their duties at regular or premium rate as required;
- to respond in writing, within 21 days, to written recommendations by the committee;
- to pay members for becoming certified at regular or premium rate, as may be proper;
- to post a copy of the annual summary of data from the Workplace Safety and Insurance Board (WSIB) (the company's safety record) on the company's accident experience;

---

**FOCUS ON TECHNOLOGY**

### Designed for Safety

Because of the need for mechanized equipment and repetitive assembly work, manufacturing is a sector that has struggled with frequent workplace injuries. The machines used on assembly lines are frequently the subject of innovative engineering modifications designed to encourage safe work practices.

For example, a common source of manufacturing injuries is the use of presses, which can cause crushing injuries if a finger or hand strays into the press during operation. In an attempt to remove this possibility, many presses are now designed so that the pressing action can only be activated if the user presses *two* separate buttons, placed shoulder-width apart. This procedure requires the use of both hands and ensures that the worker cannot have a hand in the press when it is activated.

- to provide assistance and cooperation to committee members;
- to provide the committee with the most recent inventory of hazardous materials and hazardous physical agents, along with copies of the safety data sheet (SDS);
- to provide a copy of the written assessment for hazardous materials;
- to provide information to the committee on hazardous physical agents; and
- to ensure that at least one management and one worker member are certified members.

## Security Spotlight

### OHS Representation Across the Nation

The Canadian Centre for Occupational Health and Safety (CCOHS) summarizes the legislative requirements for Health and Safety Committees for each of the provinces and territories in Figure 5.2.

**Figure 5.2** Legislation Requirements for Health and Safety Committees

| | When do I need one? | Size of committee | Representation |
|---|---|---|---|
| Canada | Mandatory: 20 or more employees | At least 2 | At least half to represent employees |
| British Columbia | Mandatory: when there are 20 or more employees or when "required by order" | Not less than 4 | At least one-half must be worker representatives |
| Alberta | As directed by the minister | At least 3 and not more than 12 | At least two employees and one employer or at least half employees |
| Saskatchewan | Mandatory: when 10 employees or more | At least 2 and not more than 12 | At least half to represent employees |
| Manitoba | Mandatory: 20 or more employees as designated by lieutenant governor | At least 4 and not more than 12 | At least half to represent employees |
| Ontario | Mandatory: 20 or more employees, when ordered by minister, or where a designated substance is in use (no minimum number of employees) | At least 2 (fewer than 50 employees); at least 4 (50 or more employees) | At least half to represent employees |
| Quebec | Mandatory: 20 or more employees and where regulated | At least 4 | At least half to represent employees |
| New Brunswick | Mandatory: 20 or more employees | As agreed upon by employees and employer | Equal representation |
| Nova Scotia | Mandatory: 20 or more employees | As agreed upon by employees and employer | At least half to represent employees |
| Prince Edward Island | Agreed upon by employees and employers | Not specified | At least half to represent employees |
| Newfoundland and Labrador | Discretionary: 10 or more employees | At least 2 and not more than 12 | At least half to represent employees |
| Yukon | Mandatory: 20 or more employees | At least 4 and not more than 12 | At least half to represent employees |
| Northwest Territories | As directed by chief safety officer | Not specified | Equal representation |

## Duties of an Employer

The Act imposes duties on "the employer," which in practice means management—those who have some degree of control over the workplace, the materials and equipment in the workplace, and the direction of the workforce. Included in these duties are

- ensuring that measures and procedures prescribed by the Act are carried out;
- ensuring that everyone performing work complies with the Act and regulations;
- protecting the health and safety of workers;
- acquainting a worker with any hazard in the workplace;
- ensuring that equipment, materials, and protective devices prescribed are provided, maintained, and used as prescribed;
- providing information, instruction, and supervision to workers to ensure their safety; and
- appointing only competent people to take the position of supervisor.

### *Workplace Violence and Harassment*

Any workplace with more than five employees is required to prepare policies with respect to workplace violence as well as workplace harassment. These policies are to be reviewed as often as necessary and no less than on an annual basis. Policies are created by assessing the risks of workplace violence based on the nature of the workplace. Other considerations include what would be common to a similar workplace and factors specific to the workplace. One of the main responsibilities of an employer is to provide a means of summoning immediate assistance when there is the likelihood or occurrence of workplace violence. These situations will generally require an intervention from the security team that will vary in relation to training and policies.

## Duties of a Safety Supervisor

"Supervisor" means a person who has charge of a workplace or authority over another worker. According to the Act, safety supervisors should ensure that workers

- work safely;
- use protective devices and clothing when required;
- follow established safety procedures;
- are advised of any actual or potential hazards of which the supervisor is aware; and
- receive every protection reasonable in the circumstances for the protection of the worker.

## Duties of a Worker

Workers also have several general duties under the Act:

- They must take responsibility for personal health and safety, insofar as they are able, and be aware of issues (and avoid taking actions) that might affect the safety of others.
- They must work in compliance with the Act and regulations.
- They must use and wear protective equipment or other safeguards required by the Act.

- They must report all hazards to their employer or supervisor.
- They must report any contravention of the Act.

The Act also makes certain limitations very clear to workers. They must *not*

- remove or make ineffective any protective devices;
- use or operate any equipment, machine, device, or thing in a manner that may endanger themselves or another worker;
- engage in any prank, contest, horseplay, etc., that could endanger the health and safety of themselves or another worker.

# Workplace Accident Investigation

As noted in the introduction, workplace accidents are, unfortunately, commonplace. Security personnel, regardless of formal health and safety roles (such as JHSC membership), are typically "first responders" in such situations. Consider, for example, the widely reported accident of December 9, 2003 during the demolition of Toronto's landmark Uptown Theatre at Bloor and Yonge streets. Instead of imploding, part of the building collapsed on the neighbouring Yorkville English Academy, killing one person and injuring 14 others. In this case, the demolition company's security management team along with provincial investigators and fire marshals participated in finding out what went wrong.

## Reporting Requirements

Part XV of the *Canada Occupational Health and Safety Regulations* requires reporting of an accident by the employer to a Labour Canada safety officer if the accident results in any of the following:

- death;
- disabling injury;
- permanent impairment of a body function;
- the loss by an employee of a body member or a part thereof or the complete loss of the usefulness of a body member or a part thereof;
- fire or rupture to a boiler or pressure vessel;
- any damage to an elevating device; or
- an explosion.

## Purpose of a Workplace Accident Investigation

The purpose of a workplace accident investigation is to determine the cause of the accident, the extent of injury, any damage (or loss) to property, and to recommend corrective or preventive measures.

The cause of an accident is "any behaviour, condition, act, or negligence without which the accident would not have happened." It is essential that a security guard investigating an accident focus on "fact finding" and not "fault finding."

Analysis of workplace investigation reports suggests that most accidents fall into one of six general categories: organizational errors, technical data insufficiency, material failure, design deficiency, human failure, and natural phenomena.

### Organizational Errors

An accident may occur through failure of the organization to properly manage planning, training, supervision, or work practices.

### Technical Data Insufficiency

An accident may occur when a hazard is not well understood because of inadequate technical data, incomplete operating instructions, omissions in data, or erroneous data.

### Material Failure

When the physical breakdown or chemical deterioration of any part, structure, or component contributes to an accident, the accident can be attributed to "material failure."

### Design Deficiency

When a part or component is designed so that failure can or should occur under predictable circumstances, the accident can be attributed to design deficiency.

### Human Failure

An accident is deemed to be caused by human failure when a person, whether due to physical or psychological limitations, including illness, fails to perform an assigned task properly and contributes to an accident.

### Natural Phenomena

An accident is attributed to natural phenomena when unusual acts of nature (such as an earthquake or hurricane) cause the accident; but this attribution of cause is not appropriate when there is evidence of failure to take normal precautions against these contingencies.

## Domestic Violence

In recent years, domestic violence has become a prominent issue in the workplace as employers are recognizing the impact on employees. Domestic violence has on occasion made its way into the workplace. When domestic violence occurs in the workplace it puts not only the intended victim but also their colleagues at risk. The *Occupational Health and Safety Act* requires the employer to work with employees to ensure that reasonable protective measures are in place. Section 32.0.4 of the Act states that "[i]f an employer becomes aware, *or ought reasonably to be aware*, that domestic violence that would likely expose a worker to physical injury may occur in the workplace, the employer shall take every precaution in the circumstances for the protection of the worker" (emphasis added). In many instances, an individual who is affected by domestic violence will not be forthcoming about the situation. There are many reasons for this, including embarrassment, stigmas involving domestic violence, and denial of an actual problem. The wording of the Act requires diligence on the part of the employer to address such issues. The most common response is the development of a safety plan to protect the worker. This will typically ensure that the necessary stakeholders have knowledge of the threat and are able to assist appropriately. From a security perspective, this could include escorts to and from the employee's vehicle or scheduled check-ins for employees who are working alone.

# Procedures for a Workplace Accident Investigation

As the first responder to an accident scene, the security guard must first focus on the need for medical attention for any injured worker(s) and the prevention of further injuries. The procedures are covered in CPR/first aid training. Once these matters have been dealt with, the workplace accident investigation must begin. The following guidelines explain how the investigation might proceed.

## Step One: Respond to Emergency

Control the accident scene by:

- *Erecting barriers*: Barriers of some kind must be established in order to prevent and/or control the movement of people and vehicles into the accident scene.
- *Shutting down machinery*: Any machinery that is in operation within the accident area, including any machinery that may have been involved in the accident, must be shut down safely and treated as evidence.
- *Following standard operating procedures (SOPs)*: The investigating security guard must follow the SOPs that govern that specific area of the workplace affected at all times.
- *Locating and identifying witnesses*: Find out what happened from those witnesses who saw the accident.

## Step Two: Collect Information

Collect information through:

- *Interviews*: Conduct interviews as soon as possible in a place that is non-threatening for the people being interviewed.
- *Photographs*: Use of a digital camera or camcorder is the most common practice. Ensure that stored images are available for legal purposes. Be certain to follow organizational policies to avoid any accusations of tampering. In court, the defence may object to any evidence that can be (or may have been) manipulated.
- *Block diagrams*: Block diagrams are useful for recording the layout of an accident scene, in addition to showing the following information:
  - the sizes of objects in relation to their surroundings;
  - the position of objects or people in relation to other objects;
  - the distance (to scale) between fixed objects within the scene;
  - the recorded location of objects and people prior to their removal from the accident scene.
- *Removal of material or equipment for testing*: It may be necessary to remove tools, substances, machinery, or other items to have them tested for any operational malfunction or physical deficiency. In many cases, the worker may have been injured due to some fault of the tools or equipment that he or she was using.

## Step Three: Analyze Information

The initial analysis of an accident scene begins as soon as the security guard arrives. It is very important that the security guard specifically write down all observations along with the facts obtained from the answers to his or her questions. In gathering information about the accident, the who, what, where, when, how, and why questions should always be asked.

*Who was involved?* The security guard should get the names of everyone who witnessed the accident and events preceding or following it, including supervisors. Workers who do the same job as the injured worker may be able to describe it in a step-by-step way. Names, phone numbers, and work locations should be recorded in case the witnesses need to be interviewed at a later stage in the investigation.

*What was involved?* Physical evidence can be removed or destroyed. For this reason, it should be one of the first things the security guard examines and records. Materials and equipment involved should be described and checked for any defects. If the security guard is unfamiliar with the equipment, one of the workers may be able to assist in the examination. If safety guards were missing or were not being used, the security guard should find out why. The security guard should check for defects or other equipment problems that might have contributed to the accident and examine the general housekeeping, weather conditions, and any other hazardous conditions that might have been a factor in the accident.

*Where did it happen?* A description of the exact location and circumstances that led to the accident must be fully provided as part of the accident report. The description should include reference to hazardous conditions such as overcrowding, noise, poor lighting, fumes, and other potential factors. It is also important to note what other jobs are carried out in the same work area. Making a rough drawing and taking photographs of the accident scene from several angles are effective ways of recording information.

*When did it happen?* The day and time that the accident occurred must be recorded and it is important to note any relevant details that might have a bearing on the accident, such as whether shift work was a factor. The responding security guard should note whether the injured worker was on overtime and if he or she was working alone. The weather conditions at the time should also be noted if they are relevant to the accident. The security guard should write down the time of arrival at the accident scene. The lapse of time between the accident occurring and the investigation beginning can make an important difference in some cases.

*How did it happen?* Because the security guard was not at the scene of the accident, asking the injured worker questions is the best way to find out what happened. The security guard should ask about any near misses prior to the accident and whether any changes have recently been made to the job or work environment. The injured worker or a witness should be asked to describe the job process in detail, noting events immediately before, during, and after the accident. A review of these descriptions may indicate ways that the accident could have been prevented.

*Why did it happen?* This is the big question that everyone wants to know and the hardest thing to find out. It is important to record suggested reasons from witnesses or employees even if they are hypothetical rather than factual. Every theory should be investigated until discounted. The security guard must find out all the causes, both direct and indirect, that contributed to the accident. Most accidents are not caused by a single problem, but by a combination of factors.

Things to consider are

- the adequacy of health and safety training;
- job procedures, quotas, and labour relations;
- supervision issues;
- previous complaints about equipment safety;
- the effects of toxic substances and poor indoor air quality; and
- other work conditions that might be related to the accident.

In order to conduct an effective investigation, it is important to look behind what appears to be the primary cause (for example, "faulty equipment") to determine what really caused the accident.

Initial impressions should be followed by questions until the security guard is satisfied that he or she knows all the causes of the accident.

Not all the information needed for a thorough investigation will necessarily be available at the accident scene. Often, information about the accident can be found in:

- reports of past accidents and hazardous occurrences reports;
- safety data sheets (SDSs);
- maintenance reports and inspection reports;
- training reports;
- first aid reports and workplace safety and insurance claims;
- blueprints and floor plans of the workplace;
- specifications of equipment and engineering reports;
- reports of similar incidents from other workplaces in the same industry with similar working conditions;
- reports supplied by the union or other labour organizations; and
- newspaper articles about the accident being investigated.

Any pertinent information should be examined to see what can be learned about other factors that might have contributed to the accident and what changes might be recommended to prevent a recurrence. This background information must be assembled and examined before doing a final analysis and reaching a conclusion about how the accident happened.

## *Step Four: Write Report*

The investigative report should be thorough and accurate and must include specific recommendations to management. Recommendations need to cover such areas as how to avoid a similar accident, safety precautions or improvements, along with information on compliance with provincial health and safety laws and regulations. The report should then be posted in the workplace in every area where workers congregate, such as the staff cafeteria, lunch rooms, change rooms, the security office, the personnel office, and on notice boards. Copies of the investigative report should be sent to the site manager, security manager, union representative department supervisor, the injured worker, the Ministry of Labour, and the joint health and safety committee.

## *Step Five: Follow Up*

Every workplace accident report should have a suggested timetable for the implementation of the recommendations. The security manager will usually advise the security guard on how to schedule the timetable. The timetable should have realistic achievable deadlines and be submitted in writing. The security manager usually reviews the health and safety training done on site after an accident has occurred. The recommendations compiled in the complete workplace investigation submitted by all official parties are adopted and an effort is made to raise awareness in all the workers about the cause of the accident. This helps to avoid a recurrence of the accident.

> ## ON THE JOB
>
> ### Accident Investigation Checklist
>
> Check the working environment. At the place of the accident, what was the state of the lighting, temperature and humidity, noise level, dust and fumes, workplace layout, flooring, and housekeeping?
>
> Check the training, job experience, and supervision of the injured worker. Consider these questions:
>
> - How long had the worker been on the job?
> - What safety training had the worker received?
> - What supervision was present?
> - What safety training had the supervisor received?
>
> Other aspects of the accident to consider are:
>
> - Was information available on the safe use of equipment and the handling of materials?
> - Was all plant and equipment maintained to standard?
> - What do maintenance reports reveal about the state of any equipment?
> - Did protective clothing hamper communications in any way?
> - If protective clothing was issued, was it suitable for the individual and the job, and was it properly maintained?
> - Are there records of other accidents or dangerous occurrences in the same work area or job? If yes, are there any common factors that could link them?
> - Is there any evidence of previous unsafe practices being condoned by management?

## Investigative Pitfalls

Listing "carelessness" as a cause of an accident is a direct admission that the investigation was worthless.

Basing the cause solely on the type of accident or injury indicates a lack of completeness. For example, listing "faulty electric wiring" as a fire cause without elaboration provides no information upon which future prevention efforts can be based.

Security guards should be careful not to assume that one single cause will be found in each and every investigation. All possible causes indicated by the evidence should be listed so that corrective action can be taken to eliminate every one of them.

# Hazards

**hazard**
a physical or behavioural condition or circumstance that poses a risk of harm to individuals

A **hazard** is anything that can cause injury to or illness in a worker.

## Hazard Classification

There are three levels of hazards: classes A, B, and C.

## Class A

*A condition or practice likely to cause permanent disability, loss of life or body parts, and/or extensive loss of structure, equipment, or material.*

- Example 1: A barrier guard is missing on a large press brake.
- Example 2: A maintenance worker is observed servicing a large sump pump in an unventilated deep pit, using gasoline.

## Class B

*A condition or practice likely to cause serious injury or illness (resulting in temporary disability) or property damage that is disruptive, but less severe than class A.*

- Example 1: Slippery oil condition observed in a main aisle.
- Example 2: Frayed carpeting at the bottom of office stairs.

## Class C

*A condition or practice that is likely to cause minor (non-disabling) injury or illness or non-disruptive property damage.*

- Example 1: Carpenter observed handling rough lumber without gloves.
- Example 2: Traces of fumes in the degreasing area.

# Hazardous Materials and WHMIS

In an effort to provide standardized, high-quality information about hazardous materials to employers and workers, the Canadian federal and provincial governments worked together to develop WHMIS. Changes have been made to align WHMIS with the Globally Harmonized System of Classification and Labelling of Chemicals (GHS), with all phases of implementation scheduled to be completed by December 1, 2018.

Because WHMIS is an occupational health and safety initiative, it required implementation at the workplace by means of a provincial law. However, because it also involves the sale and import of hazardous materials, it enters into the federal legislative domain as well. Thus, the enactment of WHMIS into law was accomplished by the passage of complementary federal and provincial legislation.

WHMIS was developed in support of the right of workers to know about the hazards of chemicals and other materials used in their workplaces. Exposure to hazardous materials can cause or contribute to many serious health problems, such as effects on the nervous system, kidney or lung damage, sterility, cancer, burns, and rashes. Some hazardous materials are safety hazards and can cause fires or explosions. WHMIS was created to help stop the injuries, illnesses, deaths, medical costs, and fires caused by hazardous materials.

The three main features of the WHMIS system are the requirement for materials safety training for workers, the requirement for warning labels on containers, and the requirement for the development and dissemination of safety data sheets (SDSs) by the manufacturers and distributors of hazardous materials. The WHMIS legislation also contains provisions allowing for the protection of trade secrets (for example, ingredient lists) by manufacturers, while complying with the level of disclosure necessary to allow users to protect themselves.

There are six classes of hazardous material regulated under WHMIS.

### Class A: Compressed Gas

Any material that is normally a gas that is placed under pressure or chilled, and contained by a cylinder is considered to be a compressed gas. These materials are dangerous because they are under pressure. If the cylinder is broken, the container can "rocket" or "torpedo" at great speeds and this is a danger to anyone standing too close.

If the cylinder is heated (by fire or a rise in temperature) the gas may try to expand and the cylinder will explode. Leaking cylinders are also a danger because the gas that comes out is very cold and it may cause frostbite if it touches the skin (for example: carbon dioxide or propane). Common examples include compressed air, carbon dioxide (fire extinguishers), propane, oxygen, ethylene oxide, and welding gases. The hazard symbol is a picture of a cylinder or container of compressed gas surrounded by a circle shown in Figure 5.3. For information on the new pictograms shown in Figure 5.3, see http://www.ccohs.ca/oshanswers/chemicals/whmis_ghs/pictograms.html and http://www.ccohs.ca/WHMISpictograms.html.

Additional dangers may be present if the gas has other hazardous properties. For example, propane is both a compressed gas and flammable. Propane would bear two hazard symbols: the one for a compressed gas and another to show that it is a flammable material.

### Class B: Flammable and Combustible Material

Flammable means that the material will burn or catch fire easily at normal temperatures (below 37.8°C or 100°F). Combustible materials must usually be heated before they will catch fire at temperatures above normal (between 37.8°C and 93.3°C or 100°F and 200°F). Reactive flammable materials are those that may suddenly start burning when they react with other materials, such as air or water.

Flammable or combustible materials may be solids, liquids, or gases. Common examples include propane, butane, acetylene, ethanol, acetone, turpentine, toluene, kerosene, spray paints, varnish, ammonia, and chlorine. The symbol for this class is a flame with a line under it inside a circle (see Figure 5.3).

### Class C: Oxidizing Material

Oxygen is necessary for a fire to occur. Some chemicals can cause other materials to burn by supplying oxygen. Oxidizers do not usually burn by themselves but they will either help the fire by providing more oxygen or they may cause materials that normally do not burn to suddenly catch on fire (spontaneous combustion). In some cases, a spark or flame (source of ignition) is not necessary for the material to catch on fire but only the presence of an oxidizer. Like flammable or combustible materials, oxidizers can also be in the form of gases (oxygen, ozone), liquids (nitric acid, chromic acid, sodium hypochlorite), and solids (chromates, potassium permanganate). Some oxidizers such as the organic peroxide family are extremely hazardous because they will burn (they are combustible) as well as provide oxygen for the fire. They can also have strong reactions that can result in an explosion. The symbol for oxidizing materials is shown in Figure 5.3.

### Class D: Poisonous and Infectious Material

Class D materials are those that can cause harm to the human body. They are divided into three major divisions.

*Division 1*: Materials causing immediate and serious toxic effects are very poisonous and immediately dangerous to life and health. Serious health effects such as burns, loss of consciousness, coma, or death within just minutes or hours after exposure are grouped in this category. Most D-1 materials will also cause long-term effects. Examples of some D-1 materials include carbon monoxide, sodium cyanide, and sulphuric acid. The symbol for class D, division 1 (D-1) is a skull and crossbones inside a circle (see Figure 5.3).

*Division 2*: Materials causing other toxic effects are poisonous as well. Their effects are not always immediate, or if the effects are immediate they are only temporary. They may still have very serious consequences, however, such as: cancer, allergies, reproductive problems or harm to the baby, changes to genes, or irritation/sensitization from small exposures over a long period of time (chronic effects). Examples of this class include asbestos fibres, mercury, ammonia, acetone, benzene, propane, silica, lead, and cadmium. The symbol (D-2) for materials causing other toxic effects is shown in Figure 5.3.

*Division 3*: Biohazardous infectious materials or the toxins they produce can cause diseases in people and/or animals. Included in this division are bacteria, viruses, fungi, and parasites. Because these organisms can live in body tissues or fluids (blood, urine), the tissues and fluids are also treated as toxic. Biohazardous infectious materials are usually found in hospitals, health care facilities, laboratories, veterinary practices, and research facilities. Workers in these places do not usually know which tissues or fluids contain dangerous organisms. For this reason, the workers assume that every sample is dangerous and proper protection is used all the time. Examples of biohazardous infectious materials include the HIV virus, hepatitis B, and salmonella. The symbol (D-3) for this division is shown in Figure 5.3.

## Class E: Corrosive Material

Corrosive is the name given to materials that can cause severe burns to skin and other human tissues, such as the eye or lung tissue, and can affect clothes and other materials,

**Figure 5.3** WHMIS Symbols and Revised GHS (WHMIS 2015) Pictograms

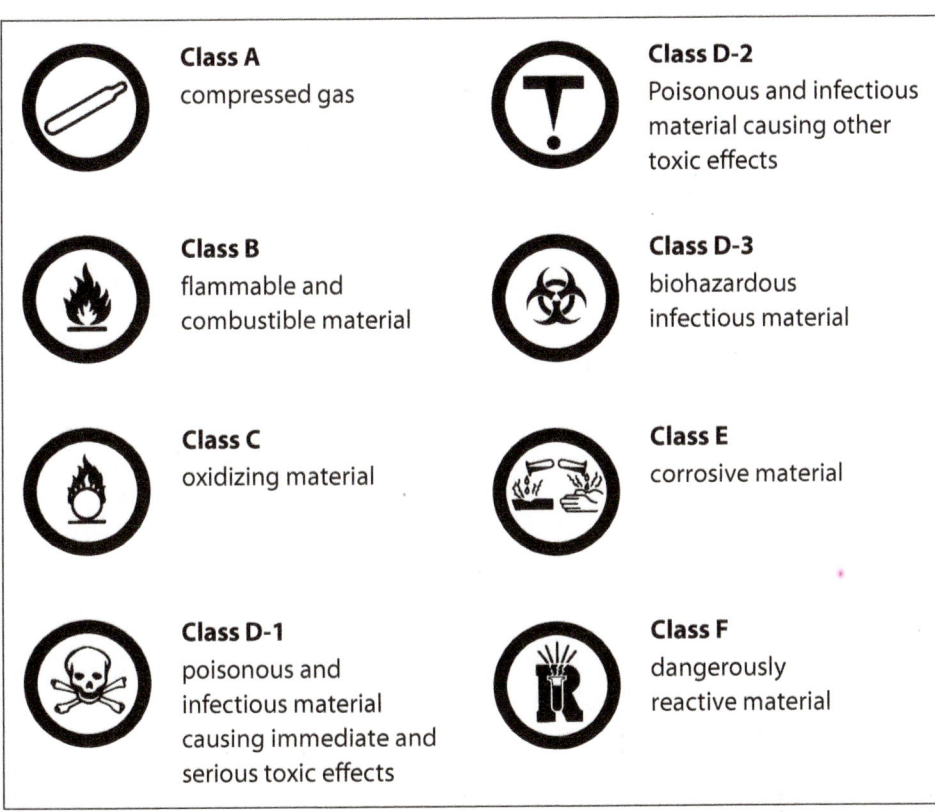

**Figure 5.3** Continued

| Symbol | Name | Symbol | Name | Symbol | Name |
|---|---|---|---|---|---|
| | **Exploding bomb** (for explosion or reactivity hazards) | | **Flame** (for fire hazards) | | **Flame over circle** (for oxidizing hazards) |
| | **Gas cylinder** (for gases under pressure) | | **Corrosion** (for corrosive damage to metals, as well as skin, eyes) | | **Skull and Crossbones** (can cause death or toxicity with short exposure to small amounts) |
| | **Health hazard** (may cause or suspected of causing serious health effects) | | **Exclamation mark** (may cause less serious health effects or damage the ozone layer*) | | **Environment*** (may cause damage to the aquatic environment) |
| | **Biohazardous Infectious Materials** (for organisms or toxins that can cause diseases in people or animals) | | | | |

\* The GHS system also defines an Environmental hazards group. This group (and its classes) was not adopted in WHMIS 2015. However, you may see the environmental classes listed on labels and Safety Data Sheets (SDSs). Including information about environmental hazards is allowed by WHMIS 2015.

including metal. Corrosives are grouped in this special class because their effects are permanent (temporary irritants are grouped in class D-2). Common corrosives include acids such as sulphuric and nitric acids, bases such as ammonium hydroxide, caustic soda, and potassium, and other materials such as ammonium, chlorine, and nitrogen dioxide. The symbol for a corrosive is a picture inside a circle of two test tubes pouring liquid on a bar (piece of metal) and a hand, both with lines rising from them (see Figure 5.3).

### *Class F: Dangerously Reactive Material*

A material is considered to be dangerously reactive if it shows one or more of the following three different properties or abilities:

- it can react very strongly and quickly ("vigorously") with water to make a toxic gas;
- it will react with itself when it gets shocked (bumped or dropped) or if the temperature or pressure increases; and/or
- it can vigorously join to itself (polymerize), break down (decompose), or lose extra water such that it becomes a more dense material (condense).

If a material is dangerously reactive, it will most likely be described as "unstable." Most of these materials can be extremely hazardous if they are not handled properly because they

> **ON THE JOB**
>
> **Anatomy of a Safety Data Sheet**
>
> A safety data sheet (SDS) contains the following information:
>
> 1. identification: product identifier (name), manufacturer's and supplier's names, addresses, and emergency phone numbers;
> 2. hazard(s) identification;
> 3. composition/information on ingredients;
> 4. first-aid measures;
> 5. fire-fighting measures;
> 6. accidental release measures;
> 7. handling and storage;
> 8. exposure controls/personal protection;
> 9. physical and chemical properties;
> 10. stability and reactivity;
> 11. toxicological information;
> 12. ecological information (non-mandatory);
> 13. disposal considerations (non-mandatory);
> 14. transport information (non-mandatory);
> 15. regulatory information (non-mandatory); and
> 16. other information.

can react in such a quick manner very easily. Examples of these products are ethyl acrylate, styrene, vinyl chloride, benzoyl peroxide, piric acid, and aluminum chloride. The symbol for dangerously reactive materials is a picture of a test tube with sparks or lines coming out of the tube surrounded by a letter "R" inside a circle (see Figure 5.3).

For every hazardous material used in the workplace, the employer must have, and provide for review, an SDS. The SDS contains much more information about the material than the label and is prepared by the supplier. It is intended to

- describe the hazards of the product;
- explain how to use the product safely;
- advise what to expect if the recommendations are not followed;
- explain what to do if accidents occur;
- explain how to recognize symptoms of overexposure; and
- advise what to do if such incidents occur.

An SDS for each hazardous material present in the workplace must be available to be read by any worker who may be exposed to a hazardous material. SDSs are usually

- kept in a file or binder in an easily accessible place—some employers keep this binder in a materials storage area;
- stored electronically;
- available to the joint health and safety committee.

## Hazardous Energy

Energy can be a workplace hazard. If a form of energy is properly directed and controlled, it will perform a useful function, but when uncontrolled, it presents a danger to workers. Several forms of energy are hazardous to workers; they are shown in Figure 5.4.

Protecting workers from dangerous energy is generally accomplished through the use of energy barriers. Energy barriers can be classified as engineering controls, work practices, administrative controls, and personal protective equipment.

## Engineering Controls

This form of barrier is designed as a form of built-in control. Examples include off switches, machine part guards, and ventilation systems.

## Work Practices

Work practices can provide a form of barrier to individual hazards and dangers in the workplace. Examples of safe work practices include worker education and training, good housekeeping, highly visible labels, proper storage, personal hygiene, compliance with rules, and behaviour reinforcement.

## Administrative Controls

This type of barrier includes the things that management can do to help avoid some workplace hazards. For example, management can rotate workers to minimize their exposure to hazardous energy. They can also install warning and alarm systems to notify workers when they have received maximum allowable exposure.

## Personal Protective Equipment

Various forms of personal protective equipment (PPE) are used to avert danger to the worker. Examples of PPE are gloves, safety footwear, safety hats, splashguards, protective glasses, face shields, respirators, and aprons.

**Figure 5.4** Hazardous Energy in the Workplace

| Type of hazardous energy | Example in the workplace |
| --- | --- |
| Gravitational | Falling from a height |
| Electrical | Contacting underground equipment |
| Mechanical | Colliding with mobile equipment |
| Chemical | Inhaling toxic chemicals |
| Noise | Working with air compressors without protective ear covering |
| Thermal | Contact with hot or cold objects |
| Radiation | Ultraviolet radiation from welding |
| Pressure | Uncontrolled release of pressure |
| Biological | Exposure to viruses |
| Body mechanics | Lifting heavy objects |

Because security guards have the responsibility for monitoring workplace safety, they should be aware of all workplace safety equipment, practices, and policies, and they should monitor all work areas regularly to assess whether workers are taking full advantage of the protections available to them, and whether safety equipment is in proper working condition.

## CHAPTER SUMMARY

Occupational health and safety is probably the most important safety issue in modern workplaces. Since security personnel are employed by a company to protect against both external and internal risks, responsibility for occupational health and safety is a natural part of the security role. In recognition of this "fit," many companies choose security personnel to play key roles with respect to occupational health and safety, such as JHSC membership. Even when security guards are not assigned formal roles, they are usually the first responders when there is a workplace accident.

Security guards are expected to understand the general principles of the OHSA, the roles of workplace parties, and how the internal responsibility system is supposed to work. They may also be given responsibility for the investigation of workplace accidents.

Keeping staff and the public safe from hazards requires being able to recognize an unsafe situation before an accident or injury occurs. The WHMIS system supports hazard recognition via labels, SDSs, and workplace training.

A key preventive step in the promotion of workplace safety is the use of energy barriers and supportive work practices. These can include anything from ventilation systems to rules with respect to smoking in the workplace. Security personnel play an important role in assuring that all safety equipment and precautions prescribed by the employer are being used and followed by the employees. The enforcement of safety rules protects everyone and can save the lives of employees and save employers' money as well.

## KEY TERMS
due diligence, 87
hazard, 98
Workplace Hazardous Materials Information System (WHMIS), 86

## REFERENCES
*Canada Labour Code*, RSC 1985, c L-2.
*Canada Occupational Health and Safety Regulations*, SOR/86-304.
*Occupational Health and Safety Act*, RSO 1990, c O.1 [OHSA].

## PERFORMANCE APPLICATION
### Multiple Choice

1. What does the acronym WHMIS stand for?
   a. Workplace Hazards Materials Information Sheets
   b. Workplace Hazardous Materials Information System
   c. Worker Hazards Management Information System
   d. Workplace Hazardous Materials Information Sheets
   e. Working Hard to Manage Information about Safety

2. According to the OHSA, corporations face potential fines of _____ per offence for violations of the rules.
   a. $100,000
   b. $250,000
   c. $500,000
   d. $50,000
   e. $1,000,000

3. In addition to potential fines of $25,000, individuals may also face 12 months in prison for OHSA violations.
   a. true
   b. false
   c. only if they have received at least 2 prior warnings
   d. only in the public sector
   e. if a fatality results from the violations

4. A person who has charge of a workplace or authority over another worker is the definition of:
   a. supervisor
   b. JHSC
   c. MOL
   d. prevention officer
   e. none of the above

5. According to the *Canada Occupational Health and Safety Regulations*, which result of an accident does *not* require reporting by the employer to a Labour Canada safety officer?
   a. death
   b. disabling injury
   c. any damage to an elevating device
   d. near miss incident
   e. loss of a limb

6. Anything that can cause injury to or illness in a worker is the definition of a _____?
   a. risk
   b. hazard
   c. threat
   d. danger
   e. material event

7. Which hazard classification does a condition or practice likely to cause permanent disability, loss of life or body parts, and/or extensive loss of structure, equipment, or material fall under?
   a. Class C
   b. Class A
   c. Class B
   d. Class E
   e. Class D

8. What does the acronym SDS stand for?
   a. safe distribution sheets
   b. safety data sheet
   c. safety data system
   d. safe disposal system
   e. secure disposal system

### Short Answer

1. Research WSIB lost-time injuries and identify the three sectors with the highest frequency of lost-time injuries. Explain why these sectors have such a high number of lost-time injuries.

2. Identify specific work environments where each of the WHMIS symbols would commonly be found.

# Emergency Response Preparation

## 6

| | |
|---|---|
| Introduction | 108 |
| **Fire Emergencies** | **108** |
| Training Requirements | 108 |
| Evacuation Procedures | 109 |
| Fire Is a Common Emergency—Be Ready | 110 |
| **Bomb Threat Response Emergencies** | **110** |
| Elements of a Bomb Threat Response Plan | 111 |
| Bomb Threat Response Procedure | 112 |
| **Explosive Devices and Suspicious Objects** | **115** |
| Identifying Explosive Devices | 116 |
| **Observed/Reported Weapon or Active Shooter Situations** | **116** |
| Security Response | 117 |
| Arrival of Law Enforcement | 118 |
| **Protection of Evidence** | **119** |
| Collection and Preservation of Physical Evidence | 119 |
| **Chapter Summary** | **120** |
| **Key Terms** | **121** |
| **Performance Application** | **121** |

## LEARNING OUTCOMES

When you have completed this chapter, you will be able to:

- Identify the different types of potential emergencies.
- Describe the elements of emergency response procedures.
- Explain the roles of a security guard in emergency situations.
- Describe the legal requirements of emergency response.
- Detail how to protect and secure evidence at a crime scene or emergency event.

# Introduction

Preparing to respond to an emergency event has become one of the most essential elements of training required by security personnel across the industry. Security guards perform front-line services in such diverse areas as shopping malls, airports, nightclubs, amusement parks, schools, government installations, hospitals, courts, office buildings, nuclear power facilities and a variety of other areas.

Emergency events that may require security response include:

- fire emergencies;
- bomb threat response emergencies;
- explosive devices and suspicious objects; and
- observed/reported weapon or active shooter emergencies.

# Fire Emergencies

One of the greatest dangers at the time of a fire emergency is panic, which can be just as deadly a threat to the welfare and safety of workers as the fire itself. Consequently, it is of vital importance that security personnel are aware of the basics of fire safety and evacuation management so that they will be able to function in a calm, orderly, and effective manner during a fire emergency. It is therefore the security guard's responsibility as first responder to ensure that he or she is capable of the required response to any fire situation.

Specific responsibilities of security personnel:

- Respond to the fire location and take immediate control.
- Activate the fire alarm (if required) and use available firefighting equipment to contain the fire, if possible.
- Assist with the evacuation of people from the affected area.
- Provide assistance to fire department personnel when they arrive.
- Facilitate post-event activities such as employee head counts, access control, re-occupation of the building, resetting of systems, and equipment repair or replacement, as required.

## Training Requirements

Security personnel must become totally familiar with all forms of firefighting equipment so that regardless of their surroundings, they are capable of using whatever type is available. They should be familiar with the technical specifications of the fire alarm system and its sensors that together make up the building's system. Since security guards are likely to work on several different sites, they should take the time to become familiar with each system. Lives, including their own, may depend on it.

Security personnel should also be trained to assume the role and responsibility of a security supervisor. If called upon to assume the position of site supervisor in a fire emergency, the guard must be familiar with the response duties of the supervisor.

Practical firefighting skills training for security guards should include instruction in

- the use of all types of fire extinguishers;
- the use of a fire blanket;
- the way to activate and hold a fire hose;
- how to check for fire at a locked door;

- evacuation procedures; and
- how to assist the elderly and those with physical disabilities.

## Evacuation Procedures

The general guidelines for building evacuation are:

- The last person leaving a room should close, but not lock, the door. Locking the door hinders the fire department's search and rescue efforts.
- Evacuees should proceed to the nearest safe exit as outlined in the Emergency Action Plan, which should be posted on every floor of a facility.
- Elevators should never be used in a fire situation.
- When smoke or toxic gases are present (or suspected to be), evacuees should be instructed to bend over and stay low. The best air is close to the floor, so crawl if necessary.
- If possible, the mouth and nose should be covered with a damp cloth to filter the air and assist breathing.
- If the facility has multiple floors, a stairway will be the primary escape route. Most enclosed stairwells in buildings over two storeys are "rated" enclosures (which means they are more fireproof than other areas) and will provide a safe means of exit. Don't panic. Descend stairs slowly and carefully. Once in the stairwell, proceed down to the first floor. Never go up.
- Once outside the building, evacuees should report to a predetermined area so that a head count can be taken.

### ON THE JOB

#### The Use of Fire Extinguishers

A security professional's employer may have a specific policy for the use of fire extinguishers in the event of a fire. Even if such a policy exists, security guards should:

- attempt to put out fires only *after* ensuring that all occupants have been evacuated;
- confirm that the fire is small enough to be completely contained using the available extinguisher;
- ensure that they know how to use the extinguisher(s); and
- ensure that there is a clear escape route if the attempt to extinguish the fire fails.

Fire extinguishers are particular to the type of fire encountered. Using the wrong type of extinguisher for the fire can *increase* the risk of harm. For this reason, it is important not to use a fire extinguisher without training.

In general, water-based extinguishers work only on Class A fires (caused by the combustion of solids such as wood, paper, or cloth). They should *never* be used on Class B (flammable liquid) or Class C (live electricity) fires; to do so can cause severe injury or death. Carbon dioxide gas extinguishers, which are designed to rob a fire of oxygen, are for use on Class B or C fires and are less effective on Class A fires.

While extinguishers and their uses may differ and guards should receive training for those available in their workplaces, most pressurized fire extinguishers work as follows:

- pull out the locking pin,
- aim the nozzle at the *base* of the fire, and
- sweep the nozzle from side to side across the base of the fire until it is completely out.

A person trying to escape a fire should never open a closed door without feeling it first with the back of the hand for excessive heat on the other side. If the door is hot, another exit should be used. If there is no other exit, the cracks around doors and vents should be sealed with anything available.

A trapped person should use a radio or telephone to call the fire department, giving them his or her exact location. If a phone or radio is not available, the person should wave for attention at a window or hang out the window a sheet, towel, or other item that can be used to signal for help.

If breathing is difficult, the person should try to ventilate the room. If the fire is on an upper floor and the window is of a type that cannot be opened, the window should *never* be broken as glass will rain down on rescuers and people exiting the building.

A person on fire should stop, drop to the floor, and roll around to smother the flames. If someone else catches fire, the flames should be smothered with a blanket. Wrapping a person in a blanket or rug can save them from serious burns or even death.

### Fire Is a Common Emergency—Be Ready

Statistics suggest that a security guard in a typical workplace will be required to deal with a fire alarm situation about once per month. Fire can do an enormous amount of damage and can cause death or serious injury much more quickly than most people expect. Reacting immediately and appropriately to both false alarms and real fire situations can mean the difference between life and death for people in the building.

While the actual firefighting responsibility lies almost exclusively with the fire department, security guards play a vital role in promoting a speedy, orderly, and effective response to a fire situation, and their assistance is crucial for evacuation management. Security guards are also expected to understand the use of fire protection equipment, to know where it is located, to report any problems with equipment, and to coordinate equipment maintenance.

## Bomb Threat Response Emergencies

The possibility of a bomb threat event is an unfortunate reality of our times. In the recent past, most Western countries, including Canada, have experienced bomb threat incidents of varying magnitude. Although most recent incidents have been politically motivated, or linked to international terrorism, some such threats are made simply as a nuisance or in an attempt to disrupt business activities. Also, not all bomb threats involve the actual placement of an explosive device.

Nevertheless, all bomb threats with any degree of credibility must be handled as though they are legitimate, which means securing the area; managing an evacuation where appropriate; and performing an exhaustive investigation, often in cooperation with public authorities, of the threat, the motives behind it, and any actual placed explosive device(s).

Any organization or facility that employs security should have a bomb threat response plan in place, no matter how remote the chance of ever receiving such a threat appears to be. The nature and level of detail of the bomb threat response plan will depend greatly on the type of organization, the size of the facility, the general risk for bomb threats, and other factors. Being prepared for a bomb threat means that, should such a threat actually materialize, security and management will have a better chance of protecting lives and property, minimizing disruption to business operations, and creating the impression that the workplace is safe and that security is being maintained.

## Elements of a Bomb Threat Response Plan

The first step in being prepared to manage bomb threats is to create a written bomb threat plan, or, if your workplace has one, to review it. Basic bomb threat response plans should address the following:

1. *Actions on receipt of threat*: The person who receives the bomb threat should know what immediate actions to take, what information to record and ask for, and whom to contact with respect to the threat.
2. *The role of security*: The authority and role of the security department, in the event of a bomb threat, should be described. Appropriate contact people (in larger organizations, a bomb threat team) should be identified.
3. *Evacuation plans*: Every facility should identify evacuation routes, evacuation rules (for example, no elevator use), and a "marshalling area" to which evacuated individuals should be brought so that they can be protected and accounted for.
4. *Search plan*: For the purpose of searching for an explosive device, security should be trained to divide the facility into search zones. Security guards should be trained on how to perform a methodical search of a zone, and how to report their findings.
5. *Plan for contacting outside authorities*: Security guards should know which public or other support authorities are to be contacted for support in the event of a bomb threat. Contact information should be kept in an easily accessible location, and provision should be made for orderly and accurate briefing of support authorities upon their arrival at the facility.

Larger, higher-risk, or more sophisticated organizations may also cover, in their bomb threat response plans, the following issues:

- identification of a bomb threat team;
- establishment of a bomb threat control centre;
- bomb threat response training for all employees;
- regular bomb threat drills;
- back-up communications, such as a loud hailer, in case of a bomb threat (some radio systems pose a risk of detonating explosives);
- purchase and storage of special supplies, such as bomb blankets, package X-ray equipment, and chemical trace detectors;
- installation of special equipment, such as bomb-proof doors or barriers between zones;
- a policy with respect to public relations and media communications in the event of a bomb threat;
- a written and/or graphic search and evacuation plan that divides the facility into zones, permitting a comprehensive search and, in appropriate cases, evacuation of only at-risk parts of the facility (this is less disruptive to business activities, and minimizes risks related to panic reactions in a large facility).

# Bomb Threat Response Procedure

An appropriate response to a bomb threat is critical for three key reasons (ranked in order of priority):

1. To preserve the safety of personnel, customers, and visitors, and to minimize damage to business assets.
2. To preserve the reputation of the employer or client by sending the message that the organization is prepared for and in control of the situation.
3. To minimize disruption of business activities.

All personnel, not only security, should be aware of the potential for bomb threats and should be alert to suspicious situations. At the same time, personnel should be encouraged to feel secure that there is a plan in place that is designed to provide for their safety and security in the event of a bomb threat.

For security personnel faced with a bomb threat, the following priorities should be observed:

- ensure personal safety at all times;
- ensure the safety of staff, contractors, visitors, and the general public;
- maintain the integrity of the site security function;
- maintain the routine operations of the site;
- obtain explosive ordnance disposal (EOD) assistance when and if required.

## *Person Receiving the Threat*

It is important to remember that bomb threats may be made to *any* employee in an organization—a bomb threat call cannot be expected to be made directly to the person best trained to handle it! For this reason, *all* employees should receive basic, well-designed training about how to respond to a threat. Simple instructions are best, as these are most easily retained.

A bomb threat can be most effectively responded to if the person taking the call can gather as much information, both objective and subjective, as possible about the threat and can later communicate that information accurately to others (for example, to security personnel, or EOD staff).

Objective information about a bomb threat may include:

- the timing of the call;
- the phone number from which the call came;
- the exact wording of the threat; and
- any background noise overheard.

Subjective information might include:

- the listener's perception of the caller's state of mind/attitude (e.g., he sounded nervous, she was trying to suppress laughter);
- perceived information about the caller (e.g., English is not his first language, she was reading from a prepared script); and
- recognition of the speaker's voice as familiar (voices are very unique).

A person who receives a threat, by listening carefully, can help security evaluate the seriousness of the threat. For example, most experts suggest that a threat should be perceived as valid if it is both *credible* and *specific*. The **credibility of a threat** might be affected by such things as the speaker's tone; for example, a person trying to suppress laughter might be rated as less credible than one speaking in a serious, even slightly nervous, tone. The **specificity of a threat** relates to details of the threat itself. A general threat such as "We've got the place wired to the max" might well be less valid than a specific threat such as "There's a pound of C4 explosive somewhere under the floor in the north end of Warehouse D; it will be detonated remotely at 0215 hours, or sooner if tampered with."

Because of the stress involved in receiving a bomb threat call, it can be very useful for employees to have a written guideline, stored near every telephone, for their reference. Figure 6.1 is an example of a form that may be used for this purpose.

**credibility of a threat**
a subjective estimate of the likelihood that the threat is legitimate, based on, for example, the identity or demeanour of the person making the threat

**specificity of a threat**
the degree to which specific details (time of detonation, location of bomb, nature of risk, expected damage, etc.) have been provided about the threatened detonation or other threat

## *Threat Response and Evacuation*

Once a bomb threat has been received, it should be immediately communicated to the director of security or his or her delegate. That person, in cooperation with the bomb threat team, if any, should quickly make a determination with respect to the validity of the threat.

When a threat is deemed valid or potentially valid, and when there is some information about the location of the explosive device, the director of security may decide to evacuate all personnel, or personnel within a particular zone or zones.

Security personnel will supervise the evacuation. Evacuees should be directed toward the safest possible exit route, taking into account the suspected location of the bomb. In general, employees are to be advised not to use elevators, telephones, or any other electrical devices. Cellphones, though often safe, should not be used unless security advises otherwise.

Evacuees should be advised to move quickly but not to run, and to maintain quiet so that instructions can be heard (and other personnel in other areas are not alarmed unnecessarily). Line managers are to take responsibility for the employees who report to them and should account for all employees who were at work that day. Where an employee cannot be accounted for, his or her absence should be brought to the attention of security.

Evacuees should be brought to a safe marshalling area, and all personnel should be accounted for. In general, evacuees should not leave the marshalling area without express permission from security.

Where there is no reliable information about the location of an explosive device, the decision to evacuate is more complicated, because there can be no assurance of the safety of the marshalling area, or the exit route. In some cases, it may actually be safer to allow personnel to remain at their workstations. This decision should be at the discretion of the director of security, sometimes in conjunction with instructions from EOD staff.

## *Search Procedure*

Once the facility, or the affected zone, is secured, a search can be performed. This usually takes place after an evacuation is complete; although in some sophisticated settings, after bomb-proof barriers are set in place. Unless the risk is deemed to be certain or very high, the initial search is conducted by security guards and/or other employees, and not by an external response force.

Where possible, all parts of the facility should be searched by individuals already familiar with those areas; for example, security guards should search areas falling within their normal patrol routes.

**Figure 6.1** Bomb Threat Checklist

---

Exact time of call _____

Exact words of caller _____

_____

_____

QUESTIONS TO ASK

1. When is the bomb going to explode? _____
2. Where is the bomb? _____
3. What does it look like? _____
4. What kind of bomb is it? _____
5. What will cause it to explode? _____
6. Did you place the bomb? _____
7. Why? _____
8. Where are you calling from? _____
9. What is your address? _____
10. What is your name? _____

CALLER'S VOICE (circle)

| Accent | Crying | Giggling | Nasal | Sincere |
| Angry | Deep | High-pitched | Nervous | Slow |
| Broken | Disguised | Lisp | Normal | Slurred |
| Calm | Excited | Loud | Rapid | Stutter |

If voice is familiar, whom did it sound like? _____

Were there any background noises? _____

Remarks _____

_____

Person receiving call _____

Telephone number call received at _____

Date _____

Report call immediately to _____

(Refer to bomb incident plan)

---

Searchers should work systematically, according to a search plan. Useful strategies include:

- stopping to look, listen, smell, etc., upon entering a new room before moving around;
- dividing the room vertically into search zones, to ensure that the whole room is searched, not just the floor space;

- walking in a set sweep pattern;
- overlapping with another searcher;
- paying attention to hidden surfaces (undersides, topsides, backs of furnishings, doors, etc.); and
- noting damage to surfaces (e.g., marks or smudges on a false ceiling tile).

Security guards should pay special attention to stairwells, washrooms, lobby areas, vacant offices, corridors, elevators, receiving areas, garbage areas, the parking garage, and the mail room.

When a suspicious item is found in the course of a search, no one should touch it. Efforts should be made to determine its source (where it came from/who brought it there) and how long it has been in place. In most cases, an immediate call for support should be made to the appropriate authorities. If there has been no evacuation, a decision may be made to evacuate in light of the discovery of the item; however, it is important to remember that there is a possibility that there might be more than one device. In appropriate cases, the search of other areas should continue while awaiting support.

## Coordination with External Response Force

When a call is made to an external response force, security should provide any available information pertaining to the incident over the phone. This information will assist in the determination of the size of the team to be dispatched and what equipment might be required.

The director of security (or his or her delegate) should be prepared to brief the external response force personnel on their arrival at the facility. Security personnel should provide ongoing support to the external response force over the course of the investigation. It is useful to have any paperwork that would assist in this task readily available—for example, a bomb threat form filled out by the person who took the call, and site plans for the facility.

## Conclusion

While only a small proportion of bomb threats relate to the actual placement of an explosive device, all such threats should be taken seriously. This means that security personnel specifically, and employees in general, should receive basic training about how to respond to a bomb threat call.

Security departments should have a bomb threat response plan in place that addresses, at minimum, the issues of how and when to evacuate, how to search for a bomb, and whom to contact for outside support in case a device or suspected device is located.

Avoiding bomb disasters requires planning, good observation skills, and an ability to assess the credibility of bomb threats.

# Explosive Devices and Suspicious Objects

**Explosive devices** exist in a wide variety. An explosive device is any object containing chemical, liquid, or gas (or combinations thereof) that is designed to do damage or create injury upon detonation, explosion, or chemical or physical reaction.

Bombs built by would-be criminals for the specific purpose of doing damage are sometimes called **improvised explosive devices** (IEDs). Mechanical or electrical IEDs commonly have an initiation system or fuse, explosive fill, a detonator, a power supply for the detonator, and a container.

**explosive device**
an object that contains a chemical, liquid, or gas (or combination thereof) that is designed to do damage or create injury upon detonation, explosion, or chemical or physical reaction

**improvised explosive device**
an explosive device built by private individuals (not a manufacturer), often made out of ordinary items commonly available to the public

Explosive devices can range in size from very tiny (consider, for example, the size of a grenade, or piece of plastique) to 200 kg or larger. Explosive devices can be made to look like everyday objects (particularly, small electronics) or can be hidden inside, or fixed to the underside of innocent objects. By contrast, harmless collections of sinister-looking materials (fuses, timers, etc.) can be assembled to look like workable explosive devices. In a threat event, any unidentified object whose ownership cannot be positively identified should be treated as a suspicious object.

Explosive devices are fairly easy to create. Instructions for making bombs abound on the Internet, and many explosive devices can be made out of easily accessible materials. This means that even fairly unsophisticated would-be criminals should, in appropriate cases, not be ruled out as posing a credible security threat.

In general, an explosive device works when an initiation system (which can be mechanical, electrical, chemical, etc.) triggers the detonation of explosive material. The resulting explosion—sudden release of energy—does damage by generating heat and/or pressure and sometimes by causing the mobilization of shrapnel or the destruction of surrounding structures and/or materials. Some bombs are specifically designed to trigger the release of another hazard—for example, in the case of the 1993 World Trade Center bomb, the propulsion of a canister of cyanide gas into the ventilation system. (It didn't work very well; the heat of the explosion rendered the gas harmless.)

## Identifying Explosive Devices

Because of the variety of explosive devices available, training security personnel and employees to identify explosives by sight is often not as effective as simply training them to identify objects that are "suspicious."

In order to be able to classify an object as suspicious, employees, including security employees, should be taught to regularly examine and observe the normal state of their working areas and the objects that surround them. When employees are familiar with what is supposed to be in the workplace, it becomes easier to note any objects that appear out of the ordinary, either because they cannot be identified or because their source or function is unknown.

When an employee notices a suspicious object in the normal course of work (i.e., not in the context of a bomb threat), security should be called. If security cannot identify the object or its origins, it may be advisable to call for appropriate outside assistance—the public **explosive ordnance disposal** (EOD) **authorities** (the bomb squad).

Where a suspicious object is noted in the context of a search that follows a bomb threat, the object will almost always provide cause for outside intervention.

Employees must be trained *never* to touch or move a suspicious package or object.

**explosive ordnance disposal authority**
a specialized team, often part of a police department or military force, deployed to remove and/or disable explosive devices

# Observed/Reported Weapon or Active Shooter Situations

If a weapon is observed/reported to security or management, the response procedures for an active shooter emergency must be implemented. Since this type of incident could easily escalate into an active shooter emergency, it is safer for all concerned if the security and employee response covers that contingency.

The term "active shooter" describes an individual who is actively engaged in killing or attempting to kill individuals in a facility or populated area. In the majority of recorded instances, active shooters use some type of firearm(s) and are indiscriminate in their selection of victims. The security response to an observed/reported weapon or active shooter incident must be consistent with an established protocol and appropriate to the environment in which it occurs.

Employers should assess the risk to their workplace and develop site-specific employee and security training that take into account the layout of the building(s), business operations, and security capability. Several training videos patterned after the US Department of Homeland Security's *Run, Hide, Fight* video about active shooter situations are available commercially. At a minimum, security and employee training should include an approved version of such a video, and response procedures developed that, at a minimum, address the possibility of events triggered by one of the following:

- current or former disgruntled employees;
- employees involved in incidents of bullying, or making threats;
- incidents of workplace violence;
- employees affected by a restraining order;
- employees recently terminated or affected by downsizing;
- the company being targeted because of the work it does;
- the company being targeted because of its social prominence, or its value as a high-profile target for radicalized groups.

## Security Response

Active shooter situations are unpredictable and evolve quickly. Security must be prepared to respond to an active shooter situation before the arrival of law enforcement. Security personnel must remain calm, and take immediate action to direct the evacuation of anyone in the vicinity who has safe access to the exterior of the facility. Anyone remaining in the facility should be advised to lock and barricade doors, and shelter in place.

During an active shooter situation, the natural human reaction, even for trained individuals, is to be shocked, feel fear and anxiety, and maybe even doubt that what you are hearing is actually happening. The sounds of gunfire, people screaming, alarms, and explosions can be disorienting. Training helps security regain control, remember their response priorities, and commit to action. The security response, whether as an individual guard or part of a security team, is to preserve the safety of the persons within their area of responsibility.

### Evacuate the Area

- If persons in your direct vicinity are not being targeted and a building exit is nearby, immediately *evacuate* everyone and direct them away from the building:
  - leave personal belongings behind and
  - designate specific individuals to assist any person(s) requiring assistance.
- Use very *loud*, very *simple* commands: GUN! — GET OUT! — RUN!
- Call 911 as soon as possible: Establish radio contact with the security team as soon as possible.
- If you are close to a public address system, broadcast the "active shooter" alert.

### Shelter In Place

- If evacuation is not a safe option, direct people to hide in as safe a place as possible.
- Lock the doors and barricade them with heavy furniture.

- Close and lock windows; pull down blinds or shades.
- Turn off the lights.
- Silence all electronic devices: cellphones, TVs, monitors, radios, computers, etc.
- *Keep silent*.
- *Stay low* and behind something solid, if possible.
- If first responders can be seen from a window, attempt to signal them, indicating how many people are in the room and the status of the individuals.
- *Remain in place* until given the "all clear" by law enforcement.

### Fight

- If neither evacuation nor shelter-in-place is possible or practical, and your life and the lives of others are threatened, the only possible action that may allow you to survive is to fight:
    - attack the shooter using any items/objects available: chairs, a fire extinguisher;
    - use any security equipment available: a baton or large flashlight.

Note: Confronting an active shooter cannot be mandated as part of the responsibilities of a security guard, or included in his or her job description. How each individual (security guard, employee, or member of the public) decides to respond if directly targeted by an active shooter is up to him or her.

## Arrival of Law Enforcement

The primary aim of the law enforcement response team is to locate and stop the shooter(s). Both security and employees should be trained to cooperate and not interfere with the response team. When law enforcement officers arrive, everyone must display empty hands with open palms. Since law enforcement may still be unsure of the number and identity of the shooters involved, everyone may be instructed to place their hands on their heads, and may be searched or kept in a controlled posture until the situation is resolved.

Once positively identified, security guards may be asked to provide information to law enforcement such as:

- location of any known victims and the active shooter;
- number of shooters, if more than one;
- physical description of shooter(s);
- number and type of weapons used by the shooter(s); and
- number of potential victims at the location.

Once positively identified, security guards may be required to assist law enforcement with tasks such as:

- the *identification* of certain individuals;
- *locating* and *providing access* to secure rooms or locked-down areas;
- *providing access* to the facility public address system;

- *delivery* of facility security surveillance video or data storage to law enforcement; and
- assisting human resources in *coordinating* liaison between law enforcement and employees, as required.

Active shooter situations are an unfortunate reality that our society cannot afford to ignore. Security guards must be aware of the possibility of an active shooter event occurring at their place of work and make all efforts to prepare for this eventuality. The development of a response program, supported by realistic training at all levels will go a long way toward mitigating this threat.

# Protection of Evidence

Security personnel involved in investigations or attending incident scenes may become involved in the securing, handling, and processing of evidence or exhibits. Different types of physical evidence can come under the control of a security guard, and each type requires particular handling and processing precautions. In certain minor incident investigations, a security guard may be responsible for exhibits from the start of an investigation to its conclusion. In the wake of more serious occurrences, security guards will play a role in securing and protecting evidence until other investigating authorities are on site and able to take over control. Procedures for investigations and the securing of evidence will be discussed in detail in Chapter 14 of this book. The following is a basic overview to keep in mind in the emergency response context.

## Collection and Preservation of Physical Evidence

When security personnel first come across an incident scene, it is critical that they stop and scan the entire area, examining everything in view for possible evidence. At the same time, they need to fix the placement of every object in their minds. No detail should be dismissed, regardless of origin. The distinctive smell of a popular cologne, cigar smoke, or chemical fumes may become key clues later in the investigation that help identify a suspect who has fled the scene. It is just as important to note what's missing from the scene: a picture from a wall or a matching bookend from a shelf.

Security guards should avoid touching or handling items found at the scene of an incident. This ensures that pieces of evidence that may identify a suspect more precisely will not be overlooked, disturbed, or damaged. Moreover, hasty, careless actions may result in depositing evidence, such as fingerprints or hair, at the scene. When this evidence is collected as part of the evidence it may slow down and burden forensics teams with misleading possibilities. This is called **contaminating the evidence**, and if the defendant's lawyer can prove the evidence has been contaminated, it is inadmissible in court.

**contaminating the evidence**
destroying, altering, or depositing physical evidence at a crime scene

Written notes should be supplemented with a diagram of the scene in the security guard's notebook. Since most security guards are equipped with cellphones, photos of the incident scene taken by the guard are often used to confirm the presence and relative position of objects to each other when completing the official occurrence/incident reports for submission.

## CHAPTER SUMMARY

In this chapter, we examined several different types of emergency situations that are commonly faced by security personnel in the course of their duty. Understanding the elements of each of these emergencies, and the response protocols that guards are required to follow in support of responding EMS and law enforcement is key to the performance of their duties.

The role of the security guard in each of the identified emergencies was discussed in detail. These included the response to fire emergencies, the actions taken by security when a bomb threat has been received, and how to identify suspicious objects when searching a building. We also discussed what constitutes an improvised explosive device, and what security guards should look for when attempting to determine whether a package or unclaimed backpack is a potential IED or suspicious object.

The increasing number of active shooter events was examined in detail and the role of security guards as first responders in schools and other venues was discussed. Weapons-based emergencies are an unfortunate reality and security personnel must be properly trained in the proper response procedures and actively practice in their primary response role and as support to responding law enforcement personnel. The legal responsibilities of security in these types of emergencies were also identified.

The chapter concluded with the manner in which physical evidence is collected and protected by security personnel in support of an active investigation. Security techniques associated with incident scene management, protection of and continuity of evidence (the chain of custody), and proper record-keeping were emphasized. These underscored the importance of preparing for emergency response, and the role of security in this process.

## KEY TERMS

contaminating the evidence, 119
credibility of a threat, 113
explosive device, 115
explosive ordnance disposal authority, 116
improvised explosive device, 115
specificity of a threat, 113

## PERFORMANCE APPLICATION
### Multiple Choice

1. Why must bomb threats, even by apparently unsophisticated would-be criminals, be taken seriously?
    a. because even bomb threats that are not particularly credible can have an impact on employee morale
    b. because bombs are fairly easy to create and many varieties require readily available materials
    c. because even false bomb threats disrupt business productivity and should therefore be investigated and deterred
    d. because bomb threats can have a negative public relations impact on businesses and agencies
    e. all of the above

2. The first action a security professional should take when a fire alarm sounds is to:
    a. follow the instructions for responding to a fire alarm that are set out in the emergency measures plan for that site
    b. evacuate the building
    c. reset the alarm
    d. notify the fire department
    e. secure confidential records

3. What information should be recorded by an individual who receives a bomb threat call? Choose the best answer.
    a. only factual information, no opinions or judgments about the caller
    b. as much factual and subjective information as possible including caller demeanour, accent, and motivations, but focusing first on specific details about precise bomb location, bomb type, and detonation time if any
    c. bomb location
    d. bomb type
    e. motivation for setting the bomb

4. A Class B fire involves:
    a. a vacant location with no risk to human lives
    b. a live source of electricity
    c. radioactive materials
    d. flammable liquids such as gasoline or cooking oil
    e. paper, wood, cloth, and similar combustible solids

5. Improvised explosive devices
    a. are designed to look like bombs but are not capable of explosion
    b. should be viewed as harmless unless touched or moved
    c. can look like ordinary objects or containers that might be found on the property
    d. look like ordinary objects except that they always have wires (sometimes concealed) going into the ground or a wall
    e. need to be connected to the building electrical system to detonate

6. What issues are taken into consideration by a director of security in deciding whether or not to evacuate personnel and others in a facility on receipt of a bomb threat?
    a. an immediate evacuation should always be conducted
    b. the credibility and specificity of the bomb threat, the security department's assessment of whether the threat is serious, and the risks inherent in the evacuation itself
    c. the credibility of the threat, but also the potential for lost productivity
    d. employee morale, lost productivity, deterrence, and public relations implications
    e. the location of the bomb and the time remaining before detonation

7. The role of security personnel during evacuations is
    a. to follow the evacuation instructions contained in the emergency measures plan for the facility
    b. to ensure all internal doors are shut
    c. to turn off all critical building operation systems
    d. to preserve physical assets and confidential records
    e. personal safety—to exit the building as soon as possible for his or her own safety

8. What instructions should be given to evacuees in the event of a bomb threat?

    a. move quickly without running

    b. avoid speaking so that instructions can be heard

    c. avoid use of cellphones

    d. meet at a pre-arranged location for head count

    e. all of the above

## Short Answer

1. A bomb threat has been received by a shelter for women and children who have fled domestic abuse. The shelter premises include a garage, a garden shed, a backyard with a treehouse, a basement storage area with laundry facilities, a basement furnace room, a basement workout room, a common area (sitting room, dining room), a kitchen, a pantry, three bathrooms, and eight bedrooms.

    a. List three useful strategies for carrying out a search incident to a bomb threat.

    b. List three parts of a facility that should receive particular attention when conducting a bomb search.

2. What kinds of information should security personnel be prepared to share with external response force members upon their arrival at a site that has received a bomb threat?

# Canadian Legal System 7

| | |
|---|---|
| Introduction | 124 |
| **The Canadian Legal System** | 124 |
| Courts Divided by Area of Law | 125 |
| Appeal Courts | 128 |
| **The Law of Evidence in Canada** | 129 |
| Evidence Statutes | 129 |
| Other Sources of the Law of Evidence | 131 |
| **The Evidence of Security Professionals** | 133 |
| Preparing for Court | 134 |
| On the Day of the Hearing | 135 |
| **Chapter Summary** | 137 |
| **Key Terms** | 138 |
| **Note** | 138 |
| **References** | 138 |
| **Performance Application** | 138 |

## LEARNING OUTCOMES

When you have completed this chapter, you will:

- Be able to describe the Canadian court system, including the levels of jurisdiction and the distinctions between civil courts, criminal courts, and administrative tribunals.
- Be able to explain the sources of evidence law in Canada and know which rules of evidence apply to which courts.
- Know what types of evidence are admissible in Canadian courts, and understand that evidence may be excluded by a court if it is collected or stored improperly.
- Understand what is expected of a security guard who is called to testify as a witness in court.

## Introduction

A security professional's job is to protect assets, information, personnel, and facilities for either the employer or the employer's clients. Part of the job is dealing with people who have taken prohibited action or committed illegal acts. This means that some security professionals will spend time in court giving evidence as part of lawsuits against or criminal trials of these individuals. The best evidence rule, a common law rule of evidence, provides that where a **witness** to an incident is alive and competent to give testimony, his or her oral testimony in court under oath—his or her "best evidence"—is required to be presented, even if it would be possible to simply present a written statement.

**witness**
person who gives evidence while under oath

To be able to discharge these duties effectively, security professionals require a basic understanding of the Canadian court system. They will also need some awareness of the rules that govern the presentation of evidence in court. This chapter will provide an overview of the Canadian justice system, with a focus on Ontario courts, as well as an introduction to the law of evidence. We will conclude with information and advice about giving testimony in court as a witness.

## The Canadian Legal System

The Canadian legal system distinguishes courts from each other on two bases: types of courts and levels of courts. Distinctions by type of court are based on the nature of the disputes heard in the court (criminal matters, family cases, tax cases, and so on). The level of a court relates to whether it is a court of "first instance"—generally, this is a court in which a full trial occurs, complete with witness and/or documentary and physical evidence; or an appeal court, in which a lower-level trial decision or administrative decision is reviewed.

For a visual representation of the Canadian court system, see Figure 7.1.

**Figure 7.1** The Canadian Court System

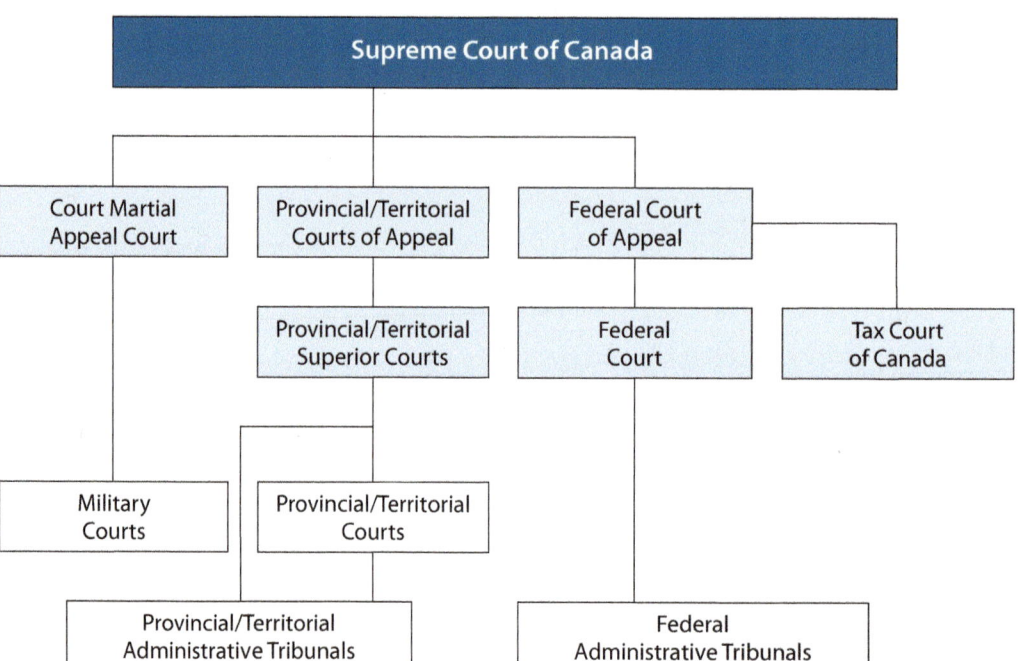

# Courts Divided by Area of Law

Within the Canadian legal system, the most important "type of court" distinction is that between criminal courts and civil courts.

## Criminal Courts and Procedure

Criminal courts hear trials of offences charged under the *Criminal Code*. The parties in a criminal trial are the prosecution (the government, represented by a **Crown Attorney**); the accused (often represented by **defence counsel**); and the **judge** and/or **jury**.

While criminal courts are subdivided into levels, they are not further specialized.[1]

The procedure for criminal trials varies depending on whether the offence charged is a **summary conviction offence** (generally less serious) or an **indictable offence**. Summary trials follow a simplified procedure that is designed to be fairly efficient and to control costs, but certain aspects of procedure (some of which are known as "protections") are not available to the accused; for example, a summary trial does not include a preliminary hearing. The trial of indictable offences is more complex, and includes the full range of available procedural protections. In cases where the penalty that can be imposed for an indictable offence is five years or more, the accused is entitled to a jury trial. The procedures that govern criminal trials are set out in the *Criminal Code* itself.

Where an accused is charged with a **hybrid offence**, the prosecution has the option to choose between either the summary procedure or the indictable procedure. While the indictable procedure requires more time and effort, more severe penalties can be imposed if a conviction is entered against the accused on an indictable charge.

Ontario summary trials are held in what is called "provincial court," the lower of two levels of courts of first instance in the province (in Ontario, the provincial court is a division of the Ontario Court of Justice). The appeal of some decisions made by the provincial court is not to the Court of Appeal, but rather to the Ontario Superior Court of Justice, a court that doubles as the court of first instance for most (but not all) indictable trials in the province.

The rules governing the introduction of physical evidence (also called "real evidence") and the giving of testimony (also called "direct evidence" or "oral evidence") are the same regardless of the type of criminal offence charged. In general, the hearing of appeals does not involve the presentation of evidence of any kind; instead, appeals usually involve a review of the way in which the judge or jury applied the law to the evidence presented

**Crown attorney**
lawyer who prosecutes the accused on behalf of the government

**defence counsel**
lawyer who represents the accused

**judge**
court official appointed to try cases in a court of law

**jury**
group of 12 people (in criminal law) or 6 people (in civil law in most provinces) who decide the case based on the evidence presented

**summary conviction offence**
a less serious offence that is tried according to summary court procedure

**indictable offence**
a serious offence tried according to the indictable criminal court procedure

**hybrid offence**
an offence that can be charged and tried either as a summary conviction offence or on indictment, according to the prosecution's choice

## ON THE JOB

### Finding My Courtroom

Should you ever find yourself wandering panicked through the halls of a courthouse trying to find the room in which a trial is to be held, it can be helpful to know that while courts are segregated by function and type, there are not always particular courtrooms permanently designated to a court type. For example, especially in a smaller city, a courthouse may run bail court out of a general purpose courtroom during certain hours of the day or day of the week; for instance, "Courtroom 2" may hold bail court in the mornings, and provincial offences court in the afternoon. See the courtroom help desk attendant or review a posted legend for the building to find the room you are looking for. The names of cases scheduled to be heard (usually by party name) are often posted somewhere on or near a courtroom door or displayed on a monitor.

at the trial in the court below. This means that you will not, as a security professional, be asked to give testimony at an appeal—only at a trial. A transcript of your evidence will form part of the "record" presented to the appeal court, as will any documentary evidence that you created and that was used in the trial (for example, notebook entries), but you will not have a chance to give that evidence again.

## Security Spotlight

### Roles of Courtroom Players in a Criminal Trial

#### The Judge

Criminal and civil trials are always presided over (directed) by a judge. In some cases, the judge is also the decision maker: he or she renders the verdict in the trial. In other cases, the jury renders the verdict, and the judge's role is to assist the jury in understanding, organizing, and considering the evidence. In all trials, the judge makes the decisions about whether to admit (let into the court record) or exclude evidence. If evidence is presented but the judge feels, based on the rules of evidence, that it is not admissible, the jury (or the judge, if there is no jury) must not consider that evidence. The judge decides what happens in the course of a trial and answers all inquiries—from lawyers, witnesses, and the jury—about how the case will proceed.

#### The Jury

Many criminal trials and some civil cases are decided by a jury. The jury's role is mostly passive—jury members say nothing during the trial, they simply listen to the evidence. If they have questions, they address these to the judge. At the conclusion of the trial, after listening to the judge's instruction with respect to the evidence, the jury members go into a private room to discuss and agree on a verdict, which they then present to the court.

#### The Crown Attorney

The Crown attorney or prosecutor, sometimes also referred to simply as "the Crown," is the lawyer who presents the case on behalf of the government. The Crown needs to work closely with police and other key witnesses, including security professionals, to build a case on behalf of the government. In order to win a criminal case, the Crown must prove beyond a reasonable doubt the necessary elements of the crime. Because of this, the Crown is said to have the burden of proof.

#### The Defence Counsel

The defence counsel is a lawyer who is either hired by the defendant privately, or, in the case of "duty counsel," provided by the court to work on behalf of the defendant. The defence's job is to refute (disprove) the Crown's case in an attempt to obtain an acquittal for the defendant. To do this, the defence needs to create, in the minds of the judge and/or the jury, a reasonable doubt as to whether the crime was committed by the accused. The defence may do this either by simply refuting the Crown's evidence, or by raising a defence (a denial or justification) on the defendant's part.

#### The Witness

A witness is any person who is called to give verbal evidence in a court case. The accused can be a witness for the defence, although he or she is not required to testify. The victim can also be a witness for the prosecution.

## Provincial Offences Court

Despite the confusingly similar name, "provincial offences court" is different from provincial court generally. A provincial offences court is part of the Ontario Court of Justice system, but instead of hearing summary conviction criminal matters, it hears provincial offences matters; that is, the trials for offences charged under statutes like the *Highway Traffic Act* or the *Trespass to Property Act*. In some cities, this court may also hear matters relating to breaches of municipal by-laws.

As a security professional, this is one of the courts in which you are likely to be called as a witness, because your work may lead to charges under the *Trespass to Property Act*. Procedures for hearings in this court are governed by an Ontario statute called the *Provincial Offences Act*. We will discuss this legislation further in the next chapter. One difference between provincial offences court and other courts is that it is very common for defendants to appear before this court without a lawyer or paralegal to represent them. To help accommodate these unrepresented defendants, the judge in a provincial offences court will often take a more active role than usual, giving instructions to the defendant about the steps in the hearing and what to do. For this reason, the proceedings tend to have a less formal tone.

## Civil Courts and Procedure

"Civil" courts, in Ontario, are courts that resolve non-criminal legal disputes (lawsuits) between private individuals or corporations, or between private parties and governments. The proceedings in these courts are commenced (started) by a party generally known as a **plaintiff** (though sometimes called "**applicant**" if the case is of a type called an "application"). The plaintiff brings a lawsuit against one or more **defendants** in an attempt to obtain "relief" from the court. This "relief" generally means money compensation, which is known as **damages**, but can also include court orders. Relief orders often require the defendant to stop a particular type of behaviour; for example, building a structure, selling a counterfeit product, or engaging in defamation. They can also require a defendant (or a "**respondent**," if the case is an application) to take some kind of action; for example, to grant an applicant access to a child after a divorce. In some cases, defendants respond to lawsuits by seeking relief of their own against the plaintiff (this is called a counterclaim), or against additional defendants (a third party claim).

In some provinces, including Ontario, civil courts are divided into both levels and types. The lowest level of civil court is Small Claims Court, a court with a simplified procedure that hears matters in which the defendant is requesting no more than $25,000 in damages. The Superior Court hears civil matters in which higher amounts of damages are being claimed, and Divisional Court is actually an appeal court, hearing appeals of some lower-level civil matters (including some family law matters) and also judicial reviews (somewhat similar to appeals) of rulings made by **administrative tribunals** (discussed below).

Within the Superior Court level, there are some courts dedicated to particular areas of law, notably family law, and, in some areas, commercial law.

As in criminal trials, the first instance trials of civil matters involve the presentation of evidence, including witness evidence. Appeals generally do not involve the introduction of new evidence.

The rules that govern the procedure in civil trials can vary depending on the subject matter. For example, family law courts have a dedicated set of rules, as do small claims courts. Where no specialized rules apply, an Ontario regulation called the *Rules of Civil Procedure* governs procedures. The *Rules of Civil Procedure* create a very complex system that includes deadlines for the completion of steps in the litigation and instructions for the imposition of particular responsibilities on the various parties.

**plaintiff**
the party who commences a civil action (lawsuit)

**applicant**
the party who commences an application (type of civil proceeding)

**defendant**
either the accused in a criminal trial, or, in a civil trial, the party against whom an action is brought

**damages**
the losses alleged by a plaintiff in a lawsuit and/or the compensation ordered to be paid to the plaintiff by the defendant

**respondent**
the party who must respond to a civil application

**administrative tribunal**
a quasi-court, typically created by statute, to hear disputes that arise within the legal framework created by the statute

There are many kinds of civil lawsuits in which security professionals might be asked to give testimony. Here are some examples:

- where an intruder has damaged a property owner's property;
- where an incident at a business (for instance, a fire) has resulted in a contested insurance claim;
- where an incident at one business (like a flood) has damaged the property owned by another business;
- where there has been an accident in which a customer or other visitor has been injured and that visitor is suing the security guard's employer; or
- where the security professional is a private investigator and has gathered evidence in support of the termination of a person's employment.

As a result, you should be aware that you could be called as a witness not only in a criminal trial or a provincial offences trial, but also in a civil trial.

### *Tribunals*

Along with criminal courts and civil courts, there is a third type of decision-making body in use in Canada: tribunals.

A tribunal (often called an "administrative tribunal") is a quasi-court, typically created by statute, to hear disputes that arise within the legal framework created by the statute. For example, disputes between landlords and tenants in Ontario are heard not within the general civil court system but, rather, by a tribunal called the Landlord and Tenant Board.

Tribunals are created to allow for the effective resolution of disputes that arise under specific legislative schemes. The evidence in these disputes tends to fall within a particular narrow scope, and the officials who make the decisions tend to be specialists with respect to the subject matter, which can sometimes be quite technical.

Here are some examples of Ontario tribunals before which security professionals might give evidence:

- the Landlord and Tenant Board;
- the Ontario Labour Relations Board;
- the Human Rights Tribunal of Ontario; and
- the Workplace Safety and Insurance Board.

Administrative tribunals have procedures of varying formality, and the rules for the presentation of evidence may be more relaxed than within the criminal and civil courts system. If you will be required to testify before an administrative tribunal, it is helpful to ask the party who is calling you as a witness to explain what you can expect when you make your appearance.

## Appeal Courts

An appeal is a review, by a higher-level court, of a decision by a lower-level court. In certain circumstances, an appeal court can overturn the decision of a lower-level court. In the civil court context, this can mean that a plaintiff who won at trial may no longer be entitled to damages, or that a plaintiff who lost may have that decision reversed and may obtain relief after all.

In the criminal context, a successful appeal of a criminal conviction either leads to the reversal of a conviction (acquittal) or to a new trial (which may or may not result in a new conviction). In some cases, criminal defendants choose not to appeal convictions, but do appeal sentences—this means that they remain convicted of the offence, but if successful on appeal, they may have their sentences reduced.

Because most appeals involve the reconsideration of the application of the law to the facts presented at trial, evidence is not generally presented at an appeal hearing.

In Canada, the number of levels of appeal available depends on where the case was heard at first instance. Some cases decided in a provincial court can be appealed to a divisional court, and from there to the Ontario Court of Appeal. A very small number of cases appealed to provincial or territorial courts of appeal (the highest level of court in the provinces and territories) go on to be heard by the Supreme Court of Canada, the highest level of court in Canada. Decisions of the Supreme Court of Canada are final.

# The Law of Evidence in Canada

As a security professional, there are two main reasons why you should have a general understanding of evidence law: 1) because you may be involved in the collection of evidence about incidents you have observed, and 2) because you may be asked to give evidence in court.

In this chapter, we discuss how the law applies to the admission of evidence in court. Procedures for collecting evidence and investigating occurrences will be discussed in Chapter 14.

The law of evidence is primarily concerned with:

- defining the types of proof that can be introduced in the effort to establish facts that may either support the conviction of an accused, or support an award of damages in favour of a plantiff;
- setting out rules for the admissibility of evidence (when it will be admitted, when it will be excluded), usually based either on issues of fairness to an accused, or on perceptions about whether the evidence was tainted in the way in which it was collected or stored; and
- setting out rules for the questioning of witnesses, including about who can be made to give testimony and what can and cannot be asked.

The bulk of the law of evidence exists as common law, and is not recorded in statutes (legislation). The common law is a collection of legal principles derived from decisions made by courts. The common law has long historical roots: some of the rules that govern how evidence is handled in modern Canadian courts date back hundreds of years, and were established in British courts.

There are, however, a few aspects of evidence law that have been incorporated into legislation, often because these aspects relate to the specific Canadian or provincial/territorial context.

## Evidence Statutes

There are two separate statutes that apply to evidence given in Ontario courts.

The Ontario *Evidence Act* applies to cases about matters over which the province of Ontario has jurisdiction—for example, the trial of provincial offences (including offences under the *Trespass to Property Act*, the *Provincial Offences Act* and the *Highway Traffic Act*). Each province and territory in Canada has its own evidence statute.

The *Canada Evidence Act* applies to proceedings in federal courts, including the Tax Court of Canada and the Federal Court of Canada. Certain immigration decisions are reviewed by the Federal Court, as are some matters relating to intellectual property (copyright, trademarks, and patents).

The *Canada Evidence Act* also applies to proceedings under federal legislation even when they take place in provincial courts, and this includes the trial of offences under the *Criminal Code*, the *Controlled Drugs and Substances Act*, and certain other pieces of legislation.

## *Notable Provisions Under the Canada Evidence Act*

The bulk of the *Canada Evidence Act* deals with **judicial notice** and with technical rules and standards for documentary evidence. For the most part, these are relevant to the lawyers introducing the evidence, not to witnesses. As a security professional, you may be asked to turn over your notebook in an investigation, or to provide copies of any witness statements you have taken. Procedures for note and statement-taking were discussed in Chapter 4, and will be touched on further in Chapter 9.

A few provisions of the *Canada Evidence Act* are relevant to **oral testimony** (the questioning of witnesses in court). Since you may be asked to give testimony, you should be aware of these.

Before giving evidence, you will be asked to, according to your choice, swear an oath or make an affirmation. An oath is a promise to tell the truth while invoking the witness of a sacred authority (e.g., God), often while placing one's hand on a holy book. An affirmation is the secular (non-religious) version of an oath: it is a promise to tell the truth. Affirmations are discussed in the legislation in sections 13 to 16.

Honesty in oral testimony is supported by provisions dealing with self-incrimination:

> **Incriminating questions**
> 5(1) No witness shall be excused from answering any question on the ground that the answer to the question may tend to criminate him, or may tend to establish his liability to a civil proceeding at the instance of the Crown or of any person.
>
> **Answer not admissible against witness**
> (2) Where with respect to any question a witness objects to answer on the ground that his answer may tend to criminate him, or may tend to establish his liability to a civil proceeding at the instance of the Crown or of any person, and if but for this Act, or the Act of any provincial legislature, the witness would therefore have been excused from answering the question, then although the witness is by reason of this Act or the provincial Act compelled to answer, the answer so given shall not be used or admissible in evidence against him in any criminal trial or other criminal proceeding against him thereafter taking place, other than a prosecution for perjury in the giving of that evidence or for the giving of contradictory evidence.

In other words, a witness is not excused from giving testimony that could incriminate him or her, but, when he or she does give incriminating evidence (as is defined by the common law), that evidence cannot be used in a trial or lawsuit, except a perjury trial (in which case, the evidence is only used to prove perjury—the crime of giving false testimony). So, for example, if a witness were asked whether she had consumed illegal drugs before having observed matters that she was testifying about and she said yes, that admission could not be used as evidence against her in the trial of criminal charges brought against her relating to the possession of illegal drugs.

---

**judicial notice**
a concept that allows judges to accept certain widely accepted facts as true without the need for evidence

**oral testimony**
a witness's verbal evidence, given in court

The *Canada Evidence Act* also touches on the use of previous statements to contradict witness testimony. For example, as a witness, you may be cross-examined in court by the defence about matters that you discussed in an earlier statement that was taken down in writing or video or audiotaped. When this happens, section 10 of the Act says that the lawyer cross-examining you must, if they intend to contradict your evidence, give you a chance first to read or listen to your former evidence.

### *Notable Provisions in the Ontario Evidence Act*

As does the *Canada Evidence Act*, the Ontario *Evidence Act* establishes detailed rules about conditions for the court's acceptance of many different types of evidence, including business records, photographs, and electronic evidence. In general, security guards do not need to know these rules in detail. More relevant to your work as a security guard are the provisions dealing with the following issues:

- administration of oaths and affirmations (s. 3);
- compellability—who can be called as a witness; in general, anyone who is competent to testify can be called, even if they have a criminal record, are the spouse of the defendant, are also a party to the case, etc. (ss. 6–8);
- special rules for testimony about a spouse or about adultery (you cannot be forced to give evidence of something your spouse said to you during marriage, and you may not have to confess to adultery (there are some exceptions)) (ss. 10–11);
- no exemption from giving self-incriminating evidence; but, as in the *Canada Evidence Act*, this evidence cannot be used against you in a civil proceeding or a prosecution under Ontario law (s. 9);
- rules for summons and subpoenas (orders to appear as a witness) and consequences for not complying with these orders (s. 19);
- rules for cross-examination that attempts to contradict your oral evidence with your prior written evidence (you have to be shown that written evidence if you ask to see it) (s. 20); and rules for cross-examination that attempts to contradict your oral evidence with your prior oral statements (you are allowed to deny the prior oral statements, and the opposing party will then have to prove them) (s. 21);
- rules about what happens if you are asked about your prior criminal record and you refuse to answer, or you deny a criminal record when the questioner alleges that you have one; in these cases, the person asking the question is allowed to enter proof of the convictions (ss. 21–22);
- rules about how far a party, through his or her lawyer, can go to "impeach" (prove wrong, prove dishonest) its own witness; in a nutshell, a lawyer who is trying to impeach his or her own witness cannot introduce "general evidence of bad character," but can, if the witness is given an opportunity to deny it, introduce evidence of past statements inconsistent with present evidence (s. 23).

Should you be asked to testify in a proceeding that is under the jurisdiction of the Ontario *Evidence Act*, you may want to read these provisions in full beforehand.

## Other Sources of the Law of Evidence

As noted earlier, the bulk of the law of evidence is not contained in either the *Canada Evidence Act* or the provincial evidence acts. Some aspects of evidence law are woven through the procedural provisions of statutes like the *Criminal Code*.

## Evidence Rules in the Criminal Code

The *Criminal Code* contains complex rules about the **burden of proof**: which party, Crown or defence, has the responsibility for proving certain facts. As you may know, the burden of proving the facts that establish the commission of crimes is on the defence. By contrast, where the accused is alleging a **defence**—a legally recognized justification for his or her actions; for example, the defence of self-defence—the burden of proof is said to "shift" to the accused.

The *Criminal Code* also contains detailed rules for many other matters related to evidence, including, for example, the use of subpoenas (orders requiring a witness to attend court and give testimony), videotaping of evidence, confessions, and more.

**burden of proof**
responsibility to provide evidence to support a particular conclusion

**defence**
legally recognized denial of or justification for an act

## Evidence Implications of Charter Rights

Other aspects of evidence law are created by the *Canadian Charter of Rights and Freedoms*, a statute that forms part of the Constitution and that, therefore, takes precedence over all other statutes. The Charter protects the rights of individuals in the context of their interactions with government, and the rights established by it have many implications for the law of evidence. The most important of these is the concept that the government should not be allowed to breach an individual's right to liberty and security (for example, by breaking down a person's door), take advantage of that breach to collect evidence, and then present that evidence in court in support of charges against the individual. Instead, the Charter provides that where evidence is collected in contravention of an individual's rights it will, in many cases, be excluded from use in court. This rule is founded on a number of Charter provisions (depending on the nature of the breach), but commonly on the interaction between sections 7, 8, and 24 of the Charter, which read:

> 7. Everyone has the right to life, liberty and security of the person and the right not to be deprived thereof except in accordance with the principles of fundamental justice.
> 8. Everyone has the right to be secure against unreasonable search or seizure.
> 24(1) Anyone whose rights or freedoms, as guaranteed by this Charter, have been infringed or denied may apply to a court of competent jurisdiction to obtain such remedy as the court considers appropriate and just in the circumstances.
> (2) Where, in proceedings under subsection (1), a court concludes that evidence was obtained in a manner that infringed or denied any rights or freedoms guaranteed by this Charter, the evidence shall be excluded if it is established that, having regard to all the circumstances, the admission of it in the proceedings would bring the administration of justice into disrepute.

In general, the Charter deals with violations of individuals' rights by the government and not by private parties (for example, a business that hires private security guards). However, the definition of what kind of entity is "government" is very complicated, and some agencies that you might not think of as government agencies are caught by the definition. This means that certain security professionals may in fact fall within the definition of government actors for the purpose of the application of the Charter, and could potentially violate the rights of individuals in a way that jeopardizes the admissibility of their evidence. Also possible is that detentions of individuals that flow from the co-operation of private security and peace officers (consider, for example, the detention of a nightclub patron for possession of drugs by security personnel that evolves into a police arrest) could result in rights violations that lead to the exclusion of evidence. For these reasons, security professionals should, in carrying out searches or citizens' arrests, comply strictly with the law (for example, by ensuring that all bag searches for patrons entering a club are truly voluntary).

### *Common Law Evidence Rules*

Finally, the majority of the rules of evidence applied in Canada come from the common law of evidence, a very old body of principles and doctrines. An explanation of these is well beyond the scope of this book, but some of them have the potential to affect your testimony in court.

The most common implication for you, as a witness, is that you may be ordered not to answer a question that one lawyer has asked after the other lawyer objects to the question and the judge "allows" the objection. If this happens, you need not (and should not) continue to answer the question. Some of the scenarios in which your testimony might be the subject of an objection include:

- the testimony you are being asked to give is expert evidence, and you have not been recognized as the right kind of expert (for example, a question may touch on the severity of an injury you observed, and the other lawyer may object on the ground that you are not a physician);
- the testimony you are being asked to give relates to a party's prior instances of behaviour similar to the behaviour that is the subject of the current trial (there are restrictions on this kind of "tendency" evidence); or
- you are being asked to share information that was given to you by another person and that you didn't independently gain; for example, you are asked to tell the court about an event that your supervisor told you about: this is "hearsay" evidence, and the party who wishes to present this evidence should call your supervisor as a witness instead; or
- you may be stopped from answering a particular question because the other lawyer has successfully objected that it is not relevant to the matter at hand (and may "prejudice" the accused improperly).

As a witness, it is not your responsibility to monitor the questions you are being asked for violations of the law of evidence; that is up to the lawyer on the other side of the case. Your only responsibility is to answer questions honestly and to pay attention to the judge's instructions about whether or not to provide an answer when the other lawyer objects.

# The Evidence of Security Professionals

Security professionals are frequently the source of multiple types of evidence used in proceedings in the criminal courts, civil courts, and before administrative tribunals. Those types of evidence include:

- physical evidence (for example, damaged property, abandoned weapons, or break-in tools);
- documentary evidence (notebooks, reports, and security camera footage); and
- oral testimony (the answers given on the witness stand).

These kinds of evidence are often presented in a connected way; for example, a security guard may be asked to confirm that he or she found, collected, and stored an exhibit (a piece of physical evidence) prior to its introduction in court; or a guard may be asked to confirm whether he or she made the notes included in a notebook that is being "entered into evidence." For this reason, the quality of a security professional's testimony and how it is perceived by the judge and/or jury can easily be influenced by events that took place long before the trial started, and how well the security professional followed procedures appropriate to his or her job.

A security guard who is aware of this can benefit from remembering, even while carrying out his or her routine day-to-day work, that anything done on the job could eventually be presented as evidence in a court. This can be an important motivation to take pride in following procedures correctly. Giving evidence in court can be stressful, but it is made much less so by the knowledge that you live up to the standards of your profession when you are on the job. If you do that, you have nothing to fear from being asked to turn over your notes or give testimony.

Since the collection and storage of physical evidence will be discussed later (in Chapter 14), and note taking and report writing were discussed earlier (in Chapter 4), this section will focus on witness testimony, including information about how documentary evidence is used in conjunction with oral testimony.

## Preparing for Court

Security guards are compensated by their employers at the regular rate of pay and/or overtime rate, depending on the company's policies, for time spent off work to make court appearances.

Employers should be advised of the date of a security guard's court appearance as soon as possible so that coverage for the work shift can be arranged.

### Be Prepared for the Process

Before security guards deliver any testimony in court, they should, if possible, seek an opportunity to ask questions about what to expect at the hearing. While it is not appropriate for a witness to discuss his or her evidence in detail or in a strategic way with the prosecution or lawyer that has called the witness in support of his or her case, it is fine to ask questions about the court process, since the procedures before various courts and tribunals do differ.

### Be Prepared for the Questions

In general, for security professionals, giving evidence in court means both stating for the plaintiff or prosecution the facts that you have observed and reported, and answering cross-examination by the defence.

The questions asked by the party who has called you as "their" witness (usually, the Crown or the plaintiff) form part of that party's "examination-in-chief"—the process of establishing evidence for all the facts they need to support their case. Questions asked during an examination-in-chief will typically feel "friendly" (not critical or challenging), and may call for longer, open-ended answers. When you are asked these questions, it will be your job to answer them fully and truthfully, but without rambling beyond the scope of the questions and without offering opinions.

Questions asked by the party who didn't call you as a witness—typically the defendant—are "cross-examination." The goal of these questions is typically to cast doubt on the evidence you provided during the examination-in-chief. Cross-examination questions are typically challenging or critical, and are generally crafted to invite one-word answers. It is appropriate to answer them with a yes or a no, and it is important to avoid getting emotional or aggressive, because provoking a reaction from you is often the defence's goal.

With this understanding of the role of examination-in-chief and cross-examination in mind, you should review your notes and think about what kinds of questions might be asked, and what answer, on your part, is honest, forthright, and concise.

You will also want to study your notes to refresh your memory about the sequence of events, including times and dates, in the same chronological detail that they were recorded, because accuracy is essential. If the defence establishes that a detail is lacking in even one area, it may be enough to cast doubt on all other aspects of your testimony.

Similarly, if you testify on the witness stand to an important fact that is not reported in either the general occurrence report or your notebook, the defence may suggest that you fabricated the fact because there is no recorded reference to it. If, upon reviewing your notes, you realize that they do not completely reflect your observations at the time, think through how you might answer questions about those gaps in a way that is truthful but concise, and without being defensive.

## On the Day of the Hearing

### Professional Appearance and Court Apparel

Security professionals can attain a high degree of credibility in the eyes of court officials and jurors simply by looking and acting professional at all times during the proceedings. As an ambassador of both the client and the company, security professionals should

- attend court in clean, ironed "civilian clothing" (not your security uniform, unless otherwise instructed);
- arrive early so that attendance can be noted by the lawyers prior to the beginning of the proceedings;
- act professionally outside the courtroom, both before and after the proceedings;
- avoid discussing the evidence with any person prior to court, except the prosecutor, the police officer in charge of the case, or a fellow security guard, should it be required;
- commit the evidence to memory;
- stand erect, and speak slowly and distinctly while in the witness box;
- look in the general direction of the jury (if there is one) when speaking, unless responding directly to a question from the presiding court official.

### Using Your Notes

After taking the stand, you should ask the judge for permission to refer to your notes—for example, to provide such precise information as distances, measurements, or the exact words of a witness.

You should be familiar with your notes so that you can quickly find the sections that apply to the case before the court. The fastest way to access the needed notes is to isolate the incident from other entries. Take one elastic band and wrap it from the first page of notes on what happened around all previous notebook entries to the front cover of the notebook. Similarly, separate the last page of the incident from all subsequent notebook entries and fasten those pages with another elastic band to the back cover of the memo book. This also prevents anyone from reading any confidential notes on other incidents not related to the case.

### On the Witness Stand

You can expect the defence counsel to challenge your notebook by examining it, asking how, where, and when the notes were taken, and asking questions such as, "What was the weather like at the time?"

Security professionals should not be afraid to admit candidly in court that they have prepared their notes in conjunction with another person, especially with respect to confirmation of objective data, such as times and street names. They should also not be afraid to admit that they have omitted or altered something or that they have made a mistake.

While providing evidence, you will most likely be asked open-ended questions. You should answer fully, but not volunteer more information than is requested. Use simple language, avoiding industry jargon—remember, your evidence needs to be understood by the jury, if there is one. If a judge rules that a particular question is not to be answered because the rules of evidence forbid it, you should not show displeasure—to do so is disrespectful of the rules of court and is unprofessional. If either the prosecution/plaintiff's lawyer or the defence asks a question that the security guard cannot answer, he or she should simply state, "I don't know."

You should *never* provide unsolicited information about a defendant's prior criminal record, convictions, or previous arrests. To do so could result in a mistrial, reversal of the decision, or an appeal.

Finally, you should listen very carefully and fully understand the defence's questions before attempting to answer during cross-examination. If a question is not understood, you should ask for it to be repeated or rephrased.

You may find, at times, that the way a question is worded feels unfair, and that it is designed to frame your answer in a negative light. It is essential that you understand that controlling the evidence received by the court and the impressions created by that evidence is not your responsibility—it is the responsibility of the lawyers. When you are in court, you will need to trust that if the defence is asking you a misleading or irrelevant question, the Crown or plaintiff's lawyer will object to the question and the judge will excuse you from answering. This means you should take your time before answering a question that makes you uncomfortable to allow an opportunity for the lawyer to object. If no objection is made, you should answer, and not second-guess the choices made by counsel.

## WHAT WOULD YOU DO?

### Testifying When Your Notes are Incomplete

You have been asked to testify in court about your fellow security guard's arrest of a teenager who was caught "keying" cars in your employer's underground parking garage.

At the time of the incident, you made only rather cursory notes, because you were busy with another security incident (a dog attack), and because you assumed that your co-worker would make detailed notes of his own. In particular, your notes about your own involvement in the early stages of the arrest—you were the first person to see the accused, and the first to approach him—are quite brief, and there is no thorough description of the accused.

By the time the trial comes around, however, your co-worker has been dismissed from his job, and cannot be located. As a result, you are being asked to testify. While you feel you remember the incident fairly well, you are worried about the sufficiency of your notes.

List at least six things you would do in this situation. Consider, for example:

- Would you add anything to your notes at this stage? Why or why not?
- What resources might you have at work to assist you in preparing for court (consider both people and things)?
- Is there anybody you should discuss your predicament with? Whom?
- How will you explain your incomplete notes in court?
- What approach will you take to answering cross-examination questions from the defence?
- How will you avoid this kind of problem in the future?

## CHAPTER SUMMARY

Security professionals may be asked to testify as witnesses in a wide range of court proceedings. In some cases, these proceedings will take place in criminal courts like the Ontario Court of Justice, Provincial Division or the Ontario Superior Court of Justice. However, security guards may also testify in civil cases (lawsuits) before other courts, or even before administrative tribunals such as the Landlord and Tenant Board.

When preparing to testify, it is useful to ask questions about court procedures, and to review the rules of evidence that will apply, whether they come from the *Canada Evidence Act*, the Ontario *Evidence Act*, or the common law. It is important for security professionals to understand that they must tell the truth, without unnecessary details and without stating opinions. It is also important to know that you cannot refuse to answer a question that might tend to incriminate you. It is useful to understand the different styles of questioning you may experience from the Crown or plaintiff's lawyer and from the defence, and how to handle them. You must also understand how you will be allowed to use your notebook in court as a memory aid.

Finally, security professionals are expected to bring the same level of professionalism to their in-court duties that they bring to their everyday employment. The demeanour, appearance, and deportment of security personnel reflects directly on the employer or client.

## KEY TERMS

administrative tribunal, 127
applicant, 127
burden of proof, 132
Crown attorney, 125
damages, 127
defence, 132
defence counsel, 125
defendant, 127
hybrid offence, 125
indictable offence, 125
judge, 125
judicial notice, 130
jury, 125
oral testimony, 130
plaintiff, 127
respondent, 127
summary conviction offence, 125
witness, 124

## NOTE

1. In Toronto and Sarnia, a special court called "Gladue Court" is held that has jurisdiction over matters in which the accused is an Indigenous person. It is designed to provide a culturally sensitive approach to these accused, in recognition of the fact that they have been found to be overrepresented in the justice system and in criminal custody. The government has plans to expand the number of dedicated Gladue Courts in the future (an Ottawa court will soon be introduced). Certain other municipalities without a dedicated Gladue Court offer "Gladue services"—for example, access to experienced preparers of Gladue sentencing reports.

## REFERENCES

*Canada Evidence Act*, RSC 1985, c C-5.
*Canadian Charter of Rights and Freedoms*, Part I of the Constitution Act, 1982, being Schedule B to the Canada Act 1982 (UK), 1982, c 11 [Charter].
*Controlled Drugs and Substances Act*, SC 1996, c 19.
*Criminal Code*, RSC 1985, c C-46.
*Evidence Act*, RSO 1990, c E.23.
*Highway Traffic Act*, RSO 1990, c H.8.
*Provincial Offences Act*, RSO 1990, c P.33.
*Rules of Civil Procedure*, RRO 1990, Reg 194.
*Trespass to Property Act*, RSO 1990, c T.21.

## PERFORMANCE APPLICATION
### Multiple Choice

1. If you wish to refer to your notebook while giving testimony in court, you should ask permission from:

   a. your supervisor

   b. the accused

   c. the prosecutor or plaintiff's lawyer

   d. the defence lawyer

   e. the judge

2. Serious criminal trials in Ontario are held:

   a. before a justice of the peace

   b. at the Ontario Superior Court of Justice

   c. at the Ontario Court of Justice

   d. at the Court of Appeal for Ontario

   e. in judges' chambers

3. The rule that where a witness is alive and can be compelled to give oral testimony, and that that testimony and not just a written statement must be introduced in court is called the:

   a. rule against perpetuities

   b. oral evidence rule

   c. best evidence rule

   d. hearsay rule

   e. impeachment rule

4. A civil trial is:

   a. brought by a plaintiff

   b. sometimes called a lawsuit

   c. an attempt by a plaintiff to obtain "relief" against a defendant

   d. one that includes the testimony of witnesses

   e. all of the above

5. Cross-examination is:
   a. not permitted in Canadian courts
   b. the questioning of one party's witness by the other party's lawyer
   c. reserved for criminal trials only
   d. not permitted as a way to impeach one's own witness
   e. a violation of the rules of evidence

6. A security guard's notebook:
   a. may be entered into evidence
   b. may be used as a memory aid during oral testimony
   c. is a type of documentary evidence
   d. is opinion evidence
   e. is a, b, and c

7. If something happened at the time of the incident and the security guard forgot to include it in her notes on the day of the incident:
   a. the security guard must admit that it happened if asked about it when giving testimony
   b. it would be illegal for the security guard to add it to her notebook the next day
   c. the lawyers asking questions in court are forbidden from asking about it
   d. the security guard should object and refuse to answer if asked about it in court
   e. it is hearsay evidence

8. When you are giving evidence in court and are asked a question by the lawyer who asked you to attend as a witness, your best answer to a question:
   a. should accurately reflect your personal opinion about the cause of the incident that occurred
   b. is a concise description of your observations, sticks narrowly to the question asked, and does not include opinion
   c. is a yes or no answer
   d. supports the theory of the case that the lawyer is trying to make
   e. is to avoid answering at all

# Legal Authorities 8

| | |
|---|---|
| Introduction | 142 |
| Privacy Law in Canada | 142 |
| Protecting Property | 144 |
| Arrest Without Warrant for a Criminal Offence | 148 |
| Canadian Charter of Rights and Freedoms | 149 |
| Search Authority | 149 |
| Protection of Persons Acting Under Authority | 150 |
| Civil Action and the Security Professional | 151 |
| Public Relations Considerations | 151 |
| Provincial Offences Act | 151 |
| Liquor Licence Act | 153 |
| Residential Tenancies | 156 |
| Employment Laws | 157 |
| Chapter Summary | 160 |
| Key Terms | 161 |
| References | 161 |
| Performance Application | 161 |

## LEARNING OUTCOMES

When you have completed this chapter, you will:

- Have a basic understanding of the general purpose of the various provincial and federal statutes that are relevant to the work of many security employees.
- Be aware of the need to protect the confidentiality of personal information.
- Have a basic knowledge and understanding of the legal authority of a security professional to restrict access, to protect property, and to arrest and detain persons.

# Introduction

Chapter 2 of this text introduced the *Private Security and Investigative Services Act* (PSISA), which regulates the private security profession in Ontario and establishes the powers and duties of private investigators and security guards. The PSISA is not the only legislation that has an impact on the work of security professionals. Depending on the kind of employer a security professional works for, many other statutes, including the *Personal Information Protection and Electronic Documents Act*, the *Trespass to Property Act*, and the *Provincial Offences Act*, may govern many aspects of the work. This chapter will introduce you to several of these statutes. Depending on what kind of work you do, you may need to familiarize yourself with additional legislation during the course of your career.

# Privacy Law in Canada

In April 2000, Parliament passed the *Personal Information Protection and Electronic Documents Act* (PIPED Act). This federal statute was created, among other purposes, to give businesses guidance for safeguarding personal information gathered by private companies and individuals.

In addition to the PIPED Act, each province has its own statute that governs the collection and use of personal information by the provincial government. The Ontario statute is called the *Freedom of Information and Protection of Privacy Act* (FIPPA). Finally, Ontario has an additional provincial privacy statute that deals specifically with the collection of health information: the *Personal Health Information Protection Act, 2004*, also known as PHIPA.

## The PIPED Act

The PIPED Act requires that organizations obtain peoples' consent when they collect, use, or disclose personal information. The general rule (there are exceptions, discussed below) is that no one else will be able to make use of a person's personal information without that person's permission. An individual will have the right to access his or her personal records held by an organization and to correct them, if needed. Personal information can only be used for the purposes for which it was collected, and if an organization plans to use it for any other reason, it must get the individual's consent again.

These requirements are relevant to private security professionals because you may collect personal information during your work, for example, when asking individuals to show identification, when taking witness statements, and when establishing identity and/or credentials before allowing visitors into secure areas. Security guards may also be in charge of protecting data that is stored on their employers' premises. For these reasons, it is important that security professionals understand the basic rules for maintaining the confidentiality of personal information.

### Application and Principles

Personal information is defined as "information about an identifiable individual" and includes things such as race; ethnic origin; age; marital status; religion; education; medical, criminal, employment, and financial history; address and telephone number; numerical identifiers (for example, Social Insurance Numbers); fingerprints; blood types; tissue and biological samples; and views or personal opinions.

The PIPED Act applies to every organization that collects, uses, or discloses personal information in the course of a commercial activity. "Commercial activity" is any buy-and-sell transaction, or one that involves bartering. The organizations governed by the Act include companies, associations, partnerships, and trade unions.

All industry sectors and companies of all sizes across the country are subject to the general principles outlined in Schedule 1 of the Act. These principles are:

- *Accountability*: The organization is responsible for the protection of any personal information.
- *Identifying purposes*: The organization *must* define what the information will be used for before it is collected.
- *Consent*: Consent *must* be obtained from the individual regarding collection, use, and disclosure of the information. (There are a few exceptions.)
- *Limiting collection*: Only necessary information will be collected.
- *Limiting use, disclosure, and retention*: The organization may not change the purpose for collection of the information after it was collected.
- *Accuracy*: The information *must* be accurate, complete, and up to date.
- *Safeguards*: The information *must* be adequately protected because of its sensitivity. Protection may include physical safeguards (for example, locked cabinets), procedural safeguards (for example, security clearances), and technological safeguards (for example, the use of passwords and/or encryption of data).
- *Openness*: Policies regarding the management of personal information *must* be readily available.
- *Individual access*: An individual shall be allowed access to and be able to challenge the accuracy of their own information.
- *Challenging compliance*: An individual may challenge the organization regarding the degree of compliance to any or all of the above principles.

## Exceptions

There are exceptions to the general principles established by the PIPED Act. For example, section 7(1)(b) allows for the collection and/or sharing of personal investigation without a person's consent for the purpose of investigating a provincial or federal offence or a breach of contract if "it is reasonable to expect that the collection with the knowledge or consent of the individual would compromise the availability or the accuracy of the information and the collection is reasonable." It is also permissible to use personal information without a person's knowledge or consent in an emergency situation, where the use of that information is to the person's benefit. For example, a security guard might be aware, based on past interactions, that a person who is a regular patron of a bar where the security guard works is a drug user. If that person is found passed out on the premises and 911 is called, the security guard would likely be justified in disclosing the person's drug use history to first responders.

## Privacy Safeguards on the Job

To some extent, ensuring that you are compliant with the provisions of the PIPED Act and other privacy statutes is a matter of common sense and professional discretion. As a starting point, keep in mind the following:

- If you have access to computer or network passwords, never write them down and never share them with individuals not authorized to use them.
- When choosing passwords, select random collections of letters, symbols, and numbers that are hard to guess, and change your passwords regularly.

- Do not leave any of the following in an unlocked office or vehicle: work smartphones, tablets, laptops, USB sticks, or any other technology that can contain data.
- Do not leave reports, notebooks, or any other records out in the open where they can be seen by the public.
- Do not allow any unauthorized person to read over your shoulder while you are making notes or writing reports.
- Keep filing cabinets locked and store keys securely.
- Do not share personal information about individuals over radios or intercom systems.
- Do not discuss work incidents, interactions with the public, or any other sensitive information with friends, family, or others outside the workplace.

Finally, you should be aware that protecting personal information also extends to ensuring that when records are destroyed, procedures are followed to ensure that they do not fall into the wrong hands. These procedures may involve destroying hard drives when computers are discarded, and guarding sensitive documents until they can be shredded and removed from the premises.

# Protecting Property

One of the key roles of security personnel is the protection of their employers' property. Property rights are a traditional aspect of the law, and some exist under the common law, which means, even where they are not explicitly covered by a statute.

The right to exclude other people from one's property is a long-standing right. If a property owner gives notice (for example, by posting a "no trespassing" sign) that another person is not welcome on the property, and that visitor does not leave, he or she is a trespasser and has committed a **tort** (a civil wrong). A visitor can also be guilty of trespassing even if he or she doesn't receive notice to leave if he or she performs a prohibited activity on the property (for example, hunting out of season).

**tort**
harm caused to a person or property for which the law requires a civil remedy

Security guards acting as agents of the property owner can exclude individuals who become trespassers through prohibited activity even if the property generally welcomes the public. For example, if the property in question is a store, and a customer enters and yells racist insults at a store clerk, a security guard can ask the person to leave even though the person was entitled to enter the store.

Section 35(1) of the *Criminal Code* provides that a person who is either the property owner or acting under the authority of the property owner is not guilty of an offence when he or she takes reasonable action to prevent a trespass, remove a trespasser from the property, or prevent the property from being stolen or damaged. This section was amended in 2012 as part of a major overhaul of the self-defence provisions of the *Criminal Code* (s. 34 defence of the person, and s. 35 defence of property). Reasonable action in the defence of property can include the use of reasonable force. For a full discussion of the use of reasonable force by security professionals, see Chapter 11 of this book.

## The Trespass to Property Act

In Ontario, many of the rules for managing trespassers are contained in a statute called the *Trespass to Property Act* (TPA).

The TPA provides some definitions that must be understood for the proper application of the Act. In particular, security professionals should understand the terms "occupier," "premises," and "trespass."

Section 1(1) of the Act describes an occupier as:

(a) a person who is in physical possession of premises, or

(b) a person who has responsibility for and control over the condition of premises or the activities there carried on, or control over persons allowed to enter the premises

even if there is more than one occupier of the same premises.

This means, for example, that both the owner of a store building and the manager on duty in the store can be occupiers.

The same section defines premises as:

lands and structures, or either of them, and includes,
(a) water,
(b) ships and vessels,
(c) trailers and portable structures designed or used for residence, business or shelter,
(d) trains, railway cars, vehicles and aircraft, except while in operation.

**Trespass** is defined in section 2 of the Act. According to section 2, a person is trespassing when he or she without legal right or authority and without the permission of the occupier enters or engages in activity on property where entry is prohibited by the Act

(a) without the express permission of the occupier, the proof of which rests on the defendant,
(i) enters on premises when entry is prohibited under this Act, or
(ii) engages in activity on premises when the activity is prohibited under this Act; or
(b) does not leave the premises immediately after he or she is directed to do so by the occupier of the premises or a person authorized by the occupier.

A person charged with trespassing can argue the defence of **colour of right**. This defence provides that a person is not guilty of trespassing if he or she reasonably believes that he or she has an ownership interest in the premises.

Where an alleged trespasser claims that he or she had colour of right to come onto property, it is up to the trespasser to prove this.

Trespassing is a tort (a harm caused by one person to another or against another person's property). As such, trespassing is a **civil wrong** rather than a **criminal offence** and cannot result in a jail term or a criminal record. However, trespassers can be liable to a fine of up to $10,000.

## Prohibiting Entry Under the TPA

In order for trespassing to occur, intruders must know that they are not welcome. In some cases, intruders are expected to understand this without specific notice. For example, people are expected to understand that they are not allowed to enter a private residence uninvited. Other areas that need not have special notices posted include gardens, fields, vineyards, agricultural woodlots, tended orchards, and enclosed outdoor areas such as livestock pastures (s. 3).

**trespass**
unlawful interference with the person, property, or rights of another

**colour of right**
circumstances that lead to an understandable but mistaken belief that one has the right to do something

**civil wrong**
non-criminal wrong that can form the basis of a civil lawsuit—either a tort or a breach of contract

**criminal offence**
act that contravenes a provision of criminal law

### Limited Permission Areas

Some locations may restrict entrance to certain individuals. For example, entry onto a construction site may be restricted to construction workers. In other cases, the general public may be allowed entry, but certain activities may be prohibited. For example, the public may be allowed to enter a park that has a pond, but people may be prohibited from swimming.

### Methods of Giving Notice

When an occupier wants to limit entry to a premises, he or she must give notice of the intended restrictions. Notice can be given orally or in writing. Most commonly, notice is given by posting signs.

There are often regulations, which may be found under a wide range of legislation and bylaws, with respect to how certain signs need to look. Some signs need to be of a particular size or colour or need to incorporate recognized symbols.

### Types of Signs

To give notice that an activity is permitted, a sign should describe the activity or provide a graphic representation (picture) of it (s. 6(1)). To prohibit the activity, the same wording or graphic representation should have an oblique line (usually red or black) crossed through it (s. 6(2)). See Figure 8.1.

Other sections of the legislation describe specific signage conventions. For example, red markings are generally used to prohibit entry, while yellow markings are used to restrict entry or activities permitted on a premise (s. 7). Section 7 gives additional information about the size and placement of warning signs.

**arrest**
legally deprive a person of liberty by touching that person to indicate that he or she is in custody

## Arrest Rules Under the TPA

Section 9 of the TPA gives security guards the authority to make an **arrest**. The section applies to police officers, occupiers, and "a person authorized by the occupier" (that is, a security guard).

**Figure 8.1** Sign Indicating Prohibited Activity

To be able to arrest a trespasser, a security guard must have "reasonable and probable grounds" to believe that the person is in contravention of section 2. As discussed above, section 2 defines trespassing and makes it an offence.

Section 9(2) further provides that "[w]here the person who makes an arrest . . . is not a police officer, he or she shall promptly call for the assistance of a police officer and give the person arrested into the custody of the police officer." At that point, the police officer will arrest the person as provided in the *Provincial Offences Act*.

### Reasonable and Probable Grounds

An important aspect of arrests under section 9 is the need for reasonable and probable grounds. "Reasonable and probable grounds" is a legal requirement that has application to many issues, both under provincial law and under the (federal) criminal law. There is a lot of **jurisprudence** (judge-made law) about what constitutes reasonable and probable grounds in various contexts. However, the basic requirement is fairly simple to understand: a security guard's reasons for making an arrest must be both reasonable—based on reason, logic, and common sense—and probable. The validity of the assumptions and conclusions that the security professional is making with respect to what the suspect has done, is doing, and may go on to do (if not arrested) must be probable—that is, more than just hypothetically possible.

**jurisprudence**
judge-made law

### Summary of Arrest Requirements

Review the requirements for a legally valid arrest under the TPA:

1. The security professional must be authorized to make arrests on behalf of the occupier.
2. The security professional must have reasonable and probable grounds to believe that the suspect either:
   a. has made a prohibited entry, or
   b. is carrying out a prohibited activity.
3. A prohibited entry or activity is one that violates the TPA.
4. The TPA allows occupiers to prohibit entry or activities by giving notice, either orally or in writing, or by posting signs.
5. The security professional must typically direct the person to leave and should generally not make an arrest until the person fails to do so.
6. Once the suspect has been arrested, the security professional must turn him or her over to the police as soon as possible.

When transferring custody of an arrested person to the police, security personnel should always obtain the name, rank, and badge number of the attending officer, and record these details in their notes for future reference.

## Requests to Vacate Premises: Practical Issues

When a suspected trespasser has been asked to immediately leave by a certain entrance and fails to respond within a reasonable time, the security guard has the right to **detain** the suspect and to turn him or her over to a peace officer. While this seems straightforward, in practice, commands to leave are a significant source of guard–public conflict. When a problem arises, it is often because the security guard either overzealously made the request,

**detain**
legally deprive a person of liberty for the purpose of asking questions

precipitating a further confrontation; or because the guard did not understand how to make the request properly—that is, did not give the person clear directions. In making a request to leave, the security guard must be both courteous and clear.

A related problem arises when security professionals fail to identify themselves properly prior to issuing a command. In these cases, the person to whom the command is made is often unsure of the guard's authority. Where the guard fails to sufficiently identify his or her position and/or authority, the trespasser may take advantage of the situation by relying on any uncertainty as a reason to prolong a confrontation. In a later defence, the person who refused to follow the security guard's direction may claim: "I was not sure the guard was who he said he was, so I was not going anywhere."

# Arrest Without Warrant for a Criminal Offence

Where the issue is not an unauthorized entry but the commission of a criminal act, or a case where the TPA does not apply, security guards can make arrests under the doctrine of "citizen's arrest." As that wording implies, any person—not just a police officer or a security guard—can make a citizen's arrest, as long as the necessary conditions are met. For this reason, for the purpose of arrest, security guards have no more—and no less—authority than do ordinary citizens.

## Enabling Provisions

The rules for making a citizen's arrest are described in section 494 of the *Criminal Code*.

Under section 494(1), anyone may arrest without warrant:

> (a) a person whom he finds committing an indictable offence; or
> (b) a person who, on reasonable grounds, he believes
>   (i) has committed a criminal offence, and
>   (ii) is escaping from and freshly pursued by persons who have lawful authority to arrest that person.

As explained in Chapter 7, an indictable offence is a serious criminal offence that carries a severe penalty. Canada's *Criminal Code* indicates whether or not an offence is indictable. Courts that have decided cases involving arrests under this section have ruled that hybrid offences can be considered indictable offences for the purpose of the right to make a citizen's arrest.

Section 494(2)(b) creates another kind of arrest that can be made by a property owner, or a person acting under the authority of a property owner, of a person found committing a criminal offence—including a summary conviction offence, and not just an indictable offence in this case—on or in relation to the property.

As was the case under the TPA, a security guard who arrests a person without warrant must immediately deliver the person to a peace officer.

## Steps to a Citizen's Arrest

In making an arrest under either the TPA or the *Criminal Code*, a security guard should take the following steps:

1. Identify himself or herself and announce directly and simply that the person is under arrest.
2. At the same time, lightly grasp the person's elbow to indicate control of the situation.

3. Give the person a reason for making the arrest as required under the *Canadian Charter of Rights and Freedoms* (Charter).
4. Advise the person of his or her right to counsel under the Charter.
5. Caution the person to remain silent.
6. Turn the person over to a police officer as soon as possible.

Following the arrest, immediately after having turned the accused over to the police, the security guard should make detailed notes about what happened and why the arrest was made.

## Canadian Charter of Rights and Freedoms

All security professionals making an arrest must protect the rights of the suspect under the Charter. The Charter requires that a person be provided with a reason for the arrest, be advised of the right to counsel, and be advised of the right to avoid self-incrimination. This is done by cautioning the suspect. A caution is a statement made at the time of arrest for the purpose of advising the suspect of his or her rights. There is no set wording for the caution; that is, there are no "magic words" that will guarantee that an arrest meets the Charter requirements. Whether or not the actual caution given will meet the requirements of the Charter depends on the circumstances of the particular case. For example, if a person speaks very limited English or appears to have a cognitive disability, a standard caution may be too complex.

As a starting point, however, it is useful to learn the following typical caution, which is consistent with current Charter jurisprudence (existing law) with respect to how the rights can best be protected.

### Notice Upon Arrest
"I am arresting you for_____." (Describe briefly the reasons for arrest.)

### Right to Counsel
"It is my duty to inform you that you have the right to retain and instruct counsel without delay. You have the right to telephone any lawyer you wish. You may also be entitled to free advice from a legal aid lawyer. If you are charged with an offence, you may apply to Legal Aid Ontario for assistance. You can call this toll free number [give the number for your local legal aid office] and it will put you in contact with a legal aid duty counsel lawyer for free legal advice right now. Do you understand? Do you wish to call a lawyer right now?"

### Caution
"You may be charged with _____. Do you wish to say anything in answer to the charge? You are not obliged to say anything unless you wish to do so, but whatever you say may be given in evidence. Do you understand?"

## Search Authority

Following or in connection with an arrest, a security guard's rights to search a suspect are very limited under the law. There are, however, some **common law** rules (that is, rules based on **case law** rather than on **statute law**) that give limited rights to search a person, or his or her belongings or property.

**common law**
rules that are formulated in judgments in case law

**case law**
body of law based on decisions of similar cases

**statute law**
laws passed by the government

## Search With Consent

A security guard can search a person or his or her property with that person's consent. In some cases, a person's contract of employment allows an employer's security staff to search employees or their property, such as purses, shopping bags, and lockers on the job site. But, according to Gerden (1998), "a forced search against employees, especially if it is a requirement before leaving the property, may very well be considered a criminal assault; at the least, it will involve civil liabilities" against the company, and possibly the security guard as well. Under these circumstances, such an "assault" violates an individual's rights under section 24(2) of the *Charter of Rights and Freedoms* and the evidence secured may be excluded in court.

## Search Without Consent

If a security guard reasonably believes the person just arrested has a weapon and that he or she is in "harm's way," the security guard can search this individual without permission.

# Protection of Persons Acting Under Authority

When a security guard makes a citizen's arrest without excessive force, the security guard may be protected from prosecution by section 25 of the *Criminal Code*, which provides:

> 25(1) Every one who is required or authorized by law to do anything in the administration or enforcement of the law
>     (a) as a private person,
>     (b) as a peace officer or public officer,
>     (c) in aid of a peace officer or public officer, or
>     (d) by virtue of his office,
>
> is, if he acts on reasonable grounds, justified in doing what he is required or authorized to do and in using as much force as is necessary for that purpose.

This section requires that security professionals base their actions on reason, and that their actions be controlled and measured, and not out of proportion to the needs of the situation. If security guards act in a firm, controlled, and rational manner, they can generally count on the protection of section 25.

## Excessive Force

There are times when people use more force than they really need to control a situation. Section 26 of the *Criminal Code* states:

> 26 Every one who is authorized by law to use force is criminally responsible for any excess thereof according to the nature and quality of the act that constitutes the excess.

This means that if a security professional goes beyond firm, controlled, and rational behaviour in handling an accused and uses excessive force, he or she has committed a criminal act and can be charged. In some cases, however, the security guard may be able to defend against using greater-than-usual force to defuse a situation.

## Self-Defence Against Assault or Threatened Assault

Section 34 provides that a person is justified in using force to repel force when that person is assaulted or threatened with assault as long as that person did not provoke the assault or use more force than was necessary to defend himself or herself. In considering whether the use of force was reasonable, the court will consider a wide range of factors, including whether the attacker had a weapon, and the parties' relative size and age, among other factors.

# Civil Action and the Security Professional

Security personnel and their employers may be vulnerable to civil lawsuits for such charges as **assault** (often, verbally threatening someone to obey your demands), **battery** (often, using excessive force in an arrest), **false imprisonment** and/or **malicious prosecution** (often, by making false accusations or arresting someone without proper grounds), **conversion** (the civil version of theft), **negligence** (failure to perform to a certain standard, and thereby causing harm), and **defamation** (injuring someone's reputation either through **slander** or **libel**). A successful civil action involves reimbursing the plaintiff (injured party) for the damage caused.

The best way security guards can avoid being personally sued in civil court (or doing something that will get their employer sued) is to perform their duties using good judgment and restraint, while complying with the law and any professional standards, codes of practice, or company policies that apply to them.

# Public Relations Considerations

A final consideration when thinking about the issue of arrest is public relations. Often, security professionals are required to consider a response to events that may fall short of an indictable crime, particularly in the case of TPA violations. In dealing with any situation, security personnel must be mindful of their role as representatives of their employer. An overzealous response to a trespass, including the use of force and/or the making of an arrest, may reflect badly on the company or, worse, attract a civil action.

# Provincial Offences Act

The *Provincial Offences Act* (POA) of Ontario is a largely administrative/procedural statute. It governs procedure in one division of the courts, and assists in the enforcement and administration of other provincial statutes. Matters of procedure, sentencing, and so on that are not specifically dealt with in an individual statute are governed by the terms of the POA. Where the POA is *not* intended to govern the application of a provincial statute, the provincial statute must set out its own procedure in detail or specifically exclude the operation of the POA.

A provincial offence is different from a criminal offence. For one thing, it is created not under the federal *Criminal Code*, but under provincial law—either the POA or another of the hundreds of provincial laws. Provincial offences tend to be less serious than federal offences and are often committed by people in the course of their everyday lives—good examples are offences like speeding under the *Highway Traffic Act*, or trespassing under the TPA.

The procedure for prosecuting provincial offences is set out in the POA and is simpler and faster than criminal procedure. In many cases, defendants represent themselves. The fines and sentences are limited and, in most cases, are lower than penalties under the criminal law.

---

**assault**
threat of imminent harm in the mind of the intended victim

**battery**
any unwelcome physical contact

**false imprisonment**
detention of a person without consent and without legal authority

**malicious prosecution**
wrongful prosecution of a person without reasonable or probable cause

**conversion**
unauthorized interference with another's property that deprives the owner of its use

**negligence**
careless conduct that causes foreseeable harm to another person

**defamation**
injury to a person's reputation by slander or libel

**slander**
oral statement that damages a person's reputation

**libel**
written or recorded statement that damages a person's reputation

## WHAT WOULD YOU DO?

### Assessing Security Personnel Responses

**Scenario One:** April is a security employee working for a department store in a large shopping mall. She observes two teenage girls leaving an aisle where sunglasses are displayed. As they approach the main aisle, the girls nervously pick up their pace and rush toward the exit. April follows at a run, leaving the department store and moving into the mall common area. One girl disappears into the food court crowd, but April catches up with the second girl. She grabs the girl's shoulder. Both women fall to the floor. April restrains the girl's arms behind her back and informs her that she is being taken back into the department store. The girl asks "Why?" and April answers "You'll know soon enough."

**Scenario Two:** Ben is a contract security guard who has been hired to provide security for the final game in a city-wide high school football playoff series. Ben is in charge of entry control and has been instructed to perform consensual searches of entrants to the stadium. There is no alcohol permitted at the event. Several boys who appear to be under the legal drinking age approach the entry door. Ben notices a bulge under one boy's jacket and requests that the boy open his jacket. The boy opens his jacket, revealing an open bottle of rye. Ben grasps the boy lightly by the elbow, explains that he is a security employee, and places the boy under arrest for underage possession of alcohol. The boy's friends attempt to intervene. They become argumentative and jostle Ben, who is attempting to explain the boy's Charter rights using appropriate wording. The situation breaks down and one of the boy's friends punches Ben. Ben attempts to place the boy who punched him in a submission hold, but fails when another boy grabs Ben from behind. Ben is overpowered and all the boys flee the scene.

**Scenario Three:** Cameron works as a security guard for a major department store. While patrolling the back of the store, he notices a female shopper moving quickly toward an employee-only area. She opens and walks through a door marked "Employees Only." Cameron catches up with the woman inside the employee area and advises her that she is not authorized to be there. The woman replies firmly, "I need the bathroom." Cameron advises the woman that the washroom is for employees only and steps between the woman, who is now in tears, and the washroom door. The woman turns around and runs back into the public area of the store. Later that day, Cameron is called into the supervisor's office to discuss a complaint from a customer. The customer, who suffers from Crohn's disease, will be making a complaint to head office about the way she was treated by security at Cameron's location.

**Scenario Four:** Dharma and Eddie work as night clerks at a large furniture warehouse store. The store is closed during their late-night shift. One of their duties is to monitor the parking lot, which bears prominent signs prohibiting parking between the hours of 11 p.m. and 6 a.m. At 1:30 a.m., Eddie observes a car pull into the parking lot, stopping in a location near the parking lot entrance and far from the building. The car stops, but no one gets out. Eddie suggests that he and Dharma immediately approach the car. Dharma prefers to wait a couple of minutes, while monitoring the car through a security camera. Five minutes later, no one has left the vehicle, which has begun rocking slightly. Dharma laughs and points this out to Eddie. The two of them walk out into the parking lot. Eddie stays back a couple of metres, and Dharma approaches the car. Dharma gives three firm knocks on the driver's side window, and says in a very loud voice: "No parking. Move along, please." The two guards return to the store, where they record the licence plate number. The car does not pull away immediately. Eddie suggests that they go back out, but Dharma says, "They're harmless. Let's give them five minutes." He checks the clock. Two minutes later, at 1:46 a.m., the car pulls out of the lot and drives away.

### Assignment

Answer the following questions for each of the above scenarios.
1. Did the security guard have the authority to intervene the way he or she did in the situation? Why or why not?
2. Was the security guard's response appropriate in the situation? Why or why not? Be specific.
3. What would an appropriate response to the situation be?

In general, a person charged with a provincial offence is not kept in jail pending trial. The POA creates no search or arrest powers. In some cases it may be appropriate to search and/or arrest a person who is suspected of committing a provincial offence, but in those cases, the search/arrest authority must either exist at common law or be provided under the individual provincial statute (for example, s. 9 of the TPA).

In many cases, charging a person with a provincial offence is done through a ticketing process. (Most people are familiar with *Highway Traffic Act* tickets—other provincial offences can be charged in the same way.) Security guards cannot charge or ticket a suspect. If charging or ticketing is appropriate, the security guard must turn the suspect over to police as soon as possible.

# Liquor Licence Act

The *Liquor Licence Act* (LLA) is enforced by security guards on a fairly regular basis, largely because many of the rules with respect to liquor possession and consumption relate to specific locations, and security guards often work to regulate access into a premises or movement of patrons within a premises. For example, there are rules that prevent bringing liquor into a hotel lounge, but it is generally permissible to possess or consume liquor in a hotel room. A security guard working in the hotel may be required to explain and/or enforce this rule to guests of the hotel. A guard needs to know the limit of the law in each situation involving liquor and his or her workplace.

The LLA is an exceptionally long act that deals with licensing, permits, individual compliance, and offences. Only the provisions that commonly affect security professionals are discussed here.

## Definitions

Section 1 of the LLA defines several terms, including the following of interest to security guards:

> "alcohol" means a product of fermentation or distillation of grains, fruits or other agricultural products, and includes synthetic ethyl alcohol; . . .
>
> "government store" means a government store established under the *Liquor Control Act*;
>
> "licence" means a licence issued under this Act; . . .
>
> "sell" means to supply for remuneration, directly or indirectly, in any manner by which the cost is recovered from the person supplied, alone or in combination with others, and "sale" has a corresponding meaning.

(The full text of the *Liquor Licence Act* is available online at https://www.ontario.ca/laws/statute/90l19.)

---

### ON THE JOB

**Not Safe for Drinking!**

These substances contain alcohol, but are not safe or legal to drink:

- rubbing alcohol,
- mouthwash,
- aftershave and perfume,
- flavouring extracts (vanilla extract, almond extract, etc.),
- some disinfectants,
- cough syrups and other alcohol-based medicines, and
- photocopier toner fluid.

## Compliance by Consumers

The Ontario LLA imposes rules on individual consumers of alcohol:

- Consumers can only buy liquor from a government store or from a person with a sale licence (for example, the bartender at a properly licensed bar).
- No person can buy, obtain, possess, or consume liquor while under the age of 19 years (there are some exceptions).
- Underage individuals are prohibited from using fake identification to obtain or consume liquor.
- Opened liquor can be possessed or consumed only in certain places.
- There are rules against public intoxication (discussed further below).
- Opened liquor cannot be transported in a vehicle (including a boat or snowmobile) unless it is stored in a separate locked compartment or in baggage that is not readily accessible by the occupants.
- It is illegal to drink, or to supply to another person for drinking, alcohol that is not designed as a drink (for example, rubbing alcohol, aftershave, or mouthwash).

## Compliance by Providers

Rules governing providers (government stores, licensed providers such as bars, and private providers such as party hosts) include the following:

- It is illegal to provide or sell liquor to a person who is, or appears to be, intoxicated.
- It is illegal to sell or provide liquor to a person who is or appears to be under the age of 19, or to "knowingly" allow him or her to consume it on licensed premises.
- It is illegal to sell or provide alcohol that is not intended for drinking to a person whom you believe will use it for that purpose.

## Enforcing the Rules

Security professionals are often called upon by their employers to enforce the provisions of the LLA, whether or not the employer has a liquor licence.

## Controlling Entry

One of the common ways security guards enforce the LLA is by controlling entry. Security guards may restrict entry to premises when a patron is attempting to bring in liquor for consumption in contravention of the law (because the patron is underage, the premises is not licensed, the licence does not allow patrons to bring in their own liquor, or the patron is violating rules with respect to motor vehicles).

Where the patron is suspected of being underage, the security guard will typically ask to see identification. If the identification is unsatisfactory, the patron can be excluded. Where the patron is suspected of attempting to smuggle liquor in, the security guard can ask the patron to volunteer to be searched (to open his or her coat or bags, or to allow him or her to be "patted down"—a same-sex guard should be available for this). Where the guard suspects improper transportation in a vehicle, the patron may be asked to submit to a voluntary vehicle search.

## Removal of Offenders

In some cases, a security guard will be required to assist in the removal from premises of a person who is or is suspected of being in contravention of the LLA.

Section 34 of the LLA deals with removal from the premises. It provides:

> 34(1) The holder of a licence or permit issued in respect of premises shall ensure that a person does not remain on the premises if the holder has reasonable grounds to believe that the person,
> (a) is unlawfully on the premises;
> (b) is on the premises for an unlawful purpose; or
> (c) is contravening the law on the premises.
>
> (2) The holder of a licence or permit may request a person referred to in subsection (1) to leave the premises immediately and if the request is not forthwith complied with may remove the person or cause the person to be removed by the use of no more force than is necessary.
>
> (3) If there are reasonable grounds to believe that a disturbance or breach of the peace sufficient to constitute a threat to the public safety is being caused on premises for which a licence or permit is issued, a police officer may require that all persons vacate the premises.
>
> (3.1) No person shall remain on licensed premises after being required to vacate the premises by a police officer under subsection (3).
>
> (3.2) No person shall re-enter the licensed premises on the same day he or she is required to vacate unless authorized to re-enter by a police officer.
>
> (4) The holder of the licence or permit for premises that are required to be vacated under subsection (3) shall take all reasonable steps to ensure that the premises are vacated.
>
> (5) A licensee or employee of a licensee who has reason to believe that the presence of a person on the licensee's licensed premises is undesirable may,
> (a) request the person to leave; or
> (b) forbid the person to enter the licensed premises.
>
> (6) No person shall,
> (a) remain on licensed premises after he or she is requested to leave by the licensee or an employee of the licensee; or
> (b) re-enter the licensed premises on the same day he or she is requested to leave.

You should read this section carefully, noting in particular:

- the need for reasonable grounds before a person can be removed or excluded;
- the prohibition against excessive use of force;
- the option of police support for a mass removal order; and
- the requirement of the licence holder to take all reasonable steps to support compliance on the premises.

Section 34.1 discusses removal/exclusion by police. This is normally used when a situation has gotten out of security's control, where a confrontation has arisen, or in an under-control situation where the licence holder or another party wants charges laid.

## Public Intoxication

It is illegal to be drunk in a public place or in the common area of a residence of a multi-dwelling residence (for example, an apartment lobby or hallway). The police (at the request of security, in many cases) can arrest without a warrant any person who is intoxicated in a public place and who is a threat to the safety of others.

## Civil Liability

Where a security guard's employer contravenes the LLA, the employer may be charged under the legislation and may be at risk of losing the liquor licence. By enforcing the LLA, security professionals protect their employers from such charges. But it is also important to know that there is also the potential for civil liability on the part of a person or corporation who fails to enforce the LLA where the failure to comply with the rules results in harm to people or property. The most common way that this happens is through over serving—that is, providing or selling liquor to intoxicated guests, who then go on to cause harm to themselves or others—for example, by driving drunk.

This liability is outside (beyond) the LLA and in addition to any charges under it, and can be very significant. To avoid civil suits, security guards must be vigilant in preventing overconsumption of liquor on their employers' premises.

# Residential Tenancies

The rights of landlords and tenants in Ontario are governed by the *Residential Tenancies Act, 2006*. This legislation is designed to allow tenants to live their lives in reasonable privacy without unnecessary intrusion by landlords, to have necessary repairs made, and to have reasonable security in knowing that they will not be thrown out of an apartment without notice. It also gives landlords rights, such as the right to gain entry to a unit to make repairs or to show it to prospective tenants, and the right to evict tenants who are disruptive, destructive, or who do not pay their rent.

Large rental buildings often employ security professionals who may have a range of duties. These duties can include:

- controlling entry to the premises;
- handling complaints by tenants about the behaviour of other tenants or trespassers;
- enforcing building rules; and
- defusing confrontations between tenants and between landlords and tenants.

Many of these duties simply require security professionals to follow the normal procedures associated with their work. In a few cases, however, security guards will need to understand which actions are permitted and which are prohibited under the *Residential Tenancies Act, 2006*.

Should you work in a residential rental facility, it will be useful to carefully read the Act so that you are fully familiar with its provisions. For the purpose of this overview, there are some key aspects of the legislation that you should be aware of.

In April 2017, while this book was in production, the government of Ontario announced its intention to introduce a number of measures intended to address rental market problems in the province. Among the measures was a promise to make certain changes to the *Residential Tenancies Act, 2006*; notably, to introduce a new standard lease form and to make it possible for landlords to evict tenants who rent an apartment for the purpose of renting it out to others (for example, via Airbnb). Security professionals who work in apartment buildings should be sure to review the new amendments when they are released to ensure that they have an up-to-date understanding of the rules.

## Landlords Must Not Interfere with Tenants Without Reason

Landlords are prohibited from harassing, obstructing, coercing, threatening, or interfering with tenants: section 23. They cannot withhold essential services such as heat or water, and if they are required to provide care services or food, they cannot withhold those: section 21.

Landlords cannot change the locks on a unit unless they give the tenants new keys: section 24. Tenants are also not allowed to change locks without the landlord's consent: section 35.

Landlords cannot interfere with tenant privacy, and can only enter units after giving notice. Notice periods are provided under the legislation, and tenants need not comply with all requests for access. In general, tenants need only give access to allow landlords to make repairs, to conduct occasional inspections to ensure that the unit complies with building or fire codes, or to show the unit to prospective tenants after the current tenant has given notice that he or she is leaving. Section 26 does permit for entry by the landlord when the tenant consents, or in cases of emergency (for example, a fire).

There are some situations in which a landlord is required to permit entry by other individuals—for example, municipal or provincial inspectors who are investigating possible offences. If a security guard is approached by such inspectors, he or she should contact the landlord, and should ask the inspectors to explain the authority under which they are requesting access.

## Evictions

Tenants can only be evicted for reasons specified under the Act. These reasons typically include serious interference with other tenants, or the non-payment of rent. Eviction for these reasons is neither automatic nor instantaneous—there are many rules that require landlords to give notice of pending eviction and to give tenants the chance to pay rent arrears or correct their behaviour.

One cause for eviction that may allow landlords to move more quickly is criminal behaviour by tenants. It is important to know that while a security professional is entitled to provide security to the landlord and/or the other tenants in the event of criminal activity, a security guard is prohibited by law from physically evicting a tenant for any reason. The landlord cannot either—only the sheriff or a representative of the sheriff's office is permitted by law to physically remove tenants from premises.

The removal of a tenant's belongings cannot be done without first giving the tenant notice, and even then, the belongings cannot be disposed of until the tenant has been given sufficient time to collect them.

As a general rule, it is important for security guards to treat tenants respectfully, and to avoid heavy-handed tactics or harassment. The legislation creates a long list of offences related to the mistreatment of tenants—for example, the locking out of tenants, obstruction of the establishment of tenant associations, or unauthorized entries. Fines for these offences can be steep—up to $25,000 for individuals or $100,000 for corporations. For this reason, security guards should take the time to review the legislation and understand how the rules can be enforced without violating tenant rights.

# Employment Laws

The final area of law that is relevant to many security professionals is employment law. While it is useful for all employees (including security guards) to have some knowledge of their rights under the law, security professionals must also take into consideration the rights of employers, because they may be called upon to support the enforcement of those rights. Because unfair treatment of employees can form the basis of wrongful dismissal and other kinds of litigation that can prove costly for employers, security personnel must walk a fine line when supporting employer actions such as escorting an employee out after he is fired, or breaking up a heated conflict between a worker and her supervisor.

For the purpose of this chapter, we will touch on two Ontario statutes in particular: the *Labour Relations Act, 1995* (LRA) and the *Employment Standards Act, 2000* (ESA).

## Conflict of Interest?

As noted above, security employees may be required to assist the employer in enforcing its own rights "against" employees. Because of this, security employees are likely the only non-management staff in an organization that are not permitted to act in only their own interest on the job. Does this constitute a conflict of interest?

The answer is that it may create a conflict of interest, but only in rare and polarized circumstances, such as a strike or lockout in the context of highly adversarial labour negotiations. Most of the time, and in the majority of workplaces, employees and managers view themselves as part of a team and act accordingly. This is in fact almost always the state of the workplace culture in non-unionized workplaces. Security personnel working in unionized settings may, however, on a few rare occasions, be called on to provide security in the context of heated protests.

For this reason, section 14 of the LRA establishes rules for unions that are entirely made up of security guards, and unions that include guards and other employees. Should you ever find yourself in the middle of a labour dispute and needing to decide whether or not to obey management directives, there will be three sources for you to consult: (1) your own conscience; (2) the advice of your union representatives, especially if you are in a union that represents only security personnel; and (3) the Code of Conduct established under the PSISA to govern the work of security professionals. As we noted in Chapter 2, regardless of by whom you are employed, you remain a representative of your profession, and you should strive to uphold the standards of ethical behaviour expected of you.

## The Ontario Labour Relations Act

The LRA was created to help maintain good relations between employers and trade unions, including by providing mechanisms for the resolution of workplace disputes.

The LRA does not apply to certain kinds of workers, including, for example, domestic workers (such as housekeepers), police, firefighters, and workers who are covered by other labour relations regimes, like agricultural workers and teachers.

The most important rights underlying the LRA are the right of workers to belong to trade unions and the right of employers to belong to employer associations.

An LRA provision of particular interest to security guards is section 78, which prohibits "strike-breaking" activities by the employer. These activities can include "a course of conduct of incitement, intimidation, coercion, undue influence, provocation, infiltration, surveillance or any other like course of conduct intended to interfere with, obstruct, prevent, restrain or disrupt the exercise of any right under this Act in anticipation of, or during, a lawful strike or lock-out." As you might imagine, an employer might seek to enlist security personnel to provide security during a strike, and so you must be mindful of to avoid taking actions that could be characterized as strike-breaking.

Unlawful lockouts are also prohibited, by section 82. If a lockout happens, it may be investigated by a labour relations officer sent by the Labour Relations Board. If the lockout is found to be unlawful, the employer can be charged with an offence for which there is a penalty, under section 104, of up to $2,000 for individuals and $25,000 for corporations, unions, or employers' associations.

Security professionals who work in unionized workplaces or in workplaces in which trade unions are seeking to organize should also be aware that the legislation creates rules to govern the activities of unions that are seeking to recruit members in a workplace, and that the general rule is that the employer must not obstruct employees' efforts to become organized (unionized).

## The Ontario Employment Standards Act

The ESA is a statute administered by the Ontario director of employment standards and overseen by the Ontario minister of labour. It establishes many of the employee rights that we now take for granted—hours of work and overtime, breaks, vacation and vacation pay, notice of termination and acceptable causes for termination, sick leave, maternity leave, etc.—that have not always existed and do not exist in all parts of the world.

As a security professional, you may occasionally find yourself called upon to provide support in the context of a dispute between employers and employees over ESA rights—most commonly, attempts to remove employees on the spot when they are terminated for cause. In these situations, it is useful to bear in mind that where an employee feels that a termination has been unnecessarily heavy-handed or humiliating, he or she might later bring a successful lawsuit for damages, or even bring a tort lawsuit or press criminal charges. For this reason, it is essential to strive for discreet and respectful treatment of all employees, even if they become belligerent.

Finally, security personnel may need to understand the ESA to appropriately handle requests for access to a workplace by employment standards officers. These government employees have rights under the legislation to come into a workplace, including in some cases without a warrant, to conduct inspections when they have grounds to believe there has been a violation of the provisions of the ESA.

The provision of the ESA that establishes this right of inspection is section 91, which reads as follows:

> 91(1) An employment standards officer may, without a warrant, enter and inspect any place in order to investigate a possible contravention of this Act or to perform an inspection to ensure that this Act is being complied with.
>
> (2) The power to enter and inspect a place without a warrant may be exercised only during the place's regular business hours or, if it does not have regular business hours, during daylight hours.
>
> (3) The power to enter and inspect a place without a warrant shall not be exercised to enter and inspect a part of the place that is used as a dwelling unless the occupier of the dwelling consents or a warrant has been issued under section 92.
>
> (4) An employment standards officer is not entitled to use force to enter and inspect a place.
>
> (5) An employment standards officer shall produce, on request, evidence of his or her appointment.
>
> (6) An employment standards officer conducting an investigation or inspection may,
>
> (a) examine a record or other thing that the officer thinks may be relevant to the investigation or inspection;
>
> (b) require the production of a record or other thing that the officer thinks may be relevant to the investigation or inspection;

(c) remove for review and copying a record or other thing that the officer thinks may be relevant to the investigation or inspection;

(d) in order to produce a record in readable form, use data storage, information processing or retrieval devices or systems that are normally used in carrying on business in the place; and

(e) question any person on matters the officer thinks may be relevant to the investigation or inspection.

Obstructing an employment standards officer is prohibited under section 91(11), and could lead to a provincial offence being charged against your employer.

## CHAPTER SUMMARY

One of the important functions of security professionals is to enforce the law. Pertaining law is contained not only in Canada's *Criminal Code*, but also in a wide range of other statutes, regulations, and by-laws at the federal, provincial, and municipal levels. This chapter provided a review of some of the legislation that is most commonly encountered by security personnel.

We introduced the Ontario *Trespass to Property Act*. The definition of trespass was discussed, and the requirements for making an arrest under the TPA were reviewed.

Also covered was the doctrine of citizen's arrest, as codified by the *Criminal Code*. The requirements for making a citizen's arrest were explained. The wording required for the protection of an arrested suspect's rights under the Charter was described, and the implications of using excessive force were explained.

Several pieces of provincial legislation may apply to the work of security professionals. In Ontario, these statutes include the *Provincial Offences Act*, the *Liquor Licence Act*, the *Residential Tenancies Act, 2006*, and employment-related legislation such as the *Employment Standards Act, 2000* and the *Labour Relations Act, 1995*. A brief overview of these acts was presented; however, security professionals will need to study legislation in greater detail if they find themselves working in settings where it is regularly applied.

CHAPTER 8 Legal Authorities 161

## KEY TERMS

arrest, 146
assault, 151
battery, 151
case law, 149
civil wrong, 145
colour of right, 145
common law, 149
conversion, 151
criminal offence, 145
defamation, 151
detain, 147
false imprisonment, 151
jurisprudence, 147
libel, 151
malicious prosecution, 151
negligence, 151
slander, 151
statute law, 149
tort, 144
trespass, 145

## REFERENCES

*Canadian Charter of Rights and Freedoms*, Part I of the Constitution Act, 1982, being Schedule B to the Canada Act 1982 (UK), 1982, c 11 [Charter].

*Criminal Code*, RSC 1985, c C-46.

*Employment Standards Act, 2000*, SO 2000, c 41 [ESA].

*Freedom of Information and Protection of Privacy Act*, RSO 1990, c F.31 [FIPPA].

Gerden, Robert. (1998). *Private security: A Canadian perspective*. Scarborough, ON: Prentice-Hall Canada.

*Highway Traffic Act*, RSO 1990, c H.8.

*Labour Relations Act, 1995*, SO 1995, c 1, Schedule A [LRA].

*Liquor Licence Act*, RSO 1990, c L.19 [LLA].

*Personal Health Information Protection Act, 2004*, SO 2004, c 3, Schedule A.

*Personal Information Protection and Electronic Documents Act*, SC 2000, c 5 [PIPED Act].

*Private Security and Investigative Services Act, 2005*, SO 2005, c 34 [PSISA].

*Provincial Offences Act*, RSO 1990, c P.33 [POA].

*Residential Tenancies Act, 2006*, SO 2006, c 17.

*Trespass to Property Act*, RSO 1990, c T.21 [TPA].

## PERFORMANCE APPLICATION
### Multiple Choice

1. A person can be given notice that entry onto a premises is forbidden:
   a. verbally only
   b. verbally or by posting "No Trespassing" signs
   c. only if signs are posted and clearly visible 24 hours a day
   d. verbally, by posting signs, or by clear indications that the property is private, such as by using a tall, locked fence
   e. none of the above

2. When making an arrest under the authority of the *Trespass to Property Act*, a security professional may:
   a. use force only in self-defence
   b. use force only if the person being arrested has a weapon
   c. use no force at all
   d. use force only if the use of force is necessary
   e. use force only if police are not present

3. An organization that possesses personal information about an individual can share it with a third party if:
   a. the organization has the consent of the person whose information is being shared
   b. the information was collected as part of the investigation of the alleged breach of a provincial offence
   c. the information was collected as part of the investigation of the suspected commission of a crime under the *Criminal Code*
   d. the information is needed by emergency responders for the benefit of the person whose information it is and that person is not able to give consent
   e. any of the above

4. Ontario's *Liquor Licence Act* establishes a legal drinking age for the province of:
   a. 16 years
   b. 18 years
   c. 19 years
   d. 21 years
   e. 25 years

5. What can happen if a security guard arrests a person without legal authority?

   a. the security guard's employer may be sued for a tort, such as false imprisonment

   b. the security guard may be personally sued for a tort, for example, for false imprisonment

   c. the security guard may lose his or her security licence

   d. the security guard may be charged with a crime under the *Criminal Code*

   e. all of the above

6. The *Canadian Charter of Rights and Freedoms* requires that a suspect who is arrested is told:

   a. the specific offence(s) with which she will be charged

   b. the maximum penalty for the offence(s) for which she will be charged

   c. the badge number of the arresting officer

   d. that she has the right to contact a lawyer without delay

   e. all of the above

7. Removing a tenant from his or her unit:

   a. can only be done by the sheriff

   b. is legal after the tenant has failed to pay three months rent

   c. can only be done between 6 p.m. and 9 p.m.

   d. can be done by security personnel using reasonable force

   e. is a legal remedy known as "distress"

8. A security guard has *not* caught a person in the process of committing an offence, but suspects that the person committed an offence just minutes before. The security guard may:

   a. not make an arrest under any circumstances

   b. make an arrest only if the suspected offence was an indictable offence

   c. make an arrest if the person is being chased by police

   d. make an arrest only if the person has a visible weapon

   e. make an arrest only in self-defence

9. When a security professional interacts with police to transfer custody of a person who has been arrested, the security professional should:

   a. make a recommendation about which *Criminal Code* charges should be laid

   b. make careful notes about the police officer's demeanour

   c. request to turn over the suspect to an officer with the rank of detective

   d. record the officer's name, rank, and badge number

   e. verify that the officer is from the appropriate force from a jurisdictional standpoint (municipal police, OPP, or RCMP, depending on the charge)

## Short Answer

Why must a security guard consider the public relations implications of his or her actions?

# Effective Communications 9

| | |
|---|---|
| Introduction | 164 |
| Image and Communication | 164 |
| Security Professionals Are Customer Service Representatives | 166 |
| Effective Verbal Communication | 167 |
| Interviewing | 168 |
| Note Taking in General | 178 |
| Radio Procedures | 179 |
| Chapter Summary | 183 |
| Key Terms | 184 |
| References | 184 |
| Performance Application | 184 |

## LEARNING OUTCOMES

When you have completed this chapter, you will:

- Be able to describe the types of communication that people use, which include verbal, para-verbal, and non-verbal communication.
- Be able to explain the importance of the awareness of one's appearance, attitude, and biases when communicating with the public.
- Be familiar with a range of professional interviewing techniques.
- Understand the procedures for the proper use of radio equipment.

# Introduction

Private security is a highly interactive profession. Security personnel communicate with members of the public every day in a wide range of circumstances, including in the wake of serious and stressful incidents. Obtaining compliance from the public and collecting information from interviewees require that security professionals have highly developed skills not only in verbal communication and listening, but also with respect to the non-verbal aspects of human interactions.

In this chapter we introduce the range of communication techniques employed by security professionals, with a special focus on interviewing, listening, and the use of two-way radio technology.

# Image and Communication

Communication is not restricted to the spoken and written word. Human beings collect information about each other and about events using all five senses, and they interpret this information through the complex filter of their own perceptions, which are based on beliefs, biases, and expectations shaped by the events of their lives. For this reason, security professionals must maintain a continual awareness of not only the verbal but also the non-verbal information they are providing in the course of their interactions with the public, with other security personnel, and with first responders.

The three basic modes of communication can be defined as follows:

- **Verbal communication:** the spoken words that are involved in communication with others.
- **Para-verbal communication:** the way in which the words are spoken during the communication process.
- **Non-verbal communication:** the body language used during communication with others.

Security professionals should always be aware that people may send out conflicting messages in their non-verbal, verbal, and para-verbal communications. Most people cannot control their non-verbal communication indicators, and therefore security professionals should learn to read the non-verbal cues that people use. Para-verbal cues are somewhat difficult to control and should also be considered when in conversation with witnesses, suspects, and even victims.

Verbal cues are typically controllable and will sometimes challenge non-verbal and para-verbal cues. A classic example is when a toddler does something wrong, and their whole body language says that they know they did something they should not have, but when confronted they say, "No, I didn't do it."

In order to communicate clear messages, security professionals should strive for lack of conflict between the verbal, non-verbal, and para-verbal cues they provide. The following sections demonstrate strategies for providing that clarity.

## Personal Appearance

**bearing**
appearance and way of holding oneself

A professional **bearing** (one's appearance and way of holding oneself) is extremely important for a security professional. The way a security professional looks and acts toward others and the way he or she carries himself or herself in relation to others allows for the non-verbal communication of a professional image.

Guards dressed in a slovenly manner, with poorly fitting trousers, running shoes, and their shirts untucked, are generally deemed less experienced and less professional than those wearing clean and neat well-fitting clothing and proper footwear.

Behaviour and manners also count, and are part of a professional security guard's image. Security professionals must bring a serious, professional attitude to their work, and must project an appearance of being observant, alert, and interested in what is going on in the facility where they are employed.

They must also appear competent and confident, a goal that is best achieved through learning about the industry. Finally, security professionals must be polite, friendly, and approachable. While they may have only limited opportunities to speak with the public, when they do so they must remember that they are representing their employer or client company. This role carries a lot of responsibility, since a clean, neat, and well-groomed security guard will influence the public's general impression of the company: a polite and well-spoken guard will support the image of a professional and well-managed company.

The following are basic standards of personal appearance:

- The uniform should be well-fitted, clean (no stains), and ironed.
- Any accessories—for example, belts—should be in good condition, well cared for, and clean.
- Proper, clean, and well-maintained footwear should be worn: boots or comfortable dress shoes.
- The name tag should be worn in a visible but secure location, and should include the security licence number and identification.
- Personal hygiene should be attended to: trimmed hair and a neat appearance are important.

A guard's bearing, the way the security professional carries himself or herself, is also important to non-verbal communication of competence. The first and most noticeable aspect of bearing is posture. Security professionals should always, when in view of the general public, stand up and sit up straight, without leaning, fidgeting, putting hands in pockets, or chewing gum. When we think of a person with a professional image, in our imagination that person is almost never leaning against something. Leaning makes people think of laziness and lack of respect. Therefore, never lean against a wall or a pole, particularly when in view of others.

Security professionals must also avoid being and even appearing distracted, for example, by a cellphone, newspaper, or book. Instead, keep your head up, look around, and pay attention to your surroundings.

It is equally important to make eye contact with everyone you come in contact with, speak with, or listen to. This will both increase your image of professionalism and allow you to concentrate on whatever is being said. Finally, keep your work area clean and tidy. This creates a professional impression for anyone who views your workspace.

## Attitude

Maintaining authority over the employer's property requires the communication of an attitude of competence. Projecting this attitude requires having the actual "credentials" to back it up.

Security professionals must have specialized knowledge about the security industry, including how to effectively respond when required to do so. They must have an education designed for the specific profession, including specialized training that equips them for the type of setting in which they work. They must also have the requisite licence. A security guard's possession of a security licence provides the public with the assurance that the guard has met the qualifications and standards imposed by the industry.

An appropriate attitude includes a commitment not only to do the job, but to perform it well. This commitment is reflected in actions such as always appearing neat and tidy, always taking notes, and always being attentive and off the phone or computer.

These actions communicate to others that the security professional takes pride in being a professional and doing what it takes to show that professionalism to others, and that he or she sees themselves as a representative of the security industry as a whole, a representative of the security company they work for and, finally, a representative of the client they are securing.

Improving professionalism and one's attitude requires taking an interest in your work, pursuing continuing education and training, and submitting to performance reviews. Reviewing job performance—determining what has worked and what mistakes have been made—both reinforces good procedure and allows security guards to learn from their mistakes.

Finally, seasoned security professionals should always help others to do the job well, and should assist in training new security professionals. This reflects a commitment to improving the security profession overall.

## Security Professionals Are Customer Service Representatives

All security professionals should consider themselves customer service representatives of the company for which they work for as well as for the company/client they are helping to secure. Therefore, a security guard should always be helpful, friendly, approachable, courteous, respectful, and professional.

A security professional should always be flexible in dealing with the general public. When communicating with people, be aware of their needs and their circumstances, and be aware that many members of the public will not have any idea what to do under certain stressful situations. By taking the time to communicate with people and behaving in a respectful and caring manner you will be able to obtain more information to assist with an emergency or other situation. Projecting an image of professionalism will assist in communicating effectively with both the public and with first responders who arrive to provide assistance.

Effective communication requires that you not allow your prejudices to interfere with your communication. When speaking with the public, the security professional must not "clock watch," must not be apathetic, and, especially, must not go on any power trips. Excessive displays of power will tend to decrease communication quality, often either discouraging responses from the public or even inspiring individuals to lie, either by omission or commission.

A customer service approach to communication should extend to dealings with the media, which may include news crews and camera operators. While every security professional will eventually encounter the media, it is essential to limit conversations with these individuals, and to pass them on as quickly as possible to appropriate spokespeople. Security professionals should direct any questions that the media may have to their employer's or client's public relations department or to management. Whenever any cameras are pointed in the direction of the security professional, he or she must be careful to project a professional image, as described above.

# Effective Verbal Communication

Communication is only effective when a security professional is clearly understood by the person with whom he or she is conversing. The converse is true in that the security professional must clearly understand what the other person is trying to communicate to them. This takes practice. Practice actively listening to and actually hearing what is said by others: take note of what is being said and take pains to remember details. If required, take notes (discussed below under "Note Taking in Interviews" and "Note Taking in General") to assist in remembering conversations.

## Overcoming Communication Barriers with Active Listening

There are a number of barriers that complicate interpersonal communication. Almost all barriers are created as a result of past experiences, past interactions with people such as teachers, parents, friends, siblings, and so on. These barriers include but are not limited to prejudices, biases, preconceived ideas, language barriers, mistrust, and failure to actually (actively) listen to others. In the security context, mistrust of a security professional or security professionals in general and any failure of a security professional to act with professionalism may create a barrier that will damage interaction.

To overcome communication barriers, security professionals must remember that their duty is to solve problems and provide service, not to simply provide an authority figure. A security professional must communicate with the general public and others within the profession in a friendly, professional, and respectful manner at all times.

An essential tool for good communication is patience. When dealing with others who are under stress, security professionals must do what they can to understand and learn about the problem. Practising patience in these situations will allow security personnel time to gather important information about the situation and make appropriate decisions about what to do. Practising patience will also allow for the accommodation of a large number of interaction styles.

As a security professional you will have contact with many different types of people, including the general public, visitors, customers, employees, contractors, service providers, management, other security professionals, police and other first responders, and criminals and suspected criminals. These individuals will present vastly different outlooks on life, enough so that communication with some of them can become difficult. That is why security professionals must be able to suppress their background non-verbal cues, show the ones that project professionalism, and adapt to the cues of others involved in any interaction.

The key to effectively communicating with unfamiliar people is active listening. The listener must take steps to ensure that they understand what the other person has said, and what it means from the point of view of the speaker. If the speaker feels that he or she is being sincerely listened to, heard, and understood, this will lead to better communication between the parties. To exercise active listening, the speaker must be given full attention, there should be no interruptions to the story being told, and the listener should paraphrase what was said to confirm understanding of it.

## Communication During Conflict

When conflict and confrontations happen, they go hand in hand with hostility and violence. Most conflicts are simply exaggerated differences of opinion. Many conflicts or confrontations are caused by or complicated by strong negative emotions. The best way to defuse or resolve a conflict is to determine the cause of that conflict and find a way to solve the problem.

When security professionals are involved in confrontations they should always recognize their own emotional responses to the conflict and keep them under control. Security professionals should always remember, especially now, with the prevalence of cellphones, that everything could be and probably will be recorded in some way: pictures, video, and audio, or a combination of all three. With recording comes scrutiny by people who were not present during a particular conflict, and who may second guess what was said and what actions were taken by the security professional involved.

Security professionals should decide what they are trying to achieve and then use words, actions, and gestures to attempt to bring about the desired outcome, which is almost always a de-escalation of the conflict. Being patient and calm in the face of conflict does more to resolve a conflict than taking action against the conflict.

When a security professional ends up in conflict with another person it generally has to do with something the security professional wants that person to do that they don't want to do, such as leave a particular location. In a situation like this it is almost always better for the security professional to convince the person to voluntarily receive direction.

Using verbal skills to attempt to build a rapport will give conflict less of a chance to interfere with communication. A rapport-building strategy can work with all types of people that a security professional interacts with. This rapport can help reduce the likelihood of use of force being required during a confrontation, thus limiting potential injury, legal liabilities, and negative public relations.

## Interviewing

An interview can be defined as a structured conversation between two people that is attempting to achieve a purpose, such as the collection of information. An interview may be required to gather complete and accurate information from a person, such as a witness or even a suspect in a crime. There is little if any formal training for security professionals in this industry and most often the interview process devolves into the most basic style of interviewing, the traditional or question and answer style of interview.

As a security professional, the main categories of individuals you will interview in the course of an investigation are witnesses, victims, and suspects. However, sometimes a security professional may use his or her skills to interview others as part of an everyday occurrence. These individuals include co-workers, suppliers, passengers, business associates, customers, job applicants, and refugee claimants. Depending on the subject and the reasons for the interview, the techniques chosen will vary widely. In choosing interview techniques, it is useful to understand human cognition.

### How the Mind Works

The mind works very similarly for everyone. The same basic physical structure of the brain leads to similar behaviours and patterns in thinking. The three basic patterns of thought are cognitive, affective, and psychomotor. These categories of thought govern the following human reactions:

- **Cognitive:** awareness, knowledge, and understanding;
- **Affective:** feelings and emotions;
- **Psychomotor:** skills, competencies, and actions.

When interviewing a subject, it is helpful to identify which domain or pattern of thought you are triggering when you ask a particular question, because it will provide insight into the subject's response. While these patterns of thought fluctuate, and work together, at any one time any one of them could be dominant in the subject's thoughts. For example, if in the wake of a traffic accident you ask a victim for technical information about direction or speed of travel, you may expect to be calling on their cognitive processes. However, in requiring them to reflect on the accident, you may be triggering an affective response (causing them to "re-live" the crash) and you may receive an emotional response instead of the technical details you are seeking.

## Common Problems in Interviews

There are a number of problems that commonly plague inexperienced interviewers. Learning how to recognize and correct these will help you more efficiently access the information you need.

Interviewers whose listening skills are not well developed may interrupt the interviewee, stopping the interviewee's train of thought, and they will not obtain all the information the interviewee had to offer. Interviewers who lack experience with crafting questions may make excessive use of closed-ended questions that lead to one-word answers, such as "yes" or "no."

Further problems include the inappropriate sequencing of questions. This error results in the interviewee moving between topics and losing his or her train of thought and can lead to the interviewer not delving as far as possible on a topic before moving on. The result is that a lot of information gets left out of the interview. Other problems include:

- negative phrasing,
- non-neutral wording,
- inappropriate language,
- distractions,
- judgmental comments,
- lack of follow-up on potential leads, and
- not noticing auditory cues: auditory cues are vocal expressions made as affirmative and negative reactions during a conversation; some examples might be "uh huh," "nh nh," and "umm," and not paying attention to these cues can lead to missing out on avenues of questioning.

### *Perception Distortions*

During the interview, perceptions can skew the response of the person the security professional is communicating with. One example is **parataxic distortion**. This refers to the interviewee projecting his or her distorted perception of any past interviewers onto the current interviewer. Parataxic distortion can occur when you try to make yourself sound too official and too much like law enforcement. The security professional must remember that this person may already have been interviewed a number of times by police, lawyers, corrections staff, probation officers, and so on. Those prior interviews will leave a residue within the person's mind that they will overlay onto their perceptions of the security professional, providing an inaccurate view of the professional and creating a barrier to the exchange of information. Of course, the opposite can be true as well: prior interviews that went well will allow the subject to perceive the security professional in a good light during the interview.

**parataxic distortion** a tendency to perceive others as we imagine them to be rather than as they actually are

> ## ON THE JOB
>
> **Parataxic Distortion**
>
> Parataxic distortion is a psychiatric term first used by Harry S. Sullivan in the 1940s to describe the inclination of a person to skew their perceptions of others based on fantasy. This distortion is a faulty perception of others, based not on actual experience with another individual, but on a projected fantasy personality attributed to the individual. For example, when a person falls in love, an image of another person as the "perfect match" or "soulmate" may be created, but in reality the other person may not live up to these expectations and may not embody the imagined traits in any way.
>
> During interviews and other interactions, security professionals may be able to avoid having individuals fall prey to parataxic distortion by not coming across as too authoritarian.

### *Interviewer Bias*

Bias can creep into an interview from both the interviewee and interviewer. Security professionals are not immune to bias and must take steps to recognize and compensate for it, because bias can have a negative impact on the interview process.

Types of biases include positive and negative "halos." A positive halo occurs when the general impression of the interviewee is positive and this thinking makes everything else about the interviewee, such as the information they provide, seem positive. A negative halo is the opposite of a positive halo: the interviewer has a negative general impression of the interviewee and therefore judges the person, and any information they provide, too harshly.

Several factors can affect whether an impression is positive or negative: the interviewee's attractiveness, the interviewee's personality, and whether the interviewer views behaviour as being fixed rather than constantly in flux and changeable.

Be aware that bias affects everyone to some degree or another, and must be taken into account in order for the security professional to carry out a proper interview.

## Voluntariness and Legality of Interviews

In Ontario, any investigator or security professional is entitled to ask anyone who is not under arrest any question they wish. An investigator or security professional does not have to advise the interviewee of the right to be silent or the right to refuse to answer unless and until that person is placed under arrest. The Charter rights of individuals under arrest were discussed in detail in the previous chapter.

An investigator or security professional may not detain anyone for the purpose of questioning without arresting them. Any person who is denied the right to leave, by the security professional, is technically under arrest. While a security professional can ask any person any question, he or she cannot demand that a person answer.

All interviews of people not under arrest must therefore be voluntary. The security professional must not put the interviewee under any form of duress (for example, must not try to force the interviewee to answer).

Ensuring that interviews are voluntary and avoiding the use of duress or coercion will make it more likely that any evidence collected during the interview will be admissible in court.

## Security Spotlight

### Historical Roots of the Rules for Statement Voluntariness

The admissibility of statement evidence will depend on compliance with legal rules for voluntariness. These rules come from both the common law and from legislation like the *Canadian Charter of Rights and Freedoms* and the *Criminal Code*. The following are some examples of legal rules that govern voluntariness.

#### The Ibrahim Rule

The Ibrahim Rule, which comes from the British decision in *Ibrahim v R* and was adopted as a legal precedent in Canada, provides that any statement made by a suspect, to anyone, such as a security professional, may be given as evidence in court only if it can be shown to have been made entirely on a voluntary basis.

#### The Judges' Rules

Again from English common law, the Judges' Rules are a set of rules drawn up by judges that set out the way in which suspects are to be reminded of their rights.

These rules became a code of "best practices" designed to ensure that statements given by a suspect in accordance with the rules would be admissible in evidence. They can be summarized as follows:

- police may question any person with a view to finding out whether, or by whom, an offence has been committed;
- police (or security personnel) must caution a suspect when they have evidence to suspect that the person has committed an offence;
- a further caution should be given when a person is charged;
- a record of questioning must be kept; and
- formal written statements are to be recorded according to a prescribed format.

As mentioned above, the content of the Judges' Rules helped to shape the content of Canadian legislation such as the Charter and the *Criminal Code*, which are more commonly cited as sources of voluntariness standards today.

# Interview Styles

A number of different interviewing strategies have been developed, and seasoned interviewers may choose different styles depending on circumstances and objectives. Because it is easy to learn and widely accepted as effective, the cognitive interview process will be the focus in this section. In general, law enforcement personnel have found that the cognitive interview style allows for more recall from the person being interviewed than other interview styles.

## The Traditional Interview

Essentially the traditional interview is a session in which the interviewer asks questions and the interviewee answers those questions. This interview process is structured for completeness and is typically a "just-the-facts" type of interview. These interviews answer the "Five W's and a How" (Who, What, Where, When, Why, How) of what happened, but typically do not go deeper for more information. Traditional interviews usually include a high ratio of closed-ended questions.

The advantages of this type of interview are that it is quick, efficient, and complete. However, it does not accomplish as much as it could. Some disadvantages are that it does not aid in any type of memory recall, does not analyze indicators from the suspect/witness, and opportunities to make determinations based on the response of the suspect/witness are limited.

## *The Cognitive Interview*

The cognitive interview, by contrast to the traditional interview, includes a number of techniques designed to enhance accurate responses from memory. This type of interview follows a step-by-step approach, using the techniques of building rapport, reconstructions, reporting of everything, changing the order of events, and changing the perspective from which the person remembers the event.

### Basic Technique of Cognitive Interviewing

The basic technique for cognitive interviewing starts with an introduction, where you introduce yourself and describe why the interview is required, what topics will be covered and so forth. This helps to establish a rapport (a close or harmonious relationship) with the individual being interviewed. The rapport that is built must be continued throughout the interview process for this style of interviewing to be effective. Essentially, the security professional is making it easier for the interviewee to talk to them because of the rapport that has been built.

The interview should begin with narrative phases so the interviewee can get his or her story out, and the interviewer can get background on the topic and determine where to go. These phases include free recall, where the interviewee just talks about what they remember, and guided recall, where the interviewer guides the interviewee through the recall process with questions. After that there is a clarification phase during which the topic discussed is repeated by the interviewer, with the interviewee supplying clarification on any inconsistencies.

Once the basic story has been remembered by the interviewee, the interviewee once again recalls the story, this time led by the security professional. This time the security professional has the interviewee reconstruct the memory so that the scenes, lighting, and surrounding objects are described in detail, and revelations about their impact on what was seen and heard by the interviewee are recorded by the security professional.

The interviewer, again using the rapport that has been developed with the interviewee, must encourage the interviewee to report everything that is remembered. There should be no holding back of any information no matter how trivial or unconnected it may seem at the time. Small, seemingly unrelated observations have sometimes turned out to be the cornerstones of challenging cases.

Next comes a difficult part, in which the interviewer strives to confirm that there is no deception going on, and at the same time assists with recall. The interviewer must repeat the interviewee's story, changing the order of the events. Starting at the end, the interviewer guides the interviewee backward in time, describing what happened. Next, the interviewer starts in the middle and moves either forward or backward. The goal is to determine whether the information remains consistent regardless of which point in the story the account is started from, or whether the process sparks new memories.

Finally, using the story provided by the interviewee, the interviewer asks the interviewee to change perspective. This is done to try to get the interviewee to remember the story from the point of view of another witness, the victim, or the suspect. This may also bring about new memories of the occurrence.

Then there is the challenge that anything that the interviewee can remember about the occurrence, that may not have been said previously in conversation, should now be said.

The final stage is the closure of the conversation and the interview. This is the time for the interviewer to re-establish rapport with the interviewee. The rebuilding of rapport will make it seem as if the interviewee is talking to a friend, which will make it easier for the security professional to return to the witness at a later date with more questions, if required.

## Interview Skills Development

Security professionals who will be involved in interviewing should work on developing good questioning skills. Some types of questions that the security professional can ask will elicit information, while others can shut down the flow of information with one word.

### Open and Closed Questions

Open-ended questions allow the interviewee to free-form a response to the question that should continue into a narrative. Open-ended questions are generally broad and are used to get the interviewee talking about the subject. Closed-ended questions, by contrast, limit the interviewee to a narrow response: typically "yes" or "no," or a similarly uninformative response such as "maybe," "not me," or "fine."

### Direct and Indirect Questions

Direct questions are designed to elicit a specific answer. Examples of direct questions are "Where were you?" and "Who else was involved?"

Indirect questions encourage the sharing of information and, at the same time, avoid making the interviewee feel threatened or interrogated. For example: "I'm wondering whether your need for alcohol is going to make you do things you wouldn't normally do?"

### Other Question Styles

Other styles of questions include linear, circular, strategic, and reflexive. These are described as follows:

- **Linear:** Direct questions with an investigative intent: who, what, where, when, (why), how.
- **Circular:** Questions with exploratory intent; using questions about the details of one event to reveal insights about another event.
- **Strategic:** Questions with a corrective intent that are used to change an interviewee's behaviour.
- **Reflexive:** Facilitative questions that allow the interviewee to "dig deeper."

## Listening

Listening is an essential skill that most security professionals need to learn in order to interview effectively. During a conversation, most people listen in order to respond;

however, a security professionals must listen to record and understand what is being said. There are five elements to listening:

1. hearing,
2. attending,
3. understanding,
4. responding, and
5. remembering.

Security professionals may make the mistaken assumption that interview subjects are following these steps effectively and may also wrongly assume that they are being good listeners. Listening, like any skill, must be practised to be of any use. Practise listening, using the five steps above to help you. Recording notes will also help you in remembering.

It can be useful, while conducting an interview, to remind yourself to consider how effectively both you and your interview subject are listening to one another. Being aware of how well your subject is listening can help you formulate appropriate questions. You can ask the best question in the world, but if the person does not effectively listen to it, it is worthless.

## *Ineffective Listening Styles*

Here are some examples of ineffective listening styles that you can watch out for in yourself and in others:

- **Pseudo listening:** Giving the appearance of listening while not actually listening.
- **Stage hogging:** Shifting a conversation back to what the listener wants to talk about.
- **Selective listening:** Responding only to selected parts of a conversation.
- **Insulated listening:** Ignoring undesirable information.
- **Defensive listening:** Taking the speaker's remarks as personal attacks.

Identifying these barriers to listening can help you tailor both your own listening and the questions you ask your subject.

## Deception

When interviewing a subject, it is important to remain aware of the possibility of deception (lying). If, while conducting an interview, you suspect that what you are hearing is not true, it is of paramount importance to determine whether the person is a liar or is just mistaken. The key factor that distinguishes a liar is *intent*. A liar intends to purposefully provide false information, whereas someone with bad information lacks intent because they may believe their information to be accurate.

There are many forms of deception. Here is an incomplete list:

- **Emphatic denial:** Strenuously denying that something was said or done in the face of evidence that it was, in fact, said or done.
- **Concealment/omission:** Withholding some of the requested information from the interviewer.
- **Fabrication:** Making up a completely fake account of events.

- **Minimization:** Making the information related seem less important than it was.
- **Exaggeration:** Making the information related seem more important than it was.

Security guards are most likely to detect deception in a high-stakes situation, such as where the interviewee realizes the information they are providing may have a direct impact on whether they will be in trouble or not.

Detecting deception takes practice. It is important to be aware that as a security professional you may not always be correct in your detection. You may sometimes conclude that an interviewee is telling a lie and being deceitful when in fact he or she is under a large amount of stress and, as a result, is forgetting details.

There are certain signs that sometimes signal deception. It is useful to bear in mind that these signs may equally result from high levels of stress. These are:

- Changes in vocal pitch.
- Obvious signs of nervousness.
- Confusion.
- Long pauses before responding.
- Interviewee takes frequent drinks of provided water.
- Masking (buying time by saying "um," "ah," and so on).
- Repeating what was just said (Interviewer: Did you have anything to do with the crime? Interviewee: Did I have anything to do with the crime?).

It can also be useful to be alert to particular manners of speaking that may reflect deception:

- inclusion and distancing;
- using the wrong tense;
- conflicts in logic;
- changes in possession (my car, the car);
- lack of conviction: interviewee says "sort of," "maybe," "kind of," "not really," and so on;
- missing or out-of-place time frames; and
- the giving of extraneous information.

An incomplete list of the many and varied motives for deception follows. Deception may be used in order to

- avoid punishment,
- obtain a reward,
- protect another person,
- gain protection from physical harm,
- win the admiration of others,
- get out of an awkward situation,
- avoid embarrassment,
- maintain privacy, and/or
- exercise power over others and control information.

## Preparing for an Interview

The time before an interview starts is known as the "pre-interview" and it can occur days or minutes before the actual interview. Use this time to anticipate the interviewee's emotional state. Are they angry, sad, confused, or despondent? Will they be an eager witness? Can they be considered a suspect? Are they under any kind of stress?

Attentive observation of the interviewee can allow an opportunity to identify questions that the interviewee should answer. Initial questions should be simple, allowing for time to build rapport before moving into a more challenging exploration of the incident. The security professional should always draft questions before the interview, but he or she should also be prepared to formulate additional questions as the interview progresses.

The security professional should anticipate areas of importance and should have specific objectives for the interview. Along with the questions to be asked, the interviewer should have a written hierarchy of important areas to cover during the interview.

Preparation for an interview should include the set up of any audio or video equipment that will be used to record the interview. Even when audio and/or video recording is used, the security professional should always make his or her own notes as the interview progresses.

## Note Taking in Interviews

An interview is useless if it is not properly recorded. The interviewer should take detailed notes and, ideally, should record the interview using audio and/or video equipment. The advantages of recording are as follows:

- Audio can be used after the interview to fill in gaps in notes, provide the interviewee's exact wording, and serve as a record of some of the verbal and paraverbal cues that were used by the interviewee.
- Video with audio provides both the exact wording and the expressions and nonverbal cues that were used by the interviewee.

Notes taken during an interview will help the security professional when it comes time to complete the interview report, and will also be useful when compiling written witness statements for use in court. A security professional may also later use notes taken during an interview to refresh his or her memory when preparing to give testimony in court.

Note taking should be done in a way that does not interfere with the interview. A security professional should always be sure that he or she is not paying more attention to the note-taking process than to the interview process, because with the focus on note taking, valuable information imparted by the interviewee may be missed.

Don't interrupt the interviewee to take the notes and don't stop the interviewee's flow when he or she is talking. To avoid gaps in the interview while writing, the security professional should not pause to write while the interviewee is silent; this will interrupt the flow developed by the interview process and may cause the interviewee to either misremember or forget entirely. The interviewer must find a way to take notes that prevents gaps in talking.

The security professional should maintain eye contact with the interviewee during the interview. This eye contact creates a sense of interest in the interviewee and a feeling of closeness develops, which helps with rapport and leads to better communication. When talking with the interviewee, the security professional should be careful to not start and stop the conversation suddenly while interviewing. The security professional should practice having smooth flowing conversation during which they don't stop or pause to look for the next question. The security professional should know what they're going to ask. If the interviewee pauses for some reason, the interviewer should try to use non-verbal cues to restart the conversation.

In order to avoid curiosity on the part of the interviewee about the notes being taken by the security professional, the interviewee should be told why the notes are being taken. At the beginning of the interview the security professional should inform the interviewee that notes will be taken, and that recording in some form—audio or video or both—will be carried out. The security professional should also let the interviewee know the purpose of the notes; for example, that they will form the basis of a written statement, a witness "will say" summary, or that they are simply going to be used as background information in the investigation.

The security professional should review the notes immediately after the interview to make any corrections or add missing information, using any recordings taken as a resource. During this immediate review of his or her notes, the security professional should add any useful observations, rather than trying to rely on memory at a later time.

## The Use of Audio and Video During Interviews

It is a good idea to use audio and video recording during an interview. In Canada, it is legal to record a conversation as long as *one* party to the conversation consents—and this can be the recording party. Recording an interview allows the security professional to concentrate more on the interviewee and take selective strategic notes during the interview, with the option to go over the audio and/or video later to recover anything that may have been missed. Furthermore, it allows the security professional to record observations during the interview and again during the review of the recording.

Even though it is legal to record an interview without the interviewee's permission (as long as the security professional is present and involved in the conversation), it is best to be sure to get that permission anyway. Permission from the interviewee is not strictly required, but it makes the person feel more a part of the process.

Always make certain that all audio and video equipment is ready before starting an interview. Equipment should be tested, and make sure that batteries are new or fully charged. Where possible, have a backup recorder running. Finally, the interviewer should make sure that the equipment is not a distraction to the interviewee—for example, there should not be a boom mic hanging in the interviewee's face.

### ON THE JOB

**Interview Basics**

Here is a useful checklist/refresher for review prior to conducting an interview:

1. Have all documentation ready.
    a. Everything that is to be shown to the interviewee should be available and ready.
2. Plan your questions.
    a. Anticipate difficulties, misunderstandings, forgetfulness, overeagerness, and so on.
    b. Have a number of questions ready and memorized.
    c. Write down new questions that arise to ask later in the interview.

*Continued*

Continued

3. Record the interview.
   a. Audio.
   b. Video.
   c. Written notes.
4. Maintain professionalism.
   a. The more professional the interviewer is, the more composed the interviewee will be during the process.
5. Seating arrangements.
   a. Make certain that the interviewee has a clear path to the door.
   b. Offer a glass of water to the interviewee.
   c. Be careful with the chair the interview subject is sitting in:
      i. A wheeled chair that easily moves about could make it difficult to read body language.
      ii. Try not to let the interviewee stare out the window (it may be distracting).
   d. Try not to let the interviewee hide his or her hands and feet under a desk or table.
6. Time management.
   a. Never rush an interview.
   b. A one-hour interview may be planned, but if the interviewee wants to tell the entire story and it will take longer than one hour, the security professional should make sure that the interview will not be interrupted.
7. Always meet the objectives of the investigation during the first interview.
   a. It may be very difficult to interview the subject again.
   b. Make sure *all* questions are asked and all topics are covered.
   c. If a response is not understood, ask questions that will clarify the matter; ask until the response is understood.

## Note Taking in General

Note taking is one of the most important skills a security professional can develop: carry a notebook of some kind and a writing instrument at all times. Notes taken during a standard shift will help you remember what happened, what order things happened in, and descriptions of people or things involved.

When situations arise that require detailed observations for reports or for evidence, a security professional's notes can be used to assist him or her in remembering the incident.

Notes should contain as much detail as possible about an occurrence, from the chance meeting of a civilian on site, to a large fire. Examples of what details should be recorded in notes are as follows:

- The time and date the security professional started his or her shift.
- Any hazards in the area being patrolled.
- Any incidents witnessed, identity of witnesses, first responders, etc.
- Improper activity observed on the site.

Notebooks must be viewed by security professionals as a complete and factual record of events that they encounter. An entry for each day worked indicating the date, location, and persons involved (other security persons, supervisors, etc.) should be created at the start of each day.

The progress of the shift should be documented as a timeline, using the time format (regular or military) preferred by the employer. Make sure all numbers are clear and precisely written, such as 17:00 hours. If non-military time is used, make sure that a.m. and p.m. designations are clearly marked.

Security guards should always make entries to their notebooks at the time of observation of any incident or immediately thereafter, not waiting until they get back to the office or their car. This allows for opportunities to confirm on-scene details (for example, a licence plate number) that might otherwise be missed.

# Radio Procedures

In the 21st century, keeping up to date on communication technology developments is more vital in the security industry than in any other commercial field. For example, the events in the United States on September 11, 2001 may not have been as tragic were it not for certain communications' failures. The radio networks of the New York fire and police departments were on separate systems. They could not hear one another, so vital information that could have saved more lives was lost. Radios also play a vital role during general and routine patrols. It is very important to be able to relay relevant information to other team members, for example, in case a security breach or hazard is discovered while conducting a patrol.

Professional security companies realize how important it is to have radios that work so they can pass critical information from point to point in their operations. Consequently, radios and radio systems used in the security industry are chosen carefully for their reliable performance under all circumstances.

A two-way radio is a device that can both transmit and receive, unlike a broadcast receiver (car radio), which only receives transmissions. A point-to-point radio communicates to another within a certain distance, depending on the output power of the radio and the size of its antenna. These radios work only within a certain distance, typically about one to three kilometres.

## Parts of a Hand-Held Radio

A hand-held radio has several parts. These parts and their uses are as follows:

1. **Antenna:** Usually helical or whip style with a threaded base, the antenna is necessary for receiving transmissions.
2. **External antenna jack:** Connects an optional 50-ohm external antenna to the radio; also used for test procedures. The jack is fitted with a threaded protective cap, which should be left in place when the jack is not being used.
3. **Universal accessory jack:** Connects the optional external speaker-microphone or surveillance accessory to the radio. When an external speaker-microphone is connected, the internal speaker and microphone audio is muted and the transmitter can be keyed via the radio PTT switch or the remote PTT switch (see point 7).
4. **Frequency select switch:** Selects the operating channel.
5. **On/off volume control:** Turns the radio on and off and adjusts the audio output level.

6. **Monitor/reset switch:** When this switch is depressed and held, the channel is monitored for voice communication.
7. **PTT (push-to-talk) switch:** When this switch is depressed and held, the radio is in transmit mode; when it is released, the radio operates in receive mode.

## Radio Storage, Retrieval, and Inspection

Usually, the radios kept on site for security guards are stored in a specific location within the main security office or operations centre. Strict control over who has access to the communication equipment is usually enforced. Upon opening the radio cabinet, the following procedure is usually followed.

### Taking the Radio Out

- Check to see whether any batteries are on green, or fully charged. If they are, move them to the top shelf.
- Remove carrying case and microphone; attach microphone to radio.
- Lock up and return the key to security supervisor.

### Replacing the Radio

- Turn radio off.
- Check to see whether any batteries are on green and charged.
- Take recharged battery and place in radio.
- Put used or drained batteries into charger.
- Store carrying case and belt attachment in the cabinet.
- Place radio in numbered slot in cabinet.
- Place microphone on top of radio.
- Lock up and return the key to security supervisor.

## Safe Use of Hand-Held Radios

Follow these rules to avoid accidents:

- Do *not* hold the radio such that the antenna is very close to, or touching, exposed parts of the body, especially the face or eyes, while transmitting. The radio will perform best if the microphone is held two to three inches (or five to eight centimetres) away from the mouth and the radio is vertical.
- Do *not* hold the PTT (push-to-talk) switch on when not actually making a transmission.
- Do *not* allow children to play with any radio equipment containing a transmitter.
- Do *not* operate a portable transmitter near unshielded electrical blasting caps or in an explosive atmosphere (for example, where there is a gas leak or bomb threat) unless it is a type specially designed for such use.

## Radio Procedures and Etiquette

When using the radio, be aware that there may be "eavesdroppers," including members of the public, who have access to the network. Because guards never know who may be listening, good radio procedures can greatly enhance their professional image. Conversely, inappropriate radio procedures or etiquette can also be overheard and must be avoided. Security professionals should adopt a courteous code of behaviour at all times. When talking on the radio the security professional should always speak carefully and clearly, and communication should be concise and to the point. When using the radio, security professionals should take care to not talk about anything that could be considered private, confidential, or personal.

To enforce proper **radio etiquette**, most employers deal severely with all instances of improper or illegal use of the radio, profanity, or the use of the radio to play games, pranks, or practical jokes.

Besides general etiquette principles and the protocols developed by employers and clients, there are regulations in place with respect to the use of radio frequencies. In Canada, radio broadcasts are regulated by the Canadian Radio-television and Telecommunications Commission (CRTC), and by the minister of Innovation, Science, and Economic Development Canada.

**radio etiquette**
standardized procedures for courteous radio use that are designed to maximize comprehension of communications and minimize interference with other users

## Security Radio Protocol

The following are general rules of protocol for operating hand-held radios:

- Do *not* cut into other people's transmissions. If you must interrupt due to an emergency, break into the communication and immediately declare that there is an emergency, identify yourself, and describe the emergency.
- Do *not* use the paging encoder when others are transmitting.
- If someone else cuts into a transmission, do not retaliate with derogatory comments, as most interruptions are unintentional.
- Avoid unnecessary transmissions such as excessive number of radio checks or time checks.
- Do not respond to the radio unless your call sign is heard.
- Do *not* use the radio for lengthy, non-urgent, and/or personal conversations.
- Speak at a normal voice level.
- Enunciate clearly.
- Think before you speak to avoid stuttering and repetitiveness.
- Be brief and to the point, using numbers and details in your descriptions. For example, state "the suspect is approximately 5 feet 10 inches tall or 180 centimetres tall, with brown hair and blue eyes," and not "the suspect is about medium height with brown hair and blue eyes."
- Do *not* use slang, and this includes CB jargon. Professional security personnel do not imitate a CB (citizens band) operation. Do not use, for example, "Roger . . . over and out," or "That's a Big 10-4."
- Use the standard **10 codes**, where possible, but also remember that clarity is the most important concern. Briefly clarify your message using plain English if required. Remember that "10-4" means "Message Understood/End of Transmission," *not* "Yes." Use "Affirmative" and "Negative" for "Yes" and "No." A list of standard radio 10 codes is provided in Appendix D of this book.
- Do *not* use proper names on the radio. Always use assigned unit designations where possible. Some non-security personnel (for example, maintenance workers) may be assigned "W" or "workplace" codes. "W" codes are used in some workplaces as a private designation for individuals or situations within that workplace only. Where

**10 codes**
a system of codes designed to increase the clarity, efficiency, and discretion of radio communications

they have been implemented, they should be recognized and used at all times. For people who do not have designated security "W" codes or private codes, refer to them by title; for example, "Please call the scheduling coordinator" or "Please see the superintendent."

- Switch radios off and store them in proper battery charger units when not in use.
- Report all damaged or malfunctioning radios immediately to the security supervisor and submit a full report. Radios that require repair should be sent out with a covering report that lists specific details of the problem. The person who picks up a radio for repair usually signs for it at the control room.

### *Code Red (Fire)*

When an alarm sounds, Control will come on the air and announce a Code Red in location X. Upon receipt of this information, units should maintain a listening watch on their radios and refrain from transmitting anything to allow Control to proceed with emergency measures without any interruptions. Shortly after the Code Red transmission, security guards should receive a call advising them of the intended entry point of the fire service. At this stage, Control will radio the various security guards on duty with directions as to who goes where and for what purpose.

When the fire department arrives at the scene, the security guard who meets the trucks and the security guard who subsequently escorts them to the location of the fire will keep in close contact with Control to report each step of the operation.

### *Radio Dead Zones*

Security guards may experience poor reception in some areas of a site and, when required, should move to another area to call for assistance. Security guards who are accustomed to a site will be able to identify communications problem zones, and these sites may require the use of TAC-2: a higher frequency range to allow confidential communications between two guards in the same general location. Be advised that TAC-2 is usually not monitored by Control and should only be used in emergencies where no other alternative is available.

---

**ON THE JOB**

### Radio Language

**phonetic alphabet**
an alphabetic system designed to eliminate any confusion when spelling out a phrase (i.e., names or vehicle plate numbers)

The **phonetic alphabet** has been in use in maritime radio communications for almost a century. Developed to assist radio operators in sending and receiving clear messages over the airwaves, it became a standardized procedure for the military services during World War II. The use of standard phonics to clarify the sound of letters and vowels has been adopted in all parts of the world, including air traffic control. Some variations exist for specific groups of users and activities, such as truckers and CB users, but the phonetic alphabet used by the security industry is based on the standard military version.

**Phonetic Alphabet Chart**

| | |
|---|---|
| **ALFA**—AL fah | **NOVEMBER**—no VEM ber |
| **BRAVO**—BRAH VOH | **OSCAR**—oss KAR |
| **CHARLIE**—CHAR lee | **PAPA**—Pah PAH |
| **DELTA**—DELL tah | **QUEBEC**—keb BECK |
| **ECHO**—ECK oh | **ROMEO**—ROW me oh |
| **FOXTROT**—FOKS trot | **SIERRA**—see AIR rah |
| **GOLF**—GOLF | **TANGO**—TANG go |
| **HOTEL**—hoh TELL | **UNIFORM**—YOU nee form |
| **INDIA**—IN dee ah | **VICTOR**—VIK tah |
| **JULIET**—JEW lee ET | **WHISKEY**—WISS key |
| **KILO**—KEY loh | **X-RAY**—ECKS RAY |
| **LIMA**—LEE mah | **YANKEE**—YANK key |
| **MIKE**—MIKE | **ZULU**—zoo loo |

**Note:** The syllables printed in capital letters are to be stressed; for example, the two syllables in BRAH VOH are given equal emphasis, whereas the first syllable of AL fah is given emphasis.

## CHAPTER SUMMARY

Security professionals are always in constant communication with others, be they clients, other professionals, suspects, or witnesses. They need to know the various ways that people communicate and to be aware that some will send out conflicting messages in their communication. Security professionals must be able to communicate well with others during regular, everyday contact and during conflicts.

The appearance, attitude, and bearing of security professionals has considerable impact on their interactions with others. Security professionals should always remember that they will be viewed as customer service representatives for their company and also for their client.

Security professionals may be involved in interviewing in the process of protection of the client's property. The ability to interview witnesses is a basic skill that is used in the collection of information. Two basic styles are discussed in this chapter: the traditional interview and the cognitive interview.

Note taking is a vital skill that must be learned by security professionals. Notes are used to create reports, in court to provide evidence, to manage the collection of information, and so on. Notes are used to provide backup for a security professional's memory.

Finally, the use of technology is important to the security professional. Cellphones, radio communication, and CCTV (as well as other types of cameras) are all technologies that the security professional will use on the job. Two-way radios are important to learn to use and the style of communicating with them is unique. The short forms, or 10 codes, for use with two-way radios must be used and understood along with the phonetic alphabet so that radio communication is not misunderstood.

## KEY TERMS

10 codes, 181
bearing, 164
parataxic distortion, 169
phonetic alphabet, 182
radio etiquette, 181

## REFERENCES

*Canadian Charter of Rights and Freedoms*, Part I of the *Constitution Act, 1982*, being Schedule B to the *Canada Act 1982* (UK), 1982, c 11 [Charter].

*Criminal Code*, RSC 1985, c C-46.

*Ibrahim v R*, [1914] AC 599 (PC).

## PERFORMANCE APPLICATION
### Multiple Choice

1. What are the three basic types of communication?
    a. speaking, listening, body language
    b. verbal, para-verbal, non-verbal
    c. notes, interviews, radio communications
    d. verbal, physical, mental
    e. verbal, oral, listening

2. Which is *not* an aspect of the professional appearance of a security guard?
    a. personal hygiene
    b. polished professional footwear
    c. erect posture (no leaning or slouching)
    d. uniform clean, pressed, and in good condition
    e. absence of facial hair

3. Which is *not* a barrier to effective communication?
    a. gender
    b. language not understood/spoken
    c. bias
    d. overuse of closed-ended questions
    e. prejudices

4. Developing a rapport with the interviewee is a significant requirement of what type of interview style?
    a. casual
    b. traditional
    c. behavioural
    d. cognitive
    e. none of the above

5. Which is *not* a purpose for the taking of notes by security professionals?
    a. as a basis for the preparation of reports
    b. as a memory aid to be used during testimony in court
    c. as a back-up for audio and video recording of interviews
    d. as a record of observations at the time of an incident
    e. all of the above are purposes of note-taking

6. What is parataxic distortion?
    a. a form of lying
    b. the interviewer's devaluation of the interviewee's information based on a poor first impression of the interviewee
    c. the interviewee's projection onto the current interviewer of a distorted perception of past interviewers
    d. distortion of the facts of an incident caused by affective responses to questions while under stress
    e. the inability of a subject to breathe when restrained in a face-down position

7. What are the three basic patterns of thought?
    a. verbal, para-verbal, non-verbal
    b. situational awareness, non-awareness, parataxic distortion
    c. cognitive, affective, psychomotor
    d. bias, prejudice, objectivity
    e. reason, emotion, reaction

8. Which is *not* a sign that a subject may be lying in an interview?
    a. subject repeats questions before answering
    b. changes in vocal pitch
    c. long pauses before answering
    d. blinking
    e. confusion

9. What are the five elements involved in skilled listening?

   a. hearing, attending, understanding, responding, remembering

   b. hearing, attending, repeating, reframing, remembering

   c. silence, non-verbal encouragement, hearing, repeating, follow-up

   d. hearing, attending, responding, reframing, remembering

   e. looking, listening, insight, perception, reflection

10. Which instruction is incorrect with respect to the correct use of a radio?

    a. avoid cutting into others' transmissions

    b. speak at a moderate volume with the radio close to your face

    c. use radio 10 codes for discretion and clarity

    d. be brief and to the point

    e. speak very loudly, holding the radio 30 centimetres from your face

## Short Answer

1. Why is a security professional's appearance important from a communications perspective?

# Sensitivity Training

## 10

| | |
|---|---|
| Introduction: Diversity in Canada | 188 |
| Immigration and Multiculturalism | 188 |
| The Canadian Human Rights Act and the Canadian Human Rights Commission | 191 |
| The Ontario Human Rights Code and the Ontario Human Rights Commission | 191 |
| Implications of Human Rights Legislation for Security Professionals | 192 |
| Diversity and the Private Security and Investigative Services Act | 194 |
| Diversity and Conflict | 195 |
| Indigenous People in Canada | 197 |
| Racial Profiling | 199 |
| Chapter Summary | 202 |
| Key Terms | 203 |
| References | 203 |
| Performance Application | 203 |

## LEARNING OUTCOMES

When you have completed this chapter, you will:

- Be able to recognize the many aspects of diversity that exist in Canada.
- Understand the human rights that each person has in Canada, and how sometimes competing rights conflict.
- Be familiar with and able to identify the laws, policies, and processes available to resolve conflicts when elements of diversity lead to conflict.
- Be able to discuss the unique rights of Indigenous people that occasionally lead to political conflict.
- Know how to analyze racial profiling in relation to the Charter.

## Introduction: Diversity in Canada

Before we discuss diversity in Canada, let's begin this chapter by acknowledging that every human being is different. No one is the same as the person sitting next to them. Many who study diversity believe that diversity is "socially constructed." That is to say, that the characteristics on which individuals and groups define themselves or are defined by others are given meaning by society. Those who study diversity in societies identify two dimensions of diversity. *Primary* dimensions include those things that cannot be controlled or changed, such as age, ethnicity, physical ability, race, and sexual orientation. *Secondary* dimensions of diversity are also important to recognize and include things that may change over a lifetime, such as education level, marital and family status, gender expression, religious belief, income level, and country of residence.

Understanding diversity and how it can affect individuals' experiences in many aspects of their life and work is important for security professionals for many reasons. First, security professionals can expect to encounter a wide range of individuals in the course of their work, and they are required by law to avoid discrimination in their interactions with those individuals—for example, human rights legislation prohibits denying access to goods and services to individuals based on grounds of discrimination. Second, as a matter of good customer service, security personnel need to be sensitive to the fact that individuals' needs may differ—for example, disabled or pregnant individuals may not be able to stand as long as others in a gathering area after an evacuation and may need to be permitted to sit down, and new immigrants from a country in which there has been political violence may be unusually wary or afraid of security personnel. Finally, knowledge about human rights will be useful to security professionals if they encounter discrimination with regard to their employment.

## Immigration and Multiculturalism

Canada ascribes to an ideology of multiculturalism. This means that Canada supports people in maintaining and promoting their diversity provided that the practices of their diverse lifestyle, religion, or culture do not conflict with the laws of Canada. Canada is host to many cultures and religions and people have come from all over the world to make their home in Canada and become truly Canadian. Immigration to Canada began with the arrival in the Americas of Europeans in 1492 and continues to this day. The fact is that all non-Indigenous Canadians are here because someone in their family history immigrated from elsewhere.

The source countries for immigration have changed over the past 50 years, and this has changed the face of Canada from primarily an English- and French-speaking and Western European immigrant based nation to a more visibly diverse country. Prior to the creation of the *Bill of Rights* in 1960, Canada could choose not to accept immigration applications from countries it deemed unsuitable or incompatible with the goals of government. Following the passage of the *Bill of Rights*, the *Immigration Act* had to be amended to be consistent with the *Bill of Rights*, which meant that immigrants could not be denied the opportunity to apply to immigrate to Canada based on the colour of their skin or their country of origin: they had to be judged suitable for immigration based on their merits as individuals who had the capacity to contribute to Canada's society and its economy.

From 2001 to 2006, Canada accepted 200,000 immigrants per year. Since then, the number has been steadily increasing. In 2015, 271,660 new permanent residents came to Canada from 190 different source countries. The largest sources of immigrants to Canada since 2015 are the Philippines, India, China, and Pakistan (see Figure 10.1). In fact, those four source countries accounted for 49 percent of the total immigration in 2015 (Canadian Magazine of Immigration, 2016a). In 2017, our target immigration number is 300,000 (Government of Canada, CIC, 2017).

People immigrate to Canada under different classes. The class that makes up the highest percentage of immigration is the economic class. The economic class is subdivided into a number of categories. In 2017, the majority of those approved for immigration to Canada were in the economic class because one of the main objectives of Canada's immigration plan is to make Canada competitive in the global market. These immigrants have either significant financial resources or highly specialized skills. See Figure 10.2.

The second largest class of immigrants to Canada in 2017 was family class. People who qualify for family class are family members of those who have already successfully immigrated to Canada and have the guaranteed economic and social supports in place for their immigration.

The group that forms the smallest segment of the 2017 target of approximately 300,000 immigrants, only 14.5 percent, is the refugee and humanitarian class. Included in part in this number are the over 20,000 Syrian refugees that Canada has agreed to accept over two years. This is a marked increase in the number accepted in the past. Nevertheless, Canada, when compared with other countries, may actually be overrating its humanitarianism and generosity in terms of how it is helping other nations and displaced persons. To put this into perspective, in 2015, the United Nations estimated the number of displaced persons in the world at 65.3 million and the number of refugees at 21.3 million; the top hosting countries range from Jordan at over 600,000 to Turkey at 2.5 million (UNHCR, 2016).

There is a difference between internationally displaced persons and refugees. "Internationally displaced persons" are those who have been "pushed" from their own country of citizenship by factors such as war, famine, and persecution. They end up in temporary shelters abroad to await assistance by the United Nations Refugee Agency. Their hope is that after a period of shelter they will be able to return to their home country. They have not yet been declared a refugee for the purpose of resettlement. "Refugees," on the other hand, are those who were once internationally displaced persons, but have applied for and been granted refugee status from the United Nations Refugee Agency because there is no hope that they will be able to return to their home countries. They are awaiting resettlement in a new country.

**Figure 10.1** Source Countries of Canadian Permanent Residents in 2016

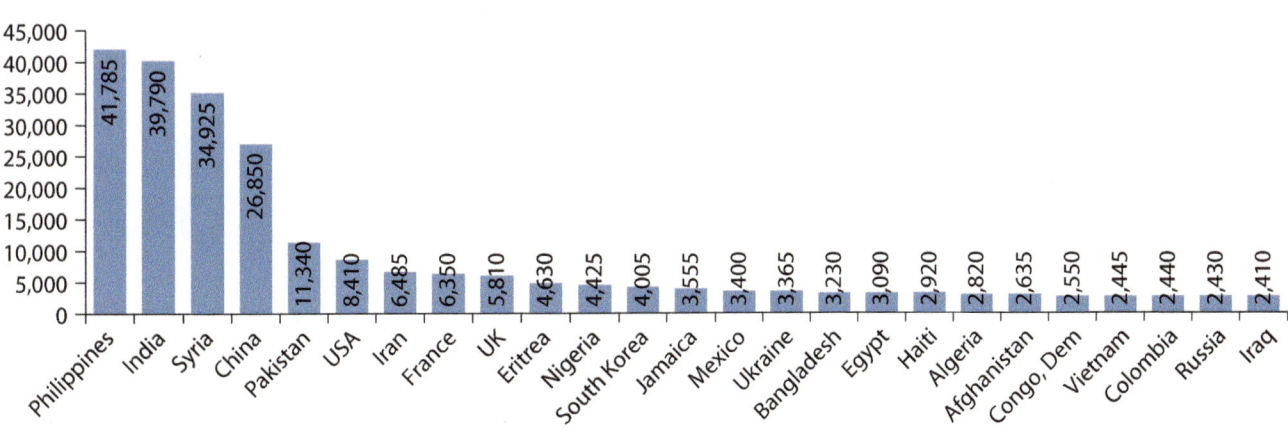

*Source*: Canadian Magazine of Immigration, 2017.

There are three ways that refugees get to Canada. The main avenue is through overseas selection in partnership with the UN High Commissioner for Refugees (the United Nations Refugee Agency). This will happen in a refugee camp or in a temporary country of refuge and the selection process will be based on how suitable the refugee is for settlement in Canada. The next most popular method is private sponsorship in which an organization in Canada agrees to sponsor a refugee for resettlement and agrees to support that person financially and socially for a minimum of two years during the resettlement process. It is most frequently Canadian religious organizations or community service clubs that engage in this type of sponsorship. Next, there are inland claims, which are quite rare. This is when a refugee flees directly to Canada and claims refugee status here at a border point. Because of our location on the globe, this is quite rare.

Finally, we should mention the number of international students who come to Canada, and especially to Ontario, to study. In 2015, there were almost 153,000 international students studying in Ontario, bringing an estimated $3.5 billion into the Ontario economy (Canadian Magazine of Immigration, 2016b). This changes the communities inside and around our post-secondary educational institutions in Ontario. For example, 19 percent of the student body at the University of Toronto are international students. Think of the additional considerations for campus security to meet the needs of all of its student body. Important things such as access to translators, education for staff on cultural norms of the cultures represented on campus, and the different perception of security and authority

**Figure 10.2** Canada's Immigration Targets for 2017 by Class of Immigrant

| Canada Immigration Targets 2017 | |
|---|---|
| **Immigration Category** | **Target** |
| Economic | |
| Federal Economic | 73,700 |
| Federal Caregivers | 18,000 |
| Federal Business | 500 |
| Provincial Nominee Program | 51,000 |
| Quebec Skilled Workers and Business | 29,300 |
| Family | |
| Spouses, Partners, and Children | 64,000 |
| Parents and Grandparents | 20,000 |
| Refugees and Humanitarian | |
| Protected Persons in Canada and Dependants Abroad | 15,000 |
| Government-Assisted | 7,500 |
| Blended Visa Office-Referred | 1,500 |
| Privately Sponsored | 16,000 |
| Humanitarian | 3,500 |
| TOTAL | 300,000 |

*Source:* Adapted from Citizenship and Immigration Canada, 2017.

figures that may be embedded in those cultures. Not all cultures perceive security personnel as "helpers"—some cultures may perceive them as a threat.

## The Canadian Human Rights Act and the Canadian Human Rights Commission

There are challenges that come along with all of the richness that is brought to Canada by so much diversity of culture. Differences can cause tension and conflict. This can happen out in the community and manifest itself in forms of violence. It can also happen in the workplace, where it affects the work environment. Fortunately there are laws and processes for dealing with this conflict.

The *Canadian Human Rights Act* (CHRA) prohibits discrimination based on race, national or ethnic origin, colour, religion, age, gender, sexual orientation, marital status, disability, or conviction for an offence for which a pardon has been granted. The agency responsible for enforcing the CHRA is the Canadian Human Rights Commission (CHRC). The CHRC is responsible for developing policies for federally regulated employers such as the Canadian Security Intelligence Service (CSIS), the Canadian Border Services Agency, Canada Post, and the military. These policies secure employees and those served by such employees against discrimination based on prohibited grounds. They develop policies around human resources recruitment and testing, mental health issues in the workplace, harassment in the workplace, and drug testing in the workplace.

If an individual who works in a workplace governed by the CHRA feels that they have been discriminated against based on protected grounds, they can make a complaint to the CHRC and the Commission will investigate and attempt to mediate a solution. If a solution cannot be reached between the employer and the complainant, the complaint will go forward to the Canadian Human Rights Tribunal (CHRT), which is a quasi-judicial board that has the authority to make an adjudicated decision in the case.

Consider the case of *Turner v Canadian Border Services Agency*. Turner had worked seasonally as a customs officer from 1998 to 2003 and had received glowing evaluations from supervisors. He twice applied to an opening for a full-time Customs Inspector position, but was unsuccessful in the competition for the position both times. The first response was that he was "unqualified," although he had been doing the job seasonally for a number of years. The second time he was the only applicant for the position, but was screened out as "ineligible." Turner took his case to the Canadian Human Rights Tribunal, asserting that he was discriminated against due to his age, race, colour, and perceived disability of obesity. The tribunal agreed and compensation was decided on by the tribunal in the 2015 decision.

## The Ontario Human Rights Code and the Ontario Human Rights Commission

The Ontario *Human Rights Code* is provincial law. It mirrors its federal counterpart with some minor differences. It guarantees all people freedom from discrimination in the provision of services, goods, facilities, accommodation, and employment based on age, creed, disability, gender identity and expression, sexual orientation, family and marital status, race and related grounds, receipt of public assistance, and record of offences. The Ontario Human Rights Commission (OHRC) sets policy on things like workplace harassment, drug testing in the workplace, disability and duty to accommodate, policy on creed and accommodation of religious observances, and much more.

If a person in Ontario feels that they have experienced discrimination or harassment, they can make an application to the Human Rights Tribunal of Ontario (HRTO) within one year of the event. The tribunal first offers an opportunity to settle through mediation within 90 days. The case is disclosed to both sides and a mediator is assigned. If a mediated settlement cannot be achieved, the tribunal can hold a hearing and provide an adjudicated decision; however, of the 70 percent of cases that go to mediation, 65 percent are settled at that point.

To give you an idea of volume and types of complaints in the third quarter of 2016 (October through December), the tribunal received 884 applications for adjudication. Of those applications 21.9 percent cited race as the source of discrimination, 16.2 percent colour, 12.2 percent ancestry, 16.3 percent ethnic origin, 54 percent disability, 5.9 percent creed, 4 percent sexual orientation, 10.6 percent family status, 13.1 percent age, 18 percent sexual harassment, and 21 percent fear of reprisal for complaint. These categories do not add up to 100 percent because each complainant can list more than one ground—for example, *Turner*, the case mentioned above, which included disability, age, colour, and race.

For clarity, the term "disability" is defined in section 2 of the *Accessibility for Ontarians with Disabilities Act, 2005* (AODA) as:

In this Act, . . .

"disability" means,
    (a) any degree of physical disability, infirmity, malformation or disfigurement that is caused by bodily injury, birth defect or illness and, without limiting the generality of the foregoing, includes diabetes mellitus, epilepsy, a brain injury, any degree of paralysis, amputation, lack of physical co-ordination, blindness or visual impediment, deafness or hearing impediment, muteness or speech impediment, or physical reliance on a guide dog or other animal or on a wheelchair or other remedial appliance or device,
    (b) a condition of mental impairment or a developmental disability,
    (c) a learning disability, or a dysfunction in one or more of the processes involved in understanding or using symbols or spoken language,
    (d) a mental disorder, or
    (e) an injury or disability for which benefits were claimed or received under the insurance plan established under the *Workplace Safety and Insurance Act, 1997*.

# Implications of Human Rights Legislation for Security Professionals

Human rights legislation is relevant to the work of security professionals in many ways. Discrimination, according to the Ontario *Human Rights Code*, is when a person is deprived of equal access to privileges and opportunities available to others because of prejudice. In the security field, because there will be times when it is your duty to deny access to property or deny entry to premises, it is important that your reasons for denying access are well-articulated and within the bounds of the law so they cannot be misconstrued as discrimination.

Considering that we are all so different and come from such diverse cultural backgrounds, we have to check our own biases to be certain that we are not acting on them in the scope of our employment. For example, do you have your own biases about transgender issues? If, perhaps because you were raised as a strict Catholic, you do have a bias, you must, despite your bias, serve transgendered persons in the scope of your employment with the same respect and decency that you serve everyone else.

Security personnel are also required to support the organization in which they work in its efforts to comply with the AODA. The AODA is legislation that requires many businesses to remove barriers to access. A barrier is anything that prevents a person with a disability from fully participating in all aspects of society because of his or her disability, including a physical barrier, an architectural barrier, an information or communications barrier, an attitudinal barrier, a technological barrier, a policy, or a practice. The AODA requires that all workplaces and venues comply with the standard of accessibility, which means that it may be your job as a security professional to assist in removing barriers to full participation. This may mean keeping ramps clear and unobstructed for the use of patrons with wheelchairs, and ensuring that signage for safety and evacuation routes includes pictures as well as text for those with literacy issues.

Avoiding discrimination is also essential in the recruitment context. If you are considering opening your own security firm, you will need to prepare written job descriptions for hiring staff. When doing so, it is important that you understand that employers have a duty to accommodate and may have to remove non-essential job requirements or adapt or adjust existing job requirements or conditions in order to enable an otherwise qualified person to carry out the essential duties or activities of the job.

If you are applying to a security role as an entry level employee, you should know what your rights are if you require accommodation. If an employer refuses to eliminate a requirement, the employer must justify that decision by proving that it is a **bona fide job requirement**. This means that the requirement is sincerely believed to be necessary to the job; is established in good faith, in an objective sense; and is reasonably necessary to assure the safe, efficient, and economical performance of the job. The onus is on the employer to prove that the requirement is "bona fide."

For example, if an employer were reviewing applications for a security position in a large-scale, multi-storey event centre such as the Air Canada Centre in Toronto, and one of the duties of the position was to be capable of assisting in evacuating thousands of people from the facility in an emergency situation, the employer might take the position that applicants who have a disability that renders them incapable of climbing stairs are not suitable for the position. If you were an applicant who wanted to challenge this position, you could make an application to the HRTO. The employer would then have to prove that the ability to climb stairs is a "bona fide" job requirement and that to adjust the job to accommodate would cause the employer "undue hardship," which is when accommodating the needs of an individual or employee would alter the essential needs of the job so substantially that it would affect the economic viability of the enterprise or present substantial risk. The burden to prove "undue hardship" also lies on the employer. Agencies such as the Canada Border Services Agency have strict physical requirements that have passed through the process and been deemed "bona fide" job requirements. They involve physical strength and stamina tests and the ability to use a firearm, which is deemed essential to the job.

The final important point to address with regard to the Ontario *Human Rights Code* and the OHRC is that they develop guidelines for policy makers in companies and government agencies for the development of harassment policies in the workplace. According to section 10(1) of the Code, "harassment" is "a course of vexatious comment or conduct that is known or *ought reasonably* to be known to be unwelcome" (emphasis added). This addresses how we treat one another in the workplace. The overarching theme is that no individual's rights supersede another's in the workplace, regardless of whether the harassment is based

---

**bona fide job requirement**
a requirement that is sincerely believed to be necessary to the job, is established in good faith, is objective, and is reasonably necessary to assure the safe, efficient, and economical performance of the job

on a protected ground such as, for example, race, colour, or creed. In fact, in November 2011, the beleaguered RCMP, condemned in the media for being rife with human rights complaints, embarked on a very public investigation into its dysfunction in the area of sexual harassment. The investigation revealed that of all the human rights complaints filed by civilian and uniformed members of the RCMP, 44 percent of complaints were filed by women and 49 percent were filed by men. Only 4 percent of complaints were of sexual harassment and 6 percent involved disability or ethnicity. This means that 90 percent of the complaints were complaints of more general harassment, which encompasses bullying, belittling, abuse of authority, and psychological abuse (Civilian Review and Complaints Commission for the RCMP, 2016).

Once again, no one person's rights supersede another's in the workplace. You are in fact *not* free to say what you think or feel if it is hurtful to another person, or if it creates a poisoned work environment. Complaints of harassment in the workplace are very common and it is the duty of the employer to address them. There can be legal repercussions if the employer does not address this type of behaviour and allows a poisoned work environment to develop. It is important before embarking on a career in security (or in any career), that you understand your responsibilities to others in your work environment and that you understand your own rights and the steps to take if your rights are being disregarded.

# Diversity and the Private Security and Investigative Services Act

The *Code of Conduct* created as a regulation under the *Private Security and Investigative Services Act* (PSISA) expresses the obligation of security professionals to treat all persons equally without discrimination based on a person's race, ancestry, place of origin, colour, ethnic origin, citizenship, creed, sex (this includes, as of 2012, gender identity), sexual orientation, age, marital status, family status, or disability. This obligation is listed under section 2(1)(d) of the regulation as it applies to the individual licensee, and under section 3(1)(b) for every licensed business. Breaches of the *Code of Conduct* can result in a guard's security licence being revoked. It can also lead to complaints to the HRTO or the CHRC.

It seems to be common sense that all security professionals would comply with this demand for equal treatment; however, the HRTO has received complaints naming both security guards individually as well as the companies that employ them.

## WHAT WOULD YOU DO?

### Lewis v Sugar Daddys Nightclub

**Case Study:** Caesar Lewis identifies as "transgender neutral questioning transgender male." His application to the Human Rights Tribunal of Ontario arises from an occurrence at Sugar Daddys Nightclub in Toronto on January 4, 2014. Lewis, who is in his twenties, attended the nightclub with three friends. Two of those friends were female and the other identifies as transgender male. After a period of time, the four friends required use of the restroom. The two females used the women's restroom, and Lewis entered the men's restroom as is his custom because he identifies as male, along with the other friend who also identifies as male.

While using a stall in the men's restroom, Lewis heard a loud banging on the door and someone yelling, "Hey, you need to get out of the male restroom." Lewis called out that he was almost done and was coming right out. Seconds later, the cubicle door was forced open and a security guard dragged Lewis out of the cubicle. This incident was witnessed by the washroom attendant, Lewis's friend, and other individuals using the washroom. Lewis's male friend told the security guard that their preference was to use the male washroom and they had the right to make that choice. He asked the security guard to let Lewis go, but the guard would not. Lewis's friend showed the security guard his passport, which gave his legal name before he transitioned, and the guard became outraged. The guard grabbed Lewis by his hair and dragged him through the club and out the front door, making degrading remarks about his sexuality the entire way. Lewis's friend followed him out.

The incident attracted the attention of many people in the club. Using offensive language, three security guards ridiculed the pair of friends, refused to retrieve Lewis's coat from the coat check, and then assaulted Lewis outside the club. The assault was sufficiently severe that Lewis sought medical treatment.

On March 17, 2016, the Tribunal ordered that the respondent to the case (the security company who employed the guards) pay $15,000 as monetary compensation for injury to the dignity of the complainant and interest on that amount from the date of injury. The Tribunal also ordered that the security company, within six months of the ruling, supply human rights training to all of its staff, including security guards, on the issue of gender identity, gender expression, and sexual orientation.

### Question

If you received a complaint at a venue at which you were employed that the incorrect gender was in a restroom, and then during your investigation you discovered that the person was transgendered, how would you defuse the situation in light of the complaint?

# Diversity and Conflict

Sometimes our diversity or differences can cause conflict, particularly when one group feels that their rights have been disregarded, and sometimes this conflict can manifest in the form of protests or **hate crimes**.

With regard to protests, one recent example is that of the emergence of the activist movement "Black Lives Matter." This movement originated in the United States in Ferguson, Missouri after the shooting of Michael Brown by police. Black Lives Matter emerged onto the scene in Ontario in 2016 and became very active following the fatal shooting of Andrew Loku, a black man with mental health issues, at a disturbance in his Toronto apartment building. The Toronto chapter of Black Lives Matter camped outside Toronto Police Service headquarters on March 20, 2016 and remained there for weeks, demanding to meet with Premier Kathleen Wynne. On April 4, 2016, Premier Wynne met with the group on the steps of the Ontario legislature. In July 2016, the group stopped the annual Toronto Gay Pride Parade en route for over an hour, protesting the presence of the Toronto Police in the parade. See Figure 10.3.

In this example, individuals with multiple aspects of diversity are competing for what they perceive to be their rights in an emotionally charged and very public situation. This can become confusing as well as dangerous: we have the voices of concerned black citizens (a visible minority) protesting over police treatment of black citizens in Toronto; the voices of LGBTQ individuals and their supporters celebrating LGBTQ and gender identity rights in the Pride Parade whose celebrations are being impeded by Black Lives Matter; and, finally,

**hate crime**
any offence committed against a person or property that is motivated in whole or in part by hate, bias, or prejudice toward an identifiable group based on real or perceived race, national or ethnic origin, language, colour, religion, sex, age, mental or physical disability, sexual orientation, or any similar factor

### Figure 10.3  Black Lives Matter Shuts Down Toronto Pride Parade

In 2016, Black Lives Matter shut down the Toronto Pride Parade until their demands were met. The group requested a signed agreement that police would not participate in future parades.

Black Lives Matter insisting that the Toronto Police not be permitted in the Pride parade, even though members of the Toronto Police Association "Serving with Pride" (LGBTQ members of the Toronto Police Service) wanted to represent their association in the parade. Emotionally charged situations like this have the potential for violence and destruction of property. Clearly, security contractors and front-line professionals are involved in all aspects of planning and securing these events. Security professionals on the front line need to understand the underlying causes of these conflicts and be skilled in completing their mandate in an unbiased manner to ensure the safety of all involved.

Thankfully, the Toronto Pride Parade continued without violence or damage. However, the situation played out differently in a more recent conflict in Vancouver (CTV News, Vancouver, 2017). In Vancouver, March 27, 2017 was the International Day to Eliminate Racism and Discrimination. A rally was held to bring attention to the issues. NDP member of Parliament Jenny Kwan was in attendance at the rally, which attracted a number of organizations, including the Coalition Against Bigotry, Antifa (anti-fascism activists who consider themselves a militant group to combat racism and discrimination), and the Soldiers of Odin, who opened chapters recently across Canada but originated in Finland as an anti-immigration group that many perceive to be tied to the white supremacist movement. These demonstrators were all very committed to their causes, and emotions were elevated. A fight broke out between members of the groups and Vancouver Police were required to intervene.

The next manifestation of conflict that must be discussed is hate crime (defined above). The world was stunned by the 2016 mass shooting at a gay nightclub in Orlando, Florida, during which 49 people were killed and 53 were left injured. Although Canada has not experienced an event of this scale, the fear it strikes into the hearts of communities when their members are targeted due to race, sexual orientation, ethnicity, or religion is a devastating effect of this type of crime. Statistics indicate that 51 percent of all hate crimes in Canada are directed at racial minorities, 28 percent at religious minorities, and

## SPOT CHECKS AND CARDING

When it comes to articulating the reason you've stopped someone for secondary inspection, a lesson can be taken from the OHRC's ruling on the practice of **carding** in the policing environment. In 2015, the OHRC released its draft regulation, which strictly prohibits the random, arbitrary collection of identifying information by police. The rules under which a person can be stopped and information collected are as follows:

- A police officer must be able to articulate detailed reasons for the stop that ensure it is for gathering information about individuals known or reasonably suspected to be engaged in illegal activities.
- An officer must inform the individual that he or she is not required to remain in the presence of the officer and the officer must explain why the information is requested.
- An officer must provide a document that gives the person the officer's identification, the date and location of the stop, and the reason for the stop. The document must contain the method to be used to file a complaint regarding the stop.

While these rules apply to police, security professionals should consider them to be an important source of guidance for their own decisions when selecting individuals for security screening—for example, when performing bag checks at a concert venue entrance.

**carding**
also known as "street checks," carding is the practice in policing of stopping persons who appear to be suspicious to ask for identification in order to connect potential suspects to criminal activity or to divert criminal activity, particularly in high crime areas

16 percent at LGBTQ people (Allen, 2015). An example of a hate crime would be the arson incident that destroyed a mosque in Peterborough, Ontario following the terrorist attacks in Paris, France in 2015. There were a number of attacks against mosques and Muslim Canadians across the country at that time. These types of crimes are investigated by police in the jurisdiction of the occurrence, and many police services have hate crime units that liaise with one another. Sometimes these incidents drive targeted groups to seek additional security through private sector contracts with security agencies. Hate crime is not limited to property damage and assault. Any crime can be a hate crime if it is motivated by hate or bias toward an identifiable group that is based on race, national or ethnic origin, colour, language, sex, age, sexual orientation, religion, or any similar factor.

It is interesting to note that in the Standing Senate Committee on National Security and Defence's report, "Countering the Terrorist Threat in Canada," it is reported that the majority of the files of the Sûreté du Québec's Division of Investigations on Extremist Threats involve members of extreme right groups operating within Canada (Standing Senate Committee, 2015, pp. 1–2), similar to the example mentioned above with the Soldiers of Odin.

A security professional should be aware that there are sections of the *Criminal Code* that address hate crime beyond acts of violence. Section 318 prohibits advocating or promoting genocide, section 319 prohibits the public incitement and wilful promotion of hatred, and section 430(4.1) addresses damage to property that is motivated by religious discrimination.

# Indigenous People in Canada

The final aspect of conflict that should be discussed is that which arises between Indigenous people and either the government of Canada or private industry. These conflicts typically arise over property and/or natural resources, and can involve non-Indigenous people who, based on environmentalism, support the Indigenous groups. There is a long history of demonstrations and **reclamations** involving Indigenous people fighting for their land and resources. This has frequently led to conflict that involves both the police and private security for large corporations involved in resource extraction on disputed territory.

**reclamation**
a form of political action employed by Indigenous people that involves physical occupation of land under negotiation, barring resource extraction or the entry of outside governments or corporations until negotiations are completed

It is important to understand that section 25 of the *Canadian Charter of Rights and Freedoms* protects Indigenous people's access to land and their rights to assert control over territories held by them. Since there are many claims to land all over Canada because of a century of questionable land purchases by the government, the Charter protects the ongoing process of unraveling who actually has rights to certain parcels of land in Canada.

When the Crown asserts ownership to land, it is generally because the Crown wants to develop the land, sell it to a third party, or sell contracts for resource extraction rights to industry. If an Indigenous group asserts rights to the same land, there is a process of negotiation and often the case must go to court to ascertain who has rights to the land and who has the right to make decisions about resource extraction. See Figure 10.4.

These cases take a very long time—sometimes as much as 30 years or more—to complete. If resource extraction continues during that time, the land sometimes becomes degraded so that it can't be used anymore or the people living on the land may be adversely affected by the industry. The land claims process in Canada aims for a lawful, fair resolution with consultation on both sides. If the process is not fair or if resources are being extracted while negotiations are ongoing, there may be a reclamation: Indigenous people may seize physical control of the land, barring resource extraction until a fair negotiation continues. These situations are complex and involve millions of dollars in resources as well as volatile emotions on all sides. Security professionals are often on the front lines, including police, ministry of transport officers, CN Rail police, and private industry security contractors. When placed in this situation, security professionals must be aware of all aspects of the conflict and be fair and patient, understanding that there is a process to resolve the dispute and a mandatory duty to consult with Indigenous people.

### Figure 10.4  Elsipogtog First Nation Faces Off with RCMP

Elsipogtog First Nation faces off with RCMP in anti-fracking demonstration. They had been blocking access to their land by Southwestern Energy Corporation, a US energy giant from Texas, to prevent shale gas extraction.

# Racial Profiling

The final discussion in this text must address an issue that is constantly in the news in Ontario and across Canada that affects all law enforcement fields and the entire security industry. This is the issue of **racial profiling**. The specific sections of the Charter that are at stake when we talk about racial profiling are:

- Section (6)(1): Every citizen of Canada has the right to enter, remain in, and leave Canada (this affects the Canada Border Services Agency).
- Section 7: Everyone has the right to life, liberty, and security of the person and the right not to be deprived thereof except in accordance with the principles of fundamental justice.
- Section 8: Everyone has the right to be secure against unreasonable search and seizure.
- Section 9: Everyone has the right not to be arbitrarily detained or imprisoned.

The Ontario Court of Appeal decision in the case of *R v Richards* introduced the following definition of racial profiling:

> Racial profiling is criminal profiling based on race. Racial or colour profiling refers to that phenomenon whereby certain criminal activity is attributed to an identified group in society on the basis of race or colour resulting in the targeting of individual members of that group. In this context, race is illegitimately used as a proxy for the criminality or general criminal propensity of an entire racial group (*R v Richards*, para. 24).

In 2017, the Ontario Human Rights Commission completed its research report entitled "Under Suspicion: Research and Consultation Report on Racial Profiling in Ontario." In the consultation process the Commission analyzed complaints to the HRTO that involved racial profiling, conducted a wide-ranging survey, and held community consultation with organizations representing people of diversity. Overall, more than 1,600 people provided information to the Commission during its research. Figure 10.5 shows the reported incidence of racial profiling among survey respondents by racial or ethnic background.

**racial profiling**
the selection of an individual for screening or questioning for purported security reasons where the selection is influenced by stereotypes about race, colour, ethnicity, ancestry, religion, or place of origin rather than on reasonable suspicion

**Figure 10.5** The Experience of Racial Profiling in Canada by Racial or Ethnic Background

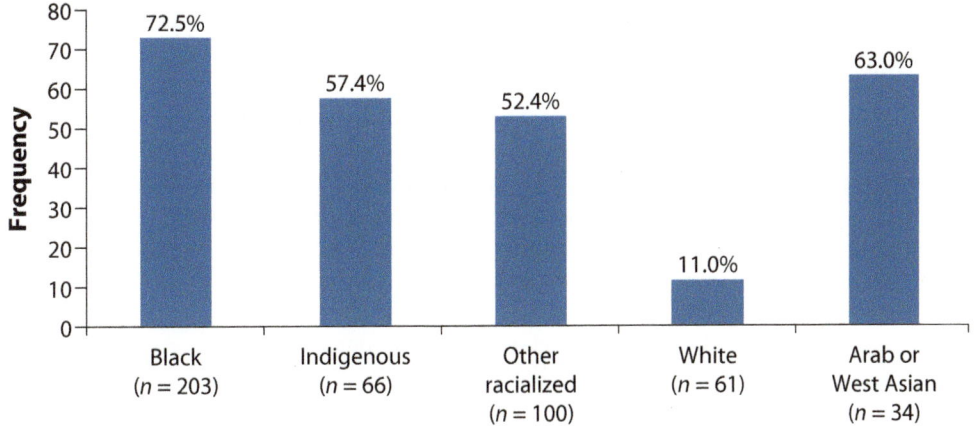

*Source*: Ontario Human Rights Commission, 2017, p. 20.

**Figure 10.6** The Effects of Racial Profiling by Quantity of Experiences

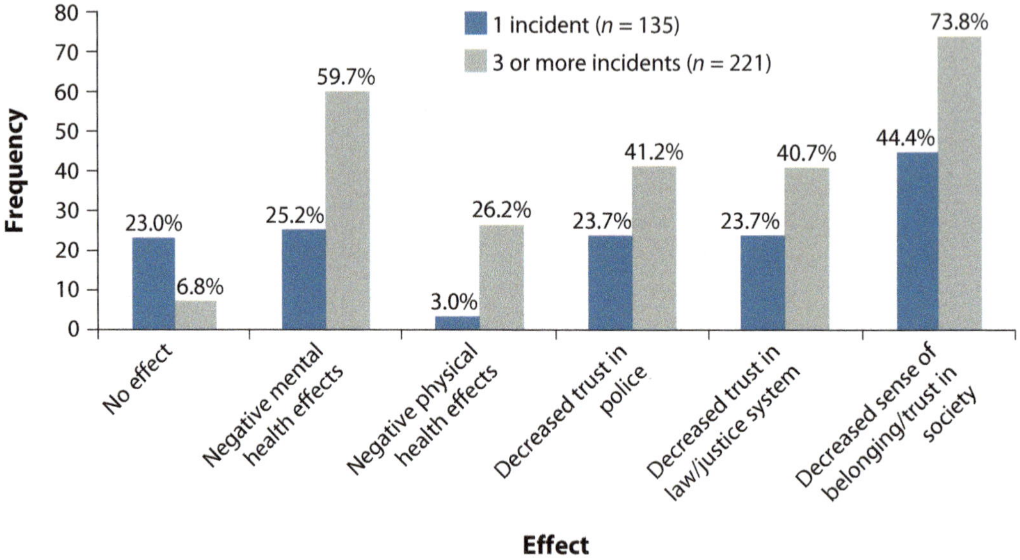

| Effect | 1 incident (n = 135) | 3 or more incidents (n = 221) |
|---|---|---|
| No effect | 23.0% | 6.8% |
| Negative mental health effects | 25.2% | 59.7% |
| Negative physical health effects | 3.0% | 26.2% |
| Decreased trust in police | 23.7% | 41.2% |
| Decreased trust in law/justice system | 23.7% | 40.7% |
| Decreased sense of belonging/trust in society | 44.4% | 73.8% |

*Source*: Ontario Human Rights Commission, 2017, p. 26.

We can all agree that when an individual feels that they have been targeted by racial profiling there is an adverse effect on both the person and the community with which that person identifies. Figure 10.6 above shows the reported effects of racial profiling by number of reported incidents over a 12-month period.

When asked about the sectors of society where racial profiling was taking place, there were a wide range of responses, including reference to barriers to education and housing. This shows that law enforcement is not alone as a perceived user of racial profiling. Not surprisingly, respondents most frequently cited police as the profilers, but National Security and Intelligence accounted for 6.5 percent of the incidents, private security accounted for 18.3 percent of the incidents, and transportation providers (including transport security) accounted for 26.6 percent of incidents (Ontario Human Rights Commission, 2017, p. 27).

## Security Spotlight

### R v Smith

As an illustration of how racial profiling works, consider the case of *R v Smith* (it will be useful to read the entire case; see the References to this chapter).

Ms. Smith was born in Jamaica but is now a Canadian citizen. She is black and she claimed that she was selected based on her race for secondary inspection by customs agents when landing in Toronto Pearson Airport in 2001, after returning from a March break trip to Jamaica with her son. Inspector Soifer was the customs agent at the primary inspection booth. Soifer asked the common questions: the purpose of her travel, where she stayed, and what she was bringing back. She examined her travel itinerary, passport, and documents. Soifer referred Smith to secondary inspection based on a number of indicators that she referred to later in court:

1. Ms. Smith's ticket was purchased just before travel;
2. the ticket was paid for in cash;

3. in the months before Ms. Smith's trip, a number of people who purchased tickets at Mirabel Travel were found to be transporting drugs;
4. when she asked Ms. Smith if she lived near the travel agency, she received no response;
5. Ms. Smith avoided eye contact; and
6. Ms. Smith said she went to visit family, but stayed in a guest house.

Ms. Smith denied that she was asked any questions by Soifer, and asserts that the questioning was fabricated by Soifer after the allegation of racial profiling was made by her legal representative.

Meanwhile, members of Canada Customs' Flexible Response Team were "roving" Ms. Smith's flight, as there had been a number of drug seizures on this flight in the past. Team members were present between the primary inspection booth and the luggage pickup, speaking to as many passengers as possible, watching for suspicious activity, and selecting passengers for secondary inspection. Inspector Boon spoke to Ms. Smith and examined her documents. She also targeted Ms. Smith for secondary inspection, independent of Inspector Soifer's selection, by making a written indication on her declaration card. Her reasons were based on the following:

1. Ms. Smith's ticket was purchased at Mirabel Travel;
2. the ticket was purchased shortly before travel;
3. she said she stayed in a villa when she was visiting her family; and
4. the person who bought the ticket did not travel with Ms. Smith.

Ms. Smith denies being asked questions by Inspector Boon, asserting again that Inspector Boon's decision to send her to secondary inspection was based on race. During inspection of Ms. Smith's luggage it was found that a pair of shoes in Ms. Smith's luggage as well as the pair of shoes on her feet contained cocaine.

Had Ms. Smith's legal representative been successful in making the argument that the secondary inspection was based on racial profiling, which contravenes the Charter, he would next have applied to have the evidence of the cocaine discovery excluded from trial. In this case, however, after considering numerous case precedents, the court concluded that both customs inspectors had valid and documented reasons apart from race to refer Ms. Smith for secondary inspection.

The lesson from this case is clear: As a security professional, if you are selecting someone to "keep an eye on" and stop in a store on suspicion of shoplifting, or if you are selecting someone to conduct a more thorough search of his or her coat or purse before allowing the person entry to a venue, you must be certain that you are not selecting that person based on prohibited grounds, particularly race. Your reason for selecting a person needs to be well-documented at the time of the stop, and those reasons may come under scrutiny later on in court.

## CHAPTER SUMMARY

In conclusion, Canadians are diverse. If we are not Indigenous, somewhere back in our family history, someone immigrated here. We chose a policy of multiculturalism for our country and we celebrate our diversity: we choose to view our diversity as a strength and we should be proud of that. But we must also be aware that our diversity can sometimes lead to conflict in the workplace, in our communities, and across our country.

This chapter introduced the human rights laws and processes that have been created to assist individuals and companies in avoiding discrimination and in navigating conflict when it arises. It also touched on the obligation of security professionals to respect diversity as required by the *Code of Conduct* established under the PSISA.

Also introduced were the issues raised when groups with differing rights and agendas come into conflict—for example, when protest groups disrupt public events to draw attention to injustice, or when Indigenous groups seek to block the extraction of natural resources while a land claim is being resolved.

Finally, the chapter introduced the problems of hate crime and racial profiling, both of which have important implications for the security profession.

Security professionals are often called upon to assist in the resolution of conflicts and ensure the safety of all involved, whether the conflict is a simple disagreement between two co-workers, or a complex and politically charged conflict. It is important that security professionals educate themselves about the issues involved and be aware at all times of the laws, policies, and processes that can be used as tools to resolve conflict. If we use these tools well, we can continue to work, play, and prosper as Canadians in a fair and just society.

## KEY TERMS

bona fide job requirement, 193

carding, 197

hate crime, 195

reclamation, 197

racial profiling, 199

## REFERENCES

*Accessibility for Ontarians with Disabilities Act, 2005*, SO 2005, c 11.

Allen, M. (2015). Police-reported hate crime in Canada, 2013. *Juristat*. Catalogue No. 85-002-X. Retrieved from http://www.statcan.gc.ca/pub/85-002-x/2015001/article/14191-eng.htm

*Canadian Bill of Rights*, SC 1960, c 44.

*Canadian Charter of Rights and Freedoms*, Part I of the *Constitution Act, 1982*, being Schedule B to the *Canada Act 1982* (UK), 1982, c 11.

*Canadian Human Rights Act*, RSC 1985, c H-6.

Canadian Magazine of Immigration. (2016a). Canada: Immigration by source country 2015. Retrieved from http://canadaimmigrants.com/canada-immigration-by-source-country-2015/

Canadian Magazine of Immigration. (2016b). Ontario international students by country (2015). Retrieved from http://canadaimmigrants.com/ontario-international-students-country-2015/

Canadian Magazine of Immigration. (2017). Canada: Immigrants by source country—2016. Retrieved from http://canadaimmigrants.com/canada-immigrants-by-source-country-2016/

Citizenship and Immigration Canada. (2017). Notice—Supplementary information 2017 immigration levels plan. Retrieved from http://www.cic.gc.ca/english/department/media/notices/2016-10-31.asp

Civilian Review and Complaints Commission for the RCMP. (2016, June 24). *Public interest investigation report into issues of workplace harassment within the Royal Canadian Mounted Police*. Retrieved from https://www.crcc-ccetp.gc.ca/en/public-interest-investigation-report-issues-workplace-harassment-within-royal-canadian-mounted

*Code of Conduct*, O Reg 363/07.

*Criminal Code*, RSC 1985, c C-46.

CTV News, Vancouver. (2017, March 27). Conflicting stories following violence at anti-racism rally. Retrieved from http://bc.ctvnews.ca/conflicting-stories-following-violence-at-anti-racism-rally-1.3343428

*Human Rights Code*, RSO 1990, c H.19.

*Immigration Act*, SC 2001, c 27.

*Lewis v Sugar Daddys Nightclub*, 2016 HRTO 347.

Ontario Human Rights Commission. (2017). *Under suspicion: Research and consultation report on racial profiling in Ontario*. Retrieved from http://www.ohrc.on.ca/en/under-suspicion-research-and-consultation-report-racial-profiling-ontario/3-what-we-heard

*Private Security and Investigative Services Act, 2005*, SO 2005, c 34.

*R v Richards*, 1999 CanLII 1602 (Ont CA).

*R v Smith*, 2004 CanLII 46666 (Ont SC).

Standing Senate Committee on National Security and Defence [Standing Senate Committee]. (2015). *Countering the terrorist threat in Canada: An interim report*. Retrieved from http://publications.gc.ca/collections/collection_2015/sen/yc33-0/YC33-0-412-18-eng.pdf

*Turner v Canadian Border Services Agency*, 2015 CHRT 10.

United Nations High Commissioner for Refugees, United Nations Refugee Agency [UNHCR]. (2016, June 20). Figures at a glance. Retrieved from http://www.unhcr.org/figures-at-a-glance.html

## PERFORMANCE APPLICATION

### Multiple Choice

1. A security guard who prohibits a person from entering a premises that is ordinarily open to the public because of that person's ethnic or racial identity:

    a. is committing an offence under the *Criminal Code*

    b. is acting in violation of human rights law

    c. is legally authorized to do so as long as the property is privately owned and he/she is an agent of the owner

    d. is legally authorized to do so if he or she has reasonable grounds to believe that the person poses a threat to security

    e. must provide the person with notice of the reasons for the prohibition

2. Canada subscribes to an ideology of

    a. pluralism

    b. multiculturalism

    c. assimilationist

    d. ethnist

    e. civics

3. Sneha is 40 years old and is immigrating to Canada from India. She has over $500,000 to invest and intends to open a business importing goods from India. She already runs an export business from India that her brother will run in

her absence. Sneha intends to bring her husband and two teenage children to Canada once she gets settled. Which class will Sneha immigrate under, and which class will her children immigrate under?

   a. economic class/family class
   b. refugee/humanitarian
   c. economic class/student visa
   d. economic class/humanitarian
   e. economic class/economic class

4. After reviewing the legislation discussed in this chapter, which statutes prohibit organizations from discriminating against a person on the basis of ethnicity, colour, religion, place of origin, citizenship, disability, and other grounds?

   a. the *Canadian Human Rights Act*
   b. the Ontario *Human Rights Code*
   c. the *Canadian Charter of Rights and Freedoms*
   d. the *Code of Conduct* under the *Private Security and Investigation Services Act*
   e. all of the above

5. In the Standing Senate Committee on National Security and Defence's 2015 report "Countering the Terrorist Threat in Canada" it is reported that the majority of the files of the Sûreté du Québec's Division of Investigations on Extremist Threats involve:

   a. ISIS (the Islamic State of Iraq and Syria)
   b. indigenous activists and eco-terrorists
   c. the extreme right
   d. al Qaeda
   e. Liberation Tigers of Tamil

6. The Human Rights Commission recently concluded a study on racial profiling. The area where people reported they experienced the greatest amount of racial profiling was with:

   a. police
   b. national security and intelligence
   c. private security
   d. transportation
   e. housing

7. Under the *Accessibility for Ontarians with Disabilities Act, 2005*, which of the following qualifies as a disability under the Act?

   a. partial paralysis
   b. blindness
   c. mental illness
   d. inability to read
   e. all of the above

8. If there is a barrier to employment for a person with a disability, such as the requirement to be able to climb stairs, the employer has a duty to accommodate by removing this barrier if possible so that the person can be employed. Sometimes the barrier cannot be removed, in which case it is referred to as:

   a. undue hardship
   b. a bona fide job requirement
   c. harassment
   d. a barrier
   e. vexatious

## Short Answer

Research the current dispute in the United States at Standing Rock North Dakota over the Dakota Access Pipeline. Then research the Elsipogtog First Nation of New Brunswick anti-fracking demonstrations. Consider the underlying environmental issues as well as the issues that involve the safety and viability of the First Nations communities affected by this development. Compare and contrast the US and Canadian handling of the matters. Give suggestions on how to minimize the risks as a security provider for the corporations involved.

# Use of Force Theory 11

| | |
|---|---|
| Introduction .................................. 206 | |
| **Legal Authority and an Employer's Use of Force Policy Choices** ............... 206 | |
| **Canadian Association of Chiefs of Police (CACP) National Use of Force Framework** ............................... 208 | |
|    The Continuous Assessment Process .......... 209 | |
|    Taking Control, Assessing a Subject's Behaviour, and Choosing a Response .................. 209 | |
|    Identifying a Person in Distress ............... 209 | |
|    Matching Response to Behaviour ............. 210 | |
|    Soft and Hard Compliance Techniques ........ 210 | |
|    Lethal Force ................................ 211 | |
| **The Framework in Action** .................... 211 | |
| **Potential Consequences of the Use of Force** 213 | |
| **Handling a Subject in Distress** ............... 214 | |
|    Responding to Excited Delirium .............. 214 | |
|    Responding to Positional Asphyxia ............ 214 | |
| **Consequences of the Use of Weapons** ...... 215 | |
| **Chapter Summary** ......................... 215 | |
| **Key Terms** ................................. 216 | |
| **References** ................................ 216 | |
| **Performance Application** ................... 216 | |

## LEARNING OUTCOMES

When you have completed this chapter, you will:

- Understand the CACP National Use of Force Framework.
- Be able to explain the potential legal consequences of the use of force and understand how courts are likely to interpret a security professional's actions/inactions.
- Understand the wide variation of use of force protocols in place in the security sector.

# Introduction

When a security professional is presented with a situation that may require use of force intervention, the guard needs to understand his or her role in this event. The guard's primary responsibility is to life and property, in that order. The responsibility to life includes the life of the security guard, the subject of interest, and anyone else that may be in the immediate vicinity. The security guard is neither expected nor required to put their life in danger for another person. The guard's role is to assess and then attempt to de-escalate the situation.

In order to accomplish this, the guard must be aware that he or she is playing a reactive role in the scenario. This means that the guard will be reacting to the suspect's actions, body language, and verbal communications. This does not mean that the guard has no means to affect the subject's actions. Through communication (sometimes referred to as tactical communication or "tac com") that is initiated immediately after the guard arrives at the scene, the guard will attempt to influence the subject's actions.

If a guard arrives at a scene alone and the situation seems volatile, then backup must be requested immediately, before the need arises. An important part of the assessment process is the guard participating in direct, active verbal communication with the suspect. To de-escalate a situation, the guard needs to slow things down, use a low-volume voice, ensure eye contact is made, ask questions, and make requests. The **Canadian Association of Chiefs of Police** (CACP) **National Use of Force Framework** ("the Framework") (CACP, 2000) is designed to aid and guide the officer in making decisions that are reasonable, based in common sense, and, most importantly, justified (for a summary of what constitutes justification for use of force, see the On the Job feature below). The process of working within the guidelines of the National Use of Force Framework will be covered in detail in this chapter.

**Canadian Association of Chiefs of Police (CACP)**
an organization led by high-ranking law enforcement officials who created the National Use of Force Framework model and continue to work on improving use of force protocols and advises the government by making recommendations

**National Use of Force Framework**
a guideline that has been implemented across Canada in public and private security sectors that helps security professionals understand use of force by enabling them to visualize the process

# Legal Authority and an Employer's Use of Force Policy Choices

As discussed in Chapter 8, it is critical for security sector professionals to understand *when* they have authorization under the law to implement their use of force practices under the *Private Security and Investigative Services Act, 2005* (often referred to as the "PSISA"). This chapter will focus more on *how* to implement use of force practices.

---

**ON THE JOB**

### Justification for the Use of Force

A person is generally considered to be legally justified in their actions if they have fulfilled the *Criminal Code* requirements of acting on reasonable and probable grounds, are either authorized or required to act with nothing personal to gain, and use only as much force as necessary (see sections 25 and 494 of the Code).

Every security professional is subject to the application of sections 25 and 494 of Canada's *Criminal Code*. As discussed in the previous chapter, these provisions pertain to the protection of persons acting under authority, and the arrest without warrant by any person (sometimes colloquially known as the "citizen's power of arrest"), respectively. However, within these broad guidelines there is variation among security organizations about what protocols they have in place with regard to which use of force methods they require their personnel to use.

The standards that will be followed in specific situations are determined based on a number of factors. These can include whether or not the personnel are providing direct/in-house or third-party services, whether or not private property and legislation such as the *Trespass to Property Act* or similar provincial legislation is applicable, and, finally, a standard liability risk assessment may be carried out by the security organization to calculate the potential harm done by allowing theft to occur versus allowing their personnel to implement use of force protocols.

Contract security companies as well as proprietary in-house security organizations will often err on the side of caution by creating policies and guidelines that prescribe forcible methods and actions that fall short of the limits provided in the *Criminal Code*. This is a risk analysis outcome designed to protect the company from costly lawsuits or criminal prosecution.

Generally speaking, avoiding the use of force will take precedence in almost every setting that involves material loss or property damage. An exception to this rule involves private investigators who work in a close-protection capacity (as body guards) where there is a level of threat that has been calculated and the guards are experienced, trained, and briefed on the anticipated threat. Specialized equipment such as batons, tasers, and firearms may be available for security work at this level.

Because factors in the chosen type of service provision model will influence use-of-force policies, it is important for security personnel to know not only what use of force is legally permissible under the law, but also what is requested and required under their organizational training and standards. Most security guards are instructed that an organization would rather absorb losses and/or liability due to theft than liability for an excessive force complaint under section 26 of the *Criminal Code*. This is discussed in more detail later in the chapter.

## ON THE JOB

### The Type of Service Provision Model Can Influence Use of Force Policies

Direct/in-house security models are those in which an individual or organizational entity secures their own liabilities (this means they field their own security force) and fields a team of security professionals who are a part of their organization. Organizational guidelines may result in these security professionals having increased ability to implement use-of-force options.

By contrast, some individuals or organizational entities contract with third-party services: a separate individual or organizational entity brought in to secure their liabilities and to field a team of security professionals. Because of the nature of this arrangement, use of force options for these security professionals may be limited.

## Security Spotlight

### Organizational Training and Standards

Organizational standards and guidelines are typically drafted in language more specific than the broader *Criminal Code* limitations on the use of force. They are entity- or operation-specific, and all security professionals must be aware that in addition to acting within the legal authority of the Code, they must also be able to apply their training and comply with the requirements established by their employers.

# Canadian Association of Chiefs of Police (CACP) National Use of Force Framework

In Canada both the public security and private security sectors rely on the National Use of Force Framework (see Figure 11.1) created by the Canadian Association of Chiefs of Police (CACP, 2000).

**Figure 11.1** National Use of Force Framework

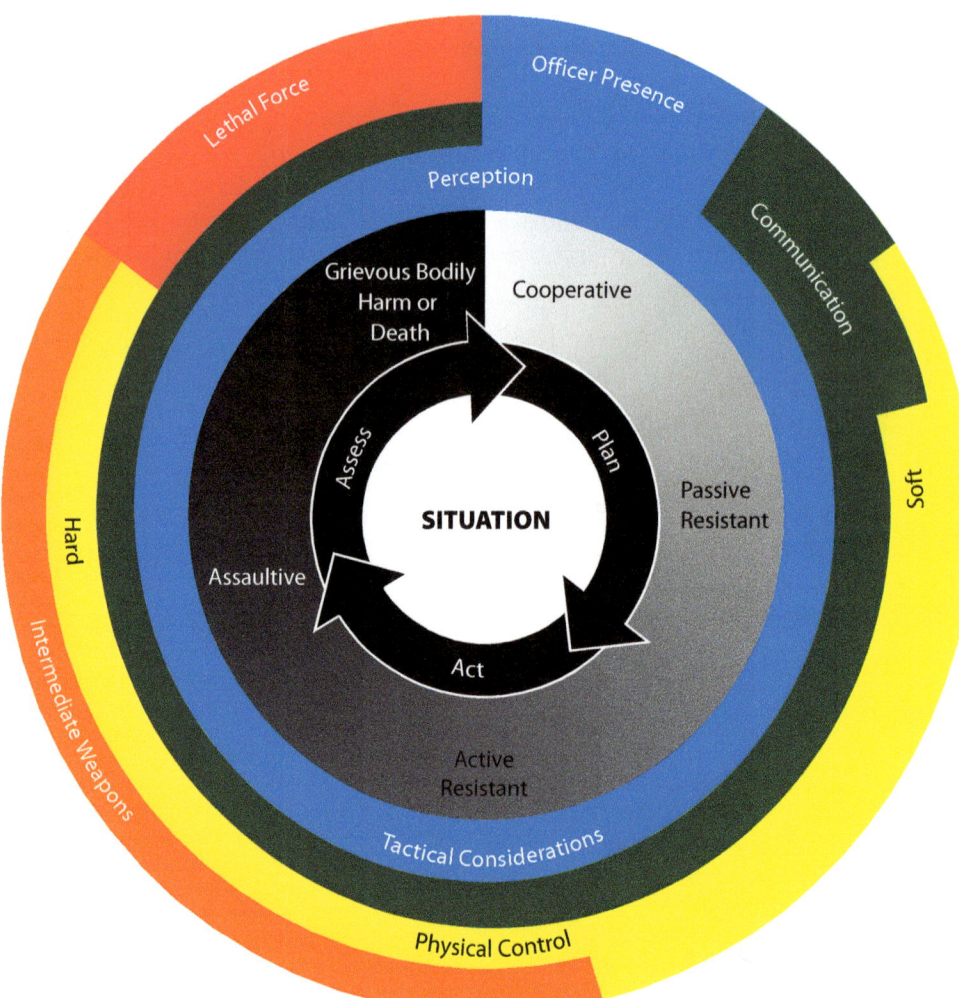

## The Continuous Assessment Process

The guiding principle behind the creation of the National Use of Force Framework model is that the security environment is so unpredictable and potentially volatile that only continuous assessment by a security professional trained to be able to assess a situations and take the initiative to implement the Framework is enough to keep up with quickly developing scenarios. This **continuous assessment process** is critical because a security professional must determine how to react to instantaneous changes in a situation. Often, situations escalate quickly. When a security professional is present at a situation, he or she must assess both the overall situation and the subject's behaviours. This assessment will allow the security professional to understand what they see and perceive, and evaluate tactical considerations and potential responses.

## Taking Control, Assessing a Subject's Behaviour, and Choosing a Response

Upon arrival at a scene or at the beginning of a situation, it is important to immediately take control and begin to de-escalate the situation. If this is done, the security professional will become the **person of authority**. It is critical that the process of de-escalation begin immediately. This is accomplished by determining the subject's position on the subject behaviour circle (the white, grey, and black ring in the Framework (CACP, n.d.)). The next step is to initiate the appropriate response.

A situation may continue to escalate—for example, a subject may progress from the cooperative category in the Framework directly into the assault category—if this happens, the security professional must adjust his or her reaction, switching from simply communicating with the subject to communicating and considering the use of hard physical controls or intermediate weapons in their response.

Alternatively, a subject who began by actively resisting compliance (which would justify the guard to initiate physical control) may suddenly become cooperative, which would require the security professional to revert to simple communication (tac com).

These fast-developing situations are why it is stated clearly at the bottom of the Framework that "[t]he officer continuously assesses the situation and acts in a reasonable manner to ensure officer and public safety." Each time a guard makes a verbal comment or request, the situation will change. This is why the guard must "re-assess, re-plan, and re-act." This three-step process (assess, plan, act) is perpetual. It must be implemented immediately upon arrival at the scene of a situation, and must not terminate until the event concludes. This principle is visually represented in the Framework by the continuous inner circle formed by the black arrows "Assess," "Plan," and "Act" (see Figure 11.1).

## Identifying a Person in Distress

Part of a security professional's assessment must be to question and determine whether the subject is under the influence of mind-altering substances or may be a **person in distress** suffering from a mental health crisis. In addition to that determination, the guard must be constantly assessing the subject's body language and observing the subject's actions.

A state of distress does not excuse the subject's behaviour, but it may mean there are additional avenues of communication that should be attempted in efforts to **de-escalate** a situation, or to resolve it without using force. If a guard does suspect that a person may be in distress, back-up and/or medical personnel should be contacted as soon as possible and the

---

**continuous assessment process**
the procedure used by security professionals to fully comprehend a possibly quickly changing security environment and situation: many factors are present at a scene that could affect the outcome and using this system ensures that the security professional is able to react appropriately within the National Use of Force Framework

**person of authority**
a person authorized by the *Criminal Code* to do anything in the administration or enforcement of the law—in most cases, refers to individuals who are peace officers or whose actions fall under the PSISA

**person in distress**
an individual suffering from a mental crisis that can include but is not limited to someone suffering a schizophrenic episode or having a flashback related to post-traumatic stress disorder

**de-escalate**
the approach used to try to resolve a security issue with a subject without resorting to force; normally accomplished through constant verbal communication and evaluation of the subject's body language

guard must continue communication by asking questions related to the subject's condition. These questions can be addressed to the subject directly, or to anyone else in the immediate vicinity who may know the subject or may have observed something relevant to the situation.

## Matching Response to Behaviour

As described above, it is important for security professionals to understand that their behaviour response (see the coloured outer circles of the Framework in Figure 11.1) must correspond to the situation and the behaviour of the subject (refer to the black and white inner circles). The Framework diagram demonstrates that security personnel must be able and willing to communicate with the subject at all times and must consider their perception of the situation and what potential tactical considerations are available to them.

Not only are these tactical considerations guided by the process laid out in the Framework, but, as mentioned above, they are contingent on the specific protocols put into place by the security organization that the security professional is working for. A straightforward example of this is demonstrated by the kinds of equipment and subsequent training provided to security personnel. Most private security professionals will not be armed with weapons of any kind and will instead rely on **soft and hard compliance techniques** for physical control when employing use of force. A few may have **intermediate (less-lethal) weapons** such as tasers and batons, and a very few others will be given actual firearms in order to more easily engage in **lethal force**.

## Soft and Hard Compliance Techniques

Soft and hard compliance techniques are physical controls and restraints placed on a subject by a security professional. Techniques can range from gently guiding individuals by the shoulder when they are trespassing on private property to forcefully moving the subject to the ground so that restraint equipment can be placed on them. Most of the time these less drastic use of force responses do not lead to permanent harm or injury to subjects. However, as discussed later in the chapter, it is important for all security professionals to keep in mind the potential consequences of any use of force techniques.

Intermediate weapons, classified as "less-lethal" equipment by public safety organizations, usually include those that can help security professionals respond to subjects when active and assaultive incidents arise. This equipment can include but is not limited to batons and tasers. Tasers are electronic devices that provide an electrical shock that is meant to incapacitate a subject and minimize resistance.

**soft and hard compliance techniques** unarmed methods for a security professional to physically control and restrain a subject

**intermediate (less-lethal) weapons** tools that essentially make security personnel lightly armed; can include tasers and batons—it is possible for these weapons to apply lethal force but they are less lethal than firearms

**lethal force** the option of last resort for security professionals that is used when an assessment demands that the threat a subject poses be eliminated immediately; this response is only readily available to public safety security personnel such as peace officers who are issued firearms; sometimes referred to as deadly force

### Security Spotlight

#### Expanded Use of Force Powers for the Protection of Nuclear Power Facilities

Most examples in this chapter discuss the limitations on the use of force that private security professionals can act under and how most organizations would rather deal with the liability of theft than the liability of an excessive force complaint. However, there are exceptions to this within Ontario where private security organizations have increased their use-of-force mandates. A lot of Ontario's power generation comes from nuclear power. Because of the sensitive nature of the material on these premises, they are heavily fortified through the use of screening procedures and guarded by a privately employed tactical team. Their use of force and training are more closely matched to the Toronto Police Service's Emergency Task Force (ETF), known elsewhere as Special Weapons and Tactics (SWAT).

## Security Spotlight

### Minimal Force Is the Norm in Retail Security

A more typical example than the one above of how security professionals implement use of force is the protocol for many plainclothes theft and loss prevention personnel. Usually, in retail security if a guard observes a subject committing a violation they are not to engage with them in any meaningful way but to merely annotate the time, location, and type of offence of the incident. They are then to submit this information to a peace officer. Alternatively, there is allowance made to call for a peace officer to respond to the offence and then to detain the person in order to turn over custody to the responding officer. Generally speaking, at no point is the theft and loss prevention professional supposed to use anything but soft and hard techniques to gain compliance.

## Lethal Force

Lethal force, sometimes referred to as deadly force, needs to be legally justified, as do all levels of force used. When confronted with deadly force, an officer must take into consideration *all other options*, including withdrawing from the situation to regroup. Unfortunately, in the security sector it is sometimes necessary to take a subject's life. This is usually the result of the subject being armed and/or threatening the lives of security personnel and/or the public. When public and private sector security personnel have greater access to this option it is usually provided through access to firearms.

Again, it is important to stress that all of these potential levels of response rely on understanding and assessing the behaviour of the subject, their level of cooperation (or lack thereof and the level of resistance), the legal authority of sections 25 and 494 of the *Criminal Code*, and the more specific guidelines issued by the security organization to its personnel.

## The Framework in Action

By referencing the National Use of Force Framework model, a step-by-step process can be determined. First, security professionals always place themselves at the centre of the model in any situation. Next, after assessing the subject, a straight line is drawn from the centre of the situation to the outer circle of the model, cutting through any observed subject behaviour. Anywhere this line intersects identifies options for use of force that can be used by the security professional.

As an example, we begin in the centre of the model, the "situation." The security professional may have been summoned to the location, or he or she may have happened upon it while making rounds. Either way, the guard now finds himself or herself in the situation. At this point it is important to note that many situations are resolved simply by the security professional arriving at the situation in a clean professional uniform, representing a "person in authority," taking charge of the situation, and communicating with the subject.

As indicated by the green circle, "communication" is initiated at "officer presence" (first arrival at the situation) and continues until the situation is concluded. The Framework shows us this: we can see that the green circle continues all the way around the model, so regardless of what "subject behaviour" we are confronted with, our straight line will always intersect communication.

If the situation persists, we continue on to "assess." The process of assessment is threefold. It involves assessing first the situation and the subject behaviours, and then the security professional's "perception/tactical considerations." How the guard will react to the situation is directly influenced by the characteristics of the situation (environment, number of subjects, potential attack signs, perceived subject abilities, knowledge of subject) and the subject behaviours (cooperative, passive resistant, active resistant, assaultive, or grievous bodily harm/death). After assessing these two categories, the guard must make a plan and act. The plan and action are directly dependent on the guard's perception of his or her personal abilities. Perception is how each individual guard perceives the situation, based on his or her personal strengths, weaknesses, and beliefs. This is why different guards confronted with similar situations react differently and are still justified in their actions. Each time a security professional "acts," the situation changes, so the security professional must continue the process of "assess, plan, and act" over and over until the situation is concluded.

Subject behaviours can and will change in the course of a situation. Changes in the situation will be influenced by the security professional's communication and interaction. There are five subject behaviours in the grey and white circle. They are listed in order of escalating violence, beginning at the one o'clock position. "Cooperative" is the desired goal; if there is no cooperation, then achieving cooperation becomes the goal. The next category, moving in a clockwise direction, is passive resistant. This is where the subject is ignoring your requests and commands to comply. The subject is not being aggressive by coming at you, but is ignoring you, hoping you will just go away. If you attempt to use soft physical controls, the subject will pull away but will not engage with you aggressively.

In the six o'clock position we escalate to active resistant. At this point, the subject is initiating contact. He may be using offensive language and is beginning to be aggressive (pushing, touching, pointing, poking). This activity can easily escalate to the assaultive level. At that level, the subject commits to fighting. This can involve kicks, punches, slaps, grabs, and strikes.

The most volatile subject behaviour is that which amounts to lethal force. Actions at this level are likely to cause serious bodily harm or death.

Although the subject behaviours in the Framework run in a clockwise, ever-increasing level of violence, and although it is common for a subject's actions to follow this pattern of escalation, it is important for the security professional to realize that subject behaviours can be volatile, changing dramatically with little notice. For example, upon arrival at a situation, a security professional may observe the subject to be passive resistant. However, if something is said that upsets the subject, he may suddenly escalate to assaultive. The guard's communications may succeed in returning the subject to a cooperative state. This is why security professionals must continually assess, plan, and act.

Once we have determined the subject behaviours, our imaginary straight line from the centre of the situation that passes through the subject behaviour will intersect with our options of action. These are the two outer circles coloured yellow and orange on the Framework in Figure 11.1. Lethal force, the short red section in the Framework, will be discussed below.

At this point, as indicated in the yellow circle, we have options of action known as soft and hard physical control. These options do not involve any weapons or tools; instead, they involve techniques to control a subject and get that person to comply. Soft techniques have a lower probability of causing injury. These methods include arm holds, joint locks, and handcuffing.

If soft physical control is not an option, it may be necessary to use hard physical control. This involves a higher probability of injury to the subject. Hard physical controls include kicks, punches, and strikes. The decision as to what kind of physical control a security professional will use is directly related to subject behaviour and the security professional's strengths (perception in the blue section of the Framework).

The outer orange circle of the Framework gives the security professional the option to use intermediate weapons. These weapons are not intended to cause **serious bodily harm** or death. Intermediate weapons available to security professionals include batons, pepper spray, and conducted electrical weapons, more commonly referred to as tasers. Employers who equip their security personnel with any of these devices are required to provide access to training in their use and in the dangers related to their use.

The last category or option in the model is lethal force, which is shown in red on the Framework. This option appears last because it is to be used only as a last resort. All other options must have been considered or exhausted (including withdrawing from the situation) before the use of lethal force can be justified. Lethal force is used when security professionals have reasonable and probable grounds to believe that if they do not act with lethal force, then they or someone else will be subjected to force that is likely to cause serious bodily harm or death.

Statistics show that an aggressive person in a standing position can cover approximately 7 metres in about 1.5 seconds. Statistics also show that most gunfights happen in low light or poor weather conditions, and that they happen at close quarters (3 to 6 metres) and are over in less than 10 seconds. When a gunfight is over there will be a winner and a loser. Initiating this level of force will never be an easy choice. A security professional should also remember that even when he or she is considering lethal force, communication must be ongoing, and it must be loud, clear, and repetitive.

Use and knowledge of the National Use of Force Framework can be enhanced through experience as well as through training with scenarios and role-playing that are followed by a debriefing by instructors and input from peers. There are two important points to remember when considering a use of force decision. First, security professionals must always be "justified" in their actions. Justified actions taken by a security professional are protected from civil or criminal liability through section 25 of the *Criminal Code*. Second, security professionals can be called into court to justify their actions. If you are required to attend court on a case you were involved in that required you to use force, you will be cross-examined by the defence counsel on your actions. The judge, Crown, and defence counsel will have reference to the Use of Force Framework model, and you will be required under oath to explain your actions according to the model.

**serious bodily harm**
lasting injuries causing permanent or temporary disability and/or lasting disfigurement (not minor injuries such as scratches, cuts, or a bloody nose)

## Potential Consequences of the Use of Force

Part of why it is so critical for security professionals to understand the legal authorities outlined in Chapter 8 and the CACP National Use of Force Framework model is because there are many potential consequences to implementing use of force. As mentioned before, a security professional who decides to use force must consider how to use only as much force as is necessary to effect his or her lawful purpose, and no more. If more force was used than a situation called for, the security professional and the organization may be open to criminal charges and/or tort and civil suits.

Within this context, a security professional might be charged with violating section 26 of the *Criminal Code*, which prohibits the unauthorized use of excessive force. Further to this, the security professional will no longer have the protection of section 25 of the Code. One of the more common scenarios that can lead to liability under section 26 is that in which, in the context of a forceful struggle to arrest a person, the subject might begin experiencing **excited delirium** (ED).

**excited delirium**
a potentially fatal condition that presents with symptoms such as profuse sweating, difficulty breathing, and a racing heartbeat when a subject is restrained; can be triggered by drug use, mental illness, brain injuries or tumours, heart disease, high blood pressure, high or low blood sugar, respiratory problems, or fever; can impart to subjects a super-human strength coupled with high tolerance for pain and low understanding of verbal communication

# Handling a Subject in Distress

Excited delirium arises when a detained subject has a physiological reaction to being physically restrained and presents symptoms such as profuse sweating, difficulty breathing, and a racing heartbeat. It can be caused by a number of factors such as drug use, mental illness, brain injuries or tumours, heart disease, high blood pressure, high or low blood sugar, respiratory problems, or fever. Furthermore, a subject can suffer from **positional asphyxia**, which is the inability to breathe effectively when restrained in certain positions. Positional asphyxia is more common if the subject is already suffering from excited delirium and if the subject is lying face-first on the ground or floor.

> **positional asphyxia**
> subject has difficulty breathing when restrained; subjects are at increased risk if they also suffer from excited delirium and/or are placed face down on the ground or floor

## Responding to Excited Delirium

In situations where a person may be suffering from excited delirium, the security professional must focus on doing everything he or she can do to determine the issue and keep the subject safe. Be calm. Take deep breaths. As a security professional, you are not expected to make medical decisions. If a subject is in distress you must continue to engage in communication. Ask the subject his or her name. Request that someone call 911, and tell them to confirm when they have an operator on the line. Describe the subject's symptoms, because the operator may have training in responding to ED.

If you suspect ED, request that medical and crisis intervention units attend. Do not restrain the subject unless it is absolutely necessary for public safety. It is best, where possible, to contain the subject in a controlled area and await personnel who are trained to handle this condition. ED is a condition that gives the subject super-human strength with a very high threshold for pain and no regard for verbal communication. Seeking backup from EMS and police personnel trained to handle this condition is the best course of action. It can also be helpful to ask whether anyone in the vicinity has medical training.

Your communication with the subject and anyone who has gathered in the immediate vicinity must be loud, clear, and simple. Your communication must involve closed-ended questions to the subject that can be acknowledged by a motion of the head or a single syllable response. Ask anyone who has gathered in the immediate area in a loud voice "does anyone know this person; does anyone know what happened?" If possible put the person in a position on their side that would be conducive to beginning CPR, and loosen the subject's clothing around the throat area. Questions that might help are:

- Can you hear me?
- Can you breathe?
- Are you on any medication?
- Do you have pain?
- Are you alone?

Other questions may be appropriate depending on the situation.

## Responding to Positional Asphyxia

You may also be required to assist a subject who presents with positional asphyxia. As noted above, this is a condition that causes difficulty in breathing due to the position the subject is in. This is most likely to present itself to security professionals during an arrest where the subject has been apprehended and is face down with the arresting officer applying downward force on the subject's back in order to control his or her movement.

This face-down position is the best, easiest, and most practical way to position a subject for the purpose of applying handcuffs; however, if a subject is in this position for an extended period of time, it can restrict the subject's breathing, especially if the capture was preceded by a chase or pressure to the subject's back is extreme. A subject who is overweight or has a respiratory condition may also be more susceptible to positional asphyxia.

Security professionals should be trained to recognize that keeping a subject in a full-frontal face-down position on the ground or floor can be fatal. If a security professional finds it necessary to have a subject in this position with the security professional's weight on the subject's back in order to control the situation, it should only be done to facilitate handcuffing, after which the subject should be rolled onto his or her side and then the subject's breathing should be checked. If the subject has stopped breathing, begin CPR immediately and call 911.

## Consequences of the Use of Weapons

The consequences of using intermediate or lethal weapons are usually obvious. Again, according to the CACP National Use of Force Framework model and the *Private Security and Investigative Services Act, 2005*, additional force that includes these tools is permitted when subject behaviour enters into the active resistant and assault categories. However, it must be understood that any use of weapons will fall under intense scrutiny from supervisors, peace officers, and the courts.

Security professionals will be guided in their use of force options by their employers' policies and guidelines. Even when they are justified under the National Use of Force Framework model, employers will likely discourage the use of intermediate weapons in non-life-threatening situations that involve loss of inventory or property damage. In situations that involve the protection of life, it is easier to justify the use of intermediate weapons even though their use may result in loss of life. Due to the potential risk of confrontation and violence when involved in this type of security, senior security professionals with extensive training and experience are the personnel of choice.

In addition to the legal concerns outlined above, it is important for security personnel to understand that the security environment in which they operate falls under public scrutiny. This is why it is critical for security personnel to be able to explain their use-of-force choices and methods and to be justified in their actions.

### CHAPTER SUMMARY

This chapter discussed the use of force by security professionals. Security professionals make decisions about the use of force by analyzing volatile situations in the context of the standards established by their employers and the principles illustrated in the CACP National Use of Force Framework model. The Framework prescribes a continuous assessment process that requires security sector personnel to monitor subject behaviour and respond accordingly.

The most common consequences of implementing use of force were discussed, including legal consequences and the requirement for justification, and physical consequences such as excited delirium and positional asphyxia.

## KEY TERMS

Canadian Association of Chiefs of Police (CACP), 206
continuous assessment process, 209
de-escalate, 209
excited delirium, 213
intermediate (less-lethal) weapons, 210
lethal force, 210
National Use of Force Framework, 206
person of authority, 209
person in distress, 209
positional asphyxia, 214
serious bodily harm, 213
soft and hard compliance techniques, 210

## REFERENCES

Canadian Association of Chiefs of Police (CACP). (n.d.). National use of force framework. [Diagram]. Retrieved from https://cacp.ca/cacp-use-of-force-advisory-committee-activities.html

Canadian Association of Chiefs of Police (CACP). (2000). A national use of force framework. [Model]. Retrieved from https://cacp.ca/cacp-use-of-force-advisory-committee-activities.html

*Criminal Code*, RSC 1985, c C-46 http://laws-lois.justice.gc.ca/eng/acts/C-46/ [Code].

*Private Security and Investigative Services Act, 2005*, SO 2005, c 34 http://www.canlii.org/en/on/laws/stat/so-2005-c-34/latest/so-2005-c-34.html.

*Trespass to Property Act*, RSO 1990, c T.21 https://www.ontario.ca/laws/statute/90t21.

## PERFORMANCE APPLICATION
### Multiple Choice

1. A security guard who wishes to use force must consider how to use
   a. only as much force as is necessary to effect his or her lawful purpose, and no more
   b. only minimum force
   c. the same amount of force as the person uses against him or her
   d. no more force than the person uses against him or her
   e. as much force as he or she wants to use, up to and including deadly force

2. Passive resistant, active resistant, and assaultive are all examples of what under the use of force model?
   a. continuous assessment
   b. subject behaviour categories
   c. tactical considerations
   d. force options
   e. reasonable force

3. The continuous assessment process can include which responses?
   a. passive resistance
   b. active resistance
   c. deadly force
   d. answers a. and b.
   e. all of the above

4. In the context of a forceful struggle to arrest a person, symptoms such as profuse sweating, difficulty breathing, and a racing heartbeat on the part of the subject should be understood as indications that the person may be
   a. about to attack
   b. lying
   c. mentally ill
   d. experiencing excited delirium
   e. trained in martial arts

5. In the context of a forceful struggle to arrest a person, if the subject appears to be unable to breathe effectively it should be understood as an indication that the person may be
   a. about to attack
   b. experiencing positional asphyxia
   c. mentally ill
   d. experiencing excited delirium
   e. trained in martial arts

6. In making a decision about the use of force, which of the following is *not* an appropriate consideration?
   a. employer use of force guidelines
   b. security professional's training, skill, and strength
   c. nature of client interest being protected (property, inventory, or human safety)
   d. subject's behaviour
   e. all of the above are appropriate considerations

7. Which of the following is not an appropriate response to a subject in distress?

   a. request for backup from medically trained bystanders
   b. release of restraints/pressure
   c. administration of a sedative
   d. continual verbal communication
   e. call to 911

8. What is the primary goal, with respect to the subject, for a security professional who attends at a situation where use of force may potentially be required?

   a. immediate arrest to preserve evidence
   b. detention for potential arrest by police
   c. obtain subject cooperation
   d. achieve subject removal from premises
   e. positional asphyxia

9. Which is not an intermediate weapon?

   a. baton
   b. taser
   c. pepper spray
   d. handcuffs
   e. all are intermediate weapons

10. Which section of the *Criminal Code* protects security professionals from liability when they use appropriate force for a justifiable purpose in the presence of reasonable and probable grounds?

    a. section 8
    b. section 25
    c. section 26
    d. section 34
    e. section 494

## Short Answer

### Scenarios

**Scenario One:** Bobby is a plainclothes security professional working for a grocery store. He observes two teenage girls leaving the chocolate bar section, laughing, and bulges can be seen in their jackets. As they approach the exit, the girls nervously pick up their pace and rush toward the exit. Bobby follows at a run, leaving the grocery store and moving into the parking lot. One girl disappears into a crowd, but Bobby catches up with the second girl. He grabs the girl's shoulder and both fall to the ground. Immediately she starts trying to throw him off, so he puts her into a compliance hold and places her facing the ground. After Bobby has cautioned her he notices that the teenager is having difficulty breathing.

**Scenario Two:** Hasan is a contract security guard who has been hired to provide security for a fenced-off private warehouse loading zone. Hasan is in charge of making sure that no one trespasses. After an alarm notification, Hasan comes across a large man who is yelling that the warehouse stores evil magic and that people should be afraid of it. Hasan notices the lack of alcohol on the subject's breath and begins to yell at the man, telling him that he is on private property and must leave immediately. The man barely notices Hasan and begins to stumble, trying to stay upright. After the man keeps ignoring him, Hasan gets into his face and again yells at the man, trying to get him to leave. The man continues to ignore Hasan, pulling away from him. Hasan decides he needs to use force because the situation must end before it becomes really dangerous. Hasan therefore punches the man, knocking him to the ground. As Hasan is informing local law enforcement that he wants to turn over custody of the man to them, he notices the man is sweating profusely and not moving.

Answer the following questions for each of the above scenarios. Make sure to discuss all relevant use of force implementation components and keywords.

1. Did the security professional act in accordance with the CACP National Use of Force Framework? Explain how the professional acted in accordance with the framework or failed to do so.

2. What potential consequences of use of force did the security professional encounter? When the scenario ends, what should the security professional's immediate response be?

# PART III

# Additional Skills and Topics

# Security Issues in the 21st Century

## 12

| | |
|---|---|
| Introduction | 222 |
| Technology on the Job | 222 |
| Liability and Risk Management | 224 |
| Terrorism and Security | 225 |
| Cybersecurity | 226 |
| Training and Education | 228 |
| Security Guard Health | 228 |
| Mental Health First Aid | 229 |
| Uniforms and Professionalism | 231 |
| Chapter Summary | 231 |
| Key Terms | 233 |
| References | 233 |
| Performance Application | 233 |

## LEARNING OUTCOMES

When you have completed this chapter, you will be able to:

- Explain the key ways in which technology is changing the work of security personnel.
- Describe the risks and liabilities that security personnel must consider.
- Be familiar with various types of terrorist attacks and understand why awareness of terrorism is important for security personnel.
- Explain the need for awareness of cybersecurity and of the potential threats involved.
- Understand the importance of lifelong skills development and improvement.

## Introduction

The security industry and its training institutions are continuously evolving to meet the changing needs of the public and private sectors. But in addition to refining the specific tasks and techniques that security professionals are required to learn, the industry must also adapt to reflect emerging trends in society as a whole, which include everything from rapid advances in technology, to an unprecedented concern over the threat of a terrorist attack in a public gathering place, and the recent increase in awareness across our society about mental health. This chapter briefly discusses some of these issues and other emerging trends that a security professional is very likely to face in his or her career.

## Technology on the Job

With advances in the world of technology, the role of the security guard continues to change as new technologies are integrated into the field. Various security roles require that security guards be familiar with the use, and sometimes maintenance, of applicable technology. Historically, guards were only required to carry out traditional core duties to perform their jobs, but as technology advances and costs fall, more and more corporations are budgeting for tech devices, with the result that security personnel are required to learn their use and maintenance.

For example, those working in bar or nightclub security once had to manually check identification for entrance into certain establishments. With the changes in cost for technology, establishments can now purchase card readers to scan and read government-issued identification (see Figure 12.1). Although such a process can create efficiency in the security guard's role, the user is still required to understand the device and be able to deal with any possible technical failures that may occur with its use. Awareness must now be shifted to deal with other factors that may arise with the use of technology.

**Figure 12.1** Electronic Card Reader

Patrolling is a common task in most security roles. Traditionally, a guard would patrol a designated area, taking notes in a notebook, documenting the times, location, and any observations that they may make on their patrol. Today, devices are available that can track this information for them. Sensors can be placed along various spots within a guard's patrol route. The guard carries a wand, and waves it over every sensor as he or she passes by it. The sensor logs the date and time of the contact to create a record of the patrol, and this record is then logged and stored for review by management. This method limits the guard's potential to interfere with the information or the records. The wands can also be assigned to certain shifts or guards, so that the log document shows which security guard did the patrol at any given time.

In addition to tools carried and used by security guards, the use of alarm systems and access control has increasingly become more popular. With ready-to-use CCTV systems now sold in retail stores, video surveillance has become more common in both private and public settings. Security guards should now be aware of how these systems operate, how they are connected to other systems, and be prepared to conduct basic troubleshooting when needed. Security guards are often called on to retrieve specific footage of an incident, and they are often responsible for some general maintenance of these systems, such as making sure that sensors are operating and that cameras maintain an unobstructed view of the area under surveillance.

A security guard's ability to monitor an area or document a crime scene has been enhanced by technology. Today, many guards carry personal devices, such as smart phones, which offer a range of useful tools. Guards can now document scenes through video or still images, take audio recordings when necessary, and stay in constant communication through video communication or via the GPS functions in their phones. Smartphones also provide valuable tools for use in emergencies, such as an audible alarm or a flashlight, and can assist in documenting a scene by, for example, providing accurate weather and road conditions. The use of biometrics has become more widely available as well: some personal devices are now able to run basic fingerprint scans.

Entire departments are now able to very quickly share information with those they are protecting. Many institutions have safety or security applications that allow users to call for assistance or monitor a situation. This ability to share information quickly is becoming a valuable asset for security teams.

Security professionals should be aware of how new technology is used in today's world. Many forms of harassment and discrimination in the workplace occur with the support of technology: inter-office chat groups, social media, and email are all areas of concern for any security department in the protection of the individuals at their establishment. Because individuals can now easily attach a camera to a drone and fly it onto a property to conduct surveillance, trespassing policies and procedures must be reviewed. Security guards should recognize these threats and be ready to address them with the assistance of their departments.

Spending on security technology continues to increase and is projected to continue to do so in the near future (IDC Research Inc., 2017). As technology changes and becomes more readily available, the role of the security guard must continue to adapt. Some industries are also moving toward automated labour, which could create a new set of security issues that a security department may be expected to deal with.

Many areas of security have changed significantly with the availability of new technology. For example, standard traffic control on a property can now be overseen using mobile speed radar devices that can be placed along the roadside in order to track vehicle speeds, vehicle types, volume of traffic, and traffic patterns. Where available, this technology allows security guards to monitor traffic patterns even when they are away from the area.

Devices continue to be developed in order to better protect people and property. In the public sector, for example, microchips are being inserted into passports to create **ePassports** for identification (Acuant Inc., 2017). In the private sector, companies such as Patriot One Technologies hope to assist the security industry by creating devices that can detect concealed weapons. These devices are hidden under floorboards and behind wall panels. They use radar technology to alert security guards to a possible concealed weapon. Scanners identify the shape and metal composition of a concealed weapon and send alerts to the guard through a computer or cellphone. The guard must then analyze these warnings and the overall situation, and take appropriate action (Juhl, 2017).

As the radar scanner example above shows, technology has the potential to completely change some ordinary security tasks. While security personnel will always be necessary, it's clear that as technology continues to quickly advance, the ways in which security guards perform their jobs will also change.

> **ePassport**
> a passport containing an electronic chip that holds information about the holder (name, birthdate, etc.) as well as a biometric identifier

## Liability and Risk Management

Liability and risk management are two elements that can affect any aspect of security. The risks relating to a security incident bring with them the possibility of being held liable for one's actions. The level of liability changes with one's specific role; however, security guards should be aware of these liabilities in order to best protect themselves and the organizations for which they work.

Liability can flow from actions such as the inappropriate use of force or the violation of privacy rights. For example, contract and in-house guards often deal with sensitive private information as they gather evidence and obtain information through statements and the use of video. The use, collection, and disclosure of this information can be subject to legal and ethical obligations. A security professional should proceed cautiously and with due diligence in order to minimize any criminal and civil liability issues.

The role that the security guard plays can have a direct impact on the level of risk. Security guards often work in environments that require ongoing familiarity with particular legislation. For example, working in a bar that serves alcohol (or at an event that has received a liquor licence) creates an entirely new set of risks and liabilities for the security guard. He or she must now be aware of the liquor licensing rules in effect at the place of employment and make sure that the policies surrounding liquor licensing are not violated. In most typical bar security roles, guards must be made aware of things such as the limits and conditions of the liquor licence, what their powers and authorities are, the authority of a liquor licence inspector, and the occupancy capacity of a bar. Something as simple as the number of people permitted to enter an establishment can be affected by a liquor licence, which allows a certain capacity at any given time. More common risks and liabilities also exist, such as physical altercations and the arrival and departure of intoxicated patrons.

Another example is event security. Security professionals should be attentive to the liabilities involved with the specific event. By-law issues, such as those for smoking and parking, become a major part of the security professional's role. The risks involved with patrons injuring themselves or being intoxicated create the potential for issues to occur. Vicarious liability often results in a company or organization being held liable for the actions of a security professional, and so it is usually in the best interests of a company to ensure that their security professionals are aware of the risks and the potential liabilities that may follow.

Because these liabilities continue to exist, organizations often respond with an increased security presence. Some major events, such as the G8 and G20 international summits hosted in Ontario in June 2010, have used a hybrid approach of both private and public security.

In these types of environments, the security professional should not only understand the power and authority granted to him or her by law, but should also be aware of the role of police presence and how to collaborate with police. In certain cases, a guard may not be able to enforce legislation that a police officer can, in which case security professionals should be working closely with police to provide a safe environment for the public.

This is why it is important for security guards to understand the legislation they are enforcing. The powers and authorities that security guards are granted vary tremendously from position to position. In addition, laws sometimes change and, as a result, security professionals must be informed and able to adapt. For example, the changing laws surrounding the use of cannabis will necessarily affect security strategies at concerts and other major events. Policies and rules must be clear in order for a security guard to perform his or her job without civil or criminal liability.

# Terrorism and Security

Although acts of terrorism may not be common in Canada in comparison with some other parts of the world, global events in the 21st century—most notably following the terrorist attacks on New York City and Washington DC on September 11, 2001—resulted in a global response from the security industry. Terrorist attacks are typically driven by a political or religious agenda, and can target members of the public either indiscriminately or in particular groups. Even the mere threat of a terrorist attack can create a hostile environment of fear. While "terrorism" may involve individuals or groups inspired by al Qaeda or the Islamic State, the term also applies to white supremacists such as the individuals who shot and killed Muslims at a Quebec City mosque in January 2017, and the individual who opened fire on students at Dawson College in Montreal in 2006. The term also applies to those inspired by other forms of hate such as misogyny and homophobia.

Recent years have seen a number of changes to the policies and procedures used to deal with these types of threats, and it is up to security professionals to adapt to changes in procedure. For example, airports and sporting events continue to increase security and change policies in order to reduce the chances of an attack occurring. Some airlines have continued to revise their restrictions on which possessions and objects a passenger may carry onboard a flight. It is now the responsibility of security professionals to enforce these policies and ensure that all passengers comply.

In the world of private security, security guards must realize that these events can occur at any time and in any place. Depending on the motives for attacks, the odds of dealing with an act of terrorism increase in many environments. In a world where information is shared so readily, society is being made more aware of attacks occurring around the world in various locations. Many locations that employ private security can be the target of a terrorist attack. Common places of gathering such as malls, schools, and sporting events may be targeted.

Although public areas are commonly secured by policing agencies, there are many locales, such as educational institutions or private corporations, that rely on private security as their primary defence. Security departments should now be training their guards to develop observational skills that may lead in the gathering of intelligence against terrorist threats. Those working in educational institutions have recently begun developing security plans to address scenarios such as those that involve active shooters. Just as fire drills are developed and practised, active shooter drills or "lock down" drills are being introduced. Security departments are now putting evacuation methods into place, combined with warning signage and defence strategies, so they will be ready in case this type of act occurs. In addition to evacuation (as commonly seen in fire scenarios), drills now include the option of barricading for safety or even fighting back against an attacker, if needed.

In Canada, security guards do not commonly carry firearms and tend to focus more heavily on barricading and evacuation support strategies rather than on direct defensive responses. In the 21st century, it is important that security guards take a proactive approach to terrorism and begin to pay attention to trends in attack patterns. Individuals suspected of having terrorist potential should not be ignored and observational awareness must be heightened to account for packages or devices that may be left behind as weapons of terrorism. Bomb threats, specifically, have led to increased training in order to deal with threats, searches, and any evacuation required. As terrorist threats evolve, security guards should be paying attention to the news and to details of attacks for insights into how they may occur.

Terrorist attacks are classified into various categories, depending on the type of situation. Six common ways that a terrorist attack might take place are:

1. Non-penetrative vehicle attack:
   - A vehicle-borne explosive that is delivered by parking a vehicle.
2. Penetrative vehicle attack:
   - A vehicle-borne explosive that is delivered by force, such as "ramming."
3. **Person-borne improvised explosive device (PBIED):**
   - An explosive delivered by a person in a suicide attack.
4. **Marauding terrorist firearms/weapons attack (MTFA/MTWA):**
   - An attack on individuals by a single person or group of terrorists with firearms or other weapons (including vehicles).
5. Postal device attack, including courier and hand deliveries:
   - An explosive, contaminant, or hoax delivered by post.
6. Placed improvised explosive device (IED):
   - An explosive device placed within an area (a suspicious package, etc.) (National Counter Terrorism Security Office, 2016).

Other areas of concern that should be addressed by the security department and staff include the development of lock-down procedures, increased security presence, staff vigilance, inter-agency cooperation, CCTV, parking, visitor identification, search regimes, and delivery management procedures. These topics, among others, should be given special attention when anticipating security against terrorist attacks (National Counter Terrorism Security Office, 2016).

**person-borne improvised explosive device (PBIED)** explosives concealed on-person, either under or within clothing, shoes, or other personal apparel

**marauding terrorist firearms/weapons attack (MTFA/MTWA)** terrorist incidents that occur across multiple sites that are perpetrated by the same attacker or group of attackers and in which firearms are the principal weapon used

# Cybersecurity

Cybersecurity is a high priority for all types of security departments. Although staff in the information technology sector mostly handle this area, awareness of the threat of an attack is important for all members of an organization. As a defence for these types of attacks, organizations should be putting in place policies and procedures that minimize the potential for anyone to infiltrate their systems. Even though firewalls and secured access can minimize threats, they do not eliminate them completely.

With advancements in technology, the types and severity of cyber threats continue to evolve. Attackers will commonly target the weakest link in the chain, often an average user, in order to penetrate a much larger system. Attacks of this nature can be detrimental to an organization because they jeopardize the security of valuable information and privacy. Often, information is stolen by an attacker, only to be offered back to the organization at a cost. Ransomware and phishing scam avoidance should be a cybersecurity priority and all users connected to the network should be familiar with these threats.

While the majority of cyber attacks begin from a remote location, there are also situations where the attackers have gained access to a system with the help of somebody within the organization. This can often be a disgruntled employee or someone trying to obtain specific information from a company. Any organization using software and computers should be aware of these threats and the best practices for mitigating them. Security guards should continue to educate themselves on these types of threats, because methods of illegal network access continue to evolve with advancements in technology.

Despite security measures, user errors that allow attacks to take place can still occur. In one example, two multinational organizations were held for ransom as the attackers used email phishing scams to trick employees into releasing millions of dollars (BBC, 2017). Other cases have seen organizations held for ransom for cash, capital, or **bitcoin** (Internet currency). Every user in an organization should be made aware of the possible points of penetration for attackers. Policies should be put into place to make sure passwords are strong and changed periodically and that users understand the risks involved with their day-to-day computer use.

**bitcoin**
an Internet-based virtual currency exchanged directly between users without banks or similar traditional authorities as intermediaries

In a Pew Research study, researchers identified four common erroneous beliefs among technology users. First: users believed the myth that email is always safe and encrypted. Second: users believed private browsing was completely private and never tracked. Third: users believed that by turning off the GPS function on their devices, they could not be tracked. And finally, users believed that passwords without a second layer of authentication were enough to protect them (Larson, 2017). Studies such as this show us how the average user could be further educated in the area of cybersecurity.

As security professionals, it is important that we recognize the reality of cyber threats. Any computer within an organization can be susceptible to attack and a security guard should be developing the observational skills necessary to minimize the number of these incidents. Working closely with information technology departments, security should be able to move quickly and efficiently to help with the company's defence. Security guards conducting patrols should be aware of signs of potential problems and should pay special attention to equipment within the organization. Computers should be shut down regularly and maintained by the organization. Security guards should be aware of devices such as USB drives and key loggers that may pose a threat to cybersecurity. Patrols should include the checking of individual computers for foreign devices and making sure that users are complying with policies regarding external drives and hardware and software installations.

Although a specialized education in cyber threats may not be realistic in every organization, security guards should be trained and made aware of how their actions could affect cybersecurity. For example, when dealing with a computer that may show signs of corruption, a security guard should know that tampering with the computer might in fact trigger a sequence that continues the attack. A computer suspected of having been tampered with should be treated as sensitive and should not be touched until a professional with a specialized background is able to attend to it. Areas of an organization that deal with the storage of information, such as a room holding servers, should have restrictions placed on access. It is crucial to protect these areas, and they should be identified as high-security zones by security departments and their staff.

Cybersecurity continues to be a complicated aspect of a security department's role. Working closely with information technology departments, security professionals should do all they can to minimize physical attacks on the system. Every minute is crucial once an attacker gains access, and organizations should be prepared and trained to quickly stop any attack.

# Training and Education

Security guard education and training is essential to the overall operation of any security department. Currently, in order to obtain a licence (specifically in Ontario, as outlined by the Ministry of Community Safety and Correctional Services and with regard to the PSISA), an individual is required to attend a 40-hour training course and pass a multiple-choice exam. Once that is completed, no further education is required in order to obtain a licence. However, in the 21st century, continuing education is of the utmost importance for all industries, and we may soon see continuing certification become a mandatory aspect of the security industry. At the present time, continuing education in the security industry is focused on the availability of special designations. Certain designations require that individuals attend a certain number of courses per year in order to maintain their certification.

As the role of security guards changes depending on the organizations for which they work and the tasks involved, training should be individualized to coordinate with this. For example, security guards that are required to use force to make arrests are mandated to recertify their use of force training on a regular basis. Certain security roles involve the use of firearms and specialized tactical weapons such as armoured car services for protecting currency; others involve work on specialized tactical teams involved with nuclear security. Continuing education has already been implemented into the standards for roles such as these.

A security guard should learn as much as possible in order to be an asset to clients and employers. Find out whether professional development courses are within your security department's budget so that you can continue to develop advanced skills. As mentioned throughout this chapter, areas such as technology, mental health, and cybersecurity threats are topics that require security guards to remain current and to be effective in their roles. An organization such as ASIS International is a good example of one with resources for the sharing of information to protect against potential threats. Organizations such as ASIS offer certification courses for advancement of staff in the security industry. ASUS certifications include Certified Protection Professional (CPP), Professional Certified Investigator (PCI), and Physical Security Professional (PSP). Many other organizations offer courses that a security guard could take in order to supplement his or her credentials and knowledge. In addition, there are also educational institutions across the country offering diplomas in security-related fields, as well as degrees in theoretical aspects (such as criminology).

Other companies offer a variety of programs for specialized security professionals. For example, organizations in the private sector may offer courses such as Pressure Point Control Tactics and Close Protection, while other companies may offer more investigative courses such as interviewing techniques and conflict management.

A security professional should invest in further education and training even if it is not provided by his or her organization. This allows the security professional to continue to develop skills and be eligible for quick career advancement. Education and training allows the security professional to stay up to date and encourages the use of best practices.

# Security Guard Health

Overall health should be a primary concern for guards and the organizations they work for. Industry standards in the private sector are still far behind those of the public sector, which requires physical and psychological testing for various security roles. In the private sector, these tests are not mandated and are therefore it is left up to each organization to decide whether an individual is mentally or physically fit for duty.

In Ontario, a security guard is not required to be tested physically or psychologically in order to obtain a security licence (PSISA). Once the province provides the licence, it is the guard's duty to make sure that they are prepared for any individual job to which they apply. Most often, due to associated costs, corporations are reluctant to go through a testing process, even though guards require a certain level of fitness in order to perform security tasks. Although the statistics are not as readily available in the private sector, it appears to be mimicking the trends of the public sector, which regularly deals with issues relating to the health of security guards.

One clear trend that has emerged in all areas of law enforcement and security during the early years of the 21st century has been a greater emphasis on mental health. It is becoming increasingly important for security professionals to pay attention to their mental and physical well-being. Improving one's physical fitness can have tremendous benefits on the job. In addition to providing relief from stress, being in good physical shape allows security guards to perform common tasks with a greater amount of ease and less chance of injury. Common tasks such as conducting patrols or making an arrest require that a security guard be ready and able in the moment. Even though this preparation is essential, it is often left up to the guards themselves to determine their overall readiness.

While dealing with individuals who face issues related to mental health, security guards put themselves at risk of developing mental health problems of their own. Simple things such as eating well and at appropriate times need to be a priority in a security guard's lifestyle. The habit of bringing doughnuts to the office is slowly being replaced with bringing fruit and other healthier options. Corporations are paying increasing attention to the relationship between employees' lifestyles and their health.

The stress of security work can be difficult for anyone because the job often comes with rotating shift work, high stress situations, and dealing with unpredictable circumstances. Because of this, security guards are at higher risk of taking time off for stress leave or developing mental health-related issues such as **post-traumatic stress disorder (PTSD)**. Organizations should be aware of these risks and offer training and preventive methods to deal with these problems. Public police are also seeing these issues with their officers and have begun to offer coping strategies to help manage them. Methods such as exercise and meditation are being offered to help reduce instances of burnout and employee turnover. Organizations now often pay for counselling and stress leave. Security guards today should be aware of these potential problems and should begin to incorporate stress reduction strategies into their daily lives.

Being physically and mentally fit for work is a lifestyle issue that should continue for guards when they are off work. Staying fit for work and fit for life requires that guards be conscious of the decisions they make outside of work and how those decisions affect them in the workplace. Training and education in the field should address this issue because its importance is crucial to any security program.

**post-traumatic stress disorder (PTSD)**
a mental health condition characterized by flashbacks, nightmares, and severe anxiety that is triggered by the victim's experience of a highly stressful event, whether personally or as a witness

# Mental Health First Aid

In many jurisdictions, including Ontario, security guards are required to obtain valid first aid training as part of the licensing process (see Appendix A to this book, which covers basic first aid). While working as a security guard, it is common to find oneself on the front line, as the first point of contact with the public, and because of this the ability to offer assistance in a medical situation is of the utmost importance. However, this concept is broadening to apply not only to assisting people with physical injuries, but also to offering assistance to those dealing with mental health issues. "**Mental health first aid**" is a term that is now commonly used in the industry because organizations are being made aware of its importance in the field.

**mental health first aid**
the help provided to a person who is developing a mental health problem or experiencing a mental health crisis

In the 21st century, the prevalence of mental health problems continues to be a factor that security guards have to manage. Many individuals in society are being diagnosed with mental illness and treated with pharmaceuticals and/or forms of counselling and therapy. As a result, there are now programs in place to offer first aid practitioners foundational knowledge in dealing with these individuals. Mental health first aid training helps security guards and other front-line staff to deal with issues as they affect the public. Limits on resources and government funding result in often insufficient availability of solutions for those suffering from mental illness. Mental health first aid is emerging as an essential component of security training, providing guards with the information and techniques they need to deal effectively with this issue.

Mental health first aid training typically includes information about substance-related disorders, mood-related disorders, anxiety and trauma-related disorders, and psychotic disorders (see also the Chapter 3 discussion on how to recognize people under the influence of specific drugs). Security guards should cultivate the ability to recognize these issues and their signs and symptoms, and to manage risk factors associated with particular conditions. In order to best serve the public and protect property, security guards should have knowledge of mental health first aid techniques, understand the common mental health issues that the public may face, and be sensitive to the need to counter the discrimination and stigma that currently remains attached to mental health problems.

Security guards working with the public should understand that mental health concerns translate into front-line issues that need to be dealt with immediately. For example, providing aid in a substance overdose or dealing with individuals facing suicidal behaviour and psychotic episodes are examples of situations that security guards may need to deal with on a daily basis. Because security guards work in various roles within the industry, the application of these skills may increase depending on the location in which a guard is working. For example, those working in a hospital environment as contract guards may deal with these types of issues every day. Guards in the educational sector may see times of the year where these issues increase. For example, at a post-secondary institution, the timing of exams may bring on an influx of mental health-related issues (caused by stress and anxiety) that need to be addressed on the front line. A similar situation may exist in corporate environments where losses in profit may trigger mental health-related situations.

The Mental Health Commission of Canada (2017) offers a course curriculum that provides a framework for dealing with these issues when they prevail. The Commission's framework is summarized by the acronym "ALGEE":

| | |
|---|---|
| A | assessing the risk |
| L | listening non-judgmentally |
| G | giving reassurance |
| E | encouraging professional support |
| E | encouraging other supports |

This framework is built into their course delivery, offering security guards options when dealing with mental health first aid situations (Mental Health Commission of Canada, 2017).

The idea behind this training is that mental health first aid must be addressed for the future of effective security. Providing security is only one aspect of security guards' work and the fact that they work on the front line places them in a position to also offer service and aid. As the industry moves forward, in addition to the already available first aid training for guards, mental health first aid should also be offered so that guards will be effective when dealing with the public.

# Uniforms and Professionalism

The presence of a uniformed guard plays a major role in the effective protection of people and property. With the increase in security guards' responsibilities and authorities, it is important for both security personnel and the public that guards are readily identifiable in a recognizable uniform. As privatization blurs the borders between police and private security, it is important to understand the benefits of a uniform and the importance of consistency within the industry. The use of uniforms in the industry projects a sense of authority and offers readily identifiable assistance in a time of need or safety.

Currently, the PSISA outlines the requirement for front-line security to wear identifiable uniforms. This stems from the public's requirement to be able to identify security guards in times of need. As expected, there are exceptions to this rule, and many of these were discussed in Chapter 2 of this text. As the role of the security guard continues to evolve, standards for uniforms will be of significant importance in the industry. Although the PSISA offers guidelines for what is *prohibited* in uniforms, the lack of prescriptive standards creates the potential for inconsistencies between organizations.

In the 21st century, it is important that industry standards are set and that front-line security guards support these standards with their uniform appearance. The issues of being readily identifiable and accountable must continue to be addressed. Security guards working in this era should understand the importance of their roles and where their authorities and powers may lie. Accountability is crucial, and the security industry should continue to enforce the use of a regulated uniform and the ability to identify the guard through the means of a nametag or identification number.

Abuse of power, discrimination, and bias are all issues being dealt with in the public and private security sectors. While public police are now wearing body cameras to capture their actions on tape, there are still security guards who wear T-shirts with "security" or "staff" printed on them who are unaware of their legal authority and are not identified by name or number. Security guards working in front-line positions should be easily identifiable to the public.

In addition to addressing accountability and providing consistency, a uniform provides a level of professionalism that is very much needed in certain areas of this industry. The professionalism and discipline involved with maintaining and wearing a uniform speak to the professionalism of the industry as a whole and how the public views security. If security guards continue to feel confident and are prepared through training and experience, they may be able to reduce the number of their negative interactions with the public.

## CHAPTER SUMMARY

As a security professional, your job will be crucial to the overall security of any organization. A security guard must deal with a variety of people and threats on a daily basis and be prepared for any situation that might arise. It is important for security professionals to understand the issues that arise on the job as they continue to protect people and property in the 21st century.

This chapter introduced some of the most important influences and changes that affect the private security industry today.

Advances in technology have enhanced the ability of security professionals to do their work, but have also made it necessary for those professionals to expand their skills so that they can operate, troubleshoot, and maintain equipment. Law is also an area that has

*Continued*

Continued

undergone change, and an increase in the public's awareness of privacy and physical security rights has led to an increase in exposure of security personnel to legal liability.

High-profile instances of terrorism and increasing media coverage of them have been met with a global response from the security industry, in which it has become increasingly common to plan for defensive responses such as evacuation, barricading, and even active defence. Cyber attacks have also prompted defensive strategies, and security professionals play an important role in counteracting these attacks.

As the industry becomes more complex, an awareness of the need for continuing education and training for guards has emerged, and programs designed to support security professionals in developing new skills have proliferated. Guards are also being urged to support their formal training with lifestyle stress-control strategies such as exercise, nutrition, and meditation, both to support on-the-job duties and to help protect against the potential mental health impacts of a demanding profession. Finally, a growing incidence of mental health problems in the population as a whole has led to the recognition of mental health first aid as an important component of work-related first aid training.

The topics introduced in this chapter are only a few of the areas of concern. Security professionals should continue to educate themselves and stay up to date on best practices in the industry. From taking care of personal health to understanding the liabilities involved in actions, the role of a security professional requires discipline and dedication. While being assets to their security departments, security guards should also strive to provide the best possible service to their clients and organizations.

## KEY TERMS

bitcoin, 227

ePassport, 224

marauding terrorist firearms/weapons attack (MTFA/MTWA), 226

mental health first aid, 229

person-borne improvised explosive device (PBIED), 226

post-traumatic stress disorder (PTSD), 229

## REFERENCES

Acuant Inc. (2017, March). Improving border security with better technology solutions: ePassports and Acuant CHIP. Retrieved from http://www.acuantcorp.com/improving-border-security-with-better-technology-solutions-epassports-and-acuant-chip/

ASIS International. (n.d.). Certifications. Retrieved from https://www.asisonline.org/Certification/Pages/default.aspx

British Broadcasting Corporation [BBC]. (2017, March 22). Two major US technology firms "tricked out of $100m." Retrieved from http://www.bbc.com/news/technology-39351215

IDC Research Inc. (2017, March 29). Worldwide spending on security technology forecast to reach $81.7 billion in 2017, according to new IDC spending guide. Press Release. Retrieved from http://www.idc.com/getdoc.jsp?containerId=prUS42425417

Juhl, W. (2017). Canadian company has high hopes for new security threat detection device. *Las Vegas Review Journal*. Retrieved from https://www.reviewjournal.com/local/local-las-vegas/canadian-company-has-high-hopes-for-new-security-threat-detection-device/

Larson, S. (2017, March 22). 4 myths—and facts—about online security. *CNN Tech: Cyber-Safe*. Retrieved from http://money.cnn.com/2017/03/22/technology/cybersecurity-misconceptions-pew/

Mental Health Commission of Canada. (2017). Mental health first aid basic. Retrieved from http://www.mentalhealthfirstaid.ca/en/course-info/courses/mhfa-basic

National Counter Terrorism Security Office. (2016, December 8). National stakeholder menu of tactical options. Retrieved from https://www.gov.uk/government/publications/national-stakeholder-menu-of-tactical-options

*Private Security and Investigative Services Act, 2005*, SO 2005, c 34 [PSISA].

## PERFORMANCE APPLICATION
### Discussion Questions

1. In what other ways has technology changed the role of the security professional?

2. How can a security guard help prevent and be prepared for future terrorist attacks?

3. What are some of the pros and cons with creating a universally mandated uniform?

4. What are some of the reasons why cybersecurity threats continue to be successful?

5. What are some of the ways that companies can encourage recognition of the importance of a security professional's mental and physical health?

# Crime Prevention Through Environmental Design

## 13

| | |
|---|---|
| Introduction | 236 |
| CPTED Defined | 236 |
| CPTED Concepts | 236 |
| Application of CPTED Principles | 237 |
| The Three Ds | 237 |
| The Nine Major CPTED Principles | 238 |
| Example 1: CPTED Applied to Storefronts | 244 |
| Example 2: CPTED Applied to Shopping Malls | 245 |
| Example 3: CPTED Applied to a Drive-Through | 246 |
| Example 4: CPTED Applied to Parking Facilities | 246 |
| Chapter Summary | 247 |
| Key Terms | 248 |
| Note | 248 |
| References | 248 |
| Further Reading | 248 |
| Performance Application | 248 |

## LEARNING OUTCOMES

When you have completed this chapter, you will:

- Understand the fundamental goals of Crime Prevention Through Environmental Design (CPTED).
- Be able to list the four core strategies that form the basis of CPTED.
- Be familiar with the nine major CPTED principles for achieving the goals of the method.
- Be able to propose improvements to the security of a facility that are based on the principles of CPTED.

## Introduction

Traditionally, the function of private security professionals has been to provide a visible and uniformed security presence on private property and to respond to and report to authorities incidents of crime. The uniformed presence of security professionals acts as both a physical and psychological deterrent to the criminal element.

Mainstream print and electronic media and, more recently, social media, have increased our awareness of the existence of crime within our communities. Traditional police and security professional response practices are not sufficient to deter and counter the effects of crime.

Over the years, there have been many attempts to address some of the root causes of deviant behaviour, social conflict, and crime. Criminologists, social workers, law enforcement, community workers, and city planners have all proposed ideas to make our communities safer. Over time, the best of these ideas have formed the basis for a new approach to crime prevention: Crime Prevention Through Environmental Design, which is known as **CPTED**.

**CPTED**
principles of design and use of built environments developed with the goals of reducing the perception of risk and incidence of crime and improving quality of life for users

## CPTED Defined

"CPTED is the proper design and effective use of the built environment that can lead to a reduction in the fear and incidence of crime and an improvement in the quality of life. The goal of CPTED is to reduce opportunities for crime that may be inherent in the design of structures or in the design of neighborhoods" (National Institute of Crime Prevention, 2015).

Traditionally, we have used physical security tools such as alarm systems, locks, and cameras to delay and deter the efforts of criminals and protect property. Today, CPTED principles can be applied to new and existing building and exterior spaces. When properly implemented, these principles can have a significant impact on the safety of communities and the quality of life of the people who live and work within them.

The results have been impressive; in some CPTED communities, criminal activity has decreased by as much as 40 percent. In Ontario, the efforts of the police in Peel Region stand as an excellent example of how the quality of life of an entire community can be positively affected by the application of these principles.[1]

## CPTED Concepts

Over time, CPTED concepts have emerged from contemporary crime prevention experiments. The application of these concepts to various sectors in our communities has had a profound effect on crime and our perceptions of safety and security. Among the many businesses, institutions, and facilities that use CPTED concepts are:

- housing projects and gated communities;
- schools, colleges, and universities;
- shopping malls and retail stores;
- commercial and light manufacturing buildings;
- restaurants and the food service industry;

- hotels and motels;
- residential and condominium complexes;
- seniors' and retirement residences;
- daycare and elementary school buildings;
- provincial and municipal facilities and offices;
- public and transit parking facilities;
- parks, green space, and community recreation facilities; and
- banks.

# Application of CPTED Principles

All private property, regardless of the community in which it is located, is at least somewhat vulnerable to crime. That vulnerability can be reduced through the application of CPTED principles. When identifying opportunities to implement CPTED principles, it is useful to remember a CPTED motto: "What are you trying to do here, and how can we help you to do it better?" Crime and losses are evidence of existing social problems. Fixing problems such as unemployment, drug use, and the involvement of youth in gang culture can and will reduce or eliminate crime. Over time, CPTED practitioners have stopped focusing solely on security and crime prevention and have started to focus on the objectives of the organizations they are trying to help.

# The Three Ds

CPTED involves the design of physical spaces for lawful use by members of a community. It influences how users of that space and the public in general react to how the space is being used. CPTED emphasizes the connection between the functional use of space and application of the principles of behaviour management to the users of the space. By using designation, definition, and design—the "three Ds"—as a guide, we can evaluate how the space is likely to be used by asking the following questions:

## Designation

- What is the designated purpose of this space?
- For what purpose was it originally intended?
- How well does the space support its current or intended use?
- Is there a conflict with its location, or between potential users?

## Definition

- How is the space defined?
- Are users aware of who owns the space?
- Where are its borders, and are they obvious?
- Do social or cultural identifiers affect how the space is used?

**Figure 13.1** Example: Application of CPTED Features on a Main Street Outside a Public Building

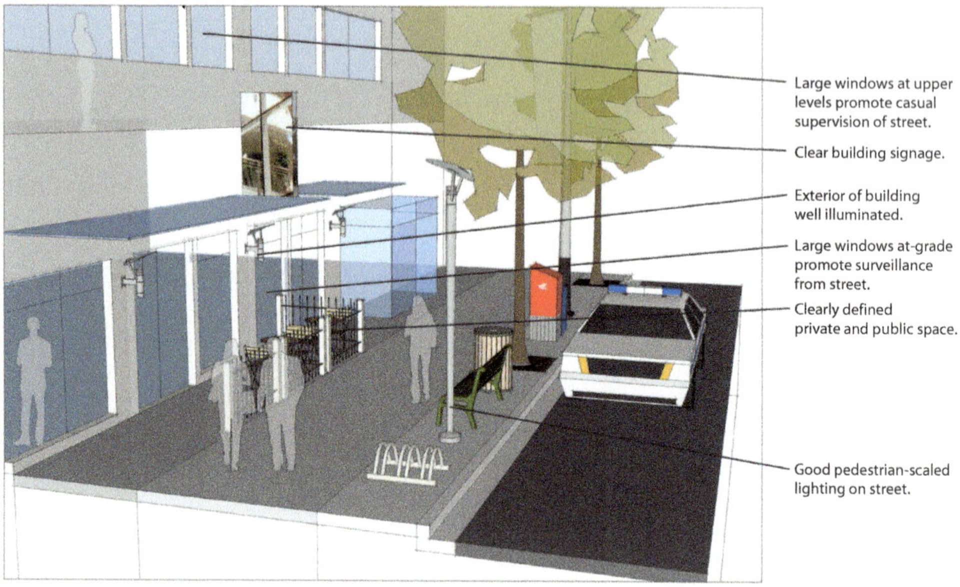

- Large windows at upper levels promote casual supervision of street.
- Clear building signage.
- Exterior of building well illuminated.
- Large windows at-grade promote surveillance from street.
- Clearly defined private and public space.
- Good pedestrian-scaled lighting on street.

- Are there clearly defined rules regarding use of the space?
- Are there signs posted?
- Is there conflict or confusion between purpose and definition?

## Design

- How well does the physical design support the intended function?
- How well does the physical design support the desired or accepted behaviours?
- Does the physical design conflict with the productive use of the space or the proper functioning of the intended human activity?
- Does the physical design clearly support the intended activities?

Once these questions have been asked, the information received may be used to determine human use of the space. Functions should be properly matched with space that can support them. The design should support the intended activity and positively influence the behaviour of anyone using the space. Figure 13.1 is an example of a plan to incorporate CPTED features into the design of a public building that fronts onto a major city street.

# The Nine Major CPTED Principles

The following principles (CPTED Ontario, 2014) are consulted by CPTED experts when planning the original design or redesign of facilities with crime control requirements. For a visual example of a redesign project, see Figures 13.2a and 13.2b.

## ON THE JOB

### Key Strategies in CPTED

CPTED is based on four key strategies. (For more information, see Toronto Police Service (2017), where resources on crime prevention and CPTED can be found.)

#### *Natural Surveillance*

This strategy is focused on keeping potential intruders under observation through a strategically positioned individual or members of the public in the course of their normal activities. It uses features that maximize the visibility of people, parking areas, and building entrances. It includes doors, windows, front porches that look out onto streets, parking areas, and sidewalks. Because criminals usually want to avoid being seen or identified when committing a crime, **natural surveillance** is supported by good lighting at night.

**Some Supporting Observations**

- Position physical features, activities, and people in ways that maximize their ability to see what is going on and discourage crime.
- Remove or minimize visual obstructions such as bushes, sheds, or shadows.
- Promote natural surveillance using landscaping and good lighting.

The security supervisor at a protected facility relies on the outer perimeter security fence as the first line of defence. To deny an intruder concealment as well as approach under cover, the supervisor will ensure that no structures are permitted within a defined space on either side of the fence, and that any vegetation is kept to a height of no more than six inches. This provides a clear field of observation over the length of the fenceline for both security guards and members of the public. This example of "natural surveillance" is as much physical as it is psychological, because the open lines of sight and lack of cover make any potential intruder feel that it will be impossible to breach the fenceline without being seen by someone and causing an alarm to be raised.

#### *Territoriality*

The manner in which a space is used defines that space. Law-abiding users of a space or area who are engaged in "normal" activities tend to develop a sense of territorial control. This tends to displace potential offenders.

**Territoriality** is usually promoted by features that define property lines and distinguish private spaces from public spaces. Elements that promote territoriality include landscape design, flower beds, pavement designs, prominent access points, and **CPTED fencing** that allows visibility from both sides.

**Some Supporting Observations**

- People are motivated to protect their own property/territory.
- People tend to respect other people's property/territory.
- Ownership can be best demonstrated by the use of fences, signs, artwork, landscaping, regular activity, and good maintenance.
- Avoid leaving areas without visible signs of "ownership." Potential users of the space should always be aware of who has authority over the space or area.

**natural surveillance**
the use of design features—for example, windows—to create both actual opportunities for surveillance and the impression of surveillance of a site

**territoriality**
in the context of CPTED, territoriality includes design elements and behaviours employed to communicate ownership and control over a space as a means of deterring illegal and nuisance activities in that space

**CPTED fencing**
fencing that is designed to support CPTED principles; for example, fencing that creates a sense of proprietary control and channels access appropriately without interfering with natural surveillance opportunities

Continued

Continued

Although most of the examples of territoriality include references to physical elements such as signs, landscaping, and prominent access points, some of the more personal examples of territoriality originate when employees demonstrate their loyalty to their company or organization by personally taking "ownership" of their space to the level where they not only observe and report suspicious persons and activities, but will approach and attempt to confirm the identity and purpose of anyone they encounter who seems out of place, is found in a restricted area, is not wearing proper ID, or seems uncertain of their surroundings.

### *Natural Access Control*

**Natural access control** is intended to decrease the opportunity to commit crimes by denying access to crime targets and creating a perception of risk in criminals and potential offenders. This is achieved by designing streets, sidewalks, building entrances, and neighbourhood gateways in ways that clearly indicate public access routes and by discouraging access to private areas by using structural elements such as low walls and hedges.

> **natural access control**
> the use of design features (including landscaping, roadway design, and fencing) to influence visitor access choices in a manner that increases security

**Some Supporting Observations**

- Properly located entrances, exits, fencing, landscaping, and lighting can channel both pedestrian and vehicular traffic in ways that discourage crime. For example:
  - Streets closed to through traffic after 3 p.m. (This can potentially reduce drug sales to minors.)
  - Neighbourhood-based parking stickers. (This can allow police to identify vehicles parked for reasons of solicitation and/or purchasing drugs.)
- Natural barriers such as thorny bushes and dense vegetation (hedges) to reinforce fence lines and other structural barriers.

A useful security strategy is to encourage public use of space that if left unused could be affected by crime or attract anti-social activity. The active social use of spaces makes it difficult for unwanted behaviour to flourish.

### *Target Hardening*

Target hardening is usually accomplished by the introduction of features that enhance the physical security of a building or structure and help to deny entry or access. These features include window locks, dead bolts for doors, and tamper resistant door hinges. While these features will not guarantee total security, they can help to deter or delay an intruder from gaining access to a target building or structure.

**Some Supporting Observations**

- Establishing legitimate activity in public places helps to discourage crime.
- Any activity that gets people to interact or work together will help prevent crime: a community clean-up day, a block party, a Neighbourhood Watch group, a civic meeting.

The key words to remember when thinking about target hardening as a CPTED strategy are "deter" and "delay." The efficacy of every physical example of target hardening can be evaluated in terms of how well it deters an intruder from entering protected space or an unwanted activity from occurring, or delaying the occurrence to the point where an appropriate security response is enabled.

**Figure 13.2a** Sightlines to Access Points: Security Guard Has No Visual Control of Access to Side Entrance and Elevators

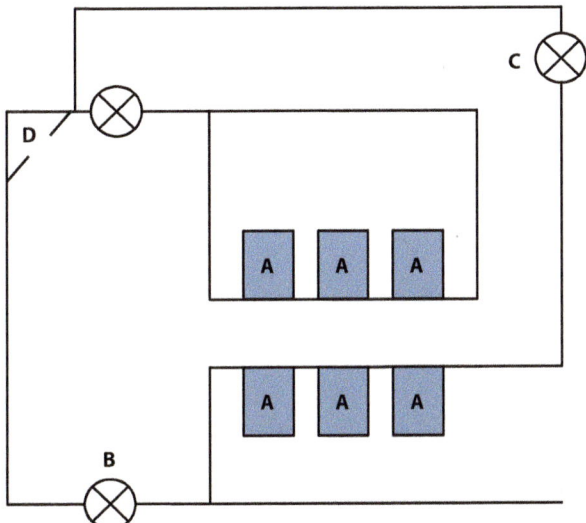

A: Elevators run from below ground to all floors above
B: Main entrance
C: Side entrance
D: Security guard station

**Figure 13.2b** Sightlines to Access Points: Security Guard Has Visual Control of Restrooms, Elevators, and Building Access Points

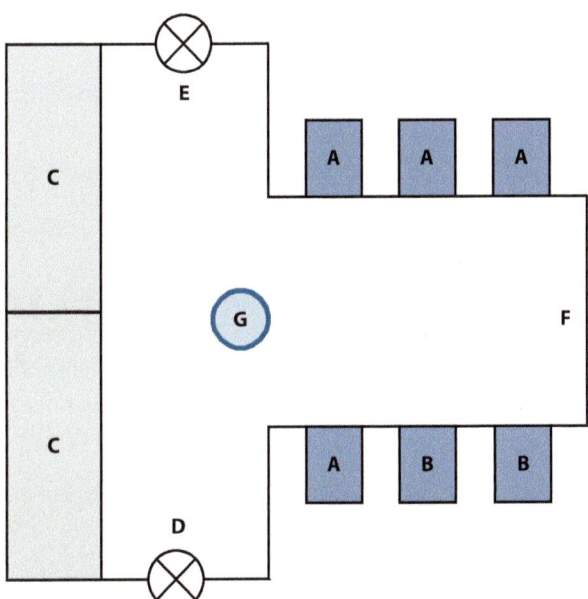

A: Elevators serving lobby and upper floors
B: Elevators serving lobby and lower floors
C: Restrooms
D: Building's main entrance
E: Main floor corridor
F: Controlled access/egress door
G: Receptionist/security guard station

## 1. Provide Clear Border Definition of Controlled Space

- It is a common law requirement that space must be defined to preserve property rights. *Boundaries may be physical or psychological. Fences, hedges, or signs help define private property.*
- The underlying principle is that a "reasonable individual" must be able to *recognize the defining line between public and private space.*
- Furniture arrangement and colour definitions may be used to *identify different types of interior spaces.*
- Murals and paintings on walls and in hallways help to *define ownership* and are powerful environmental cues that affect the behaviour and predisposition of owners, visitors, and other members of the public.

## 2. Provide Clearly Marked Transitional Zones

- It is important to *provide clearly marked transitional zones* when moving from public to semi-public, and semi-private to private space.
- *User behaviour should be influenced to conform to transitional definitions.* The user must recognize and acknowledge movement into a controlled space.

For example: A large resort that includes guest buildings, maintenance buildings, and staff residences may opt for different landscaping and outdoor lighting choices in the guest areas as distinguished from the maintenance and staff areas, and may place signs at the perimeter of the guest areas to indicate that the area beyond the signs is "staff only."

## 3. Relocation of Gathering Areas

- *Gathering or congregating areas should be placed in locations with good natural surveillance and access control.*
- In some cases, *gathering areas may be placed in positions that are out of the view* of undesired users *to decrease the potential for attracting unwelcome attention* from undesirable individuals or the criminal element.

For example: If a sports stadium has a history of fights breaking out between opposing fans or between fans and the public in the area outside the stadium's entry gates, the owner of the stadium might choose to relocate the entry gate from the remote end of the stadium (which may have originally been chosen because it's near parking lots) to a sheltered location out of plain view of the public and closer to an obviously staffed building with windows.

## 4. Place Safe Activities in Unsafe Locations

- Within reason, this strategy may be used to overcome problems on school campuses, in parks and offices, or in institutional settings.
- *Safe activities serve as magnets for normal users who exhibit challenging or controlling behaviours* (for example, staring) that leave other normal users unconcerned, but make abnormal users feel that they are at greater risk of scrutiny or intervention.
- *Be careful to not place a safe activity in an unreasonable position* that it cannot defend.

For example: If a university has problems with students being followed by would-be assailants down a particular dark pathway on weekend nights, it might establish a program that encourages buskers to perform in the area for tips during the late evening hours and for a period after the closing time for bars.

## 5. Place Unsafe Activities in Safe Locations

- *Placing vulnerable activities within sight of occupied space*, or in a well-supervised area, *will help to overcome risk* and make the users of these areas feel safer.

For example: Where a school has concerns about children being approached by outsiders during recess, it may choose to move the playground so that it is directly outside the school administrative office windows, and to enlarge those windows so that individuals who approach the playground can see school administrators watching.

## 6. Redesign the Use of Space to Provide Natural Barriers

- *Certain activities should be separated by distance, natural terrain, or other functions in order to avoid conflict.* For instance, the "trash talk" coming from a basketball court or other sports field may be upsetting to those in a nearby area used by young children or the elderly.
- The threat does not have to be real to create the perception of risk in the normal or desired user.

## 7. Improve Space Management

- *The effective and productive use of space reduces risk and the perception of risk for normal users.* Conversely, abnormal users feel at greater risk of surveillance and intervention in their activities in busy areas.
- Well-designed spaces improve profit and productivity, while increasing the control of behaviour.

For example: When choosing a facility for a business—for example, a warehousing and shipping business—the business owner should avoid renting too large a facility, even where large spaces are affordable. Having regular foot and vehicular traffic in all areas deters crime, while unused or lightly used storage areas offer hiding places and may attract break-ins.

## 8. Redesign Space to Increase the Perception of Natural Surveillance

- The *perception of surveillance* is more powerful than its reality.
- *Hidden cameras do not affect the behaviours of either law-abiding citizens or criminals* because they are unaware of the presence of these devices.
- Windows, clear lines-of-sight, and other natural techniques are often as effective as the use of surveillance cameras and security guards (see Figure 13.3).

**Figure 13.3** Landscaping Choices Can Improve Natural Surveillance

BEFORE | AFTER

## 9. Overcome Distance and Isolation

- Good communications *increase the perception* of natural surveillance and control.
- Facility managers and maintenance personnel should carry portable radios to improve communications and *create the perception* of immediate access to help.
- Common use areas such as restrooms and entranceways can be designed to increase convenience and reduce the cost of maintenance.

# Example 1: CPTED Applied to Storefronts

Retail stores are responsible for improving the safety of their workers and customers. Simple design features such as positioning cash registers near the main entrance and keeping ATMs visible can accomplish much in the way of making customers feel safe and secure.

## 1. Natural Access Control

- Cash registers should be located in view of the main entrance.
- Public paths should be clearly marked.
- Signs should direct patrons to parking and entrances.
- Access to the roof should be denied.
- Rear access to shops should be provided from rear parking lots.

## 2. Natural Surveillance

- Windows should overlook parking lots for increased visibility.
- Advertising should cover no more than 15 percent of windows.
- Interior shelving and displays should be no higher than five feet for increased visibility.
- The exterior of buildings should be well lit.
- Loading areas should be well lit and uncluttered.
- Clear visibility should be maintained from the store to the street, sidewalk, parking areas, and passing vehicles.
- All entrances should be under visual or electronic surveillance.

## 3. Territorial Reinforcement

- Define property boundaries using hedges, low fences, or gates.
- Private areas should be easily distinguishable from public areas.
- Shops should be identified by wall signs for those parking in the rear.
- Awnings should be installed over rear doors and windows.
- Parking areas should be clearly visible from the building or street.

## 4. Management

- Operating hours should coincide with those of other neighbouring businesses.
- ATM locations should be well lit and under surveillance at all times.
- Interior spaces should be well lit.

# Example 2: CPTED Applied to Shopping Malls

Shopping malls often provide much of the public space in suburban communities and attract many types of users. They often function as a gathering place for the community, and can attract criminal activity. While modern shopping malls have grown larger and more complex, they have also become a haven for abnormal users and the site of a growing number of parking lot crimes. It is therefore more important than ever that architects and contractors implement CPTED principles.

## 1. Natural Access Control

- Signs should clearly mark public entrances.
- Sidewalks and public areas should be clearly marked using special paving and/or landscaping.
- Loading zones with designated delivery hours should be separate from public parking.
- The parking garage should provide no exterior access to adjacent rooftops.

## 2. Natural Surveillance

- Restroom doors should be visible from main pedestrian areas and away from outside exits.
- Parking areas should be well lit.
- Loading areas should be well lit and uncluttered.
- All levels of the parking garage, and especially the stairwells, should be visible from the street or ground floor with high intensity lighting to minimize hiding places.

## 3. Territorial Reinforcements

- Property perimeters should be defined by landscaping, post and pillar fencing, or gates.
- Signs should clearly identify interior businesses.

### 4. Management

- Nighttime employee parking should be closest to the property.
- Business associations should work together to promote shopper and business safety.

## Example 3: CPTED Applied to a Drive-Through

Drive-throughs are potentially perfect places for criminal activity. They are used at odd hours, often hidden from view, and those using them will often be carrying cash. Visibility is the key to a safe and well-designed drive-through.

### 1. Natural Surveillance

- Locate ATMs in front of banks that face main roads or as drive-throughs in drive-in teller lanes.
- Put exterior restaurant ordering stations within sight of the interior of the restaurant.

## Example 4: CPTED Applied to Parking Facilities

In both urban and suburban environments, parking structures tend to attract the most problems. These structures isolate people. Most garages are not only badly designed—with many blind spots and hiding areas—but are poorly maintained as well. CPTED guidelines can be used to improve parking structure safety with minimal cost. The simple addition of high intensity lighting, for example, can improve the safety of a garage.

### 1. Natural Access Control

- Garages should be attended or openly monitored by cameras and intercoms that are indicated by posted signs.
- Pedestrian entrances should be adjacent to vehicle entrances.
- Use glass or screening on stairwell walls to allow visibility to and from the exterior.
- Position elevators close to the main entrance so the entire interior of the elevator is in view when the doors are open.
- Do not install a permanent stop button in elevators.
- Observation of the ground level should be enhanced by using wire mesh or stretch cable as perimeter barriers.
- Access should be limited to no more than two designated, monitored entrances.

### 2. Natural Surveillance

- Elevators should be monitored by cameras.
- Elevator walls should be made of clear materials.
- Retaining walls should be replaced with stretched cable railings for maximum visibility.
- Parking areas and driving lanes should be well-lit.

## 3. Management

- There should be no free access to adjacent buildings without direct monitoring.
- Public and private parking spaces should be designated.
- Hours of use should reflect that of local businesses, with secure closing during non-use hours.

### CHAPTER SUMMARY

This chapter provided an introduction to the principles of Crime Prevention Through Environmental Design (CPTED). CPTED principles aim to reduce crime and increase both the experience and perception of public safety through the thoughtful design of user spaces.

CPTED owes its origins to many contributors. The collective experience of police officers, military personnel, and community leaders has brought common sense, self-preservation, and a sense of pride and ownership to bear on the design of our surroundings. Security professionals should seek to understand the principles of CPTED, and use its lessons as much as possible in the application of their duties.

Crime Prevention Through Environmental Design guidelines can go a long way in creating a safe environment. While it has contributed toward a decline in criminal activity, CPTED needs to be used in conjunction with regular security initiatives to keep communities safe.

CPTED can eliminate problem areas: the badly lit parking lot, the blind alley, and the ATM stuck in the dark corner. It is hoped that along with the feelings of safety and security that CPTED brings will come a feeling of responsibility for our neighbour. That is the greatest crime prevention technique of all.

## KEY TERMS

CPTED, 236
CPTED fencing, 239
natural access control, 240
natural surveillance, 239
territoriality, 239

## NOTE

1. For a list of CPTED resources recommended by Peel Regional Police, see https://www.peelpolice.ca/en/crimeprevention/securityaudits.asp

## REFERENCES

CPTED Ontario. (2014). CPTED strategies. In *Crime Prevention Through Environmental Design*. Retrieved from http://cptedontario.ca/mission/cpted-strategies/

National Institute of Crime Prevention. (2015). Training courses. Retrieved from http://www.cptedtraining.net/

Peel Regional Police. (2015). Crime prevention through environmental design. Retrieved from https://www.peelpolice.ca/en/crimeprevention/crimepreventionthroughenvironmentaldesign.asp

Toronto Police Service. (2017). Crime Prevention Through Environmental Design (CPTED). In *Crime Prevention*. Retrieved from www.torontopolice.on.ca/crimeprevention/

## FURTHER READING

Crowe, T. (1991). *Crime prevention through environmental design: Application of architectural design and space management concepts*. Louisville, KY: National Institute of Crime Prevention.

Gardner, R. A. (1995). *Crime Prevention Through Environmental Design*. Retrieved from http://www.crimewise.com/library/cpted.html

McKay, T. (n.d.). What is CPTED? Retrieved from www.peelpolice.ca/en/crimeprevention/resources/whatiscpted.pdf

## PERFORMANCE APPLICATION
### Multiple Choice

1. Under CPTED, which of the following statements is *not* a part of "definition"?
   a. How is the space defined?
   b. For what purpose was it originally intended?
   c. Do social or cultural identifiers affect how the space is used?
   d. Are there clearly defined rules regarding use of the space?
   e. Are there signs posted?

2. Under CPTED, which of the following elements is *not* a part of "target hardening"?
   a. window locks
   b. dead bolts
   c. tamper resistant hinges
   d. neighbourhood watch
   e. impact resistant glass

3. Which one of the following is *not* one of the nine major CPTED principles?
   a. provide clearly marked transitional zones
   b. place safe activities in unsafe areas
   c. ensure that adequate insurance is provided
   d. provide clear border protection of controlled space
   e. relocation of gathering areas

4. Which one of the following is *not* one of the nine major CPTED principles?
   a. support security technology with manpower
   b. place unsafe activities in safe areas
   c. redesign the use of space to provide natural barriers
   d. improve space management
   e. overcome distance and isolation

5. Which one of the following is *not* an example of natural surveillance as applied to a store?
   a. windows should overlook parking lots for increased visibility
   b. advertising should not cover more than 15 percent of window area
   c. signs should direct patrons to parking and entrances
   d. exterior of buildings should be well lit
   e. entrances should be under visual or electronic surveillance

6. Which one of the following is an example of territorial reinforcement?
   a. place safe activities in unsafe areas
   b. shops should be identified by wall signs for those parking in the rear
   c. loading areas should be well-lit and uncluttered
   d. operating hours should coincide with those of other businesses
   e. provide clear border protection of controlled space

7. CPTED is based on four key strategies. Which of the following is *not* one of these?
   a. natural surveillance
   b. territoriality
   c. natural access control
   d. target hardening
   e. space management

8. Using glass panels or open metal grating as walls in a parking lot stairwell is an example of which of the following CPTED strategies?
   a. natural surveillance
   b. territoriality
   c. natural access control
   d. target hardening
   e. space management

## Short Answer

1. When thinking of applying CPTED to an existing facility, it is advisable to use the three Ds of CPTED as a guide. These provide a series of questions that should be asked before making decisions about how to proceed. Choose a facility and apply the questions that fall under the first of the three Ds: Designation. Be prepared to discuss your answers in class.
   Be prepared to answer the following questions as they apply to your chosen facility:
   a. What is the designated purpose of this space?
   b. For what purpose was it originally intended?
   c. How well does the space support its current or intended use?
   d. Is there a conflict with its location, or between potential users?

2. Choose a location in your community, such as a school, mall, library, or restaurant. Take a photograph of an area at your chosen location that illustrates an example of a "clearly marked transitional zone" and be prepared to explain how this CPTED strategy was used in your photo example.

3. Using the Internet, locate two photographs that show the before and after of a building or facility that has used CPTED to improve its security profile. Identify each of the changes implemented and identify which one of the four CPTED principles or the nine CPTED strategies they fall under.

# Evidence and Investigation

## 14

| | |
|---|---|
| Introduction | 252 |
| **Types of Security Investigations** | 252 |
| **Conducting an Investigation** | 252 |
| **Vehicle Accident Investigation** | 252 |
| **Evidence** | 253 |
| Types of Evidence | 253 |
| **Expert Testimony** | 255 |
| **Standards of Proof** | 255 |
| **Admissibility of Evidence** | 255 |
| **Collection and Preservation of Physical Evidence** | 255 |
| **Evidence Control** | 256 |
| **Securing Evidence** | 256 |
| **Protecting Evidence** | 257 |
| **Control and Continuity of Evidence** | 258 |
| **Record-Keeping** | 258 |
| **Consequences** | 258 |
| **Chapter Summary** | 258 |
| **Key Terms** | 259 |
| **References** | 259 |
| **Performance Application** | 259 |

## LEARNING OUTCOMES

When you have completed this chapter, you will:

- Have an understanding of how a security professional investigates incidents that occur at his or her place of work.
- Be familiar with procedures for specific incidents.
- Know how to collect, protect, and dispose of evidence and protect an incident scene.

# Introduction

Security personnel involved in investigations or who attend incident scenes may become responsible for securing, handling, and processing evidence (or, as evidence is eventually called in court, exhibits). A wide range of types of physical evidence can come under the control of a security professional, and each type requires particular handling and processing precautions. In certain minor incident investigations, a security guard may be responsible for exhibits from the start of an investigation to its conclusion. In the wake of more serious occurrences, security guards will play a role in securing and protecting evidence until other investigating authorities are on site and able to take over control.

# Types of Security Investigations

Security personnel typically conduct internal investigations if an incident falls under one of two categories: illegal activities or security breaches.

An illegal activity is any security violation or any activity or action contrary to any federal or provincial statute, such as the *Criminal Code* or *Trespass to Property Act*. This includes activities such as theft, fraud, mischief, assault, trespassing, and weapons offences.

A **security breach** is defined as any violation of a workplace policy, procedure, practice, or direction. This class of security breach includes all non-criminal security incidents.

**security breach** any violation of a workplace policy, procedure, practice, or direction; this class of security breach includes all non-criminal security incidents

# Conducting an Investigation

Security guards have to respond to every incident, conduct initial assessments, and submit incident reports to the security supervisor. The security supervisor may direct the guard to conclude the incident report or assign someone to assist in the investigation.

If during the course of an investigation it becomes apparent that a criminal act has taken place, the security supervisor must be notified immediately. The security supervisor will then call the external policing agency that has jurisdiction in the area and advise them of the circumstances.

The most common investigation a security guard is asked to conduct is an investigation of an accident on the employer's or client's property.

If the investigation is not conducted properly, the security company may be held responsible for any actual or perceived acts of omission or negligence found to have violated the rights of the accused. It is therefore essential for the security guard to perform in a way that preserves the rights of the accused and supports the credibility of the client and the security company.

# Vehicle Accident Investigation

Security personnel are usually the first responding authority to vehicle accidents on site. The guard's responsibilities here depend on existing conditions at the time of the incident.

**Minor accidents** have the following characteristics:

- Damage to vehicles is less than $2,000 in loss of value or repair costs.
- The accident is non-reportable according to the rules established by the province.
- There are no injuries.
- No serious driving or criminal violations are noted.

**minor accident** any incident that is non-reportable to the provincial authority and in which there are no injuries, no serious vehicle or criminal violations, and damages are under $2,000

In accidents of this nature, a security guard assesses the scene of the accident, controls traffic, offers assistance where possible, obtains vehicle and driver particulars for an incident report, clears the scene of any hazards, and files an incident report.

**Serious or injury accidents** are incidents with the following characteristics:

- Vehicles have incurred damage over $2,000 in value.
- Persons are injured.
- Criminal or motor vehicle operation violations are noted.

In accidents of this nature, a security guard assesses the scene of the accident, notifies the security supervisor, contacts the required assistance agency (police/ambulance/fire/tow truck), calls for assistance (if required), tends to the injured, secures the scene of the accident, and awaits arrival of the external policing agency. Security personnel are also required to secure and protect any obvious evidence (liquor/drugs/weapons), control traffic and any crowds that may have gathered, and, as soon as is practical, document his or her involvement and submit an incident report.

**serious or injury accident**
any incident in which there are injuries, vehicle or criminal violations, and damages are over $2,000

# Evidence

Evidence is the means by which facts or points of dispute can be supported or established. In general terms, evidence is something that tends to prove or give grounds for belief, in accordance with legal principles, of various elements that are necessary to support or establish that a specific act was in fact committed by the subject or an accused individual.

## Types of Evidence

A successful investigation will involve, as its primary goal, the collection of three kinds of evidence: witness (oral/verbal) evidence, physical (or "real") evidence, and documentary evidence.

### Witness Evidence

Witnesses give evidence under oath by describing events that they have witnessed. Witness evidence can be classified as direct, circumstantial, or hearsay evidence.

- A witness gives **direct evidence** when they can testify that the knowledge of it came from one or more of the five senses (taste, smell, sight, touch, or hearing); for example: *I saw the suspect shoot the victim*.
- A witness gives **circumstantial evidence** when relevant conclusions can be derived from their testimony by inference; for example: *I saw the suspect standing over the victim's body with a smoking gun*.
- A witness gives **hearsay evidence** when he or she reports information received from other individuals, rather than reporting information observed directly; for example: *Bob told me that he saw the suspect shoot the victim*.

**direct evidence**
evidence that the witness observed using his or her own senses

**circumstantial evidence**
evidence that suggests a conclusion but only by inference; for example, an electronic record showing that an individual's access card was tapped on a card reader

**hearsay evidence**
witness evidence that is "second-hand" in that it comprises an account of another person's description of direct evidence

### Physical Evidence

Physical evidence can be of any material or size. Whatever its nature, conclusions can generally be drawn from direct examination of physical evidence.

Although the investigator may not be able to analyze the evidence personally, its documentation and preservation should never be neglected. Once it has been damaged or destroyed, it can never be recreated.

Once physical evidence of any type has been collected, it is the responsibility of the investigator to ensure its safekeeping until the case is completed. This means that if ever the evidence is handed to another person, that person should be required to sign for his or her acceptance of it. Should anything happen to the evidence while in the new holder's possession, this individual can be held accountable.

When physical evidence is eventually produced in court, the party presenting it is required to prove the integrity of the evidence. In other words, that party must show that it has not been tampered with in any way. For physical or real evidence to be admitted into the court record as an exhibit, it must first be identified by a witness. This will often be the person who discovered or collected the evidence at the crime scene (for example, a security guard). The witness (or additional witnesses) must also prove to the court's satisfaction that the evidence has been kept in continuously traceable possession, and that it has been protected from any influences (water, other people's fingerprints, fibres, etc.) that could affect its original state at the time of collection.

## *Documentary and Secondary Evidence*

Documentary evidence includes documents, of course, but it also extends to other representations of information, such as photographs and recordings.

In a few cases, documentary evidence is treated by the court as a form of physical evidence—for example, where the document was either the subject of the crime (for example, in the case of a stolen manuscript), or was handled or altered by a suspect (for example, if a suspect signed a guestbook at a wedding at which a crime took place). When introduced in these kinds of situations, documentary evidence can be **primary evidence**, which is somewhat analogous to the term physical evidence.

Much more often, however, documentary evidence is **secondary evidence**, which means it is admitted in court as a representative copy of the real (physical) evidence in cases where the actual evidence (such as a bank's vault door that has been tampered with) cannot be brought into the courtroom. When a witness endorses a specific drawing or photograph as an accurate representation of the original object, it becomes acceptable secondary evidence. Other forms of secondary evidence are documents that provide written support for an oral agreement; for example, a written contract.

To identify and confirm the legitimacy of any written document or secondary evidence, such as, for example, a contract or will, a witness must:

- have seen the person writing it at the time it was written to recognize and identify the handwriting;
- have personal knowledge of the person's handwriting to recognize and identify it; or
- be an expert in handwriting analysis to identify the person's handwriting.

Today, documentary evidence has gone beyond the traditional written or typed page to embrace computer data stored on drives and cloud storage. Likewise, e-commerce and email over the Internet produce the new phenomenon of virtual evidence. The analysis of these forms of evidence is typically outside a security guard's job function. However, it is important for security personnel to be aware of how traditional crimes can be committed using one or more computers as tools. Investigating these crimes effectively depends on the careful collection and preservation of computer hardware and software, which should be subject to the same precautions applied to physical evidence (to be discussed below).

---

**primary evidence**
evidence that stands alone and can be analyzed directly; for example, a chemical substance or a piece of fabric

**secondary evidence**
evidence that is a representation of primary evidence; for example, a photograph of a damaged vault door

Computer investigations rely on the analysis of both stored data and details on the use and creation of that data; for example, dates and times that files were created, modified, and/or last accessed by the computer user.

## Expert Testimony

Some evidence can be very complicated. In these cases, the court requires a specialist or expert with knowledge, skill, experience, training, or education in the subject to help a judge and jury understand the significance of the evidence offered, so that they can feel confident enough to make decisions that will affect their verdict.

## Standards of Proof

For the Crown to win a conviction in a criminal prosecution, the evidence presented in court must prove beyond a reasonable doubt that the accused has committed the offence with which he or she was charged. This is called the **standard of proof**.

In a civil lawsuit, the standard of proof is lower: the claimant (plaintiff) must simply prove that the odds probably favour his or her version of events over the defendant's; in other words, that there is at least a 51 percent chance that the plaintiff's allegations are well-founded. This standard of proof is known as the balance of probabilities.

**standard of proof**
the level of certainty with respect to facts and events that must be established in a particular kind of proceeding (criminal or civil) to allow the proving party (prosecution or plaintiff) to succeed

## Admissibility of Evidence

Regardless of the quality of evidence, unless there are overwhelming reasons to override the general rule, evidence will only be admitted in court if it was obtained through means that respected the law and the rights of the accused.

The most common reason for physical evidence to be deemed inadmissible (not admissible in court) is that the evidence cannot be "placed" at the scene of the crime by a witness's testimony, or that it has been contaminated.

The most common reason for statement evidence to be excluded is that the evidence was collected in the context of a violation of a suspect's rights under the *Canadian Charter of Rights and Freedoms* (see Chapter 8, Legal Authorities).

## Collection and Preservation of Physical Evidence

When security personnel first come across an incident scene, it is critical that they stop and scan the entire area, examining everything in view for possible evidence. At the same time, they need to fix the placement of every object in their minds. First impressions are important and security guards should use all their senses. A perfume's scent, or the smell of chemical fumes or cigarette or cigar smoke may later in the investigation become key clues in identifying a suspect who has fled the scene.

It is equally important to note what's missing from the scene: a picture from a wall or a matching bookend on the mantel.

It takes discipline to resist the urge to rush in, help victims, and snatch up evidence. Such careless action, however, can compromise the Crown's case in court. Why? Tiny shreds of evidence that may identify a suspect more precisely may be overlooked, disturbed, or damaged. Moreover, hasty actions may result in depositing evidence, such as careless fingerprints or hair, on the scene. Later, these are collected as part of the evidence and they tie up forensics teams with misleading possibilities. This is called **contaminating the evidence**, and if the defendant's lawyer can prove the evidence has been contaminated, it will be inadmissible in court.

Instead, a security guard should pause, take everything in, note where pieces of evidence are, and then cautiously move through the scene without disturbing anything.

**contaminating the evidence**
altering evidence by tainting it with non-evidence; for example, getting one's own fingerprints on a glass handled by a suspect

# Evidence Control

When security personnel control evidence following minor incidents, they are expected to:

1. photograph any evidence at the scene, whenever possible;
2. mark all exhibits for identification, including the time, date, and initials (on the item when possible or on an attached tag or seal), and this includes photographs after they are processed;
3. keep a list of exhibits secured as evidence;
4. wear latex gloves when handling (collecting or examining) the evidence;
5. use appropriate packaging for storage: liquids are stored in sterile jars or vials and solids are to be put in evidence bags;
6. in the case of large evidence that cannot be moved or preserved as a whole (large spill of liquids on the ground), ensure that the samples collected are accurate representatives of the actual evidence;
7. create a sketch plan that shows where any representative samples of evidence were found—the sketch plan should be preserved with the samples collected;
8. seal the exhibit in an exhibit bag, if possible, and keep it in personal possession or under lock and key;
9. maintain a control ledger that details any movement of the exhibit from the time it is secured;
10. dispose of exhibits (as directed by the security manager) at the conclusion of an investigation or at the end of appeal periods if the exhibits have been used in court as evidence; and
11. maintain entries in their notebooks, documenting all details of their involvement with any evidence that has come into their possession.

# Securing Evidence

When a security guard is responsible for securing and protecting evidence that is related to more serious incident scenes or criminal investigations, he or she must:

1. keep visual contact with the scene at all times;
2. not touch or move any exhibits;
3. not permit unauthorized persons to move or touch any evidence;
4. assist external investigators where possible;
5. account for evidence coming into their possession or under his or her control; and
6. keep detailed notes about any role he or she played in securing or protecting an incident scene. If necessary, a diagram of the scene should be drawn to show where original evidence was found. Security personnel may be required to give supportive evidence in court.

# Protecting Evidence

Evidence can be contaminated in a variety of ways, depending, for instance, on the type of evidence or weather conditions at the time of collection. Security guards need follow only a few basic rules to control or secure evidence to make sure it is not contaminated and therefore inadmissible in court:

1. Do not handle or touch exhibits that may contain fingerprints—for example, paper, glass, or other solid items. If it is necessary to handle exhibits, wear disposable gloves.
2. Items like clothing and other soft material should be placed in plastic exhibit bags.
3. Any fluids, including blood or other body fluids, should be protected and left for the experts.
4. Any evidence exposed to weather should be covered where possible or moved to a protected area. If it becomes necessary to move or bag it, do so as carefully as possible.
5. Protect tire and footwear impressions, etc., until all investigations involving them are completed.
6. Weapons or tools should be protected and left for the experts or moved with caution with a minimum of handling and using all appropriate protection.

Figure 14.1 summarizes the duties of security guards with respect to the collection and preservation of evidence.

**Figure 14.1**  Security Guard Duties for Evidence Preservation

| Evidence Control | | Protection of Evidence | Continuity of Evidence | Record-Keeping |
|---|---|---|---|---|
| **Minor Incidents** | **Major Incidents** | | | |
| Photograph each piece of evidence | Maintain visual contact with scene | Avoid touching any item that could contain fingerprints | ID each item with an evidence tag | Photos, evidence tags, and memo book |
| ID each item with an evidence tag | Do not touch or move any items | Wear disposable gloves | Secure items in evidence bags under lock and key | Evidence tags, evidence bags, and memo book |
| Keep/secure a list of evidence items | Do not permit unauthorized contact with anything at the scene | Place clothing and soft items in plastic evidence bags | Keep control of evidence key until evidence goes to court or is turned over to other authorities | Evidence bags, secured items list, and memo book |
| Seal item in an evidence bag and keep it locked up | Assist external investigators | Protect blood and body fluids from contamination until experts arrive | Document any movement of evidence in an evidence log | Evidence bags, evidence log, and memo book |
| Keep control of all items in an evidence log | Keep track of all events at the scene in memo book | Cover evidence exposed to weather or move it to a protected area | Record any movement of evidence in memo book | Evidence log and memo book |
| Dispose of evidence according to protocol | Draw a diagram of the scene that shows the position of evidence items. Prepare incident report | Protect footprints and tire impressions until investigations are completed | | Crime scene diagram and memo book |
| Keep track of personal contact with evidence in memo book | Be prepared to attend court to give supportive evidence | Protect but do not move weapons or tools until experts arrive | | Memo book and incident reports |

## Control and Continuity of Evidence

In the course of an investigation, evidence may pass from one person to another. Such a transfer constitutes a change in the **continuity of possession**. A security guard has to show the chain of custody of the item from the time it was received until it is admitted as evidence in court. Once the evidence is handed over to another individual, accountability for that item passes to that person. When unexplainable breaks in the continuity of any evidence occur, it immediately suggests that there was an opportunity to tamper with an exhibit, and based on that doubt, renders the evidence inadmissible in court.

When it is a security guard's responsibility to ensure continuity, he or she must:

1. Tag all evidence, showing his or her initials and the time and date. This begins continuity.
2. Secure under lock and key any evidence that is to remain in his or her possession. Keep control of the key until the evidence goes to court or it is turned over to another authority.
3. Document any movement of evidence on a control sheet to support total continuity. This control sheet must remain with the evidence.
4. Document the continuity of evidence in his or her notebook as well. This record may have to be used in court for reference, especially when evidence is turned over to another authority.

> **continuity of possession**
> an unbroken chain or account of possession of an item of evidence with no gaps during which can no one account for the location of the evidence

## Record-Keeping

It is important to maintain accurate records relating to the handling of evidence. Again, record all procedures that take place with respect to the protection of the evidence at the scene of an incident. The notebook should contain information about the incident scene and any evidence involving security. Any logs or other records about the evidence can then be cross-referenced with these notes.

## Consequences

The main consequence of mishandling evidence is the possibility of failing to bring an investigation to a successful conclusion. There is nothing more disheartening than having a case dismissed in court because of poor procedures in the handling, protection, and continuity of evidence. Even worse, the court's dismissal of a case presented by the security company may result in a lawsuit against the company, its client, and any participating security guard.

### CHAPTER SUMMARY

This chapter discussed the types of incidents that are most commonly investigated by security personnel. It also discussed the involvement of security personnel in more serious investigations requiring the assistance of public law enforcement agencies. The basic rules of evidence, standards of proof, and requirements for preserving the admissibility of evidence were introduced.

The preservation and protection of incident scenes, and the collection and storage of physical evidence were described. The concept of continuity of evidence was introduced, and procedures for maintaining and documenting continuity were suggested.

Security personnel must learn to use the utmost care and caution whenever they become involved with any items of evidence and make sure they apply the required procedures at all times.

## KEY TERMS

circumstantial evidence, 253
contaminating the evidence, 256
continuity of possession, 258
direct evidence, 253
hearsay evidence, 253
minor accident, 252
primary evidence, 254
secondary evidence, 254
security breach, 252
serious or injury accident, 253
standard of proof, 255

## REFERENCES

*Canadian Charter of Rights and Freedoms*, Part I of the Constitution Act, 1982, being Schedule B to the Canada Act 1982 (UK), 1982, c 11.

*Criminal Code*, RSC 1985, c C-46.

*Trespass to Property Act*, RSO 1990, c T.21.

## PERFORMANCE APPLICATION
### Multiple Choice

1. Which of these is *not* a recognized type of evidence?
   a. primary evidence
   b. hearsay evidence
   c. documentary evidence
   d. testamentary evidence
   e. witness evidence

2. What is the first thing a security guard should do upon arriving at an incident scene (after ensuring his or her own immediate safety, of course)?
   a. provide first aid to injured victims
   b. cover the scene with a tarp to prevent contamination
   c. pause on the threshold of the scene and use all of his or her senses (sight, hearing, smell, etc.) to observe the undisturbed scene
   d. gain authority and control of all individuals present
   e. none of the above

3. Where there is a break in the continuity of possession of a piece of evidence, the judge may:
   a. conclude that the evidence may have been tampered with
   b. file perjury charges against the person who had possession of the evidence
   c. order a discontinuation
   d. declare the evidence to be hearsay
   e. all of the above

4. Which is *not* a follow-up step that security personnel should undertake in the wake of a major motor vehicle accident on private property?
   a. contact police
   b. secure the scene with barriers to keep other traffic away
   c. provide information to investigating police personnel
   d. move vehicles and debris to the roadside
   e. prepare an incident report for the client

5. Which of these incidents are security professionals *not* likely to investigate while on the job?
   a. dumping of residential garbage on the client's premises
   b. collision of a delivery truck into a loading platform causing minor damage and no injuries
   c. destruction of landscaping plantings, apparently by vandals
   d. abduction of a resident's child in an apartment complex
   e. repeated reports of excessive noise in the parking lot of a client's private establishment

6. Mishandling of an investigation by a security professional can lead to:
   a. acquittal of the accused
   b. a ruling that evidence is inadmissible
   c. an inference that evidence may be contaminated
   d. a civil suit against the professional's employer
   e. all of the above

7. When collecting evidence after a spill incident, which is *not* a standard procedure for security personnel?
   a. cover the incident scene with a canopy or tarp if there is possibility of rain contamination
   b. photograph the spill, marking the location from which samples are collected
   c. collect samples of the spilled material in sterile vials
   d. collect the entire spill to ensure continuity
   e. cordon off the area to prevent contamination by passersby

8. What is the most common reason for exclusion from evidence of an accused's statement?

   a. the statement was obtained in circumstances in which the accused's Charter rights were violated
   b. the statement is circumstantial
   c. the statement is hearsay
   d. the statement is uncorroborated
   e. the statement mentions physical evidence that has been shown to be contaminated

## Short Answer

1. Why might a security guard who collected a piece of evidence (say, a chisel left at the crime scene) be required to testify in court? What types of questions do you expect would be asked?

2. If you were charged with collecting evidence at a crime scene, how would you collect or protect:

   a. a dropped access control card?
   b. scrape marks on a parking garage pillar?
   c. drops of blood on a concrete floor?
   d. an abandoned car?

# Retail Security

## 15

| | |
|---|---|
| **Introduction** | 262 |
| **Principal Sources of Loss** | 262 |
| **The Nature of Retail Crime** | 263 |
|     National Figures | 264 |
| **Categories of Shoplifters** | 265 |
| **Asset Protection** | 265 |
|     Human Surveillance | 265 |
|     Closed-Circuit Television Cameras | 266 |
|     Electronic Article Surveillance | 266 |
|     CheckInk II | 266 |
|     Tamper-Evident Seals | 266 |
|     Signs | 267 |
|     Mirrors | 267 |
|     Merchandise Display | 268 |
|     Packaging | 269 |
|     Store Layout | 269 |
|     Fitting Room Policy | 270 |
|     Refund Procedures | 270 |
| **Special Tips and Strategies** | 271 |
|     Training Tips | 271 |
|     Undercover Security Tips | 271 |
| **Chapter Summary** | 273 |
| **Key Terms** | 274 |
| **References** | 274 |
| **Performance Application** | 274 |

## LEARNING OUTCOMES

When you have completed this chapter, you will:

- Have a basic knowledge and understanding of retail security, as well as how merchants can protect themselves from losses due to theft and shoplifting.
- Be familiar with common technologies used to secure merchandise in the retail sector.
- Be able to explain strategies for detecting and deterring suspicious activity.
- Be able to explain the elements of a theft and why continuity of observation is essential to a successful prosecution.

# Introduction

Retail security forms one of the basic duties of many security guards, and a major chain store that employs professional security personnel can save millions of dollars a year.

This chapter covers retail security in two sections. The first section discusses the principles of retail security and conditions that support retail theft. In the second section, the specifics of asset protection are outlined and the resources available to combat theft and shoplifting are considered.

The statistics on retail crime reveal how serious the problem is and how much it affects Canadian business. Some security professionals even believe that shoplifting may be more lucrative than robbing banks.

How could that be? For many people, the perception of shoplifting is that it's a petty crime. Many retailers are making a conscious effort to change this perception by not referring to theft from their stores as shoplifting anymore. Terms such as "retail theft," "shop theft," or simply "theft" are being used more commonly. Whether perceived as petty or not, when losses are totalled, shop theft significantly impacts retailers' profitability.

Retail **shrink** is described in terms of a percentage of sales, with 1 percent being the threshold that retailers commonly strive to stay below, depending on the type of retail. The higher a store's sales, the lower its shrink percentage will be, if shrink can be contained below a certain cost. Demand from consumers for the freedom to roam through store aisles to buy goods on open display presents a significant challenge to security professionals, who must focus not only on apprehending criminals, but also on developing strategies to prevent retail crime. Depending on which retailer a security professional works for, there could be thousands of customers coming into the store every day. Knowing who to spend time watching and who not to bother watching is fundamental to being a valuable member of a retail security team.

> **shrink (also called "shrinkage")**
> retail inventory losses attributed to shoplifting, employee theft, and administrative error

# Principal Sources of Loss

There are five principal sources of loss to retailers (see Figure 15.1):

1. **External theft:** Thirty-eight percent of losses stem from shoplifting, break and enter, and robbery.
2. **Internal theft:** Employees who steal from employers, including that innocent "extra box of pencils or bottle of nail polish," contribute to $3 million nationally per day, or 33 percent of retailers' total losses.

**Figure 15.1** Loss Categories in Canada, 2012

|  | 2012 | 2008 |
| --- | --- | --- |
| Internal theft | 33.4% | 19.0% |
| External theft | 43.0% | 65.0% |
| Paperwork errors | 19.9% | 16.0% |
| Vendor fraud | 3.7% |  |

*Source*: Retail Council of Canada/PwC, 2012, p. 8.

3. **Operational errors:** Errors made in the way retailers record and account for their inventory contribute to 21 percent of retailers' total losses. These errors are most often the result of human error or carelessness.
4. **Vendor fraud:** Suppliers who overcharge or double-charge shipments or in some way cheat retailers contribute to 8 percent of total losses. In fairness, many times these errors are unintentional and, as a result, can lead to overages as well as shortages.
5. **Return fraud. Return fraud** is a more recent type of threat that occurs when customers intend to "borrow" merchandise: they use it and then return it; or where thieves return stolen goods without a receipt to get a refund. The costs in losses from these practices are just beginning to be tracked. Retailers have learned strategies to discourage this kind of behaviour without directly impacting the honest customer's store experience. Retailers whose return policies lean toward maintaining customer loyalty will ultimately suffer.

**return fraud**
where an individual either purchases items to use them with no intention of keeping them, or attempts to return stolen merchandise for a cash refund

# The Nature of Retail Crime

The following statistics from the 2012 Retail Council of Canada security survey help illustrate where theft opportunities lie. The retailers that participated in the survey reported that:

- 43 percent of their shrink was a result of external theft (non-employees);
- 33.4 percent of their shrink was attributed to internal or employee theft;
- the average dollar value per external theft was $180;
- the average dollar value per internal theft was $1,056; and
- 4.2 percent of all refunds were fraudulent (Retail Council of Canada/PwC, 2012, p. 8).

## Security Spotlight

### Special Challenges

Some retail businesses face special challenges when it comes to internal theft. Retailers who do most of their business in a specific season often hire short-term, seasonal staff who may be less committed to the employer (and thus less honest) and less traceable than permanent staff. Completing thorough background checks on people who are being considered for a position with your company is a worthwhile investment.

In addition, there is high staff turnover in the retail sector, in part because the average salary is low, often starting at minimum wage. The need to continually hire new staff and the frequent staff changes that result create a climate of staffing impermanence in the retail industry, which poses a significant challenge from the perspective of curtailing employee theft. Retail employers should be aware of these factors and take extra steps. It's important that, when hiring, an employer takes the time to hire well. Employers should spend time interviewing candidates to help ensure the business is hiring people that have many of the core competencies required for them to be successful and that the individuals hired are looking for employment for the right reasons. To offset increased risks, employers might want to consider having security personnel engage in closer supervision of newly hired staff.

**Figure 15.2** Canadian Retail Industry Shrink Rates as a Percentage of Sales

| Sales Range | Low | High | Average |
| --- | --- | --- | --- |
| 0–$500M | 0.04% | 2.19% | 0.95% |
| $500M–$1B | 1.29% | 1.29% | 1.29% |
| $1B–$5B | 0.06% | 2.00% | 1.20% |
| >$5B | 0.58% | 1.34% | 0.94% |

*Source*: Retail Council of Canada/PwC, 2012, p. 6.

With shrink often expressed as a percentage of sales, the types of stores that feel the effects of shoplifting the hardest are smaller retailers with up to $500 million in annual sales. This category of businesses reported an average shrink rate of 2.19 percent (p. 7). See Figure 15.2.

## National Figures

Losses due to shrink for Canadian retailers were measured to be approximately $4 billion annually in 2008 (p. 7).

Shrink is money lost off the store or company's bottom-line profit as a result of inventory inaccuracies. Shrink is typically caused by criminal activity such as theft or fraud, and can also be caused by unintentional human error. As a result, shrink losses don't include the cost that retailers incur in fighting shrink, such as hiring and training employees, including security professionals; installing camera systems; purchasing or developing data mining software; and any physical security that might be needed, such as locks, inventory control tags, and showcases.

> **RFID tag**
> a security tag that uses radio technology to communicate information to a monitoring system so that specific items can be tracked

## FOCUS ON TECHNOLOGY

### Disposable Surveillance Tags and Strips

The electronic surveillance tags of the past were bulky and occasionally interfered with the appearance of merchandise, but new technological innovations have led to the development of very small and unobtrusive tags and strips that, instead of being removed at the point of purchase, are simply de-activated and left on merchandise packaging. These tags seldom interfere with a customer's ability to examine and/or try on merchandise, and provide some measure of security against theft.

Again, with shrink measured as a percentage of sales, one easy way to decrease shrink is to increase sales while minimizing the risk of theft. This is one reason why these types of tags have gained popularity.

One of the main disadvantages of such tags is that they are often designed to be applied not to merchandise itself, but to packaging; so, if a thief manages to remove the article's packaging before leaving the store, the theft may well go undetected.

There is now a new type of tag that has the potential to offer better ways for retailers to monitor and control their inventory (see Figure 15.3). RFID technology allows a retailer who has applied **RFID tags** to their merchandise to instantly know how many of that item are within a store or building.

Retailers typically apply these tags to high-risk items such as tablet computers, cameras, computers, high-end clothing, jewellery, and so on. The retailer is then able to take an accurate inventory of the tagged items multiple times per week. Doing this can greatly increase the ability to control losses. When a retailer takes an inventory and notices one less item than should be present, the retailer knows not only that the item has been stolen, but also within what time frame it disappeared. From an investigative standpoint, this information greatly increases the retailer's chances of identifying how an item went missing. Who had access to the relevant areas during the time in which the theft occurred? Pinpointing the theft could then simply be a matter of reviewing video for the relevant time period.

RFID tags also work the way a normal inventory control tag would work by alerting employees when an unpaid item is leaving the store. However, in addition to setting off the alarm, RFID will give the store information about what specific item set off the alarm.

Although the cost of RFID has come down over the past few years and many retailers are experimenting with it, it is still relatively expensive. However, now that the technology exists, we can expect that most retailers will use it in the future.

**Figure 15.3** RFID Tag

## Categories of Shoplifters

Professional shoplifters account for 20 percent of all shoplifters and for very high dollar losses. They target items with high resale value, such as jewellery, electronics, and high-end clothing. Often working in organized groups, they sometimes use children as decoys. Professional shoplifters are well-rehearsed, aggressive, and difficult to detect. When they are detected, they often resist capture.

Amateurs (including kleptomaniacs and the poor) make up 80 percent of shoplifters and are responsible for the bulk of losses. Motivated by greed or need, they usually steal on impulse when opportunity presents itself.

Among the pool of amateur shoplifters are addicts—who may steal based on a need for money or for substances to which they are addicted—and thrill seekers (often youth) who steal on a dare or just to see if they can get away with it.

## Asset Protection

There are eight basic countermeasures employed throughout the retail industry to combat shoplifting and theft. These are human surveillance, closed-circuit television cameras (CCTVs) and other types of camera installations, **electronic article surveillance, CheckInk II, tamper-evident seals,** signs, mirrors, and merchandise display.

### Human Surveillance

Store employees trained in surveillance are the most effective deterrent to shoplifters, according to Toronto Eaton Centre Director of Security Jim McDermott. First on his list is the "power of observation." He trains his security employees to be attentive and alert. It's important to have security professionals who can identify a potentially dishonest customer

**electronic article surveillance**
a loss control method that relies on the use of electronic tags on merchandise and a reader at the store exit that warns of a tagged item being removed from the store

**CheckInk II**
a tag that discharges ink onto an item when a thief attempts to remove it without the specialized removal device

**tamper-evident seals**
seals that break and show tampering if a thief attempts to open packaging or item compartments

quickly and easily. However, it's equally important to transfer the same skills to store employees. If more employees know what to watch for and can easily identify a customer that may be considering doing something illegal, a store will be more profitable.

## Closed-Circuit Television Cameras

Properly sited closed-circuit television cameras (CCTVs) used in a retail store are an integral part of a retail security plan. These cameras come in many forms and sizes and may be used in almost any environment. They can be hidden or camouflaged (for example, inside the clothing of a store mannequin) or may be openly visible in places such as domes mounted on a ceiling or as monitors angled so that customers can see themselves when they walk into a bank or store.

## Electronic Article Surveillance

Electronic article surveillance (EAS) systems have at least three components: tags, sensors, and alarms. There are various types of tags, with three system types currently in common use.

First, there is the VHF/microwave system. In this system, the tag contains a semiconductor chip that, when radiated by the transmitter frequency, reflects a signal to the receiver.

The second type of system incorporates a magnetic field rather than radio waves. Here, the tag contains a strip that is sensed by a magnetometer. Most components are reusable, but some newer systems have tags that can be desensitized and thrown away.

The third type is RFID technology or Radio Frequency Identification. This system represents the future of inventory protection, giving the retailer the ability to determine within seconds the total number of a particular tagged item in the building, as well as identifying which specific item set off an alarm at the exit.

Some EAS systems use large plastic tags that attach to clothing with a metal pin. These tags can be removed only with a special tool and can be reused. They not only aid in apprehension, but also serve as loss-prevention devices. The tags serve as a deterrent by decreasing the incentive to steal.

There was an overall reduction of less than 1 percent in inventory shrinkage over three years after EAS systems were first introduced into stores. Users claimed that there was a return on investment in the first year and that they were better able to identify employees who were committing internal theft. Also, retailers who implemented EAS were able to increase sales on items that were formerly kept under lock and key. EAS provides retailers with an opportunity to protect their merchandise in a way that is unobtrusive to their honest customers.

## CheckInk II

CheckInk II, a non-sensor-based system, is an ink-based "denial" system (see Figure 15.4). When the tag is removed without the use of a special tool, ink explodes out of the tag to deface the attached clothing.

## Tamper-Evident Seals

Some merchandise may carry seals that reveal tampering when they are removed. For example, in the case of a leased laptop whose hard drive may be exchanged for a less expensive type, the seal cannot be re-affixed, because it would now read "void."

## Figure 15.4 Ink-Based Clothing Security Tag

## Signs

There are conflicting viewpoints as to the usefulness of signs that warn against shoplifting. While some merchants feel that such signs are an insult to the great majority of honest shoppers who may become angry and take their business elsewhere, others believe that such signs have no effect on honest people because they have no criminal intent. Ultimately, customers who intend to steal will be reminded of the seriousness of their actions when they see these signs and may change their minds. Anti-shoplifting signage in stores is a low-cost strategy that will prevent at least some retail theft.

There are no statistics available to demonstrate the effectiveness of these signs, but there is also no denying the psychological impact on an amateur dishonest customer.

The most common types of anti-shoplifting signs are the following:

- Signs that warn of the presence of "store security professionals."
- Signs that warn of "prosecution" or of the repercussions of shop theft. Some are even humorous, offering "free ride in a police car" or "free bracelets for anyone caught shoplifting!"
- Signs that warn of the use of CCTV.

## Mirrors

Many types of mirrors can be used to enhance security within a retail environment. Mirrors can offer another low-cost solution when trying to make shop theft more difficult for thieves. Mirrors must be sited according to the layout of the store, and care should be taken to select the type most suited to the immediate area. Remember that although curved mirrors can enlarge the viewing area, they also distort the image. Flat mirrors are best for direct observation and offer the least distortion.

Mirrors most often used for security purposes are convex, regular, and one-way.

Convex full-dome mirrors provide full 360° visibility and are usually positioned above a lane intersection.

Convex half-dome mirrors afford 180° visibility and are usually positioned above a three-way "T" intersection.

Convex quarter-dome mirrors afford 90° visibility and are usually positioned above a two-way "L" intersection.

Many retailers have abandoned one-way mirrors in favour of CCTV and other types of camera systems; however, you may still find yourself working for a retailer that has one-way mirrors set up. These allow a security professional to stand or sit behind the mirror and monitor an area of a store that is hard to watch from the sales floor, contains high theft items, or is used by thieves to conceal items from other areas of the store.

## Merchandise Display

With shrink expressed as a percentage of a store's sales, anything that can be done to increase sales will ultimately lower that store's percentage of shrink. The trick is to find a balance between sales-friendly displays that still allow the retailer to secure and protect theft-sensitive items.

There are several strategies used by merchants to accomplish this. A few important ones are outlined below.

### Secured Samples

A secured sample on display will have wires attached to it that do not detract from the appearance of the item but will still allow a customer to pick up, handle, and sometimes even use the item. This type of security is used most often in stores that sell electronics—items that previously remained under lock and key. In stores using secured samples, customers can handle or even try cameras, cellphones, and even computers before purchasing them.

### Lockup Display

One of the most widely used forms of display security is the lockup display or showcase. The lockup display is often used when small, valuable items need to be displayed. Jewellery, watches, expensive sunglasses, personal electronics, and perfumes are some of the items protected in this manner. This ensures that the items are handled only in the presence of a salesperson. For showcases to be effective they must be maintained. Security personnel may be asked to perform audits on areas where high theft items are stored or displayed on the sales floor and in the stockroom. Ensuring that showcase doors and locks haven't been tampered with, and that the keys to these showcases are controlled and kept secure at all times is imperative for the successful secure use of showcases.

### Choice of Location

Where items are displayed within a store also influences whether they will be more or less likely to be stolen. Items close to the store exit invite snatch attacks. In small leather-goods stores, leather jackets near an exit are often secured using cables. The cables can be strong, cut-resistant cables or thinner electronic cables that, if cut, will sound an alarm. In department stores with multiple entrances and exits and with multiple items displayed near doors, stores often hang merchandise and alternate the directions in which the hangers hang. Doing this makes it more difficult for a thief to quickly grab several items and run to a waiting car. Thieves are instead forced to remove the items one at a time, which slows them down and attracts attention. Both methods reduce the possibility of a snatch attack. Inexpensive items can be placed in store areas that are the most difficult for staff to observe.

### *Symmetry*

This simple technique works on the principle that our eyes are drawn naturally to any break in a pattern. Anything different tends to stand out. Consequently, if items are displayed close together in a distinct pattern, when one (or more) is removed, the disruption of symmetry is recognized very quickly. This allows employees and security staff to react quickly to a loss, possibly before the thief has left the premises.

## Packaging

From meat to video games, the technology of packaging for security has developed to keep pace with the increase in losses from stores. Several techniques are employed in the design and application of security packaging. Here are a few examples:

- Wired wraps that allow retailers to secure high theft items such as electronics and display them on the sales floor. Using these items allows customers to pick up, handle, and even read about the item's features on the box. The customer can then take the item to the register without being asked to wait while an employee unlocks the item.
- Bulky cardboard packaging may be used for small items, again making it difficult to hide an item under clothing or in a pocket.
- With online shopping becoming increasingly popular, small high-theft items sold online are often shipped by retailers in packaging several times larger than the item itself in order to make theft in transit more difficult.
- Plastic packages with EAS bar codes printed on them as part of the package design. This makes it difficult for a thief to remove the item without completely removing the packaging.

## Store Layout

The overall design and layout of a store can complement security. Here are some points to consider:

- Ensure that there are clear lines of sight from the cash point to all expensive item display areas. Lower racks can help employees more easily identify where customers are so that they can offer to help them or quietly monitor their activities.
- Avoid the creation of isolated corners where shoppers will be hidden from sight. If areas like this exist, they are good places in which to mount mirrors or cameras.
- Avoid cluttered displays by having adequate shelving and rack space. A clean, organized environment will make it easier to identify empty packaging and items that are missing. It is also more appealing to legitimate customers.

- Use symmetry whenever possible when displaying items.
- Use lights and mirrors to create the illusion of space and to assist with visibility.
- Use a combination of overt and covert cameras (including dummies) to create the desired psychological anti-theft effect.
- Ensure that maintenance is carried out on cameras and mirrors on the sales floor. Mirrors and cameras that have an excessive amount of dust and dirt built up on them will send the message that these items aren't in use. Clean, well-maintained mirrors, cameras, and personal view monitors at entrances will send the right message.
- Select signage appropriate to the aesthetics of the store.

## Fitting Room Policy

One basic philosophy that retailers would be wise to understand is that to effectively reduce theft in their stores they must "remove the opportunity." If fitting rooms aren't monitored and controlled they become an opportunity that dishonest customers will exploit. The privacy afforded by fitting rooms provides customers with an excellent opportunity to steal. Employees must be trained to control the fitting room environment.

### *Physical*

Fitting rooms should be kept clean and clear of all merchandise and minimally furnished. Floor-to-ceiling walls will prevent shoplifters from passing garments to an accomplice in an adjacent cubicle. Mirrors mounted on the wall inside the fitting room must be caulked to prevent a dishonest customer from hiding tags behind the mirror. The same should be done with cracks in any bench seating, walls, or anywhere else where tags could be hidden.

### *Procedural*

Stores should have a process in place that limits the number of items customers are allowed to take into a fitting room with them. They should also have a system that allows employees to place a number on the door that shows how many items that customer took in. This tells the customer that the store knows how many items they went in with, and also helps the fitting room employee to remember the number—especially useful on busy days. Stores should ensure that the employee takes the items from the customer when they enter and exit so that they can be counted and accounted for. Employees must "remove the opportunity," because dishonest customers will hide extra items underneath the clothes they want to take into a fitting room.

## Refund Procedures

Refunds on the return of merchandise should be issued with the original sales slip only. Unfortunately, this doesn't always happen. Retailers have long been searching for a solution that will allow them to be able to issue refunds to legitimate customers, and not make refunds attractive to dishonest customers. Point-of-sale technology now allows retailers to issue a store credit in lieu of cash when a customer has no receipt. This discourages dishonest customers who often are looking for cash. Putting the refund on a store credit also allows the retailer to track where it was issued and where it was redeemed. Refund fraud can be committed by the employee working at the refund desk. To mitigate the risk of this happening, "no bill" refunds should require a manager's approval. In addition, managers or even loss-prevention staff may be asked to audit returns at the refund desk. The refund employee would be required to lay out all items they have refunded with the refund slip beside the item containing the customer's name and signature. If an item is found at the returns area without a matching receipt, it could be an item that was returned fraudulently by the refund employee, with no real customer present. Instances such as this should be investigated.

## Special Tips and Strategies

Educating employees on how to identify a potential shoplifter will make your store much more secure. Employees and security professionals should watch for customers who are different from the average customer in almost any way. Some things to watch for include:

- Anyone who appears nervous and is very conscious of who is around them is nervous for a reason. It would be wise for security professionals to keep an eye on these people. Asking employees to simply approach nervous-looking customers to ask whether they need any help will also deter potential shoplifters. If an employee were to make small talk with a nervous customer and say something like, "I really like that red shirt you're wearing," it would be considered a compliment to a legitimate customer, but could send a potential shoplifter a message, letting them know the employee has taken notice of them.
- People loitering either inside or outside the store for long periods of time.
- People entering the store just to "browse."
- Professionals thieves, who have many ways to distract store security, such as using children to sidetrack cashiers and salespeople while they steal something.
- Baby carriages, which provide excellent cover for stolen merchandise.
- Customers wearing out-of-season clothes, such as people wearing bulky sweaters or long coats in summer, under which they can hide items; or customers shopping in winter, but wearing no coat.
- Customers who linger near back walls or in secluded areas of the store.
- People who walk with an awkward gait, which can signify that merchandise is hidden somewhere on their person.
- People who move items from one area to another to enable an accomplice to retrieve them later—items should be returned to their proper location as soon as possible.
- Non-paying customers who ask for store bags.

## Training Tips

1. Do not identify new employees with "Trainee" tags.
2. Create attentive clerks. Implement a "10-foot rule" that requires staff to greet all customers within 10 feet of them by saying "Hello" and making eye contact.
4. Develop a "zone" system that makes each employee responsible for security in a particular area.
5. Develop a code system so employees can alert one other when they notice suspicious activity.

## Undercover Security Tips

Security professionals should

- dress like they belong in a shopping environment—to be effective, investigators would need to blend in and not be easily identified as store employees;

- rehearse a communication plan with employees;
- know which managers are working and which ones they can rely on for physical backup ahead of time, in case an arrest needs to be made; and
- ensure that there is unbroken observation of the event—that is, that the observer does not have to stop to call for backup.

Another tip for security professionals concerns the law. In Canada, to be in a position to make a lawful arrest, loss prevention security professionals must *find a person committing a criminal offence*, per section 494(1)(a) of the *Criminal Code*. What this means is that a security professional must be 100 percent sure that the customer has stolen something before deciding to approach and arrest them. The only way to be 100 percent certain of this is to personally observe all the elements of a theft. These elements include:

1. **Selection:** The security professional must see the customer select the item, they must know where the customer found the item.
2. **Concealment:** Most times, a dishonest customer will conceal an item to hide the fact that they have it. The security professional must see the person conceal the item. Is it in their right coat pocket, up their sleeve, in a bag, in a baby stroller, etc.?
3. **Continuity:** The security professional must not lose sight of the customer, even for a second. To be 100 percent sure of this, continuity of observation must be maintained; if the store security professional loses sight of the customer, it is possible the customer could put the item back on the shelf or "ditch" it. Should this occur and the security professional does not see it as it happens, it could lead to a false arrest.
4. **Exit:** The security professional must let the customer leave with the item. This is necessary to prove the customer had the intent to steal, should the matter go to court. Letting the customer leave the store makes this much easier. If a security guard were to arrest a customer inside the store, the customer might say, "Oh no, I wasn't going to steal it, I was just about to go to pay for it." If the suspected person is still inside the store, it will be difficult to prove intent.

In loss-prevention audits or checks, security professionals should look for

- empty containers/boxes on the sales floor;
- empty hangers on clothes racks;
- empty hangers in the fitting rooms;
- discarded price tags in washrooms;
- switched price tags;
- a missing piece of a set;
- an increase in refunds compared with sales; and
- merchandise returned for refund instead of exchange.

Taking the time to track where tags and empty packages are found will give visibility to some important data:

- which items are being stolen: "hot items";
- where items are being stolen within the store: "hot spots";
- depending on how often you take inventory, you could even learn when items are being stolen.

Having this information can help better protect hot items and look at why hot spots are so attractive to dishonest customers. Taking inventory can provide some visibility into how big a theft problem exists, and what percentage of shrink can be attributed to theft.

## CHAPTER SUMMARY

The retail industry is an excellent example of a setting in which the application of total security can be clearly observed. Well-trained security professionals can make a difference in reducing and preventing losses from theft and shoplifting.

This chapter provided an overview of the problem of retail theft, describing both its prevalence and patterns.

The chapter explores a wide range of theft-prevention security technologies, including security tag systems, theft-resistant packaging, camera installations, security mirrors, and secure display technologies. Non-technological theft-management methods were also discussed, including the use of strategic use of store space and symmetry.

Finally, the benefits of trained observation and monitoring, both for security personnel and sales staff, are introduced.

With the application of the various retail security strategies discussed here, it is possible to create a retail establishment that will welcome honest shoppers, encourage good customer relations, emphasize employee awareness, and "remove the opportunity" for theft and shoplifting.

## KEY TERMS

CheckInk II, 265

electronic article surveillance, 265

return fraud, 263

RFID tag, 264

shrink (also called "shrinkage"), 262

tamper-evident seals, 265

## REFERENCES

*Criminal Code*, RSC 1985, c C-46.

Retail Council of Canada/PricewaterhouseCoopers [PwC]. (2012). *Securing the bottom line: Canadian retail security survey 2012*. Retrieved from https://www.pwc.com/ca/en/retail-consumer/publications/pwc-security-survey-2012-10-29-en.pdf

Staples. (2016). *Protection and prevention: Investing in security tags*. Retrieved from http://www.staples.com/sbd/cre/retail/security/inventory-security/security-tags/protection-and-prevention-investing-in-security-tags/

## PERFORMANCE APPLICATION

### Multiple Choice

1. Why must a security guard arrest a shoplifter outside the premises where the theft occurred?

    a. to avoid embarrassing the individual in front of other customers

    b. shoplifting, as an offence, is not established until the merchandise is removed from the store—it must be possible to prove intent

    c. a citizen's arrest is valid only on public property

    d. to avoid damage to displays

    e. to avoid the application of the *Occupiers' Liability Act*

2. Which of the following is not a principal source of retail losses today?

    a. external theft

    b. internal theft

    c. foreign currency transactions

    d. vendor shipment count errors

    e. return fraud

3. Which of these is an example of a shoplifting countermeasure that can be employed by retail staff?

    a. strict return policies

    b. human surveillance

    c. good fitting room policies

    d. symmetry

    e. all of the above

4. Which of these security technologies works by triggering an alarm when goods are removed from the store?

    a. RFID tags

    b. tamper-evident seals

    c. CCTV

    d. CheckInk II

    e. all of these technologies trigger an alarm

5. What information can be gained by keeping a record of signs that a theft has taken place, such as having found empty packages and price tags that have been removed?

    a. the kinds of items that are being stolen ("hot items")

    b. which display areas are vulnerable to theft ("hot spots")

    c. if inventory is taken regularly, what times and on which days particular articles are being stolen

    d. investigators would be concerned with learning when items are being stolen; if they update their log regularly they can learn what days and even at what times thieves are more active

    e. all of the above

6. Which elements of a theft must security professionals observe to be in a position to make an arrest?

    a. intent, taking, concealment, removal

    b. selection, concealment, continuity of possession, exit

    c. selection, concealment, failure to pay, exit

    d. opportunity, taking, intent to remove, removal

    e. suspect enters the store, removes item from a package, fails to pay, enters the parking lot

7. Return fraud
   a. can be reduced by requiring manager authorization for "no bill" returns
   b. can involve the return of items for a refund after they were stolen in the first place
   c. can involve the processing of returns by a cashier where no item is actually returned
   d. can involve the "borrowing" of an item, for example where a customer buys a necklace to wear to an event, wears it, and then returns it for a refund
   e. all of the above

## Short Answer

1. How can you train new store employees to be an effective part of your security team?

# Safes, Vaults, Locks, and Alarms

## 16

| | |
|---|---|
| Introduction | 278 |
| **Electronic Access Control** | 278 |
| Types of Access Control Technologies | 278 |
| **Biometric Access Control** | 281 |
| **Cabinets, Safes, and Vaults** | 282 |
| Safe-Keeping Needs | 283 |
| Types of Filing Cabinets, Safes, and Vaults | 284 |
| Security Filing Cabinets | 284 |
| Safes | 284 |
| Industry Standards for Security Safes in Canada | 285 |
| How to Select a Safe | 286 |
| **Locks** | 286 |
| Mechanical Locks | 287 |
| Warded Locks | 287 |
| Lever Locks | 287 |
| Modern Pin Tumbler Locks | 287 |
| Wafer or Disc Tumbler Locks | 287 |
| Tubular Cylinder Locks | 287 |
| Lock Evaluation | 288 |
| Pick-Resistant Features | 288 |
| Security Applications for Mechanical Locks | 289 |
| Key Control | 290 |
| **Alarms** | 291 |
| Alarm System Capabilities | 291 |
| Elements of an Alarm | 291 |
| Alarm System Monitoring | 292 |
| **Chapter Summary** | 292 |
| **Key Terms** | 293 |
| **References** | 293 |
| **Performance Application** | 293 |

## LEARNING OUTCOMES

When you have completed this chapter, you will:

- Have a thorough grounding in the operation of electronic access control systems and the role they play in total facility protection.
- Have a basic knowledge and understanding of the important role that filing cabinets, safes, and vaults play in protecting valuable assets.
- Have a basic knowledge and understanding of mechanical locks and the role they play in protecting property.
- Understand the general types of alarms available for facility protection.

# Introduction

While protection of a building (its grounds, objects on its grounds, and its inner and outer perimeters) is the first step to take against property loss and damage, it is equally important to keep the interior of a facility secure.

Securing the contents of a building depends in large part on access control. Various technologies have emerged to help organizations control the movement of employees, customers, and individuals into and through a facility.

Depending on their nature, valuables are best secured with cabinets, locks, safes, vaults, or alarms, or a combination of these devices. This chapter will introduce technologies used on the two innermost lines of a facility's defence.

# Electronic Access Control

Technology is advancing rapidly, and keeping abreast of it is a never-ending challenge for security managers whose top priority is access control. Businesses and industries must continually invest in new access control products to keep ahead of criminals who are working diligently to defeat today's systems. Decisions on what equipment to purchase depend on the size, function, and number of buildings being managed within a complex, as well as the location of facilities that security guards are protecting.

Effective access control systems must

- identify who wants in and verify their admission;
- permit access only to those who have authorized admission into designated areas of a building or facility;
- prevent access by unauthorized personnel and limit access to designated work areas;
- trigger alarms for any security breaches of access or invalid identification;
- record every entrance and exit through an access point; and
- support and retrieve all evidence so that it remains intact and in an easy-to-understand format.

## Types of Access Control Technologies

Until recently, there were three types of electromechanical locks: code-operated, key-operated, and card-operated. With the expansion of Internet connectivity through the use of smartphones, a new type of access control technology has emerged: wi-fi enabled or "smart" locks.

### Code-Operated Locks

A code-operated lock does not use a physical key. A series of numbered keys are pressed in a preset sequence to activate an electromagnetic switch that releases the door. For some code-operated locks, an alarm sounds if a wrong number is keyed. The sequence combinations can be quickly changed in an emergency. One drawback is that more than one person can slip in behind a person who is cleared to enter. This is called **tailgating**. So, to be truly effective, this type of access requires the presence of a monitoring security guard or receptionist.

**tailgating**
to gain access by slipping in behind a person cleared to enter

## Key-Operated Locks

Electronics enhance the best features of a regular pin-tumbler lock with a key that activates an electric switch (a **solenoid**). The solenoid draws power from a battery to move a strike plate or keeper to open the lock. Unfortunately, intruders can bypass a key-operated lock by tailgating or using a dry-cell battery.

The use of a voltage shroud or voltage discriminator makes a key-operated lock more reliable. A voltage shroud protects the lock from attack by an intruder who tries to use a dry-cell battery to defeat it. It channels the electric current away from the solenoid and dispels it harmlessly. A voltage discriminator blocks any incoming voltage, except the specific voltage level designed for the lock, thereby preventing access. This prohibits an intruder from using a dry-cell battery to "jump-start" the lock.

**solenoid**
electric switch that draws power from a battery to open a lock

## Card-Operated Locks

Card-operated locks are mainly electromagnetic. The key is a plastic card with a magnetic stripe, notches, or holes. It looks and feels like a credit card and contains coded information. When the card is passed through an electronic reader, it matches the name on the card with its authorized list of users and records the time of entry. This card is also used for company ID. Using a computer, the code can be changed at the door or from a remote location. This system has two flaws: an intruder can tailgate through an access point and, because the reader identifies only the card and not the person, an intruder can steal or borrow a card to get in. There are several types of card-operated lock systems on the market.

### Magnetic-Coded Cards

There are two basic designs for magnetic-coded cards: one contains a flexible magnetic sheet sealed between two sheets of plastic, and the other contains a magnetic strip along one edge of the card.

The code is contained in magnetized spots on the sheet or strip. If the card is exposed to a strong magnetic field or is stored in a wallet or purse with the magnetic side facing another magnetic-coded card—for example, a credit card—the code will be erased from both cards. The flaw with this card is that it is easy to copy the magnetic pattern onto a duplicate card.

### Wiegand-Effect Cards

Up to 26 magnetic wire bits are embedded in Wiegand-effect cards. These bits of magnetic wire can store millions of code combinations. The card is immune to demagnetization and difficult to copy.

### Optical-Coded Cards

Bar codes, similar to those found on products in stores, are implanted in optical-coded cards and are scanned the same way that products in stores are. Originally, the bar codes were visible, which made it easy to copy them. Now the bar codes are visible only under ultraviolet or infrared light.

### Proximity Cards

Proximity cards send a code to a receiver via magnetic, optical, or ultrasonic pulses. A reader or scanner is not required.

### Wi-Fi Enabled or Smart Locks

With the expansion of Internet connectivity through the use of smartphones, wi-fi, and Bluetooth technology, and the introduction of thousands of applications (apps) designed to integrate the use of mobile devices with everyday functions, it was inevitable that a new form of security application would evolve. This fourth type of electromechanical lock, known as a "smart lock," offers cutting-edge access control features to any home or business. Proximity sensors like Bluetooth and NFC (near-field communication) are used to enable a door to unlock when a user with an authorized smartphone approaches. With a special app, users can remotely lock or unlock the door, transfer access to another person's smartphone or deny access to a previously authorized user, if necessary. In some cases, this new type of lock has code or key-operated functionality, an OLED (organic light-emitting diode) display, and fingerprint technology as additional layers of security.

Some convenient smart lock functions include:

- Connectivity choices include wi-fi, Bluetooth, NFC, and cellular.
- They connect to an existing wi-fi router in a home or business, without the need for additional equipment.
- Emails or text messages are received whenever a guest or client arrives, or when anyone accesses the door.
- The door can be opened remotely using a mobile device or phone, allowing a guest or client access even when no one is present. This function is optimal for facilitating access to Airbnb listings, which are rapidly expanding in Canada.
- Creation of virtual keys for family and friends. This enables effective monitoring and management of all users.

**Figure 16.1**   Wi-Fi Door Lock

# Biometric Access Control

Dwayne Mercredi is director of engineering for SAFLINK in Edmonton, Alberta. In "Beyond Passwords and Pins," in the October 2003 issue of *Canadian Security*, he noted that: "According to Meridien Research, between 500,000 and 700,000 people are affected by identity theft each year in the United States alone" (Mercredi, 2003).

**Identity theft**—one person's misuse of another's identity for an illegal purpose (such as fraud)—has led to increased support for **biometrics**, a class of security technology that recognizes a person's unique physical characteristics: fingerprints, hand geometry, signature, voice print, iris, and retina (see Figure 16.2). No password, PIN number, or identification is required.

Facial imaging reliability is still being developed. By contrast, the error rate for a retinal scan is one out of every 10 million individuals identified. The iris scan is less accurate: one out of every 131,000. Fingerprint and hand geometry recognition follow with one error out of every 500. The least accurate is signature and voice recognition with one error out of every 50 for each (Ruggles, 2002). This is because the recognition of these identifiers is based on behaviour rather than physical characteristics. How you write and how you speak will vary from situation to situation, and from mood to mood, and this affects the results,

**identity theft**
misuse of another person's identity for illegal purposes

**biometrics**
branch of security technology that allows access based on recognition of a person's physical attributes

**Figure 16.2** Current Biometric Methods

| Physical attribute | Biometric method |
|---|---|
| Fingerprints | Fingerprint recognition systems optically scan a chosen fingerprint area and compare the scanned area with the file of the person to be admitted. |
| Palm recognition | Hand geometry recognition systems use the geometry of the hand. The system basically measures finger lengths and compares them with the authorized files. |
| Signature | Signature recognition systems rely on the fact that no two people write with the same motion or pressure. Although forgers can duplicate the appearance of the signature, the amount of pressure and motions used in creating the signature will differ. |
| Voice print | Speaker verification systems use the uniqueness of voice patterns to determine identification and control admittance. The system uses soundproof booths and requires that the person to be identified repeat a simple phrase, usually four words in length. |
| Retina | Retina recognition systems analyze the blood vessel pattern in the retina of the eye. These patterns vary widely, even between identical twins. The chance of false identification using this system is one in 10 million. |
| Iris scan | The iris is the ring of colour that surrounds the pupil in the human eye. Under a digital scanner, everyone's iris has a unique pattern that provides an accurate method of identification and authentication. This pattern is turned into a special code that is stored in a computer biometrics database for reference when access is required. Currently less accurate than the retina scan, improvements are still being made to this technology. |

*Source*: Adapted from Ruggles, 2002.

making it possible for a good imitator to mimic your voice pattern, and a good forger to duplicate your signature, although the scanner is so sensitive that it usually defeats such attempts because it's almost impossible to precisely imitate the timbre of a voice or the pressure applied in a signature.

Of the various biometric techniques, retinal scanning is the most accurate access control method available today. Accuracy in detecting intrusions through fingerprint verification also increases when two fingers are registered and compared for identification. Overall, the more biometric elements used to verify identity, the more accurate the results will be, making biometrics the most reliable technology for access control at high-risk facilities.

If there is any drawback to the use of biometrics, it is that people change because of age, injury, stress, illness, and fatigue. Technical experts recommend that biometric records be updated on a regular basis or after a significant change in any employee's life.

## Cabinets, Safes, and Vaults

Cabinets, safes, and vaults provide means of protecting valuables by enclosing them in a container that is meant to be secure. The concept of secure containment is ancient—consider the example of a pirate's locked treasure chest.

**FOCUS ON TECHNOLOGY**

### Emerging Technologies in Access Control

**Figure 16.3**  Smartphone Used for Home Security

Card manufacturers now provide "modules" of coded information that can be added to one access card. This technology is based on smart-card technology for retail credit cards. In the future it will be possible for people to carry one card that includes all their information: birth certificate, social insurance number, passport, banking data, credit information, medical records, shopping discounts, tax payments, employment authorization, and everything else that comprises one person's life—one card for all purposes.

Also, as the smart phone and other mobile devices continue to be integrated into our daily functions, it seems inevitable that we will come to depend more and more on these devices to play a role in our security.

Wi-fi connected mobile phones and one-card systems will make our security processes more convenient, but one thing technology can never do is replace the security guards in any access control system. Someone has to answer alarms and deal with people, including individuals who require protection or aid and any unauthorized intruders.

The art of lock breaking is equally ancient, and as thieves have grown more sophisticated, safe technology has had to remain continually one step ahead of them. When safe crackers used explosives to shatter locks and security systems on safe doors, safe manufacturers introduced anti-explosive devices that automatically secured the bolts of the safe to the door. Security experts estimate there is a three-month window between the introduction of the newest security device and the introduction of resilient criminals' counter tools or techniques to overcome it.

Serious thieves carry what is called a safecracker's tool kit, and today's tools are quite sophisticated. They range from hand picking tools to electric drills, saws, jackhammers, and **plastique**, to digital decoders, gas-powered circular saws, and **liquid nitrogen**. Security personnel who work with key valuables should understand the most common safe-breaking techniques, and should understand the limitations of the technology in place at their worksites.

## Safe-Keeping Needs

It is important to remember that theft is not the only adverse event that safes are meant to protect against. For some valuables, fires, floods, and natural disasters present equally serious threats, and many container technologies are designed specifically for protection during these events.

Understanding which type of filing cabinet, safe, or vault is best suited to a situation depends on the type of valuables that require protection. For example, a storekeeper protecting his or her inventory and cash receipts worries more about fire and petty theft, while a financial institution is more concerned about keeping cash deposits, investment bonds, and highly valued objects out of the hands of sophisticated burglars. The protection of sensitive and valuable documents is an issue for all companies, large and small, and cabinets, safes, and vaults play critical roles in security.

The most common items that security services are asked to protect are cash, jewellery, investment metals such as gold and silver, coin and stamp collections, antique collectibles and heirlooms, deeds and wills, firearms and ammunition, and confidential information in document form or on flash drives or portable hard drives.

Unfortunately, many security or loss prevention managers are pressured by the client or their own budgets to let the price tag of a protective container guide the selection of a security purchase, and it is only after a fire or burglary occurs that they pay attention to the flaws in the safeguard that was chosen and failed. To ensure that they do not fall into this trap of wrong thinking, security managers should educate themselves on how security containers are built, the materials used and why they are used, and the standards set by the industry.

**plastique**
plastic explosives

**liquid nitrogen**
a substance that can be injected into a safe's lock in an effort to affect metal parts in the opening mechanism (they may freeze instantaneously and shatter), allowing the safe to be opened

## Security Spotlight

### Insurance Considerations

Insurers are increasingly refusing to pay claims for loss when safes or vaults described in a policy do not meet industry standards.

An important feature of a quality safe or lock is that it should show evidence of tampering if it is broken. Insurers will resist paying for losses when they find that there is no adequate evidence of break-in.

## Types of Filing Cabinets, Safes, and Vaults

Filing cabinets, safes, and vaults are three expressions of the same concept: a locked metal container used for storing valuables. There are many shapes and sizes, but, in general, they are classed according to their use.

There are five main types:

1. safes designed specifically for in-wall mounting;
2. floor safes designed to be embedded in a floor;
3. chests or cabinets that stand alone on a floor;
4. depositories designed with a hopper or slot for easy deposit of valuables without allowing access; and
5. vaults large enough for walk-in entry.

## Security Filing Cabinets

In most organizations, everyday administrative files are stored in filing cabinets. Although some contain confidential information, most do not. Losing these paper files to a fire would be a nuisance, but as long as the computer files are not also lost, everything is recoverable. Because filing cabinets are normally located in busy traffic areas in offices, someone wanting to steal something from a locked filing cabinet would need about half an hour of undisturbed time to pry one open. That's not a likely scenario. So, in general, when it comes to everyday files, fire is the biggest concern. A standard filing cabinet that can withstand fire for one hour and is fitted with a lock will meet most office needs.

What works for paper files, however, does not work for preserving computer data files. Microfilm, microfiche, thumb drives, portable encrypted hard drives, and CDs are vulnerable to humidity, dust, and magnetic fields. They also self-destruct in temperatures over 52°C (125°F). These items are too sensitive to store in a standard filing cabinet and must be stored in an indestructible fireproof container known as a security filing cabinet or in a safe.

## Safes

For larger items of value, most organizations will need to consider safes and vaults. They are more expensive than security cabinets, with cost increasing with the number of protective features. Most safes protect against either fire or burglary, or both.

### FOCUS ON TECHNOLOGY

#### Gardex Filing Cabinet

The Gardex filing cabinet is typical of current security filing cabinet technology. It has

- fire-resistant insulation;
- a ULC-listed key-operated plunger lock system;
- a selective locking system that allows any combination of drawers to be locked while leaving the remainder open;
- an inner steel jacket that prevents access to a locked drawer from an unlocked compartment; and
- independent insulation for each drawer so that if one drawer is left open, the others remain fire-protected.

In burglary-resistant safes, the key is preventing access. Doorjambs are angled in such a way that the safe door cannot be driven inward; the doorway works like a set of puzzle pieces, with doorway edges fitting into the matching pieces of the frame on both sides. Because burglars can also break into the walls of a safe, quality safes incorporate offset panel seams along their sides.

## *Fire-Resistant Safes*

Protecting valuables from fire is more complicated than protection from theft. It is critical to understand how fire-resistant the physical composition of the items to be stored in a safe are before deciding on the components required in the safe that will be used to preserve them. For instance, the insulation designed to line the walls of most fire safes contain compounds that suspend moisture. This insulation looks like plaster and in an Underwriters' Laboratories of Canada (ULC) test, where the safe is placed inside an oven and the temperature is set at 982°C (1,800°F) to mimic an actual fire, the insulation inside the safe must remain cool, sustaining a temperature of less than 177°C (350°F) (which burns paper) for over an hour, and, at the same time, trapped moisture must be released in the form of steam. After an hour, if the cash and papers stored in the safe are still intact, it receives the basic ULC paper rating. An hour would give a fire department sufficient time to put out a fire in most emergencies of this kind.

Primary considerations would include: What do you wish to secure? If material is primarily paper-based, fire protection rating is essential. If material is primarily metal, such as coins, jewellery, etc., then impact/burglar resistance is essential. Dual rated safes may be used for all items.

Storing a combination of paper and computer disks together presents a problem because the disks can't tolerate humidity and they self-destruct at 52°C (125°F). Thus, dry insulation to keep the temperature under 52°C (125°F) for at least one hour and a special surround that seals the safe against water leaking through from the firefighters' high-powered hoses are required.

## *High-Security Composite Safes*

The best solution for most situations is a composite safe that protects contents from both burglary and fire. These, however, are the most expensive because they exceed all industry standards.

# Industry Standards for Security Safes in Canada

The safety ratings originally introduced by the insurance industry for safes were introduced as a guide for setting insurance rates for clients in the event that safes were lost due to fire, theft, or some kind of irreparable damage. For want of another guideline, these ratings set the industry standards.

In Canada, the testing authority for safes is ULC (Underwriters Laboratories of Canada), located in Scarborough, Ontario. The international label of equivalent authority is the Chicago-based Underwriters' Laboratories Inc. (ULI). Insurance charts list levels of acceptable insurable standards. To qualify for a class 2 rating, a burglary-resistant filing cabinet or safe, for instance, must meet either a minimum materials standard of a 3.8 cm (1.5 inch) steel plate body and a minimum 2.5 cm (1 inch) steel plate door with combination lock *or* a minimum performance standard. For a safe to meet the remaining qualifying classes from 3 to 5, it must pass a performance test in the ULC labs. Once a safe

> ## ON THE JOB
>
> ### Cover All the Bases
>
> Constable Henri Bérubé of Peel Regional Police in Brampton, Ontario always ends his burglary workshops for security managers with this eye-opening anecdote: "When none of the tools that thieves used to break into a safe in a Kingston-area department store worked, they simply lifted it up and hauled it away. The safe provided excellent protection, but the retailer's detection system did not."
>
> So always remember that nothing done in security can be done in isolation. Every step between outer and inner defence lines is connected.

manufacturer achieves a ULC standard, its products are randomly tested to make sure they continue to meet that level of guaranteed performance.

These performance tests measure three things: how long a safe will resist the most recent tools in a safecracker's kit, how long it will resist fire damage, and how well it resists explosive devices.

## How to Select a Safe

Industry experts give the following sorts of advice when asked about selecting the right filing cabinet, safe, or vault to suit a facility's needs:

- Analyze the physical properties of the assets to be protected.
- Start with realistic specs based on budget, not a wish list.
- Look for a safe with interior features, such as multiple compartments, filing drawers, shelving, or custom racks that best match the facility's needs.
- Choose a safe with only the accessibility required.
- Be aware that basic ULC standards may not be sufficient for the situation and that they represent only a minimum.
- Choose a safe with the most affordable security features.
- Research the dealer's reputation and service record.

# Locks

Consider this statement: "There is no locking device on earth that can't be opened." True or false? It's true.

Lock pickers on the Internet not only brag about how they can open "anything with a keyhole, dial, or access port" with their picking tools, they have posted a manual telling any criminal who wants to know how to do it. Under these conditions, how can any security manager ever be confident of locks as a means of defence against break-ins?

The difference between a standard lock and a high security lock is how long it takes to open the lock using lock pickers' tools. For instance, a high security Medeco lock can take up to two hours or longer to pick open. If the rest of your security system is working effectively, the thief should be detected and apprehended long before he or she finishes unlocking the door under attack. So, the deterrent aspect of using a high security lock is the length of time it takes a thief to open it using criminals' tools.

## Mechanical Locks

The traditional lock consists of a key, the operating mechanism, and a bolt. Although these fundamental elements have essentially remained unchanged, over time there have been hundreds of innovative design changes made to the operating mechanism of different types of locks. In addition, the use of specially hardened metals and the introduction of pick-resistant features have combined to provide locks for every level of security.

## Warded Locks

Warded locks are generally found in pre-World War II construction. A warded lock has a single plate that includes both the doorknob and the keyway. The security value of these locks is almost nil.

## Lever Locks

First used in the 18th century, lever locks are difficult to define in terms of security because they vary greatly in effectiveness. In this type of lock, there are usually four or five levers. When the key is inserted, it lifts each lever to a different height to allow the notch in the lever to align with the post of the bolt. As the key continues to turn a full 360°, it moves the locking bolt through the notch into the second gate and opens the lock. The best lever locks are used in safe deposit boxes and are nearly pick proof. The simplest of these locks are used in desks, lockers, and cabinets and are generally less secure than pin tumbler locks.

## Modern Pin Tumbler Locks

Over half the locks in use today are the pin tumbler locks that you see on house and garage doors, padlocks, and mailboxes. Invented by Linus Yale, this design usually has five tumblers, which provide about one million different key combinations for each lock. When the key is inserted, the grooves along both sides of the key edge connect with the five tumblers to align them in a straight line, which then allows the plug to turn to release the locking mechanism. Despite multiple key combinations, the delay factor for picking a pin tumbler lock is only 10 minutes or less.

If the wrong key is inserted, some of the pins will not rise to the correct level, while others will rise too high. Without alignment, the cylinder cannot turn.

## Wafer or Disc Tumbler Locks

Wafer or disc tumbler locks are less secure than pin tumbler locks. The tumblers are shaped like thin flat wafers instead of pins but are similarly spring-loaded with less distance between the wafers. They are used for garage and trailer doors, desks, padlocks, filing cabinets, most autos, window locks, and older vending machines. The life of these locks, however, is limited because of their soft metal construction. The delay afforded is approximately three minutes. A higher security version is the double-wafer lock used in old pop and candy machines, gas caps, filing cabinets, and window locks.

## Tubular Cylinder Locks

Tubular cylinder locks are pin tumbler locks arranged on a circular plane. Unlike conventional pin tumbler locks, all of the pins are visible to the eye. The central section of the lock rotates to operate the cam when all of the seven pins have reached their breaking points. When the proper key is inserted into the lock, the tumblers are pressed into position so that the central plug can be turned. This manual operation of inserting the key places the tumblers in position so that the lock can be operated and ensures that frost, dust, salt, or unfavorable climatic conditions will not affect the smooth operation of the lock. Used for alarm control systems, newer vending machines, car-wash control boxes, and higher security applications for protection of property, merchandise, and cash, they comprise about 25 percent of the locks in use today. They provide the maximum amount of security for their price range.

## Lock Evaluation

The security value of a lock is determined by how well it resists forcible entry and the use of common tools and lock picks. Overall, the factors that determine how effective a lock really is depend on four things: design, construction, installation, and maintenance.

### Design

Locks are designed to accommodate several categories of security: low, medium, and high. Low and medium security locks are mainly used in the residential industry. High security locks are generally reserved for use where the level of protection required is above the norm, and reflects the importance of the property, artifact, or information requiring protection. High security locks have been designed for banks, casinos, museums, research laboratories, the military, detention centres, and many other specialized areas. Design elements have been developed for these areas that reflect the security challenges specific to the environment in which the lock is used.

### Construction

Good security locks are usually constructed of solid forged materials, with reinforced moving parts, for durability and resistance to impact. These materials can include brass, tempered and stainless steel, and various alloys. Some designs make use of a series of laminated steel sections surrounding the working parts of the lock, held together by retaining bolts. This design can withstand the impact of a bullet from a high calibre rifle and still remain secured.

### Installation

Installation of a good security lock should be easy to accomplish with a minimum of special tools. If the installation process is difficult or lengthy, there is a risk that the lock will not be installed correctly.

### Maintenance

Maintenance of a good security lock should be simple and require simple tools. The design of the lock and its functional parts need to support this.

## Pick-Resistant Features

Pin tumbler locks can be designed with improved security features. These are known as pick-resistant features. Here are some of the more popular examples found in the security industry today.

## Mushroom-Head Pins

The rounded shape of the head on the pin fools the lock picker into thinking it is picked when in fact it isn't. When upward pressure is applied, the pins seem to be aligned with the spring tumblers in the keyway, but the additional spools or mushroom heads above the pins are not. They continue to block the cylinder from turning all the way to release the lock.

## Six- or Seven-Pin Tumblers

Most pin tumbler locks carry five pins. High-security pin tumbler locks are available with six or seven pins, and the additional pins offer an increased level of pick resistance.

## Medeco Lock Sidebar

This security feature allows the key to move each of the pins in sequence as well as the side bar when the key is inserted.

## Multiple Direction Pins

An even greater level of pick resistance is afforded when the pins are mounted at right angles to each other. Only the most expensive locks carry this feature.

## Biaxial Pins

Biaxial pins are cut out at an angle of about 45° and form a "V" within the cylinder. This feature makes them extremely difficult to pick.

## MIWA Four-Pin and Magnetic Disc Locks

Designed on the principle of magnetic polarities, each "key" or plastic card contains a set of small magnets arranged in a coded pattern to attract and repel other magnets in the lock, thereby allowing the spring-loaded bolt or cam to open the lock and allow entry. These are used in access control systems.

# Security Applications for Mechanical Locks

There are three main types of pin tumbler locks used for security applications: rim, mortise, and deadbolt.

## Rim Lock

The rim lock is a style of pin tumbler lock that is activated entirely by the action of the key being turned. It has no external latch, bolt, or handle. Rim locks can be keyed from both sides of the door. It is generally considered to be a low security lock.

## Mortise Lock

The mortise lock is widely used on doors where a combination of aesthetics (looks) and security are required. These locks operate on a pin tumbler system. The main body of the lock is inserted into the frame of a door so that only the handles and keyway are visible on the surface of the door. Mortise locks have a very slim profile that allows them to be fully inserted into the thin width of a door.

### Deadbolt Lock

Used for higher security applications, deadbolt locks are those mounted above the knob on a door. They are not spring-loaded, and cannot be opened by sliding a plastic or metal card through to the bolt in order to work it open. The deadbolt design uses the basic pin tumbler lock with one important addition: when the lock is in the closed position, the person occupying the interior of the room can turn a latch or shift a button/lever that will engage a separate bolt into the frame of the door. This bolt cannot be disengaged using the key from outside the room. The only way to disengage the bolt is to activate the lever or latch on the door from inside the room.

## Key Control

Although selecting the right lock is an important concern, it's not the whole picture. You also need to consider who controls the master key and how custody and use of the key will be managed.

Alan Heaney, security consultant and former president of Medeco Canada, notes that more than 75 percent of thefts occurring today happen internally. In hospitals, for instance, it's not people breaking in causing thefts. They are caused by employees or patients who have keys or access to places they shouldn't.

Below we review a few things that security officers can arrange in order to ensure that security keys stay in the hands of authorized personnel only.

### Copying Restrictions

In this case, someone wishing to cut a copy of a key would be required to produce written authorization, as the original keys to the lock would bear a manufacturer's stamp advising "Do Not Copy." In addition, the lock may have an extended warranty as well as an individual serial number.

### Key Accountability

In buildings where a cleaning service requires keys to clean the offices, it is foolhardy to issue pass keys for an extended period of time to all workers. In such settings, there is often a high turnover of workers, and workers usually clean unoccupied offices and stores at night.

The best policy is to have the cleaning service report to the security reception desk where specific interior keys are issued only to the housekeepers cleaning these areas. When the housekeepers have completed their work, they sign out and return the key they used.

Also, because employees who are issued entrance keys can lose them or forget to return them when they leave the company's employ, it is wise to change the lock cylinder in the entrance every few months and issue new keys to the authorized personnel. This also applies to tenants in residential buildings who may lose their entrance key or move out, taking it with them.

### Key Inventory

When a key is issued, security should maintain strict records, showing the name of the person who received the key, along with any employee number, position, and department data; the date key was issued; and the date the employee returned the key on leaving the company's employ.

Keys issued during non-working hours to temporary or contracted staff should be kept in a locked location and accounted for daily by the security officer on duty; the log should be checked and signed by the security supervisor at the end of each shift.

> ## ON **THE JOB**
> 
> **Keep a Log**
> 
> Keeping records about to whom keys have been issued, at what time or on what date, and whether they have been returned minimizes uncertainty about potential exposure to security breaches. Knowing whether or not a lock is compromised means locks need to be changed or reprogrammed less often, which saves money and administrative effort.

### Lost Key Policy

When a key is reported lost, security personnel should write up an investigative report. They should check to see whether the key was used to access a sensitive area. If it was, or if there are other suspicious concerns that arise during the investigation, locks should immediately be changed and new keys issued.

## Alarms

An alarm is a means of giving early warning of intrusion or any other condition the system is designed to detect. There are three standard categories: intrusion alarms, fire alarms, and special-use alarms. **Intrusion alarms** warn of entry of trespassers beyond authorized zones. They are commonly found in homes, businesses, and vehicles. **Fire alarms** warn of smoke, heat, carbon monoxide, or fire, depending on their nature. They may sound a local or remotely monitored alarm and/or trigger the operation of a sprinkler system. **Special-use alarms** warn of other dangers, including changes in temperature and humidity, toxic fumes, and machinery malfunctions.

**intrusion alarm**
warning that trespassers have entered beyond authorized zones

**fire alarm**
warning of smoke, heat, carbon monoxide, or fire

**special-use alarm**
warning that a danger, such as toxic fumes or machine malfunctions, has occurred

## Alarm System Capabilities

Alarm systems can be designed to provide total facility protection. Accordingly, there are elements of each system that provide the best security protection for certain areas. These elements have been developed to complement the four lines of defence—grounds perimeter protection, building perimeter protection, space/area protection, and object protection.

## Elements of an Alarm

Alarms serve to warn you that something is happening and that your immediate attention and reaction are required. Alarm systems are of many types, but all have three common elements: a sensor detector, a circuit or sending device, and an enunciator or sounding device.

### Alarm Sensor Detector

A detector must initiate an alarm when sensing a condition to which it was designed to react, even if primary power fails, and back-up power fails to come on immediately.

### Circuit or Sending Device

The circuit or sending device transmits the alarm to the sounding device, where it will be heard or seen by security personnel, or to a remote monitoring station where the appropriate response action will be initiated.

### Enunciator or Sounding Device

The enunciator or sounding device is a light, a bell/buzzer, or a punch tape located at the monitoring station. It alerts security personnel that the alarm sensor has detected something.

## Alarm System Monitoring

There are several different ways that an alarm system can be monitored for response purposes. A facility's choice of monitoring system is usually based on perceived risk, cost issues, and facility size.

A large facility will most likely have a proprietary alarm monitoring station—alarms of all kinds (intrusion, fire, and specialized) are set up to trigger a signal at a central location, from which the facility's own security and/or fire personnel will be deployed. This kind of system permits a very rapid response.

Residences and small commercial facilities without 24-hour security personnel may choose an alarm that sends a signal to a remote monitoring station that is staffed by contract security. When the alarm is triggered, the monitoring station sends personnel to the scene (and in some cases, contacts on-site security personnel). The response time with such a system is slower than with a proprietary system.

Somewhat similar to this kind of alarm is a system designed to dial one or more contact phone numbers when triggered. This system can lead to delayed response times and its reliability is contingent on the unimpaired operation of the public phone system. Alarm systems can also be configured to contact a smartphone using wi-fi connectivity to contact the property owner, security, or other responders directly, while displaying the location and type of alarm. When supported by surveillance cameras, unauthorized activity can be recorded for evidence and transmitted to police and/or other first responders in real time.

A third kind of alarm may be localized to a specific area or zone within a facility. This kind of alarm will sound or light up only in the vicinity of the disturbance. It's designed to alert security personnel working close by. To the extent that it may take extra time to get back-up for a major emergency (since local guards may have to call or radio other personnel), it has limitations; however, there are advantages: it is more discreet than a building-wide alarm, and therefore less likely to trigger panic among people in the building, or to disrupt operations unnecessarily in other areas.

### CHAPTER SUMMARY

Access control systems are designed to control the movement of individuals into and within a protected facility. The most common systems include keypad systems, electronic keys, and card-based systems. Biometrics is a cutting-edge class of technology based on the principle of unique physical characteristics. Technology that measures these characteristics can be designed to control access based on an individual's features.

Many thieves are very sophisticated criminals who know the strengths and weaknesses of every make of security filing cabinet, safe, or vault better than most owners, bankers, and security managers. When it comes to preserving a company's assets and critical data or designs, security personnel need to look beyond the obvious and provide the best-made security filing cabinet, safe, or vault the company can afford.

Mechanical locking systems are among the most widely used security devices in the world. Understanding how they should be used, as well as their strengths and weaknesses, will allow security officers to provide a higher standard of protective services during their career.

Finally, alarm systems allow a facility to detect and warn of intrusion, fire, or other hazards even where they arise in locations not monitored by live guards.

## KEY TERMS

biometrics, 281
fire alarm , 291
identity theft, 281
intrusion alarm , 291
liquid nitrogen, 283
plastique, 283
solenoid, 279
special-use alarm, 291
tailgating, 278

## REFERENCES

Mercredi, D. (2003, October). Beyond passwords and pins. *Canadian Security Magazine*.

Ruggles, T. (2002, July). Comparison of biometric techniques. Biometric Technology Inc. Retrieved from http://www.bioconsulting.com/bio.htm

## PERFORMANCE APPLICATION

### Multiple Choice

1. A "solenoid" is a type of electric switch used in which of the following locks?
   a. code-operated locks
   b. key-operated locks
   c. card-operated locks
   d. pin tumbler locks
   e. mortise locks

2. Magnetic force is used in the operating process of which of the following access cards?
   a. proximity card
   b. optical-coded card
   c. Wiegand-effect card
   d. magnetic-coded card
   e. both c and d

3. The use of biometrics as a form of access control has increased significantly in the last few years. Which of the following has the lowest reported error rate?
   a. retinal scan
   b. iris scan
   c. fingerprint and hand geometry
   d. signature recognition
   e. voice recognition

4. The difference between a standard lock and a high-security lock is:
   a. the quality of the metal used in construction
   b. its ability to withstand blows from a sledgehammer
   c. how long it takes to open the lock using lock picker's tools
   d. based on the reputation of the manufacturer
   e. price

5. These locks were first introduced in the 18th century, and are commonly used in safety deposit boxes:
   a. warded locks
   b. lever locks
   c. pin tumbler locks
   d. wafer or disc tumbler locks
   e. tubular cylinder locks

6. Pin tumbler locks can be designed with different pick-resistant features. Which of the following is *not* a pick-resistant feature?
   a. biaxial pins
   b. multiple direction pins
   c. Medeco lock sidebar
   d. mushroom head pins
   e. deadbolt

7. Which of the following elements of "key management" best covers the temporary issue of keys to outside contractors or a cleaning service?
   a. key control
   b. copying restrictions
   c. key accountability
   d. key inventory
   e. lost key policy

8. Which of the following locks is primarily chosen for reasons of aesthetics?

   a. rim lock

   b. deadbolt lock

   c. pin tumbler Lock

   d. mortise lock

   e. warded lock

9. Which is *not* true of a proprietary alarm monitoring station?

   a. it is dependent on the local telephone system being intact

   b. it allows on-site personnel to respond to alarms immediately

   c. it requires guards to be on-site to monitor alarms

   d. it permits very fast response times

   e. all are characteristics of a proprietary alarm monitoring station

## Short Answer

1. Why do some facilities incorporate automated access control? List four common access control systems.

2. On the Internet, find four manufacturers of smart locks in the United States and/or Canada and, in your role as a security supervisor or manager, select one sample lock from each manufacturer that is suitable for access control of a large residential housing complex where approximately 30 percent of the owners use their residences as Airbnb locations.

3. Why is key control even more important than the locking system itself?

# Emergency First Aid

> **Note to readers:** The following material in this appendix is intended for quick reference and review purposes only. It illustrates key first aid skills for security guards, however all candidates for an Ontario security guard license are required to obtain a St. John Ambulance First Aid Certificate or its equivalent. (Check the requirements in your province.)
>
> **Source:** This material is excerpted from: *First Aid Reference Guide*, 2016, published by St. John Ambulance. Reprinted by permission.

Emergency scenes generally begin with confusion as people realize there is an emergency unfolding in front of them. No one knows what to do first, who should be in charge, or how they can help. In this situation, the first aider needs to follow a sequence of actions that ensures safe and appropriate first aid is given and everyone's safety is protected. First aiders use emergency scene management (ESM) to do this. Emergency scene management is the sequence of actions you should follow to ensure safe and appropriate first aid is given.

## Four Steps in ESM:

1. scene survey—during the scene survey you take control of the scene, find out what happened and make sure the area is safe before assessing the casualty
2. primary survey—assess each casualty for life-threatening injuries and illnesses, and give life-saving first aid
3. secondary survey—the secondary survey is a step-by-step way of gathering information to form a complete picture of the casualty's overall condition
4. ongoing casualty care—during ongoing casualty care you continue to monitor the casualty's condition until medical help takes over

These steps are generally done in the order above. The initial scene survey, primary survey and the start of life-saving first aid usually happens within one or two minutes. The secondary survey is not always necessary.

## Step One: Scene Survey

- Take charge of the situation
- Call out for help to attract bystanders
- Assess hazards and make the area safe
- Find out the history of the emergency, how many casualties there are and the mechanism(s) of injury
- Identify yourself as a first aider and offer to help, get consent
- Assess responsiveness

Send or go for medical help as soon as you identify a serious problem and then begin the primary survey. If you have a mobile phone, you can dial 9-1-1 or your local emergency number, and put the device on speaker phone, if possible. This allows the first aider to remain with the casualty.

## Step Two: Primary Survey

Check for life-threatening conditions, the ABCs:

A = Airway
B = Breathing
C = Circulation

The sequential steps of the primary survey should be performed with the casualty in the position found unless it is impossible to do so.

The primary survey should begin immediately after the scene survey.

1. Check the airway

   If the casualty is conscious, ask "what happened?" How well the casualty responds will help you determine if the airway is clear. Use a head-tilt-chin-lift to open the airway of an unresponsive casualty.

   If you suspect a head or spinal injury and have been trained, use a jaw-thrust without head-tilt.

2. Check for breathing

   If the casualty is conscious, check by asking how their breathing is.

   If the casualty is unconscious, check for breathing for at least five seconds, and no more than 10 seconds. If breathing is effective, move on to check circulation. If breathing is absent or ineffective (gasping and irregular, agonal), begin CPR.

3. Check circulation
   - Control obvious, severe bleeding
   - Check for shock by checking skin condition and temperature
   - Check with a rapid body survey for hidden, severe, external bleeding and signs of internal bleeding

### *Rapid Body Survey*

The rapid body survey is a quick assessment of the casualty's body which is performed during the primary survey. By running your hands over the casualty's entire body from head to toe (and under heavy outwear), you are able to feel for severe bleeding, internal bleeding and any obvious fractures.

## Step Three: Secondary Survey

A secondary survey follows the primary survey and any life-saving first aid. It is a step-by-step way of gathering information to form a complete picture of the casualty. In the secondary survey, the first aider is looking for injuries or illnesses that may not have been revealed in the primary survey. You should complete a secondary survey if:

- the casualty has more than one injury
- medical help will be delayed for 20 minutes or more
- you will transport the casualty to medical help

The secondary survey has four steps:

1. History
2. Vital signs
3. Head-to-toe exam
4. First aid for any injury or illness found

### History

A SAMPLE history is used to gather a brief medical history of the casualty. This information may be useful for health care professionals who will continue to assist the casualty. If the casualty is unable to respond, some of the SAMPLE history could be answered by a close family member.

- S = symptoms—what the casualty is feeling (such as pain, nausea, or weakness)
- A = allergies—any allergies, specifically allergies to medications
- M = medications—any medications or supplements they normally take, have taken in the past 24 hours, or any doses they may have missed
- P. = past or present medical history—any medical history, especially if it is related to what they are experiencing now. Ask if they have medical alert information
- L = last meal—last meal they ate and when, anything else taken by mouth
- E = events leading to the incident—what was happening before the injury/illness? How did the injury occur?

### Vital Signs

There are four vital signs to check on the casualty:

1. Level of consciousness (LOC)
2. Breathing
3. Pulse
4. Skin condition and temperature

#### Level of Consciousness (LOC)

A common method of obtaining a casualty's LOC is using the acronym AVPU. When using AVPU to indicate LOC, it is a scale which ranges from good (A), to not as good (V), to bad (P), to worse (U).

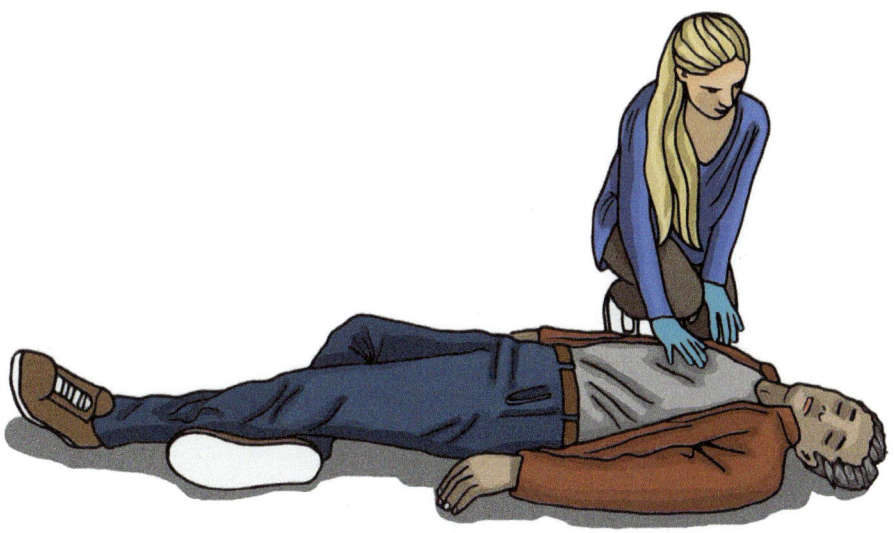

- A = Alert—An alert casualty will have their eyes open and will be able to answer simple questions. An alert casualty is oriented to person, place and time.

V = Verbal—The casualty will respond when spoken to, but may not be able to effectively communicate. They may not be oriented to person, place or time.

P = Pain—This casualty will only respond when a painful stimuli is delivered, such as pinching them or rubbing your knuckles on their sternum. They may move or make noise, but they will not communicate.

U = Unresponsive—the unresponsive casualty will not respond to any stimulus.

Please note that an alternative to quickly estimate a casualty's LOC is to evaluate their eye, verbal and motor skills. If their eyes are open, they can clearly speak, and obey a command such as "squeeze my fingers," they are alert.

*Breathing*

To assess the breathing rate, watch the casualty closely for a total of 30 seconds. It is OK to place your hand on their upper abdomen to feel the rise and fall. Check the quality of the breathing. Carefully count each breath over the 30 seconds and multiply that number by two for breaths per minute.

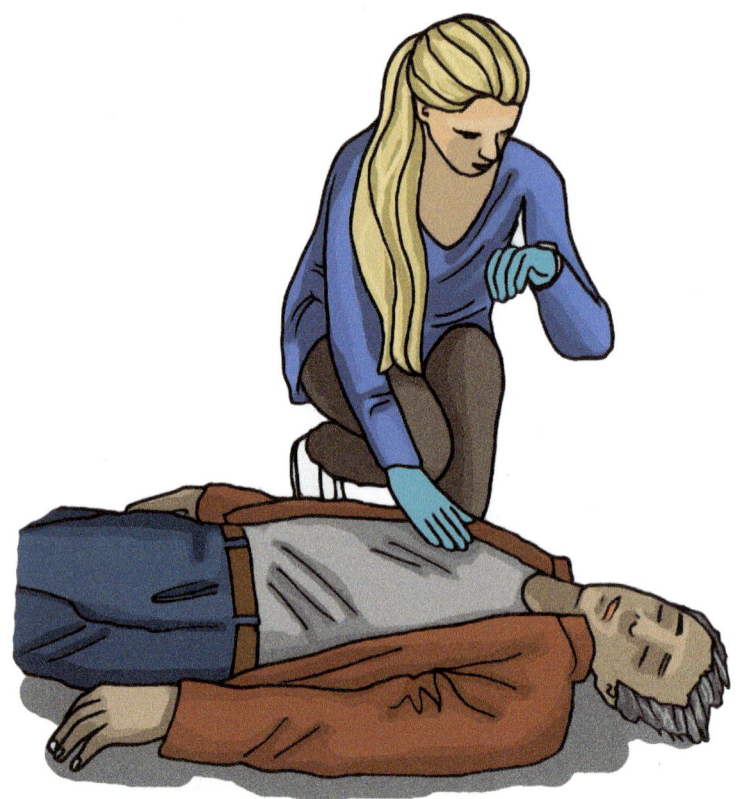

| Normal breathing rates | | | |
|---|---|---|---|
| Age | Too slow | Normal | Too fast |
| Infant | Below 25 | 30–50 | Above 60 |
| Child | Below 15 | 20–30 | Above 40 |
| Adult | Below 10 | 10–20 | Above 30 |

*Pulse*

The pulse rate is the number of beats your heart takes in one minute, and it is an essential skill for assessing all casualties. The most common places to assess a pulse is at the wrist or neck, and for infants, the inside of the upper arm.

To assess the pulse, use two fingers and gently place them on either the inside of the wrist (just below the hand on the thumb side), or on the side of the neck (carotid artery), or for infants, the inside of the upper arm, on the brachial artery. Press just gently enough to feel the pulse. You may have to feel around the area until you find it. Once you have found the pulse, count the number of beats over 30 seconds and multiply that number by two.

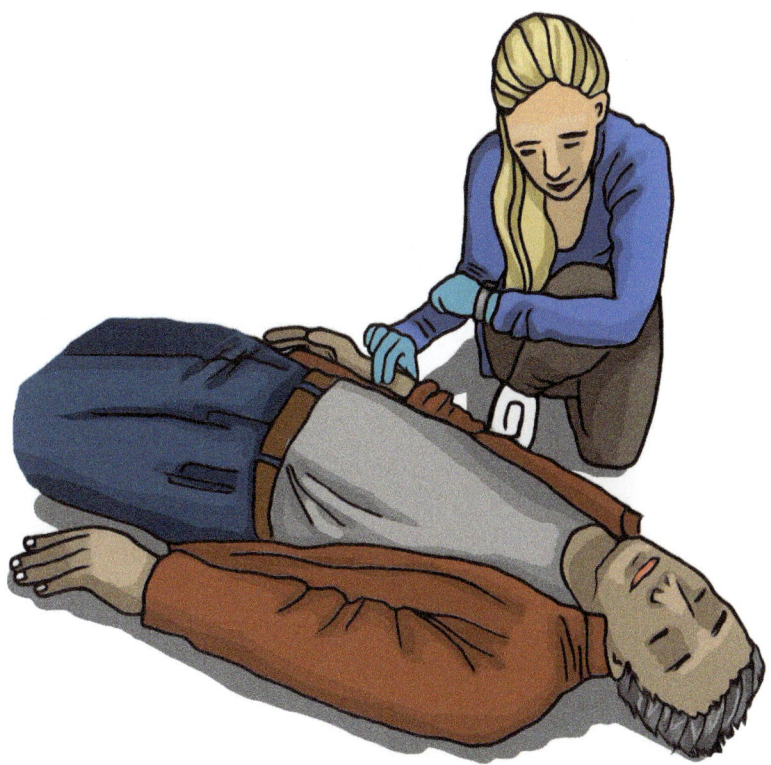

| Normal pulse rates | |
|---|---|
| **Age** | **Normal pulse range** |
| Infant | 120–150 |
| Child | 80–150 |
| Adult | 60–100 |

*Skin Condition and Temperature*

When assessing the skin we look for the temperature (warm or cold), the colour (normal skin tones or pale) and whether the skin is dry or wet. Use the back of your gloved hand to feel the casualty's forehead and cheeks. If their skin normal, they will have normal skin colour, and their skin will be warm and dry. If the skin is pale, cold and wet (sweaty), this could be an indication of shock.

### Head-to-toe exam

The head-to-toe exam is a complete and detailed check of the casualty for any injuries that may have been missed during the rapid body survey. Do not examine for unlikely injuries. You may need to expose an area to check for injuries, but always respect the casualty's modesty and ensure you protect them from the cold. Only expose what you absolutely have to.

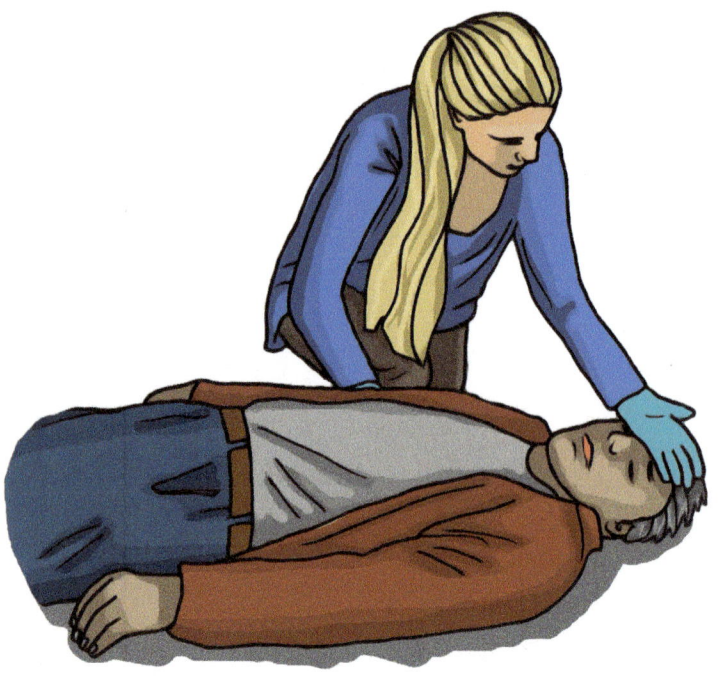

*First Aid for Injuries Found*

When you have completed your exam, give appropriate first aid for any injuries or illnesses found. If the casualty has more than one injury, give first aid to the more serious injuries first.

*Document*

Upon completion of the secondary survey, document your findings as accurately as possible. This information may be valuable to medical professionals who will continue to assist the casualty.

## Step Four: Ongoing Casualty Care

Once first aid for injuries and illnesses that are not life-threatening has been given:

- the first aider will hand over control of the scene to the casualty (or someone else) and end their involvement in the emergency
- the first aider will stay in control of the scene and wait for medical help to take over, or
- the first aider will stay in control of the scene and transport the casualty to medical help

The first aider must maintain the casualty in the best possible condition until handover to medical help by:

- Giving first aid for shock
- Monitoring the casualty's condition

APPENDIX A   Emergency First Aid   **301**

- Recording the events of the situation
- Reporting on what happened to whoever takes over

Instruct a bystander to maintain manual support of the head and neck (if head/spinal injuries are suspected). Continue to steady and support manually, if needed.

*How to put a casualty into the recovery position*

This position protects the casualty and also reduces bending and twisting of the spine. This position protects the airway if you must leave the casualty.

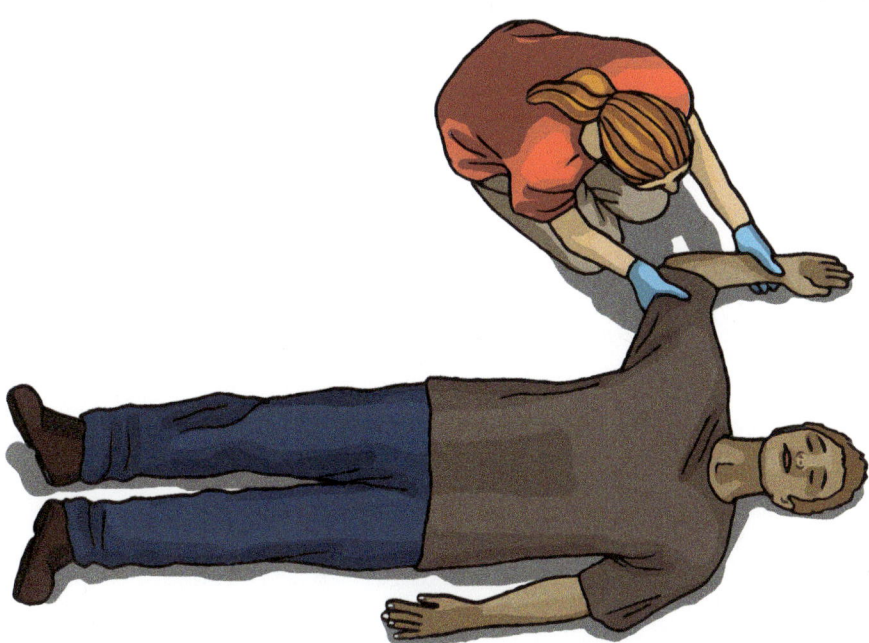

1. Position the arm closest to you at 90 degrees in front of the casualty, keeping it out of the way when rolling them.

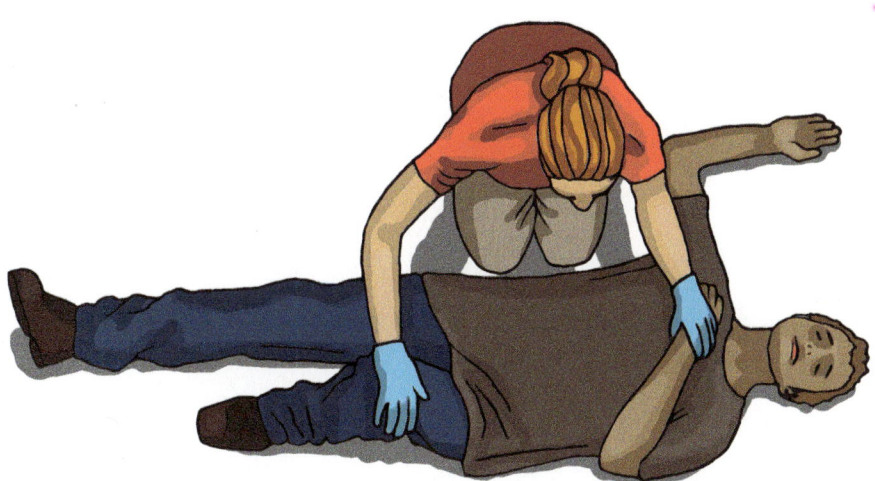

2. Position the arm furthest from you on the casualty's chest. Bend the far knee.

3. Reach behind the casualty's shoulder and roll casualty towards you by pulling on the far knee.

4. Adjust the position of the arms, leg and shoulder so the casualty is in a stable position. Place the far arm at 90 degrees to the casualty with the palm down.

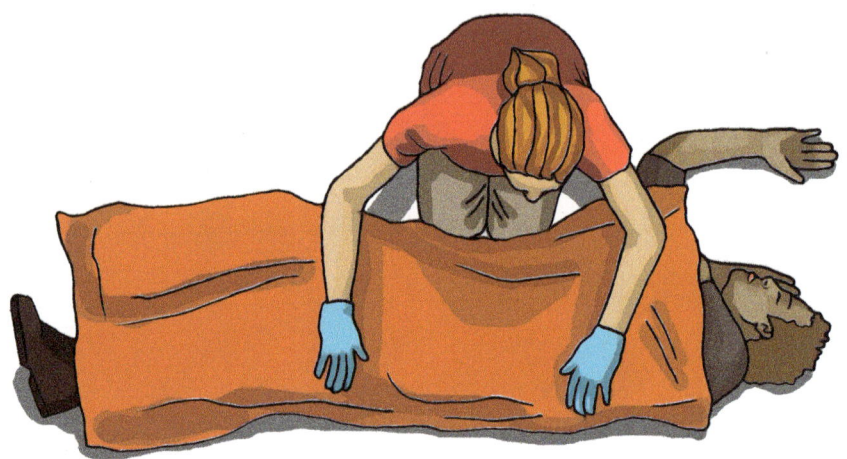

5. Give ongoing care.

### Shock

Shock is a circulation problem where the body's tissues don't get enough oxygenated blood.

Shock is a danger because any physical injury or illness can be accompanied by shock, and it can quickly progress into a life-threatening condition. Pain, anxiety and fear do not cause shock, but they can make it worse, or make it progress faster. This is why reassuring a casualty and making them comfortable is important.

Medical shock should not be confused with electrical shock or being shocked and surprised. Medical shock is life-threatening, as the brain and other organs cannot function properly.

The following information provides some causes of shock. Severe shock can also result from medical emergencies such as diabetes, epilepsy, infection, poisoning or a drug overdose.

| Common causes of severe shock ||
|---|---|
| **Cause of shock** | **How it causes a circulation problem** |
| severe bleeding—internal or external (includes major fractures) | not enough blood to fill blood vessels |
| severe burns | loss of blood plasma (fluid) into tissues—not enough blood to fill blood vessels |
| crush injuries | loss of blood and blood plasma into tissues—not enough blood to fill blood vessels |
| heart attack | heart is not strong enough to pump blood effectively |
| spinal cord or nerve injuries | brain can't control the size of the blood vessels—the blood can't get to the tissues properly |
| severe allergic reactions | many things can be affected—breathing, heart function, etc. |

| Signs and symptoms of shock ||
|---|---|
| **Signs** | **Symptoms** |
| • pale skin at first, turns blue-grey* | • restless |
| • blue-purple lips, tongue, earlobes, fingernails | • anxious |
| • cold and clammy skin | • disoriented |
| • breathing shallow and irregular, fast or gasping for air | • confused |
| • changes in level of consciousness | • afraid |
| • weak, rapid pulse—radial pulse may be absent | • dizzy |
|  | • thirsty |

\* For casualties with dark skin colour, colour changes may be observed in the following areas of the body: lips, gums and tongue, nail beds and palms, earlobes, membrane of the inner eyelid.

## First aid for shock

The following actions will minimize shock:

1. Give first aid for the injury or illness that caused the shock
2. Reassure the casualty often
3. Minimize pain by handling the casualty gently
4. Loosen tight clothing at the neck, chest and waist
5. Keep the casualty warm, but do not overheat—use jackets, coats or blankets if you have them
6. Moisten the lips if the casualty complains of thirst. Don't give anything to eat or drink. If medical help is delayed many hours, give small amounts of water or clear fluids to drink—make a note of what was given and when
7. Place the casualty in the best position for their condition
Continue ongoing casualty care until handover

The above first aid for shock may prevent shock from getting worse. Whenever possible, add these steps to any first aid you give.

### Positioning a casualty in shock

Putting the casualty in the right position can slow the progress of shock and make the casualty more comfortable.

The position you use depends on the casualty's condition. The casualty should be as comfortable as possible in the position you use.

*No suspected head/spinal injury; fully conscious*

Place the casualty on their back, if injuries permit. Once the casualty is positioned, cover them to preserve body heat, but do not overheat.

*No suspected head/spinal injury; less than fully conscious*

Place the casualty in the recovery position. When there is decreased level of consciousness, airway and breathing are the priority—the recovery position ensures an open airway.

| Signs of choking ||
|---|---|
| **Mild obstruction** | **Severe obstruction** |
| able to speak | not able to speak |
| signs of distress—eyes show fear | signs of distress—eyes show fear |
| forceful coughing | weak or no coughing |
| wheezing and gagging between coughs | high-pitched noise or no noise when trying to breathe |
| red or "flushed" face | grey face and blue lips and ears |

## First aid for choking

First aid for a choking adult or child

1. Perform a scene survey.
2. If the casualty can cough forcefully, speak or breathe, tell them to try to cough up the object. If a mild obstruction lasts for a few minutes, get medical help.

If you think there might be a severe obstruction, check by asking, "Are you choking?" If the casualty cannot cough forcefully, speak or breathe, use back blows followed by abdominal thrusts to remove the blockage.

3. Give back blows and abdominal thrusts:
   - Support the casualty and give up to five blows between the shoulder blades using the heel of your hand.
   - If the obstruction is not cleared, step behind the casualty ready to support them if they become unconscious.
   - Make a fist, place it on the casualty's abdomen at the belly button, in line with the hip bones. Grasp the fist with the other hand and give five forceful inward and upward abdominal thrusts.

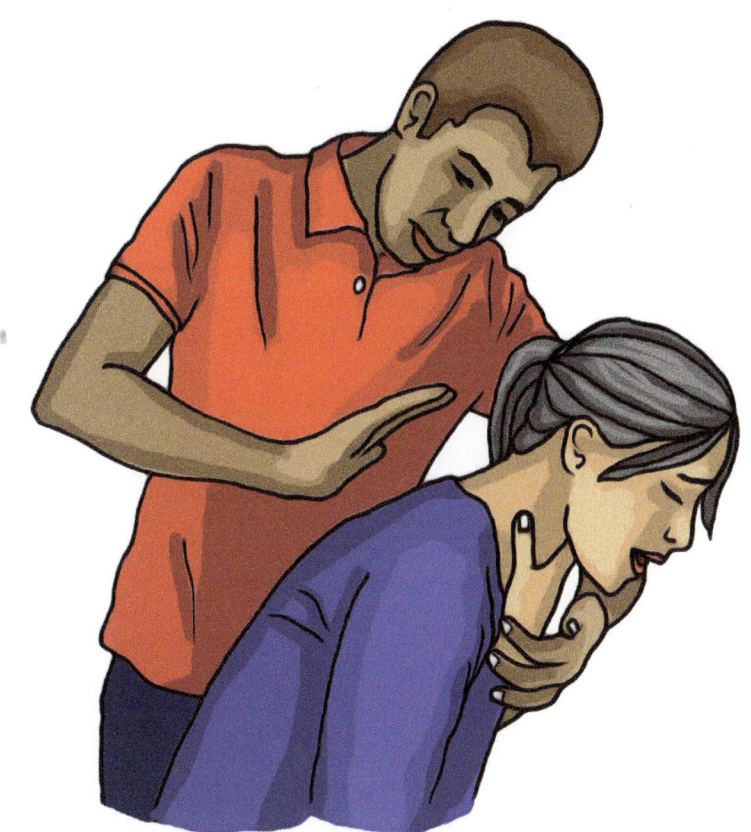

4. If the object is not removed, repeat back blows and abdominal thrusts.
5. If the casualty becomes unconscious, lower them to the ground. Call for medical help and get an AED if available.
6. Begin chest compressions immediately. After the first 30 compressions, check the mouth. Remove any foreign object you can see. Try to give 2 breaths. If air does not go in, continue to give chest compressions and inspecting the mouth before ventilations.

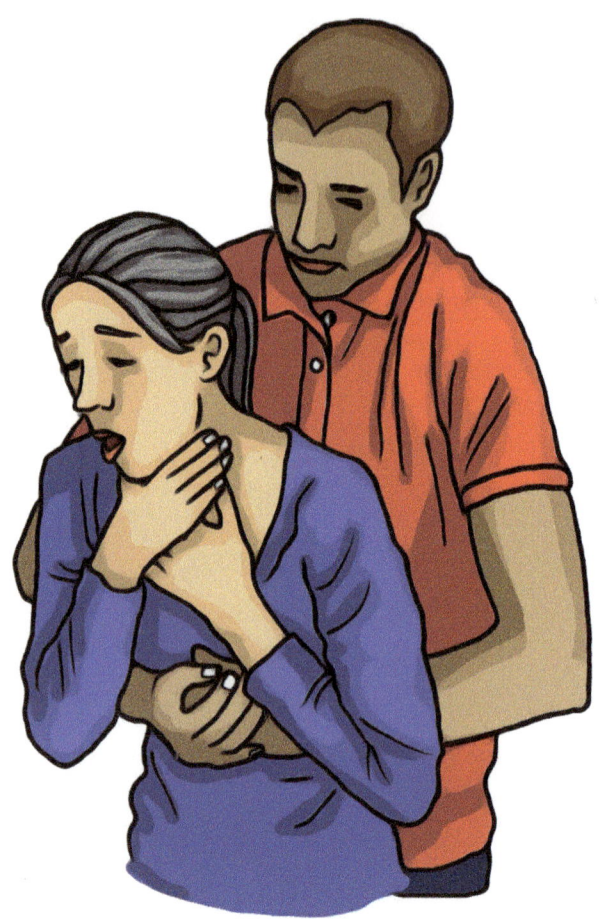

### First aid for a choking casualty much larger than the rescuer

If a choking casualty is very large or is in the late stages of pregnancy, give back blows as normal, followed by chest thrusts.

1. While supporting the casualty, give up to five back blows between the shoulder blades, using the heel of your hand.
2. If the obstruction is not cleared, stand behind the casualty.
3. Keep your arms horizontal and snug up under their armpits.
4. Place your fist against the lower half of the breastbone, thumb-side in.
5. Hold your fist with your other hand. Pull inward forcefully.
6. Continue giving back blows and chest thrusts until either the object is removed or the casualty becomes unconscious.

## Bleeding

Bleeding is the escape of blood from the blood vessels. In external bleeding, blood escapes the body through a surface wound. In internal bleeding, blood escapes from tissues inside the body.

In arterial bleeding, the blood is bright red and spurts with each heartbeat.

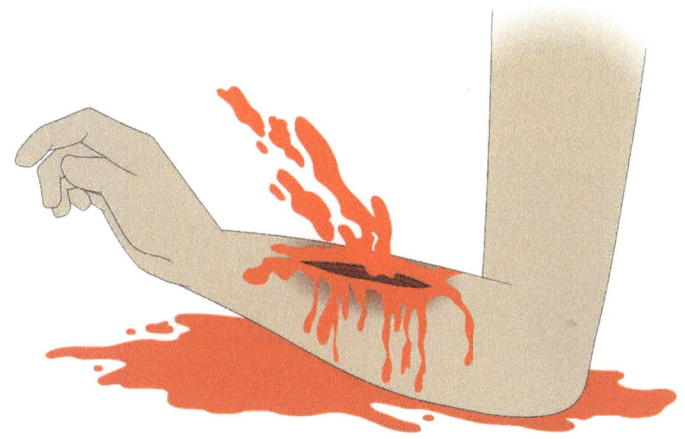

In venous bleeding, the blood is dark red and flows more steadily.

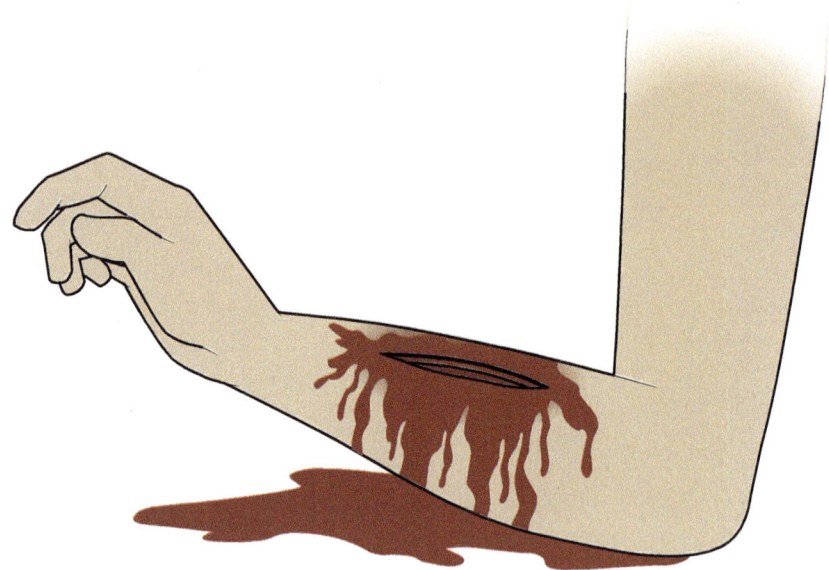

Severe blood loss will result in the following signs and symptoms of shock:

- pale, cold and clammy skin
- rapid pulse, gradually becoming weaker
- faintness, dizziness, thirst and nausea
- restlessness and apprehension
- shallow breathing, yawning, sighing and gasping for air

### First aid for severe external bleeding

1. Perform a scene survey, then do a primary survey.
2. To control severe bleeding, apply direct pressure to the wound.
3. Place the casualty at rest.
4. Once bleeding is under control, continue the primary survey, looking for other life-threatening injuries.
5. Before bandaging the wound, check circulation below the injury. Bandage the dressing in place.

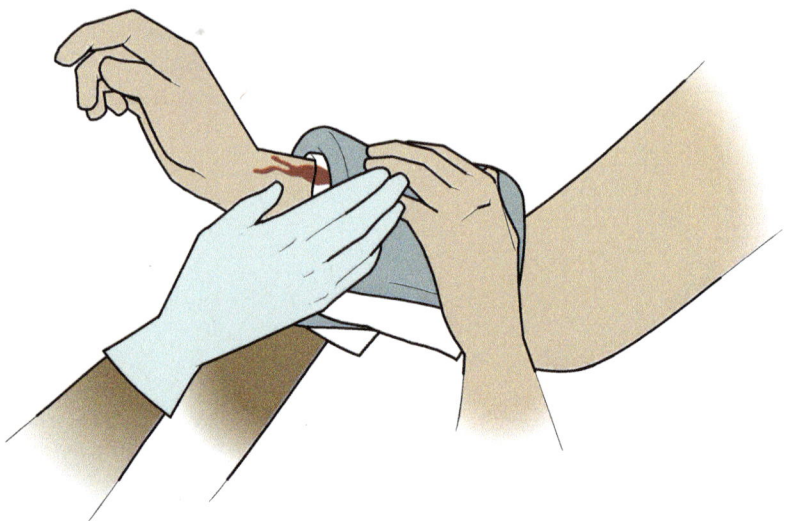

6. Check the circulation below the injury and compare it with the other side. If it is worse than it was before the injury was bandaged, loosen the bandage just enough to improve circulation if possible.
7. Give ongoing casualty care.

If the dressings become blood-soaked, don't remove them—add more dressings and continue pressure. Removing the blood-soaked dressings may disturb blood clots and expose the wound to further contamination.

*Tourniquets and hemostatic dressings*

For catastrophic wounds, where it will be difficult to control bleeding, the use of a tourniquet, a constricting bandage, to stop all blood flow to a limb, or hemostatic dressings to promote blood clotting may be considered. First aid kits for use by the military, law enforcement or wilderness first responders may contain specialized dressings or purpose built tourniquets to control bleeding.

## Cardiac arrest

When the heart stops pumping blood properly, it is called cardiac arrest, and the casualty is considered clinically dead, though they may still be resuscitated. The first aid for cardiac arrest is cardiopulmonary resuscitation (CPR) and rapid defibrillation.

## Cardiopulmonary Resuscitation (CPR)

CPR is artificial respiration and artificial circulation. Artificial respiration provides oxygen to the lungs. Artificial circulation causes blood to flow through the body. The purpose of CPR is to circulate enough oxygenated blood to the brain and other organs to delay damage until either the heart starts beating again, or medical help takes over from you. CPR is most effective when interruptions to chest compressions are minimized.

## CPR—Adult casualty

1. Perform a scene survey.
2. Assess responsiveness.
3. If there is no response, call for medical help on a mobile device, and place the phone on speakerphone, and send someone for an AED. If no mobile phone is available, send or go for medical help and the AED, if available. Perform a primary survey:
   Open the airway.
   Check for normal breathing for at least 5 and no more than 10 seconds.

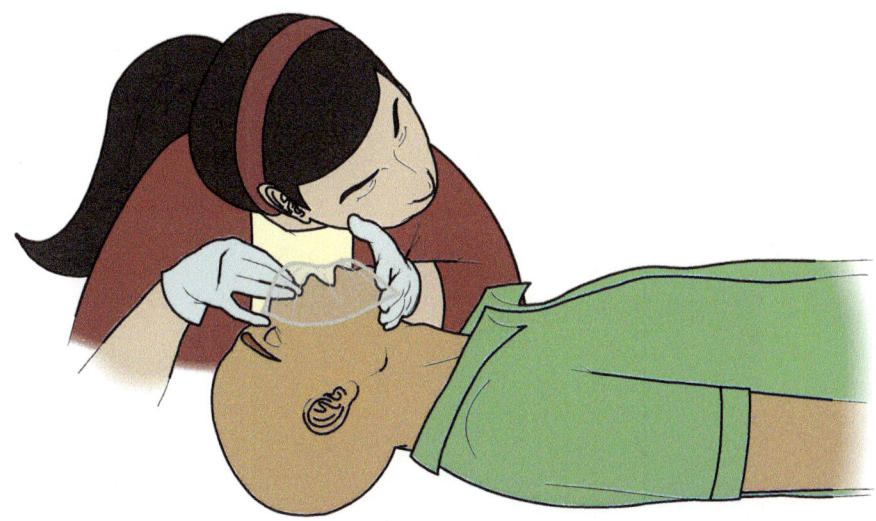

4. If the casualty is not breathing, or not breathing effectively (agonal breaths) position your hands in the centre of the upper chest and your shoulders directly over your hands. Keep your elbows locked.
5. Give 30 compressions—Push hard—Push fast!

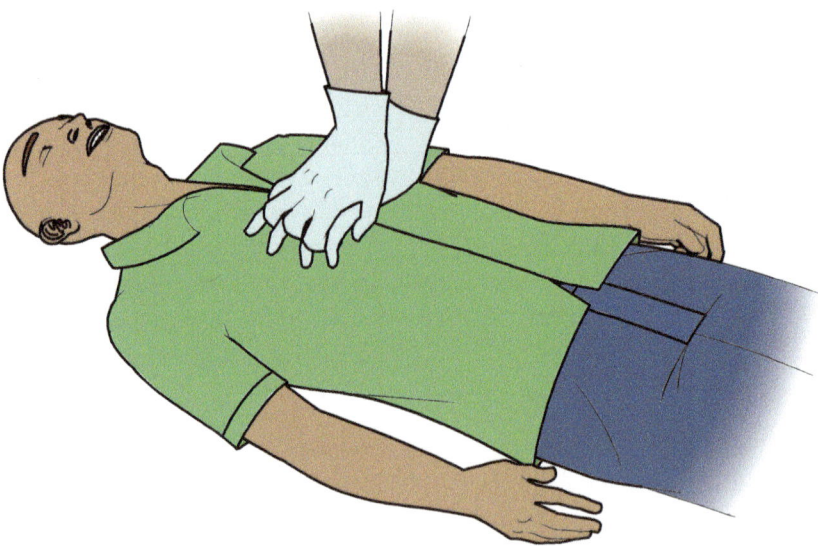

- Press the heels of the hands straight down on the breastbone. The depth of each compression should be at 5–6 cm (2–2.4 inches).

- Release pressure and completely remove your weight at the top of each compression to allow chest to return to the resting position.

- Give compressions at a rate of 100 to 120 per minute. Count compressions out loud to keep track of how many you have given, and to help keep a steady rhythm.

6. Open the airway by tilting the head and lifting the chin.
7. Position a barrier device and breathe into the casualty twice. For an adult casualty, each breath should take about for 1 second, with just enough air to make the chest rise.

    This is one cycle of 30:2 (30 compressions to 2 ventilations).
8. Continue CPR until either an AED is applied, the casualty begins to respond, another first aider or medical help takes over or you are too exhausted to continue. The AED should be applied as soon as it arrives at the scene.

## *Agonal breathing*

Agonal breathing is an abnormal pattern of breathing driven by a brainstem reflex, characterized by irregular gasping respirations at times accompanied by strange vocalizations. This can occur with cardiac arrest and lead bystanders to believe the casualty is breathing. A casualty with agonal breathing should be treated as though they are not breathing.

## CPR—Child casualty

1. Perform a scene survey.
2. Assess responsiveness.
3. If there is no response, send or call for medical help and an AED if available. If you are alone with no phone perform 5 cycles of CPR (two minutes) then go for medical help. Carry the child with you if possible. Perform a primary survey:
4. Open the airway.

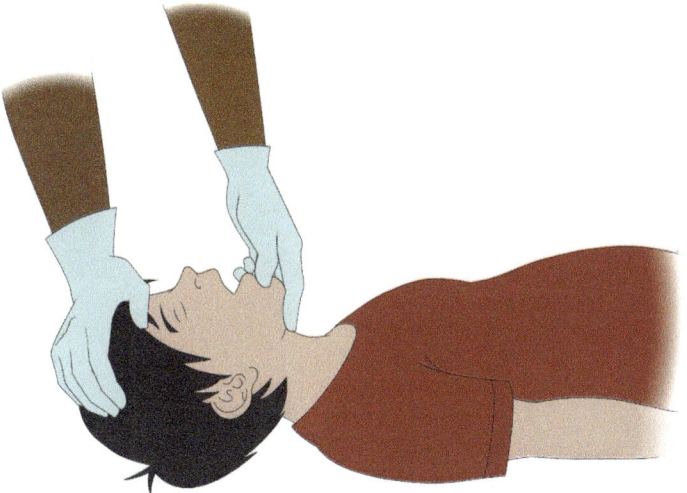

5. Check for breathing for at least 5 and no more than 10 seconds.

# Private Security and Investigative Services Act, 2005

SO 2005, c 34

Last amendment: 2015, c 30, s 27.

## CONTENTS

### PART I: INTERPRETATION AND APPLICATION
1. Definitions
2. Application

### PART II: ADMINISTRATION

#### REGISTRAR
3. Registrar

#### TYPES OF LICENCES
4. Types of licences

#### REGISTRATION
5. Registered employer

### PART III: PROHIBITIONS
6. Individual licence
7. Licence to engage in the business
8. Change in business entity
9. Licensee may not act as collector, etc.

### PART IV: LICENSING

#### MANDATORY REQUIREMENTS
10. Mandatory requirements

#### APPLICATION
11. Application for licence
12. Licences—general rules
13. Issuance of licence
14. Conditions
15. Revocation
16. Notice and hearing
17. Appeal
18. Further application

### PART V: COMPLAINTS AND INVESTIGATIONS

#### COMPLAINTS
19. Complaint to Registrar

#### INVESTIGATIONS
20. Appointment of investigators
21. Initiation of investigations
22. Search warrant
23. Searches in exigent circumstances
24. Admissibility of copies
25. Possession of licence

#### INSPECTIONS
26. Appointment of inspectors
27. Inspection
28. Warrant
29. Possession of licence
29.1 Arrest without warrant

### PART VI: GENERAL DUTIES AND STANDARDS OF PRACTICE
30. Insurance required
31. Appropriate licence
32. Information to be filed with Registrar
33. Name of business
34. Identification as private investigator
35. Security guard licence must be carried
36. Display of licence to engage in business
37. Return of licence
38. Other duties re licences
39. Holding out as police
40. Certain terms prohibited

### PART VII: GENERAL
41. Service
42. False, misleading or deceptive representation
43. Offence
44. Offence-directors or officers
45. Penalties
46. Testimonial immunity
47. Court order for compliance
48. Protection from liability
49. Fees
50. Information concerning licensee
51. Rules
52. Transition—licences

### PART VIII: REGULATIONS
53. Code of conduct
54. Regulations

## PART I: INTERPRETATION AND APPLICATION

**Definitions**

1. In this Act,

"business entity" includes a corporation, partnership or sole proprietorship;

"employee" includes a person, whether or not employed under a contract of employment, who performs work or services for another person for remuneration on such conditions that he or she is in a position of economic dependence upon, and under an obligation to perform duties for, that person more closely resembling the relationship of an employee than that of an independent contractor;

"licensee" means an individual or business entity that holds a licence under this Act, and "licensed" has a corresponding meaning;

"Minister" means the member of the Executive Council to whom the administration of this Act is assigned under the *Executive Council Act*;

"prescribed" means prescribed by the regulations;

"provincial offence" means an offence under an Act of the Legislature or under a regulation made under the authority of an Act of the Legislature;

"Registrar" means the Registrar of Private Investigators and Security Guards appointed under section 3;

"Tribunal" means the Licence Appeal Tribunal established under the *Licence Appeal Tribunal Act, 1999*.

**Application**

2(1) This Act applies to private investigators within the meaning of subsection (2) and to security guards within the meaning of subsection (4).

**Private investigators**

(2) A private investigator is a person who performs work, for remuneration, that consists primarily of conducting investigations in order to provide information.

**Same**

(3) Examples of the types of information referred to in subsection (2) include information on,

(a) the character or actions of a person;

(b) the business or occupation of a person; and

(c) the whereabouts of persons or property.

**Security guards**

(4) A security guard is a person who performs work, for remuneration, that consists primarily of guarding or patrolling for the purpose of protecting persons or property.

**Same**

(5) Examples of the types of work referred to in subsection (4) include,

(a) acting as a bouncer;

(b) acting as a bodyguard; and

(c) performing services to prevent the loss of property through theft or sabotage in an industrial, commercial, residential or retail environment.

**Soliciting or procuring services**

(6) A person who performs work, for remuneration, that consists primarily of acting for or aiding others in soliciting or procuring the services of a private investigator or security guard shall be deemed to be in the business of selling private investigator or security guard services.

**Non-application**

(7) This Act does not apply to,

(a) barristers or solicitors engaged in the practice of their profession;

(b) persons who perform work, for remuneration, that consists primarily of searching for and providing information on,

(i) the financial credit rating of persons,

(ii) the qualifications and suitability of applicants for insurance and indemnity bonds, or

(iii) the qualifications and suitability of persons as employees or prospective employees;

(c) a person who is acting as a peace officer;

(d) insurance adjusters licensed under the *Insurance Act* while acting in that capacity, and their employees while acting in the usual and regular scope of their employment;

(e) insurance companies licensed under the *Insurance Act* and their employees while acting in the usual and regular scope of their employment;

(f) persons residing outside Ontario who are licensed employees of a private investigation agency licensed or registered in a jurisdiction outside Ontario, but elsewhere in Canada who,

(i) on behalf of a person situated outside Ontario, make an investigation or inquiry partly outside Ontario and partly within Ontario, and

(ii) come into Ontario solely for the purpose of such investigation or inquiry;

(g) persons who receive remuneration for work that consists primarily of providing advice with respect to security requirements but who are not soliciting or procuring the services of private investigators or security guards for the purposes of subsection (6);

(h) persons who receive remuneration for work that consists primarily of providing an armoured vehicle service;

(i) locksmiths; and

(j) any class of persons exempted by the regulations.

**Remunerative work**

(8) In subsections (2), (4), (6) and (7), a reference to performing work for remuneration includes performing work pursuant to an agreement that provides that the remuneration paid is contingent, in whole or in part, on the completion of the work.

**"Peace officer"**

(9) For the purposes of clause (7)(c),

"peace officer" means a person or a member of a class of persons set out in the definition of "peace officer" in section 2 of the *Criminal Code* (Canada).

## PART II: ADMINISTRATION

### REGISTRAR

**Registrar**

3(1) The Lieutenant Governor in Council shall appoint a Registrar of Private Investigators and Security Guards.

Deputy registrars

(2) The Lieutenant Governor in Council may appoint one or more deputy registrars who may act as Registrar during the Registrar's absence or inability to act.

### TYPES OF LICENCES

**Types of licences**

4. The following are the types of licences that may be issued under this Act:

1. A licence to act as a private investigator.
2. A licence to act as a security guard.
3. A licence to engage in the business of selling the services of private investigators.
4. A licence to engage in the business of selling the services of security guards.
5. A licence to act as both a private investigator and a security guard.
6. A licence to engage in the business of selling the services of both private investigators and security guards.

### REGISTRATION

**Registered employer**

5. If a business entity, other than a business entity that engages in the business of selling the services of private investigators or security guards to the public, employs a private investigator or security guard, that business entity shall,

(a) register as an employer in accordance with the prescribed requirements; and

(b) provide the Registrar with a mailing address for service in Ontario, and notify the Registrar of any change in its mailing address within five days of the change.

## PART III: PROHIBITIONS

**Individual licence**

6. No person shall act as a private investigator or a security guard or hold himself or herself out as one unless the person holds the appropriate licence under this Act and,

(a) is employed by a licensed business entity, a registered employer under section 5, or an employer that is not required to be registered; or

(b) is the sole proprietor of a licensed business entity or is a partner in a licensed business entity.

**Licence to engage in the business**

7(1) No person shall sell the services of private investigators or security guards or hold themself out as available to sell such services, unless,

(a) the person holds the appropriate licence under this Act; or

(b) the person is an employee of a licensee described in clause (a) and is acting on behalf of that licensee in the normal course of his or her duties.

**Branch offices**

(2) No person shall engage in the business of selling the services of private investigators or security guards from more than one place at which the public is invited to deal unless the person is licensed, with one place designated by the licensee as the main office and the remainder as branch offices.

**Change in business entity**

8(1) Subject to subsection (2), if there is a change in the officers, directors or partners of a business entity that is a licensee, the business entity shall not continue to act or offer services under the licence.

**Same**

(2) Where there is a change in the officers, directors or partners of a business entity, the Registrar may consent, in writing, to the business entity continuing to act or offer services under the existing licence, in which case subsection (1) does not apply.

**Sole proprietorships**

(3) Where the holder of a licence who is a sole proprietor dies or becomes incapable, the Registrar may issue a temporary licence, that is valid for the time stipulated in the licence, to permit the sole proprietor's business to be maintained or wound down.

**Licensee may not act as collector, etc.**

9(1) No person who holds a licence to act as a private investigator or security guard shall act or hold himself, herself or itself out as being available to act with respect to,
   (a) the collection of accounts;
   (b) acting as a bailiff; or
   (c) an eviction under the *Residential Tenancies Act, 2006*.

**Protected witnesses**

(2) No person who holds a licence to act as a private investigator or security guard shall act or hold himself, herself or itself out as being available to act with respect to,
   (a) locating a person known or suspected by the licensee to be a member of a witness protection program; or
   (b) gathering information about any person known or suspected by the licensee to be a member of a witness protection program for the purpose of enabling the person to be located.

## PART IV: LICENSING

### MANDATORY REQUIREMENTS

**Mandatory requirements**

10(1) No person is eligible to hold a licence under this Act unless,
   (a) the person possesses a clean criminal record; and
   (b) in the case of an individual,
     (i) the person is 18 years old or older,
     (ii) the person is entitled to work in Canada, and
     (iii) the person has successfully completed all prescribed training and testing.

**Loss of requirement**

(2) If, at any time subsequent to being issued a licence, a person ceases to meet a requirement set out in subsection (1), the person shall not continue to act or offer services under the licence and shall return the licence to the Registrar as required under section 37 within five days, excluding Saturdays, Sundays and public holidays, within the meaning of the *Employment Standards Act, 2000*.

**Notice by Registrar**

(3) Where the Registrar becomes aware that a person no longer meets a requirement set out in subsection (1), the Registrar shall promptly give the person notice that the Registrar's records have been changed to show that the person no longer has a valid licence.

**Request to reconsider**

(4) Where the Registrar has given notice under subsection (3), the person to whom notice has been given may request that the Registrar reconsider the change to the Registrar's records, and the Registrar may consider any relevant information in doing so.

**"Clean criminal record"**

(5) For the purposes of subsection (1), a person possesses a "clean criminal record" if,
   (a) the person has not been convicted of a prescribed offence under the *Criminal Code* (Canada), the *Controlled Drugs and Substances Act* (Canada) or any other Act of Canada; or
   (b) the person has been convicted of such an offence and a pardon under the *Criminal Records Act* (Canada) has been issued or granted.

### APPLICATION

**Application for licence**

11(1) A person who applies to the Registrar for the issuance or renewal of a licence shall,
   (a) provide a mailing address for service in Ontario;
   (b) pay the required fee for the issuance or renewal of the appropriate licence;
   (c) provide a declaration that lists,
     (i) all of the person's convictions for and findings of guilt for offences under a law of Canada up to the date of the declaration for which a pardon under the *Criminal Records Act* (Canada) has not been issued or granted,
     (ii) all of the person's convictions for and findings of guilt for a provincial offence or an offence under a law of any other province or territory of Canada,
     (iii) all fines levied against the person for a provincial offence that remain unpaid on the date of the declaration,

(iv) all of the person's convictions for criminal offences under the laws of other jurisdictions for which a pardon has not been issued or granted,

(v) all charges for allegedly committing an offence against a law of Canada that have been laid against the person and that have not been resolved on the date of the declaration, and

(vi) all charges for allegedly committing a criminal offence against the laws of another jurisdiction that have been laid against the person and that have not been resolved on the date of the declaration;

(d) provide consent for the Registrar to collect information on any matter mentioned in clause (c);

(e) if the person is a business entity, provide the things required under clauses (c) and (d) in respect of the business entity and of every officer, director or partner, as the case may be, of the business entity;

(f) if the person is an individual, provide proof,
   (i) of his or her age,
   (ii) of his or her entitlement to work in Canada, and
   (iii) that he or she has successfully completed all prescribed training and testing; and

(g) in the case of a licence to engage in the business of selling the services of private investigators or security guards, provide proof of the insurance required under section 30.

**Registrar may require**

(2) The Registrar may require an applicant to provide,

(a) his or her fingerprints;

(b) a clearly recognizable photograph of the applicant;

(c) his or her consent for the Registrar to conduct or have local police conduct a background check, including information regarding convictions and findings of guilt;

> Note: On a day to be named by proclamation of the Lieutenant Governor, clause 11(2)(c) of the Act is repealed and the following substituted: (See: 2015, c 30, s 27)
>
> (c) a criminal record and judicial matters check under the *Police Record Checks Reform Act, 2015*, or his or her consent for the Registrar to conduct such a check or have one conducted;

(d) his or her consent for the Registrar to investigate the person's immigration status in Canada; and

(e) any other information or material as the Registrar considers necessary, including personal information within the meaning of the *Freedom of Information and Protection of Privacy Act*, in order to determine,
   (i) whether the applicant meets the requirements for the issuance or renewal of a licence, and
   (ii) whether, in the Registrar's opinion, any of paragraphs 1 to 7 of subsection 13(2) applies in respect of the applicant.

**Business entity**

(3) If the applicant is a business entity, subsection (2) applies in respect of any officer, director or partner, as the case may be.

**How information provided**

(4) An applicant shall provide information or material required under this section in a form and manner as may be required by the Registrar.

**Licences—general rules**

12. The following rules apply in respect of licences and licensees:

1. A licence shall clearly indicate what type of licence it is.
2. A licence shall clearly indicate the date on which it expires.
3. A person may be issued more than one type of licence, but, regardless of the licences a person holds, the person may not act as a security guard and a private investigator at the same time.
4. Every licence shall display a clearly recognizable photograph of the holder, if the holder is an individual.
5. A licence is not transferable.

**Issuance of licence**

13(1) An applicant who meets the requirements set out in this Act and the regulations for the applicable licence is entitled to the issuance or renewal of a licence unless subsection (2) applies.

**Registrar may decline**

(2) The Registrar may decline to issue or renew a licence if the Registrar is of the opinion that one of the following applies, and if the Registrar is of the opinion that the matter is relevant to the applicant's fitness to hold a licence:

1. The applicant or an interested person in respect of the applicant is carrying on activities,
   i. that are in contravention of this Act or the regulations, or

ii. that will be in contravention of this Act or the regulations if the applicant is issued a licence or a licence is renewed.
2. The past conduct of the applicant or of an interested person in respect of the applicant affords reasonable grounds to believe that the applicant will not carry on business in accordance with the law and with integrity and honesty.
3. The applicant, an employee or agent of the applicant makes a false statement or provides a false statement in an application for a licence or for a renewal of the licence.
4. The applicant is a business entity and,
    i. having regard to its financial position or the financial position of an interested person, the applicant cannot reasonably be expected to be financially responsible in the conduct of its business,
    ii. having regard to the financial position of its officers, directors or partners or of an interested person, the applicant cannot reasonably be expected to be financially responsible in the conduct of its business,
    iii. the past conduct of its officers, directors or partners or of an interested person affords reasonable grounds for belief that its business will not be carried on in accordance with the law and with integrity and honesty, or
    iv. an officer, director or partner of the business entity makes a false statement or provides a false statement in an application for a licence or for renewal of a licence.
5. The applicant,
    i. has been convicted of or found guilty of an offence under a law of Canada for which a pardon under the *Criminal Records Act* (Canada) has not been issued or granted,
    ii. has been convicted of or found guilty of a provincial offence or an offence under a law of any other province or territory of Canada,
    iii. is liable to pay a fine for a provincial offence that has not been paid,
    iv. has been convicted of a criminal offence under the law of another jurisdiction for which a pardon has not been issued or granted.
6. A ground exists that is prescribed as a ground for which an application for the issuance or renewal of a licence may be refused.
7. It is in the public interest to refuse to issue or renew the licence.

**Interested persons**

(3) For the purposes of subsection (2), a person is an interested person in respect of an applicant if, in the opinion of the Registrar,

(a) the person has or may have a beneficial interest in the applicant's business;

(b) the person exercises or may exercise control either directly or indirectly over the applicant; or

(c) the person has provided or may have provided financing either directly or indirectly to the applicant's business.

**Conditions**

14(1) A licence is subject to such conditions as are prescribed or that are imposed by the Registrar under subsection (2).

**Same**

(2) The Registrar may issue or renew a licence subject to such conditions as he or she considers appropriate and may, at any time, attach such additional conditions as he or she considers appropriate to an existing licence.

**Revocation**

15(1) The Registrar may revoke a licence,

(a) for any reason for which the Registrar could refuse to issue or renew a licence under subsection 13(2); or

(b) if the licensee is in breach of a condition of the licence.

**Immediate suspension**

(2) If the Registrar proposes to revoke a licence and he or she considers it to be in the interest of public safety to do so, the Registrar may by order suspend the licence and any such order takes effect immediately.

**Duration of suspension**

(3) Despite anything contained in the *Statutory Powers Procedure Act*, a suspension under subsection (2) continues in effect until,

(a) if the licensee requests an opportunity to be heard under subsection 16(3), a final determination has been made in respect of the proposed revocation as a result of there being no further right of appeal;

(b) the Registrar receives new information that leads the Registrar to believe that the licence should not be revoked; or

(c) if the licensee does not request an opportunity to be heard within the time permitted under subsection 16 (3), the Registrar revokes the licence.

**Notice and hearing**

16(1) The Registrar shall serve written notice on an applicant or licensee if he or she proposes to,

(a) refuse to issue or renew a licence under subsection 13(2);

(b) apply conditions to a licence or renewal of a licence; or

(c) revoke a licence under section 15.

**Content of notice**

(2) The notice referred to in subsection (1) shall state the reasons for the Registrar's proposed action and shall inform the applicant or licensee that he, she or it is entitled to an opportunity to be heard before the Registrar to show cause why the Registrar should not take the proposed action.

**Request for opportunity to be heard**

(3) Within 21 days after service of a notice under subsection (1), an applicant or licensee may, in writing, request an opportunity to be heard before the Registrar to show cause why the Registrar should not take the proposed action.

**No request for opportunity to be heard**

(4) If an applicant or licensee does not request an opportunity to be heard within the time permitted under subsection (3), the Registrar may take the proposed action.

**Opportunity to be heard**

(5) If an applicant or licensee requests an opportunity to be heard under subsection (3), the Registrar shall give the applicant or licensee an opportunity to appear before the Registrar in person to show cause why the Registrar should not take the proposed action no later than 90 days after the notice referred to in subsection (1) was served or at a later date if the applicant or licensee consents.

**Right to counsel**

(6) An applicant or licensee may be represented by counsel or an agent when appearing before the Registrar under subsection (5).

**Registrar's decision**

(7) If the Registrar decides that an applicant or licensee has not shown cause why the Registrar should not take the proposed action,

(a) the Registrar shall inform the applicant or licensee in writing; and

(b) if, within 14 days of being informed under clause (a), the applicant or licensee requests written reasons, the Registrar shall serve written reasons for his or her decision on the applicant or licensee within 14 days of the request being made.

**Registrar to advise**

(8) The Registrar shall, at the time of serving the written reasons, advise the applicant or licensee of the right to appeal under section 17.

**Appeal**

17(1) Within 21 days after service of reasons under subsection 16(7), the applicant or licensee may appeal the Registrar's decision to the Tribunal.

No stay

(2) Despite section 25 of the *Statutory Powers Procedure Act*, an appeal does not have the effect of staying the Registrar's decision, and neither the Registrar nor the Tribunal has the authority to stay the decision pending the hearing of the appeal.

**Registrar retains authority**

(3) During the time that an appeal is in progress, the Registrar retains the authority to reconsider the decision that is being appealed.

**Registrar a party**

(4) The Registrar is a party to an appeal.

**Authority of Tribunal**

(5) On hearing an appeal, the Tribunal may uphold the Registrar's decision, vary or set aside the Registrar's decision, grant or restore a licence or impose conditions on a licence.

**Further application**

18. A person who is refused a licence or renewal of a licence may reapply for a licence if new or other evidence is available or it is clear that material circumstances have changed.

## PART V: COMPLAINTS AND INVESTIGATIONS

### COMPLAINTS

**Complaint to Registrar**

19(1) The Registrar may receive a complaint from any person alleging that a licensee has breached the code of conduct established under the regulations or alleging that a licensee has failed to comply with this Act or the regulations or has breached a condition of a licence.

**Form of complaint**

(2) A complaint shall be in writing, signed by the complainant, and filed with the Registrar within 90 days after the subject-matter that gives rise to the complaint arose or at a later date with the Registrar's consent.

**Registrar to inform**

(3) The Registrar may, in writing, inform the licensee of the nature of the complaint.

**Registrar may decline**

(4) The Registrar may decline to deal with a complaint related to a breach of the code of conduct if, in the

Registrar's opinion, the complaint is frivolous, vexatious or not made in good faith.

**Notice**

(5) If the Registrar declines to deal with a complaint under subsection (4), the Registrar shall give notice of the decision to the complainant and shall specify the reasons for the decision.

**Referral to facilitator**

(6) Unless subsection (4) applies, and if in the opinion of the Registrar the complaint is in regard to a breach of the code of conduct established under the regulations, the Registrar shall refer the complaint to a facilitator, unless the complainant does not wish the matter to be referred.

**Rules for facilitations**

(7) The Registrar may establish rules concerning facilitations under this section, and a facilitator shall comply with any applicable rules.

**Attendance**

(8) A facilitation shall not take place without the participation of the complainant and the licensee must attend any meetings required by the facilitator.

**Facilitation**

(9) The facilitator shall attempt to resolve the complaint, and at the end of the facilitation shall communicate to the Registrar the results of the facilitation and either,

(a) his or her decision to make no recommendation; or

(b) his or her recommendation that the Registrar require the licensee to take appropriate remedial instruction.

**Registrar to act**

(10) Where the facilitator has made a recommendation under clause (9)(b), the Registrar shall act in accordance with the facilitator's recommendations by imposing the taking of the remedial instruction as a condition of the licence.

**Registrar's authority not affected**

(11) This section does not prevent the Registrar from exercising his or her authority under any other provision of this Act in respect of a licensee against whom a complaint has been made, whether or not the Registrar has dealt with the complaint under this section.

## INVESTIGATIONS

**Appointment of investigators**

20(1) The Registrar may appoint persons to be investigators for the purposes of this Act.

**Certificate of appointment**

(2) The Registrar shall issue to every investigator a certificate of appointment bearing the Registrar's signature or a facsimile of it.

**Police officers**

(3) Police officers, by virtue of office, are investigators for the purposes of this Act and the regulations, but subsection (2) does not apply to them.

**Proof of appointment**

(4) Every investigator who exercises powers under this Act shall, on request, produce the certificate of appointment as an investigator or identification as a police officer, as the case may be.

**Initiation of investigations**

21. The Registrar or an investigator may,

(a) initiate an investigation based on a complaint alleging a contravention of this Act, the regulations or a condition of a licence; or

(b) initiate an investigation even if no complaint has been made.

**Search warrant**

22(1) Upon application made without notice by an investigator appointed under this Act, a justice of the peace may issue a warrant, if he or she is satisfied on information under oath that there is reasonable ground for believing that,

(a) a person has contravened or is contravening this Act or the regulations; and

(b) there is in any building, dwelling, receptacle or place anything relating to a contravention of this Act or the regulations.

**Powers**

(2) A warrant obtained under subsection (1) may authorize an investigator named in the warrant to,

(a) enter premises, including a dwelling, specified in the warrant;

(b) examine money, valuables, documents, records and other things relevant to the investigation;

(c) seize anything on the premises that is relevant to the investigation for the purpose of being used as evidence;

(d) require a person, other than a person on the premises of the licensee being investigated, to produce anything mentioned in clause (b) that is relevant to the investigation;

(e) remove, for the purpose of making copies or extracts, anything mentioned in clause (b) that is relevant to the investigation;

(f) use any data storage, processing or retrieval device or system used in carrying on business in order to produce a document or record in readable form;

(g) conduct such tests as are reasonably necessary;

(h) remove materials or substances for examination or test purposes subject to the owner, or other occupant of the premises, being notified thereof; and

(i) use any other investigative technique or procedure or do anything described in the warrant if information and other evidence concerning the offence will be obtained through the use of the technique or procedure or the doing of the thing.

**Conditions on search warrant**

(3) A warrant obtained under subsection (1) shall contain such conditions as the justice of the peace considers advisable to ensure that any search authorized by the warrant is reasonable in the circumstances.

**Expert help**

(4) The warrant may authorize persons who have special, expert or professional knowledge to accompany and assist the investigator in respect of the execution of the warrant.

**Expiry of warrant**

(5) A warrant issued under this section shall name a date of expiry, which shall be no later than 30 days after the warrant is issued, but a justice of the peace may extend the date of expiry for an additional period of no more than 30 days, on application without notice by the investigator named in the warrant.

**Use of force**

(6) The investigator named in the warrant may call upon police officers for assistance in executing the warrant and the investigator and the police officers may use whatever force is reasonably necessary to execute a warrant.

**Obstruction**

(7) No person shall obstruct an investigator carrying out an investigation under this section or withhold from him or her or conceal, alter or destroy anything that is relevant to the investigation.

**Obligation to produce and assist**

(8) A person who is required to produce anything under clause (2)(d) shall produce it and shall, on request by the investigator, provide any assistance that is reasonably necessary, including assistance in using any data storage, processing or retrieval device or system, to produce a document or record in readable form.

**Return of removed things**

(9) An investigator who removes or seizes anything from premises under subsection (2) shall return it when it is no longer required.

**Searches in exigent circumstances**

23(1) Although a warrant issued under section 22 would otherwise be required, an investigator may exercise any of the powers described in subsection 22(2) without a warrant if the conditions for obtaining the warrant exist but by reason of exigent circumstances it would be impracticable to obtain the warrant.

**Dwellings**

(2) Subsection (1) does not apply to a building or part of a building that is being used as a dwelling place.

**Use of force**

(3) The investigator may, in executing any authority given by this section, call upon police officers for assistance and the investigator and the police officers may use whatever force is reasonably necessary under the circumstances.

**Admissibility of copies**

24. A copy of a document or record certified by an investigator as being a true copy of the original is admissible in evidence to the same extent as the original and has the same evidentiary value.

**Possession of licence**

25(1) An investigator may take possession of a licence if, while acting in the course of his or her duties, the investigator believes on reasonable grounds that the licence,

(a) is required to be returned to the Registrar under section 37; or

(b) is being used contrary to section 38.

**Same**

(2) An investigator who takes possession of a licence under subsection (1) shall promptly forward it to the Registrar.

## INSPECTIONS

**Appointment of inspectors**

26(1) The Registrar may appoint persons to be inspectors for the purposes of ensuring compliance with this Act, the regulations and the conditions of a licence.

**Certificate of appointment**

(2) The Registrar shall issue to every inspector a certificate of appointment bearing the Registrar's signature or a facsimile of it.

**Proof of appointment**

(3) Every inspector who exercises powers under this Act shall, on request, produce the certificate of appointment as an inspector.

**Inspection**

27(1) Subject to subsection (2), the Registrar or an inspector appointed under section 26 may at any time initiate and conduct an inspection and may, as part of that inspection, enter and inspect at any reasonable time the premises of a licensee that is licensed to sell private investigator or security guard services for the purposes of ensuring that the licensee is complying with,

    (a) this Act and the regulations; and

    (b) the conditions of its licence.

**Limitations on entry**

(2) An inspector shall not, except under the authority of a warrant issued under section 28,

    (a) enter any part of a licensee's premises used as a dwelling unless the occupier consents; and

    (b) use force to enter and inspect premises under this section.

**Powers on inspection**

(3) While carrying out an inspection, an inspector may,

    (a) examine all money, valuables, documents, records and things that are relevant to the inspection;

    (b) require a person on the premises being inspected to produce anything mentioned in clause (a) that is relevant to the inspection;

    (c) on giving a receipt for it, remove, for the purpose of making copies or extracts, anything mentioned in clause (a) that is relevant to the inspection;

    (d) inquire into negotiations, transactions, loans or borrowings of a licensee and into assets owned, held in trust, acquired or disposed of by a licensee that are relevant to an inspection;

    (e) use any data storage, processing or retrieval device or system used in carrying on business in the place in order to produce a document or record in readable form;

    (f) conduct such tests as are reasonably necessary; and

    (g) remove materials or substances for examination or test purposes subject to the licensee, or other occupant of the premises, being notified thereof.

**Return of removed things**

(4) An inspector who removes anything from premises under subsection (3) shall return it when it is no longer required.

**Obligation to produce and assist**

(5) A person who is required to produce anything under clause (3)(b) shall produce it and shall, on request by the inspector, provide any assistance that is reasonably necessary, including assistance in using any data storage, processing or retrieval device or system, to produce a document or record in readable form.

**Obstruction prohibited**

(6) No person shall obstruct an inspector conducting an inspection or withhold from him or her or conceal or destroy anything that is relevant to the inspection.

**Admissibility of copies**

(7) A copy of a document or record certified by an inspector to be a true copy of the original is admissible in evidence to the same extent as the original and has the same evidentiary value.

**Warrant**

28(1) On an application without notice, a justice of the peace may issue a warrant authorizing an inspector named in the warrant to enter premises of a licensee specified in the warrant and to exercise any of the powers referred to in subsection 27(3) if the justice of the peace is satisfied on information under oath that,

    (a) the inspector has been prevented from exercising a right of entry to the premises under subsection 27(1) or has been prevented from exercising a power under subsection 27(3); or

    (b) there are reasonable grounds to believe that the inspector will be prevented from exercising a right or power referred to in clause (a).

**Warrant to enter dwelling**

(2) On an application without notice, a justice of the peace may issue a warrant authorizing an inspector to enter premises of a licensee being used as a dwelling and exercise any of the powers referred to in subsection 27(3) if the justice of the peace is satisfied on information under oath that entry into the dwelling is necessary for the purpose of ensuring that the licensee is complying with this Act, the regulations or the conditions of his, her or its licence.

**Expiry of warrant**

(3) A warrant issued under this section shall name a date of expiry, which shall be no later than 30 days

after the warrant is issued, but a justice of the peace may extend the date of expiry for an additional period of no more than 30 days on application without notice by the inspector named in the warrant.

**Time of execution**

(4) An entry into premises used as a dwelling under a warrant issued under this section shall be made between 6 a.m. and 9 p.m., unless the warrant specifies otherwise.

**Use of force**

(5) An inspector may call upon police officers for assistance in executing a warrant issued under this section and the inspector and the police officers may use whatever force is reasonably necessary to execute a warrant.

**Possession of licence**

29(1) An inspector may take possession of a licence if, while carrying out an inspection, the inspector believes on reasonable grounds that the licence,

    (a) is required to be returned to the Registrar under section 37; or

    (b) is being used contrary to section 38.

**Same**

(2) An inspector who takes possession of a licence under subsection (1) shall promptly forward it to the Registrar.

**Arrest without warrant**

29.1 If a police officer finds a person apparently in contravention of this Act or apparently in contravention of a prescribed provision of the regulations and the person refuses to give his or her name and address or there are reasonable grounds to believe that the name or address given is false, the police officer may arrest the person without warrant.

## PART VI: GENERAL DUTIES AND STANDARDS OF PRACTICE

**Insurance required**

30. No person shall hold a licence to engage in the business of selling the services of private investigators or security guards unless that person is insured by an insurer licensed under the *Insurance Act* for the kinds of liability and in the amounts prescribed.

**Appropriate licence**

31. No business entity shall employ a private investigator or a security guard unless the private investigator or the security guard has an appropriate licence.

**Information to be filed with Registrar**

32. Every licensee under this Act shall ensure that the following information is on file with the Registrar and shall inform the Registrar in writing of any change within five business days of the change occurring:

1. The licensee's mailing address for service.
2. The mailing address of every branch office of the licensee.
3. The street address of the licensee's office and branch offices, if different from the mailing address.

**Name of business**

33. No person who holds a licence to engage in the business of selling the services of private investigators or security guards shall carry on business in a name other than the name in which the person is licensed.

**Identification as private investigator**

34(1) Every person who is holding himself or herself out as a private investigator shall,

    (a) carry his or her licence;

    (b) on request, identify himself or herself as a private investigator; and

    (c) on request, produce his or her licence.

No other evidence of authority

(2) No person who is acting as a private investigator or holding himself or herself out as one shall possess any identification or symbol of authority other than the licence issued to him or her under this Act.

**Security guard licence must be carried**

35(1) Every person who is acting as a security guard or holding himself or herself out as one shall,

    (a) carry his or her licence;

    (b) on request, identify himself or herself as a security guard; and

    (c) on request, produce his or her licence.

Security guard uniform

(2) Subject to subsection (3), every person who is acting as a security guard or holding himself or herself out as one shall wear a uniform that complies with the regulations.

**Exception**

(3) Subsection (2) does not apply to a person who is,

    (a) acting as a bodyguard; or

    (b) performing services to prevent the loss of property through theft or sabotage in an industrial, commercial, residential or retail environment.

No other evidence of authority

(4) No person who is acting as a security guard or holding himself or herself out as one shall

possess any identification or symbol of authority other than his or her uniform, the licence issued to him or her under this Act, and any other form of identification or symbol of authority provided for in the regulations.

**Display of licence to engage in business**

36(1) No person who holds a licence to engage in the business of selling the services of private investigators or security guards shall do so unless the licence is displayed in a conspicuous spot in the office at which the public is invited to deal.

**Branch office**

(2) The licence issued by the Registrar that is applicable to a branch office shall be displayed in each branch office.

**Return of licence**

37. Every licence is the property of the Crown and a person shall immediately return his, her or its licence to the Registrar in the following circumstances:
1. The licence is suspended or revoked.
2. The licence names a branch office at which the public is invited to deal and the business entity discontinues business at that office.
3. The licence is to engage in the business of selling the services of private investigators or security guards and the licensee discontinues the business.
4. The person ceases to meet a requirement set out in subsection 10(1) and is prohibited under subsection 10(2) from acting or offering services under the licence.

**Other duties re licences**

38. No person shall,
   (a) possess, display or permit to be displayed a fake, altered or fraudulently obtained licence;
   (b) lend a licence to another person or permit another person to use it;
   (c) display or represent as his, her or its own a licence that was not issued to him, her or it;
   (d) display or represent as valid a licence that has been suspended or revoked; or
   (e) display or represent as valid a licence when the person to whom the licence was issued no longer meets a requirement under subsection 10(1).

**Holding out as police**

39. No person who holds a licence under this Act shall hold himself, herself or itself out as providing services or performing duties connected with police.

**Certain terms prohibited**

40. No private investigator, security guard or person who engages in the business of selling the services of private investigators or security guards shall use the following terms or variations of them:
1. Detective or Private Detective.
2. Law enforcement.
3. Police.
4. Officer.

## PART VII: GENERAL

**Service**

41. A notice under this Act is sufficiently given or served if it is,
   (a) delivered personally;
   (b) sent by registered mail to the address for service on file with the Registrar;
   (c) delivered to the address for service on file with the Registrar in another manner if the sender can prove receipt of the notice.

**False, misleading or deceptive representation**

42. If the Registrar believes on reasonable grounds that a person licensed under this Act is making a false, misleading or deceptive representation in an advertisement, circular, pamphlet or material published or transmitted by any means, the Registrar may,
   (a) order the person to immediately cease making the representation; and
   (b) order the person to retract the representation, publish a correction of equal prominence to the original publication, or both.

**Offence**

43(1) A person is guilty of an offence if he, she or it,
   (a) knowingly furnishes false information in any application under this Act or in any statement or return required under this Act or the regulations;
   (b) fails to comply with any order or other requirement made under this Act or the regulations;
   (c) fails to comply with a condition of a licence; or
   (d) contravenes or fails to comply with any provision of this Act or the regulations.

**Limitation**

(2) No proceeding under this section shall be commenced more than one year after the Registrar first became aware of the facts on which the proceeding is based.

**Offence—directors or officers**

44. Where a business entity is guilty of an offence under this Act, every director, officer or partner of the business entity who authorizes, permits or acquiesces in the offence is guilty of an offence.

**Penalties**

**Individuals**

45(1) Every individual convicted of an offence under this Act is liable to a fine of not more than $25,000, imprisonment for a term of not more than one year, or both.

**Business entity**

(2) Every business entity convicted of an offence under this Act is liable to a fine of not more than $250,000.

**Testimonial immunity**

46. No person engaged in the administration or enforcement of this Act shall be required to give testimony in any civil proceeding, except in a proceeding under this Act, with regard to information obtained in the discharge of the person's duties.

**Court order for compliance**

47(1) If a person fails to comply with a Registrar's order made under this Act, the Registrar may, in addition to any other action he or she may take, make an application to a judge of the Superior Court of Justice for an order directing the person to comply with the Registrar's order.

**Judge's power**

(2) On hearing the application, the judge may make such order as he or she thinks fit.

**Appeal**

(3) An appeal lies to the Divisional Court from the judge's order.

**Protection from liability**

48(1) No action or other proceeding for damages may be instituted against the Registrar or anyone engaged in the administration or enforcement of this Act for any act done in good faith in the execution or intended execution of a duty under this Act or for any alleged neglect or default in the execution in good faith of the person's duty.

**Crown liability**

(2) Despite subsections 5(2) and (4) of the *Proceedings Against the Crown Act*, subsection (1) does not relieve the Crown of liability in respect of a tort committed by a person mentioned in subsection (1) to which it would otherwise be subject.

**Fees**

49. The Minister may, in writing, set out fees that are payable under this Act in respect of the issuance, renewal or replacement of licences and other administrative matters.

**Information concerning licensee**

50. The Registrar may make available to the public a person's status as a licensee,
  (a) on being provided with a person's name; or
  (b) on being provided with a person's licence number.

**Rules**

51(1) The Registrar may make rules concerning the exercise of any of his or her powers under this Act.

**Not regulations**

(2) A rule made by the Registrar is not a regulation for the purposes of Part III (Regulations) of the *Legislation Act, 2006*.

**Transition—licences**

52. A person who holds a licence under the *Private Investigators and Security Guards Act* on the day this section comes into force shall be deemed to be licensed under this Act until the day the person's licence would have expired under that Act.

## PART VIII: REGULATIONS

**Code of conduct**

53(1) The Minister may, by regulation, establish a code of conduct.

**Same**

(2) It is a condition of every licence issued under this Act that a licensee shall comply with the code of conduct.

**Regulations**

54(1) The Minister may make regulations,
  (a) prescribing classes of licences;
  (b) respecting applications for the issuance or renewal of a licence;
  (c) prescribing grounds on which an application for the issuance or renewal of a licence may be refused;
  (d) prescribing the term of validity of a licence;

(e) governing the training requirements for the issuance or renewal of a licence;

(f) governing the testing requirements for the issuance or renewal of a licence;

(g) exempting any person, class of person or class of licensee from any provision of this Act and attaching conditions to the exemption;

(h) governing the documents, records and information that must be kept by licensees, including prescribing types and classes and time periods for retaining each type and class, and authorizing the Registrar to specify the location at which they must be kept;

(i) prescribing documents, records or information that must be provided to the Registrar, respecting the time and manner in which they must be provided and requiring that specified information may be verified by affidavit;

(j) respecting the uniform that must be worn by a person when acting as a security guard, and providing for badges, insignia and colours;

(k) governing the equipment on vehicles and the appearance of vehicles used by a licensee or to identify the business of a licensee;

(l) prescribing requirements for the registration of a business entity that employs a private investigator or security guard for the purposes of section 5;

(m) requiring that any information required under this Act be in a form approved by the Registrar, as specified in the regulations;

(n) prescribing the kinds of liability and amounts of insurance required by a business entity that holds a licence to engage in the business of selling the services of private investigators or security guards;

(o) prescribing types of equipment and animals that may or may not be used by a licensee and prescribing conditions for the use of any equipment or animal;

(p) governing the method of terminating or disposing of the business of selling the services of private investigators or security guards;

(q) defining, for the purposes of this Act and the regulations, any word or expression used in this Act that has not already been expressly defined in this Act;

(r) prescribing offences for the purposes of clause 10(5)(a);

(s) prescribing grounds for which an application for the issuance or renewal of a licence may be refused for the purposes of paragraph 6 of subsection 13(2);

(t) prescribing any matter or thing that may be or is required to be prescribed in this Act and respecting any matter that is required by this Act to be done in accordance with the regulations.

**General or particular**

(2) A regulation under this section may be general or particular in its application.

# Code of Conduct

O Reg 363/07

**Under** *Private Security and Investigative Services Act, 2005*, SO 2005, c 34

**Breach of code of conduct**

1. A licensee is in breach of the code of conduct if the licensee contravenes or fails to comply with this Regulation.

**Individual licensees**

2(1) Every individual licensee, while working as a private investigator or security guard, shall,

(a) act with honesty and integrity;

(b) respect and use all property and equipment in accordance with the conditions of his or her licence;

(c) comply with all federal, provincial and municipal laws;

(d) treat all persons equally, without discrimination based on a person's race, ancestry, place of origin, colour, ethnic origin, citizenship, creed, sex, sexual orientation, age, marital status, family status or disability;

(e) refrain from using profane, abusive or insulting language or actions or actions that are otherwise uncivil to any member of the public;

(f) refrain from exercising unnecessary force;

(g) refrain from behaviour that is either prohibited or not authorized by law;

(h) respect the privacy of others by treating all information received while working as a private investigator or security guard as confidential, except where disclosure is required as part of such work or by law; and

(i) co-operate with police where it is required by law.

(2) No individual licensee shall,

(a) be unfit for duty, while working, through consumption of alcohol or drugs;

(b) conspire with another person or aid or abet another licensee in a breach of this code of conduct;

(c) wilfully or negligently make a false statement or complaint against another licensee; or

(d) misrepresent to any person the type, class or conditions of his or her licence.

(3) Clause (2)(d) does not apply to an individual licensee who is concealing his or her identity as a private investigator or security guard in order to carry out his or her duties.

**Licensed business entities**

3(1) Every licensed business entity and every officer, director, partner and sole proprietor of a licensed business entity shall, in the course of conducting the licensed business,

(a) comply with all federal, provincial and municipal laws;

(b) treat all persons equally, without discrimination based on a person's race, ancestry, place of origin, colour, ethnic origin, citizenship, creed, sex, sexual orientation, age, marital status, family status or disability;

(c) respect the privacy of others by treating all information received in the course of conducting the licensed business as confidential, except where disclosure is required for conducting the licensed business or by law; and

(d) co-operate with police where it is required by law.

(2) No licensed business entity and no officer, director, partner and sole proprietor of a licensed business entity shall,

(a) conspire with another person or aid or abet another licensee in a breach of this code of conduct;

(b) wilfully or negligently make a false statement or complaint against another licensee; or

(c) misrepresent to any person the type, class or conditions of the licensee's licence.

4. Omitted (provides for coming into force of provisions of this Regulation).

# Standard Radio 10 Codes

| 10-0 | Use Caution |
|---|---|
| 10-1 | Signal Weak |
| 10-2 | Signal Good |
| 10-3 | Stop Transmitting |
| 10-4 | Message Received |
| 10-5 | Relay |
| 10-6 | Standby Unless Urgent |
| 10-7 | Out of Service |
| 10-8 | In Service |
| 10-9 | Repeat |
| 10-10 | Fight in Progress |
| 10-11 | Animal Problem |
| 10-12 | Stand By |
| 10-13 | Report Conditions |
| 10-14 | Prowler Report |
| 10-15 | Civil Disturbance |
| 10-16 | Domestic Problem |
| 10-17 | Meet Complainant |
| 10-18 | Urgent |
| 10-19 | Go to Station |
| 10-20 | Advise to Location |
| 10-21 | Phone _____ |
| 10-22 | Disregard |
| 10-23 | Arrived at Scene |
| 10-24 | Assignment Complete |
| 10-25 | Report to _____ |
| 10-26 | Detaining Suspect |
| 10-27 | Driver's Licence Information |

| | |
|---|---|
| 10-28 | Vehicle Registration Information |
| 10-29 | Check Records for Want |
| 10-30 | Unauthorized Use of Radio |
| 10-31 | Crime in Progress |
| 10-32 | Person with Gun |
| 10-33 | Emergency—All Units Stand By |
| 10-34 | Riot |
| 10-35 | Major Crime Alert |
| 10-36 | Correct Time |
| 10-37 | Suspicious Vehicle |
| 10-38 | Stop Suspicious Vehicle |
| 10-39 | Respond with Siren and Flashers |
| 10-40 | Do Not Use Siren and Flashers |
| 10-41 | Beginning Shift |
| 10-42 | End Shift |
| 10-43 | Information |
| 10-44 | Permission to Leave |
| 10-45 | Dead Animal |
| 10-46 | Assist Motorist |
| 10-47 | Emergency Road Repair |
| 10-48 | Traffic Control |
| 10-49 | Traffic Signal Out |
| 10-50 | Traffic Accident |
| 10-51 | Request Tow Truck |
| 10-52 | Request Ambulance |
| 10-53 | Roadway Blocked |
| 10-54 | Livestock on Roadway |
| 10-55 | Intoxicated Driver |
| 10-56 | Intoxicated Pedestrian |
| 10-57 | Hit and Run Accident |
| 10-58 | Direct Traffic |
| 10-59 | Escort |
| 10-60 | Squad in Vicinity |

| | |
|---|---|
| 10-61 | Personnel in Vicinity |
| 10-62 | Reply to Message |
| 10-63 | Prepare to Copy |
| 10-64 | Local Message |
| 10-65 | Net Message |
| 10-66 | Cancel Message |
| 10-67 | Clear for Net Message |
| 10-68 | Dispatch Information |
| 10-69 | Message Received |
| 10-70 | Fire Alarm |
| 10-71 | Advise Nature of Alarm |
| 10-72 | Report Progress of Alarm |
| 10-73 | Smoke Report |
| 10-74 | Negative |
| 10-75 | In Contact with _____ |
| 10-76 | En Route to _____ |
| 10-77 | Estimated Time of Arrival |
| 10-78 | Request Assistance |
| 10-79 | Notify Coroner |
| 10-80 | Pursuit in Progress |
| 10-81 | Breathalyzer Report |
| 10-82 | Reserved Lodgings |
| 10-83 | School Crossing Assignment |
| 10-84 | If Meeting … Advise Estimated Time of Arrival |
| 10-85 | Arrival Delayed |
| 10-86 | Operator on Duty |
| 10-87 | Pick Up |
| 10-88 | Advise Telephone Number |
| 10-89 | Bomb Threat |
| 10-90 | Bank Alarm |
| 10-91 | Pick Up Subject |
| 10-92 | Illegally Parked Vehicle |
| 10-93 | Blockage |

| | |
|---|---|
| 10-94 | Drag Racing |
| 10-95 | Subject in Custody |
| 10-96 | Detain Subject |
| 10-97 | Test Signal |
| 10-98 | Prisoner Escape |
| 10-99 | Wanted or Stolen |

Ministry of Community Safety and Correctional Service. (2016). Retrieved from https://www.mcscs.jus.gov.on.ca/english/PSIS/BasicTesting/SecurityGuardStudyGuide/AppendixBAPCO/SG_appendixb_apco.html

# The Security Guard Licensing Process

*Neil Gonsalves, Durham College*

In Ontario, the security guard industry—along with its administrative policies and regulations—is regulated by the Ministry of Community Safety and Correctional Services (MCSCS) under the *Private Security and Investigative Services Act, 2005* (PSISA). The Private Security and Investigative Services Branch is responsible for the oversight of licensing requirements and the licensing process for security guards. All new security guards must complete a basic training course and pass the basic ministry test before applying for a licence. (In addition, all candidates for an Ontario security guard licence are required to obtain a St. John Ambulance First Aid Certificate or its equivalent. Check the requirements in your province.) The following information is intended to provide a summary of the process one must complete in order to be licensed in Ontario:

**Step One**—A candidate must complete a ministry-approved security guard training program delivered by a ministry-approved training provider. The program must be at least forty hours in length, may be delivered in class or online, and must cover all the curricula mandated under the legislation. Once the candidate has successfully completed the program, the training provider will issue the candidate a unique Training Completion Number (TCN). This TCN is required in order to book a licensing examination with the ministry test vendor (MCSCS 2016c.)

**Step Two**—Once the candidate has the TCN from the training provider, he or she may book a security guard licensing examination. The licensing examinations are conducted at select DriveTest centres across Ontario, and candidates may register online at www.ontariosecuritytesting.ca. The test consists of 60 multiple choice questions that must be completed within 75 minutes. Upon successful completion of the test, the candidate will be issued a Testing Completion Number, which is required to apply for a security guard licence (MCSCS 2016b.)

**Step Three**—Once the candidate has completed the first two steps, he or she is eligible to apply for a security guard licence. Over and above the previous two regulatory requirements, candidates must be 18 years of age or older, must be eligible to work in Canada and must possess a clean criminal record. (For more information on criminal records, see below.) The ministry may take up to thirty days to process the licence, and the licence is valid for two birthdays after the day it is issued (MCSCS 2016a.)

## Relevant Sections from the Private Security and Investigative Services Act, 2005

**Definition of a Security Guard (Who do the licence requirements apply to?)**

    (4) A security guard is a person who performs work, for remuneration, that consists primarily of guarding or patrolling for the purpose of protecting persons or property.

**Training Providers (Who can provide a ministry-approved security guard training course?)**

**Under Ontario Regulation 26/10, s. 2(3), the training program must be provided by:**

    (a) a public university;
    (b) a college established under the Ontario Colleges of Applied Arts and Technology Act, 2002;
    (c) a private career college registered under the Private Career Colleges Act, 2005 as part of a program approved under that Act;
    (d) a licensed business entity; or
    (e) a registered business entity that employs the applicant or that has made a conditional offer of employment to the applicant.

**Criminal Record Eligibility**

For the purposes of the security guard licence application, a person is considered to not possess a clean criminal record if he or she has been convicted of, and not been granted a pardon for, any of the eighty-one offences from the criminal code and/or the two offences from the *Controlled Drugs and Substances Act* listed in the PSISA). Prescribed offences that result in a candidate being deemed to not have a clean criminal record (under Ontario Regulation 37/08):

    1. For the purpose of section 10 of the Act, a person does not possess a clean criminal record if he or she has been convicted of, and not been granted a pardon for, any of the offences set out in Table 1 or 2.

## TABLE 1 Offences Under the Criminal Code

| Item | Provision | Description |
|---|---|---|
| 1. | Subsection 57(1) | Forgery of or uttering forged passport |
| 2. | Section 83.02 | Providing or collecting property for certain activities |
| 3. | Section 83.03 | Providing, making available, etc., property or services for terrorist purposes |
| 4. | Section 83.04 | Using or possessing property for terrorist purposes |
| 5. | Section 83.18 | Participation in activity of terrorist group |
| 6. | Section 83.19 | Facilitating terrorist activity |
| 7. | Section 83.21 | Instructing to carry out activity for terrorist group |
| 8. | Section 83.22 | Instructing to carry out terrorist activity |
| 9. | Section 83.23 | Harbouring or concealing terrorists |
| 10. | Section 83.231 | Hoax regarding terrorist activity |
| 11. | Subsection 121(1) | Frauds on the government |
| 12. | Section 129 | Offences related to public or peace officer |
| 13. | Section 130 | Personating peace officer |
| 14. | Section 151 | Sexual interference |
| 15. | Section 152 | Invitation to sexual touching |
| 16. | Section 153 | Sexual exploitation |
| 17. | Section 153.1 | Sexual exploitation of person with disability |
| 18. | Section 163.1 | Child pornography—making, distributing, etc. |
| 19. | Section 170 | Parent or guardian procuring sexual activity |
| 20. | Section 172.1 | Luring a child |
| 21. | Section 220 | Causing death by criminal negligence |
| 22. | Section 235 | Murder—first or second degree |
| 23. | Section 239 | Attempt to commit murder |
| 24. | Section 244 | Causing bodily harm with intent—firearm |
| 25. | Section 245 | Administering noxious thing |
| 26. | Section 264 | Criminal harassment |
| 27. | Section 267 | Assault with a weapon or causing bodily harm |
| 28. | Section 268 | Aggravated assault |
| 29. | Section 269.1 | Torture |
| 30. | Paragraph 270(1)(a) | Assaulting a peace officer |
| 31. | Section 270.1 | Disarming a peace officer |
| 32. | Section 272 | Sexual assault with a weapon, threats to a third party or causing bodily harm |

# APPENDIX E  The Security Guard Licensing Process

| Item | Provision | Description |
|---|---|---|
| 33. | Section 273 | Aggravated sexual assault |
| 34. | Subsection 279(1) | Kidnapping |
| 35. | Section 279.1 | Hostage taking |
| 36. | Section 280 | Abduction of person under sixteen |
| 37. | Section 281 | Abduction of person under fourteen |
| 38. | Section 282 | Abduction in contravention of custody order |
| 39. | Section 283 | Abduction |
| 40. | Section 318 | Advocating genocide |
| 41. | Section 319 | Public incitement of hatred, wilful promotion of hatred |
| 42. | Section 324 | Theft by bailee of things under seizure |
| 43. | Section 326 | Theft of telecommunication service |
| 44. | Paragraph 334(a) | Theft over $5,000 |
| 45. | Subsection 342(1) | Theft, forgery, etc. of credit card |
| 46. | Section 344 | Robbery |
| 47. | Section 345 | Stopping mail with intent |
| 48. | Section 346 | Extortion |
| 49. | Section 348 | Breaking and entering with intent, committing offence or breaking out |
| 50. | Section 356 | Theft from mail |
| 51. | Revoked: O. Reg. 71/10, s. 1. | |
| 52. | Section 362 | False pretence or false statement |
| 53. | Section 363 | Obtaining execution of valuable security by fraud |
| 54. | Section 367 | Forgery |
| 55. | Section 368 | Uttering forged document |
| 56. | Section 374 | Drawing document without authority, etc. |
| 57. | Section 375 | Obtaining, etc., by instrument based on forged document |
| 58. | Paragraph 380(1)(a) | Fraud over $5,000 |
| 59. | Section 382 | Fraudulent manipulation of stock exchange transactions |
| 60. | Section 385 | Fraudulent concealment of title documents |
| 61. | Section 386 | Fraudulent registration of title |
| 62. | Section 387 | Fraudulent sale of real property |
| 63. | Section 388 | Misleading receipt |
| 64. | Section 389 | Fraudulent disposal of goods on which money advanced |
| 65. | Section 390 | Fraudulent receipts under *Bank Act* |
| 66. | Section 392 | Disposal of property to defraud creditors |

## TABLE 1  Continued

| Item | Provision | Description |
|---|---|---|
| 67. | Subsection 393(1) | Fraud in relation to fares, etc. |
| 68. | Section 394 | Fraud in relation to valuable minerals |
| 69. | Section 394.1 | Possession of stolen or fraudulently obtained valuable minerals |
| 70. | Section 396 | Offences related to mines |
| 71. | Section 407 | Forging trade-mark |
| 72. | Section 423 | Intimidation |
| 73. | Section 423.1 | Intimidation of a justice system participant |
| 74. | Subsection 430(4.1) | Mischief relating to religious property |
| 75. | Section 433 | Arson/disregard for human life |
| 76. | Section 434 | Arson/damage to property |
| 77. | Section 434.1 | Arson/own property |
| 78. | Section 435 | Arson for fraudulent purpose |
| 79. | Section 436 | Arson by negligence |
| 80. | Section 462.31 | Laundering proceeds of crime |
| 81. | Section 467.11 | Participation in activities of criminal organization |

## TABLE 2  Offences Under the Controlled Drugs and Substances Act (Canada)

| Item | Provision | Description |
|---|---|---|
| 1. | Subsection 5(1) | Trafficking in substance |
| 2. | Subsection 6(1) | Importing and exporting |

O. REG. 37/08, s. 1; O. Reg. 71/10, s. 1

## REFERENCES

Ministry of Community Safety and Correctional Services. (2016a). *Apply for a security guard or private investigator license*. Retrieved from http://www.mcscs.jus.gov.on.ca/english/PSIS/ApplyforaLicence/PSIS_apply.html

Ministry of Community Safety and Correctional Services. (2016b). *Security guard and private investigator basic testing*. Retrieved from http://www.mcscs.jus.gov.on.ca/english/PSIS/BasicTesting/PSIS_testing.html

Ministry of Community Safety and Correctional Services. (2016c). *Security guard training and private investigator basic training*. Retrieved from http://www.mcscs.jus.gov.on.ca/english/PSIS/Training/PSIS_training.html

*Private Security and Investigative Services Act, 2005*, SO 2005, c. 34.

# Glossary

**10 codes:** a system of codes designed to increase the clarity, efficiency, and discretion of radio communications

**access control:** procedures designed to limit entry to premises to individuals authorized to enter, and to ensure that visitors comply with rules such as rules prohibiting bringing in alcohol or weapons

**administrative tribunal:** a quasi-court, typically created by statute, to hear disputes that arise within the legal framework created by the statute

**ADVOKATE:** an acronym for a protocol for assessing the accuracy of an eye witness's statement

**agents:** first private detectives hired by merchants and private owners to recover stolen property

**appeal:** a new hearing (oral or in writing) to review an administrative or judicial (court) decision

**applicant:** the party who commences an application (type of civil proceeding)

**arrest:** legally deprive a person of liberty by touching that person to indicate that he or she is in custody

**assault:** threat of imminent harm in the mind of the intended victim

**battery:** any unwelcome physical contact

**bearing:** appearance and way of holding oneself

**biometrics:** branch of security technology that allows access based on recognition of a person's physical attributes

**bitcoin:** an Internet-based virtual currency exchanged directly between users without banks or similar traditional authorities as intermediaries

**bona fide job requirement:** a requirement that is sincerely believed to be necessary to the job, is established in good faith, is objective, and is reasonably necessary to assure the safe, efficient, and economical performance of the job

**burden of proof:** responsibility to provide evidence to support a particular conclusion

**Canadian Association of Chiefs of Police (CACP):** an organization led by high-ranking law enforcement officials who created the National Use of Force Framework model and continue to work on improving use of force protocols and advises the government by making recommendations

**carding:** also known as "street checks," carding is the practice in policing of stopping persons who appear to be suspicious to ask for identification in order to connect potential suspects to criminal activity or to divert criminal activity, particularly in high crime areas

**case law:** body of law based on decisions of similar cases

**CheckInk II:** a tag that discharges ink onto an item when a thief attempts to remove it without the specialized removal device

**circumstantial evidence:** evidence that suggests a conclusion but only by inference; for example, an electronic record showing that an individual's access card was tapped on a card reader

**citation:** the code that incorporates the elements of a statute (or case's) bibliographical "address" so that researchers can find it

**civil wrong:** non-criminal wrong that can form the basis of a civil lawsuit—either a tort or a breach of contract

**colour of right:** circumstances that lead to an understandable but mistaken belief that one has the right to do something

**common law:** rules that are formulated in judgments in case law

**contaminating the evidence:** altering evidence by tainting it with non-evidence; for example, getting one's own fingerprints on a glass handled by a suspect

**continuity of possession:** an unbroken chain or account of possession of an item of evidence with no gaps during which can no one account for the location of the evidence

**continuous assessment process:** the procedure used by security professionals to fully comprehend a possibly quickly changing security environment and situation: many factors are present at a scene that could affect the outcome and using this system ensures that the security professional is able to react appropriately within the National Use of Force Framework

**control room:** a central and secure location where dispatch officers are located. This location can be used as a hub for all secondary operations such as report writing, conducting interviews, statement taking, shift briefing, etc.

**conversion:** unauthorized interference with another's property that deprives the owner of its use

**CPTED:** principles of design and use of built environments developed with the goals of reducing the perception of risk and incidence of crime and improving quality of life for users

**CPTED fencing:** fencing that is designed to support CPTED principles; for example, fencing that creates a sense of proprietary control and channels access appropriately without interfering with natural surveillance opportunities

**credibility of a threat:** a subjective estimate of the likelihood that the threat is legitimate, based on, for example, the identity or demeanour of the person making the threat

**criminal offence:** act that contravenes a provision of criminal law

**Crown attorney:** lawyer who prosecutes the accused on behalf of the government

**damages:** the losses alleged by a plaintiff in a lawsuit and/or the compensation ordered to be paid to the plaintiff by the defendant

**de-escalate:** the approach used to try to resolve a security issue with a subject without resorting to force; normally accomplished through constant verbal communication and evaluation of the subject's body language

**defamation:** injury to a person's reputation by slander or libel

**defence:** legally recognized denial of or justification for an act

**defence counsel:** lawyer who represents the accused

**defendant:** either the accused in a criminal trial, or, in a civil trial, the party against whom an action is brought

**detain:** legally deprive a person of liberty for the purpose of asking questions

**direct evidence:** evidence that the witness observed using his or her own senses

**discretion:** a decision-maker is said to have discretion when he or she is left free to apply his or her professional judgment in deciding an issue, rather than being strictly bound to rule in a particular way when particular facts are proven

**due diligence:** taking every reasonable precaution to avoid an undesirable consequence

**electronic article surveillance:** a loss control method that relies on the use of electronic tags on merchandise and a reader at the store exit that warns of a tagged item being removed from the store

**ePassport:** a passport containing an electronic chip that holds information about the holder (name, birthdate, etc.) as well as a biometric identifier

**excited delirium:** a potentially fatal condition that presents with symptoms such as profuse sweating, difficulty breathing, and a racing heartbeat when a subject is restrained; can be triggered by drug use, mental illness, brain injuries or tumours, heart disease, high blood pressure, high or low blood sugar, respiratory problems, or fever; can impart to subjects a super-human strength coupled with high tolerance for pain and low understanding of verbal communication

**explosive device:** an object that contains a chemical, liquid, or gas (or combination thereof) that is designed to do damage or create injury upon detonation, explosion, or chemical or physical reaction

**explosive ordnance disposal authority:** a specialized team, often part of a police department or military force, deployed to remove and/or disable explosive devices

**express authorization:** admission to private roadways by invitation of the property owner

**false imprisonment:** detention of a person without consent and without legal authority

**feudalism:** medieval social system based on an exchange of military protection for protection and labour

**fire alarm:** warning of smoke, heat, carbon monoxide, or fire

**form report:** a report template that includes blank spaces and/or check boxes and that provides for the standardized entry of essential data relating to specific incidents

**general occurrence report:** a report describing the preliminary investigation of an incident by the security professional who was the first to encounter it

**hate crime:** any offence committed against a person or property that is motivated in whole or in part by hate, bias, or prejudice toward an identifiable group based on real or perceived race, national or ethnic origin, language, colour, religion, sex, age, mental or physical disability, sexual orientation, or any similar factor

**hazard:** a physical or behavioural condition or circumstance that poses a risk of harm to individuals

**hearsay evidence:** witness evidence that is "second-hand" in that it comprises an account of another person's description of direct evidence

**high-risk patrol:** patrol that takes place in an area known for dangerous activity or in an area that may be dangerous due to a particular situation, such as a labour dispute

**human environment:** personnel at the worksite

**hybrid offence:** an offence that can be charged and tried either as a summary conviction offence or on indictment, according to the prosecution's choice

**identity theft:** misuse of another person's identity for illegal purposes

**implied authorization:** admission to private roadways is not prohibited by the property owner

**improvised explosive device:** an explosive device built by private individuals (not a manufacturer), often made out of ordinary items commonly available to the public

**indictable offence:** a serious offence tried according to the indictable criminal court procedure

**intermediate (less-lethal) weapons:** tools that essentially make security personnel lightly armed; can include tasers and batons—it is possible for these weapons to apply lethal force but they are less lethal than firearms

**intrusion alarm:** warning that trespassers have entered beyond authorized zones

**judge:** court official appointed to try cases in a court of law

**judicial notice:** a concept that allows judges to accept certain widely accepted facts as true without the need for evidence

**jurisprudence:** judge-made law

**jury:** group of 12 people (in criminal law) or 6 people (in civil law in most provinces) who decide the case based on the evidence presented

**lethal force:** the option of last resort for security professionals that is used when an assessment demands that the threat a subject poses be eliminated immediately; this response is only readily available to public safety security personnel such as peace officers who are issued firearms; sometimes referred to as deadly force

**libel:** written or recorded statement that damages a person's reputation

**liquid nitrogen:** a substance that can be injected into a safe's lock in an effort to affect metal parts in the opening mechanism (they may freeze instantaneously and shatter), allowing the safe to be opened

**malicious prosecution:** wrongful prosecution of a person without reasonable or probable cause

**marauding terrorist firearms/weapons attack (MTFA/MTWA):** terrorist incidents that occur across multiple sites that are perpetrated by the same attacker or group of attackers and in which firearms are the principal weapon used

**mental health first aid:** the help provided to a person who is developing a mental health problem or experiencing a mental health crisis

**minor accident:** any incident that is non-reportable to the provincial authority and in which there are no injuries, no serious vehicle or criminal violations, and damages are under $2,000

**National Use of Force Framework:** a guideline that has been implemented across Canada in public and private security sectors that helps security professionals understand use of force by enabling them to visualize the process

**natural access control:** the use of design features (including landscaping, roadway design, and fencing) to influence visitor access choices in a manner that increases security

**natural surveillance:** the use of design features—for example, windows—to create both actual opportunities for surveillance and the impression of surveillance of a site

**negligence:** careless conduct that causes foreseeable harm to another person

**night watchmen:** guards hired by merchants in the 1700s to patrol their properties at night and to protect their shops and warehouses from thieves and vandals

**observational skills:** the ability to critically observe one's surroundings with a heightened awareness so that details of and changes in the physical environment can be readily detected

**oral testimony:** a witness's verbal evidence, given in court

**parataxic distortion:** a tendency to perceive others as we imagine them to be rather than as they actually ar

**parochial police:** regional guards hired by clergy in the 18th century to protect church property and parishioners within major city districts or dioceses

**person in distress:** an individual suffering from a mental crisis that can include but is not limited to someone suffering a schizophrenic episode or having a flashback related to post-traumatic stress disorder

**person of authority:** a person authorized by the *Criminal Code* to do anything in the administration or enforcement of the law—in most cases, refers to individuals who are peace officers or whose actions fall under the PSISA

**person-borne improvised explosive device (PBIED):** explosives concealed on-person, either under or within clothing, shoes, or other personal apparel

**phonetic alphabet:** an alphabetic system designed to eliminate any confusion when spelling out a phrase (i.e., names or vehicle plate numbers)

**physical environment:** surroundings or particular locations at the worksite

**plaintiff:** the party who commences a civil action (lawsuit)

**plastique:** plastic explosives

**positional asphyxia:** subject has difficulty breathing when restrained; subjects are at increased risk if they also suffer from excited delirium and/or are placed face down on the ground or floor

**post-traumatic stress disorder (PTSD):** a mental health condition characterized by flashbacks, nightmares, and severe anxiety that is triggered by the victim's experience of a highly stressful event, whether personally or as a witness

**primary evidence:** evidence that stands alone and can be analyzed directly; for example, a chemical substance or a piece of fabric

**provincial offence:** an offence established under a provincial statute that is administered by a provincial offences court (for example, an offence under the PSISA itself, or under a provincial highway traffic statute)

**racial profiling:** the selection of an individual for screening or questioning for purported security reasons where the selection is influenced by stereotypes about race, colour, ethnicity, ancestry, religion, or place of origin rather than on reasonable suspicion

**radio etiquette:** standardized procedures for courteous radio use that are designed to maximize comprehension of communications and minimize interference with other users

**reclamation:** a form of political action employed by Indigenous people that involves physical occupation of land under negotiation, barring resource extraction or the entry of outside governments or corporations until negotiations are completed

**record suspension:** the official name under the *Criminal Records Act* for what used to be called a "pardon"

**regulation:** a rule that supports and is subordinate to legislation, and that often deals with practical aspects of administration of a statutory scheme

**respondent:** the party who must respond to a civil application

**return fraud:** where an individual either purchases items to use them with no intention of keeping them, or attempts to return stolen merchandise for a cash refund

**RFID tag:** a security tag that uses radio technology to communicate information to a monitoring system so that specific items can be tracked

**ride shotgun:** job of riding atop Wells Fargo stagecoaches to protect passengers and cargo from robbers during the late 1800s

**secondary evidence:** evidence that is a representation of primary evidence; for example, a photograph of a damaged vault door

**security breach:** any violation of a workplace policy, procedure, practice, or direction; this class of security breach includes all non-criminal security incidents

**serious bodily harm:** lasting injuries causing permanent or temporary disability and/or lasting disfigurement (not minor injuries such as scratches, cuts, or a bloody nose)

**serious or injury accident:** any incident in which there are injuries, vehicle or criminal violations, and damages are over $2,000

**shrink (also called "shrinkage"):** retail inventory losses attributed to shoplifting, employee theft, and administrative error

**silent hours:** time outside of normal business hours

**situational awareness:** the ability to draw accurate, real-time inferences from observations; for example, the ability to determine whether the presence of a particular individual poses a risk to others

**slander:** oral statement that damages a person's reputation

**soft and hard compliance techniques:** unarmed methods for a security professional to physically control and restrain a subject

**solenoid:** electric switch that draws power from a battery to open a lock

**special-use alarm:** warning that a danger, such as toxic fumes or machine malfunctions, has occurred

**specialized report:** a report used for complex and detailed investigations or for non-routine matters

**specificity of a threat:** the degree to which specific details (time of detonation, location of bomb, nature of risk, expected damage, etc.) have been provided about the threatened detonation or other threat

**standard of proof:** the level of certainty with respect to facts and events that must be established in a particular kind of proceeding (criminal or civil) to allow the proving party (prosecution or plaintiff) to succeed

**statute:** a piece of legislation passed by a government (either federal or provincial/territorial)

**statute law:** laws passed by the government

***Statute of Winchester:*** legislation passed in 1285 that established local law enforcement in parishes throughout England

**summary conviction offence:** a less serious offence that is tried according to summary court procedure

**supplemental report:** a report added at a later time to a general occurrence report by, for example, other personnel assisting in the investigation

**suspect statement:** a written account or the transcript of a verbal account of an incident in the words of and from the perspective of an individual who has been identified as the suspect in the incident

**tailgating:** to gain access by slipping in behind a person cleared to enter

**tamper-evident seals:** seals that break and show tampering if a thief attempts to open packaging or item compartments

**territoriality:** in the context of CPTED, territoriality includes design elements and behaviours employed to communicate ownership and control over a space as a means of deterring illegal and nuisance activities in that space

**tort:** harm caused to a person or property for which the law requires a civil remedy

**trespass:** unlawful interference with the person, property, or rights of another

**vassal:** person who exchanged labour and loyalty for protection in feudal society

**victim statement:** a written account or the transcript of a verbal account of an incident in the victim's words and from the victim's perspective

**witness:** person who gives evidence while under oath

**witness statement:** a written account or the transcript of a verbal account of an incident in the words of and from the perspective of an individual who observed the incident

**Workplace Hazardous Materials Information System (WHMIS):** a regulatory scheme that classifies hazards and communicates information about them and about means of reducing risk

# Index

10 codes, 181

## A

access control
    biometrics, 281–282
    crowd control, 50–51
    electronic, 278–280
    home security, 282
    ID systems, 47–49
    natural, CPTED, 240
    need for, 45
    technologies, 278–280
    traffic control, 51–58
    visitor control, 45–46
*Accessibility for Ontarians with Disabilities Act, 2005* (AODA), 192, 193
administrative tribunal, 127
admissibility of evidence, 255
ADVOKATE (acronym), 80
agents, 6
aide-memoire, 66
alarm systems
    elements of, 291–292
    fire alarm, 291
    intrusion alarm, 291
    monitoring, 292
    parts of, 291–292
    primitive, 6
    special capabilities, 291
    special-use alarm, 291
alcohol, individuals under the influence, 59
ALGEE framework, 230
appeal, 28, 128–129
applicant, 127
arrest, 146
    citizen's arrest, 148–149, 150
    defined, 148
    request to vacate premises, 147–148
    rules under the *Trespass to Property Act*, 148
    without warrant, 148–149
assault, 151
associations, for security professionals, 10

## B

battery, 151
bearing, 164
*Bill of Rights*, 188
biometric access control, 281–282
biometrics, 281–282
bitcoin, 227
Black Lives Matter, 195–196
Bluetooth lock, 280
bodyguards, 29
bomb threat, 110
    checklist, 114
    coordination, external response team, 115
    evacuation, 113
    response plan, 111
    response procedure, 112–115
    search procedure, 113–114
bona fide job requirement, 193
burden of proof, 132

## C

CACP, *see* Canadian Association of Chiefs of Police
*Canada Evidence Act*, 130–131
*Canada Occupational Health and Safety Regulations*, 93
Canadian Association of Chiefs of Police (CACP), 206, 208
Canadian Border Services Agency, 191
*Canadian Charter of Rights and Freedoms*, 132–133, 149, 150, 198
*Canadian Human Rights Act* (CHRA), 191
Canadian Human Rights Commission (CHRC), 191
Canadian Human Rights Tribunal (CHRT), 191
Canadian Nuclear Safety Commission (CNSC), 13
Canadian Security Intelligence Service (CSIS), 191
*Canadian Security* magazine, 10
Canadian Society for Industrial Security (CSIS), 10
carding, 197
card-operated locks, 279
case law, 149
cellular lock, 280
ChecknInk II, 265, 266

circumstantial evidence, 253
citizen's arrest, 148–149
civil court, 127–128
civil wrong, 145
CNSC, *see* Canadian Nuclear Safety Commission
cocooning, 12
code-operated locks, 278
colour of right, 145
common law, 132–133, 149
communication, 164–168
computer-generated ID cards, 48–49
conflict, diversity and, 195–197
contaminating the evidence, 119
continuity of evidence possession, 258
continuity of possession, 258
continuous assessment process, 209
control room, patrols, 42
*Controlled Drugs and Substances Act*, 25
conversion, 151
court
    appeal procedures, 128–129
    Canadian system, 124
    civil procedures, 127–128
    criminal procedure, 125–126
    provincial offenses, 127
    tribunals, 128
CPTED
    application of principles, 237
    concepts of, 236–237
    defined, 236
    definition of space, 237–238
    design of space, 238
    designation of space, 237
    drive-through application, 246
    fencing, 239–240
    key strategies of, 239–240
    mall application, 245–246
    natural access control, 240
    natural surveillance, 239
    parking application, 246–247
    principles, major, 238–244
    storefront application, 244–245
    target hardening, 240
    territoriality, 239–240
credibility of a threat, 113
*Criminal Code*, 8, 10, 25, 57, 132, 148, 150, 207, 213, 272
criminal offence, 145
*Criminal Records Act*, 25, 26
criminal trial, 125–126
crowd control, 50–51
Crown attorney, 125, 126
CSIS, *see* Canadian Society for Industrial Security or Canadian Security Intelligence Service
cybersecurity, 226–227

# D

damages, 127
de-escalate, 209–210
defamation, 151
defence, 132
defence counsel, 125, 126
defendant, 127
detain, 147
direct evidence, 253
disc tumbler locks, 287
discretion, 26
distress, person in, 214–215
diversity
    conflict and, 195–197
    *Private Security and Investigative Services Act* (PSISA), 194–195
documentary evidence, 254
domestic violence, 94
"door person," 23

# E

electronic access control
    considerations, 278
    types of, 278–280
electronic article surveillance, 265, 266
electronic card reader, 222
emergency response
    bomb threat, 110–115
    evidence protection, 119
    explosive devices, 115–116
    fire emergencies, 108–110
    weapon or shooter situations, 116–119
employment laws, 157–160
*Employment Standards Act*, (ESA), 18, 159–160
ePassports, 224
evidence
    admissibility, 255
    *Canada Evidence Act*, 130–131
    *Canadian Charter of Rights and Freedom*, and, 132–133
    circumstantial, 253
    collection, 119
    common law, 132–133
    contamination of, 119, 256
    continuity of, 258
    control of, 256, 258
    *Criminal Code*, and, 132
    expert testimony, 255
    mishandling, consequences of, 258
    Ontario *Evidence Act*, 129–130, 131
    preservation of, 257
    protection, 119, 257
    record-keeping, 258
    securing, 256

security professionals, 133–136
standard of proof, 255
statutes, 129–133
testimony, expert, 255
types of, 253–255
excessive force, 150
excited delirium, 213
expert testimony, 255
explosive devices, 115–116
explosive ordnance disposal authority, 116
express authorization, 52

# F

facial imaging, 281
false imprisonment, 151
feudalism, 4
filing cabinets, security of, 284
finger prints, 282
fire alarm, 291
fire emergency
    evacuation procedures, 109–110
    fire extinguisher use, 109
    fire safety plan, 108, 110
    preparation for, 110
    training requirements, 109
fire-resistant safes, 285
five "Ws," 70–71
form report, 74

# G

general occurrence report, 74

# H

harassment, 193
hate crimes, 195
hazard
    defined, 98
    see also workplace hazards
hearsay evidence, 253
high-risk patrol, 42
high-security composite safes, 285
*Highway Traffic Act*, 53, 57, 152
human environment, 44
Human Rights Tribunal of Ontario (HRTO), 192, 193, 194, 199
hybrid offence, 125

# I

identity control systems
    elements of good system, 47–48
    ID card standards, 47–48
    temporary ID cards, 49
    types of ID cards, 48–49
    visitor passes, 46
identity theft, 281
immigration
    classes of, 189
    *Immigration Act*, 188
    international students, 190
    internationally displaced persons, 189
    multiculturalism, and, 188
    refugees, 189–190
    source countries of, 189
implied authorization, 52
improvised explosive device (IED), 115, 226
indictable offence, 125
Indigenous people, 197–198
insurance considerations, 283
intermediate (less-lethal) weapons, 210
International Day to Eliminate Racism and Discrimination, 196
internationally displaced persons, 189
interviewing
    audio use, 177
    cognitive style, 172–173
    common problems, 169–170
    deception during, 174–175
    legality of, 170
    listening, 173–174
    note taking, 176–177
    parataxic distortion, 169–170
    pattern of thought, 168–169
    preparation for, 176, 177
    skill development, 173
    traditional style, 171–172
    video use, 177
    voluntary, 170, 171
intrusion alarm, 291
investigations
    conducting, 252
    rules of evidence, 253–255
    types of, 252
    vehicle accident, 252–253

# J

Joint Health and Safety Committee (JHSC), 88–91
judge, 125, 126
judicial notice, 130
jurisprudence, 147
jury, 125, 126

# K

key-operated locks, 279
keys, control of, 290–291
*Kostyra v Victoria Police Department*, 27

## L

*Labour Relations Act* (LRA), 158–159
laminated ID cards, simple, 48
laws of evidence, 129–133
lethal force, 210
lever locks, 287
liability management, 224–225
libel, 151
light-sensitive badges, 48
liquid nitrogen, 283
*Liquor Licence Act* (LLA)
    civil liability, 156
    compliance by consumers, 154
    compliance by providers, 154
    defined, 153
    public intoxication, 155–156
    removal of offenders, 155
    rule enforcement, 154
locks
    card-operated, 279
    code-operated, 278
    control of keys, 290–291
    disc tumbler locks, 287
    evaluation of, 288
    key-operated, 279
    lever, 287
    lock breaking, 283
    mechanical, 287, 289–290
    modern pin tumbler locks, 287
    pick-resistant features, 288–289
    smart, 280, 282
    tubular cylinder locks, 287–288
    types of, 286–287
    warded, 287
    wi-fi enabled, 280

## M

Magna Carta, 5
magnetic-coded card locks, 279
malicious prosecution, 151
marauding terrorist firearms/weapons attack (MTFA/MTWA), 226
mechanical locks, 287, 289–290
mental health first aid, 229–230
minor accident, 252
modern pin tumbler locks, 287
MTFA/MTWA, 226

## N

National Use of Force Framework
    compliance techniques, 210
    continuous assessment process, 209
    de-escalate, 209–210
    defined, 206
    diagram, 208
    lethal force, 210, 211
    person in authority, 209
    person in distress, 209–210
    response to behaviour, 210
    step-by-step process, 209, 211–213
    weapons, use of, 210, 215
natural access control, 240
natural surveillance, 239
negligence, 151
NFC lock, 280
night watchmen, 6
non-verbal communication, 164
North West Mounted Police, 7; see also RCMP
note taking
    abbreviations, use of, 70
    five "Ws," 70–71
    notebook purpose, 66–67
    notebook safekeeping, 68
    notebook specifications, 67
    prioritizing information, 68–71
    rules, 68–69
    vehicle descriptions, 71
NWMP, *see* North West Mounted Police *and* RCMP

## O

observational skills, 40–41
*Occupational Health and Safety Act*, 53, 93
Ontario *Evidence Act*, 129–130, 131
Ontario *Freedom of Information and Protection of Privacy Act* (FIPPA), 142
Ontario *Human Rights Code*, 191–192, 193, 194
Ontario Human Rights Commission (OHRC), 191–192
*Ontario Occupational Health and Safety Act* (OHSA)
    due diligence program, 87
    employer duties, 92
    employer responsibilities, 90–91
    Health and Safety Representatives, 88
    Joint Health and Safety Committee (JHSC), 88–91
    safety supervisor, 92
    structure, 87–88
    worker duties, 92–93
    Workplace Hazardous Materials Information System (WHMIS), 86
optical-coded card locks, 279
oral testimony, 130
Orlando Nightclub shooting, 196

## P

parataxic distortion, 169–170
para-verbal communication, 164
parochial police, 6

patrol procedures
    communications, 42
    control room, 42
    foot patrols, 42–43
    functions, 41–42
    heightened recall, 44
    high-risk patrol, 42
    human environment, 44
    mobile patrols, 43
    objectives, 41
    physical environment, 43–44
    planning, 41
    routes, 42
    sensor use, 223
    shift handover, 58
    silent hours, 42
    site coordination, 42
    situational awareness, 43–45
    substance abuse, 59–60
    survival mental state, 44
    switching on and off, 45
PBIED, 226
person in distress, 209
person of authority, 209
*Personal Health Information Protection Act* (PHIPA), 142
*Personal Information Protection and Electronic Documents Act* (PIPED), 142–144
person-borne improvised explosive device (PBIED), 226
phonetic alphabet, 182–183
physical environment, 43–44
physical evidence, 253–254
pick-resistant features, locks, 288–289
PIPED Act, *see Personal Information Protection and Electronic Documents Act*
PISGA, *see Private Investigators and Security Guards Act*
plaintiff, 127
plastique, 283
police
    development in Europe, 6
    parochial, 6
    versus private security, 8, 9–10
positional asphyxia, 213
post-traumatic stress disorder (PTSD), 229
primary dimensions, 188
primary evidence, 254
*Private Investigators and Security Guards Act* (PISGA), 18–19
*Private Security and Investigative Services Act* (PSISA)
    administration of, 24, 28–29, 30
    application of, 21–23
    *Code of Conduct*, 31–33, 194
    code of conduct portion, 31–33
    complaints, 28
    diversity and, 194–195
    general duties, 28–29
    general offense provision, 29
    interpretation of, 21
    investigations, 28
    licensing, 24–28
    need for, 18–19
    overview of, 8, 19–20
    prohibitions of, 24
    regulations under, 30–33
    standards of practice, 28–29
    structure, 20–30
    testing, 31
    traffic control and, 53
    training under, 31
    weapons, use of, 215
*Provincial Offences Act* (POA), 142, 151–153
provincial offense, 25
proximity card locks, 279
PTSD, 229
public intoxication, 155–156

# R

racial profiling, 199–200
radio
    10 codes, 181
    code red, 182
    dead zones, 182
    etiquette, 180–181
    inspection, 180
    language, 182
    hand-held, 180
    parts of, 179–180
    phonetic alphabet, 182–183
    procedures, 179–183
    regulation of use, 181
    safe use of, 180
    security protocol, 181–182
    standard 10 codes, 181
    storage, 180
RCMP, 7, 194, 198
reclamation, 197
record suspension, 25
refugees, 189–190
regulation, 20
reports
    basic skills required, 72
    facts, inferences, opinions, differences, 72–73
    five "Cs," 78
    form reports, 74
    general occurrence reports, 74
    note taking, 66–71
    principles, effective report writing, 77–78
    specialized reports, 74–76
    supplemental reports, 76
    suspect statements, 79
    traffic report, 75–88

reports (cont.)
    types of, 73–77
    victim statements, 79
    witness statements, 79, 80
*Residential Tenancies Act*, 156–157
respondent, 127
retail security
    CheckInk II, 265
    closed-circuit television cameras, 266
    disposable surveillance tags and strips, 264
    electronic article surveillance, 265, 266
    employee training, 271–272
    fitting room policy, 270
    human surveillance, 265–266
    merchandise display, 268–269
    minimal force norm, 211
    mirrors, 267–268
    packaging, 269
    principal sources of loss, 262–263
    refund procedures, 270–271
    retail crime, nature of, 263–265
    shoplifting, 265
    shrinkage, 262, 264
    signs, 267
    special challenges, 263
    store layout, 269–270
    tamper-evident seals, 265
    technology, 264–265
    undercover security, 271–272
retinal scanning, 282
return fraud, 263
RFID tag, 264–265
ride shotgun, 6
risk management, 224–225
Royal Canadian Mounted Police (RCMP), 7, 194, 198

## S

safe-keeping needs, 283
safes
    fire-resistant safes, 285
    high-security composite safes, 285
    industry standards, 285–286
    insurance considerations, 283
    selection of, 286
search
    authority, 149
    with consent, 150
    without consent, 150
secondary dimensions, 188
secondary evidence, 254
security breach, 252

security legislation, 18–19
security profession
    *Accessibility for Ontarians with Disabilities Act*, 2005 (AODA), 193
    ALGEE framework, 230
    attitude, 164–165
    bearing, 164–165
    bona fide job requirement, 193
    carding, 197
    certification, 228
    civil actions against, 151
    *Code of Conduct*, 194
    communication skills, 164–166
    customer-service approach, 166
    development in Canada, 7–11, 18–19
    development in Europe, 6
    development in United States, 6–7
    diversity and, 194–197
    education, 228
    evidence of, 133–136
    first aid training, 228–229
    growth of, 11–12
    hate crimes, 197
    health, 228–229
    human rights legislation implications, 192–194
    legal authority of, 8–9
    liability management, 224–225
    mental health first aid, 229–230
    Middle Ages, 4–5
    observational skills, 40–41
    occupations within, 10–11
    personal appearance, 164–165
    post-traumatic stress disorder (PTSD), 229
    privacy safeguards, 143–144
    professional associations for, 10
    professional certification, 10
    professionalism, 230
    versus public police, 8, 9–10
    public relations considerations, 151
    reason for growth, 11–13
    risk management, 224–225
    technology on the job, 222–224
    terrorism, 225–226
    training requirements, 228
    types of security providers, 10–11
    uniform requirements, 29, 231
    verbal communication, 167–168
security technology, 5, 11
self-defence, 151
sensitivity training
    carding, 197
    conflict, 195–197
    diversity, 188, 195–197

hate crimes, 197
human rights legislation implications, 192–194
immigration, 188–190
Indigenous people, 197–198
legislation, 191–194
multiculturalism, 188
racial profiling, 199–200
serious accident, 253
serious bodily harm, 213
shoplifting, 265
shrinkage, 262, 264
silent hours, 42
situational awareness
    heightened recall, 44
    human environment, 44
    level of concentration, 45
    physical environment, 43
    survival mental state, 44
slander, 151
smart locks, 280, 282
soft and hard compliance techniques, 210
solenoid, 279
specialized report, 74
special-use alarm, 291
specificity of a threat, 113
St. John Ambulance Emergency First Aid Certificate, 31
standard of proof, 255
statement taking
    ADVOKATE (acronym), 80
    professional statements, 79–80
    suspect statements, 79
    victim statements, 79
    witness statements, 79
statute, 20
statue law, 149
*Statue of Winchester*, 5
substance abuse, individuals under the influence, 59–60
summary conviction offence, 125
supplemental report, 76
surveillance, disposable tags and strips, 264
suspect statements, 79

# T

tailgating, 278
target hardening, 240
technology
    access control, 278–280
    bitcoin, 227
    CheckInk II, 266
    cybersecurity, 226–227
    disposable surveillance tags and strips, 264
    electronic article surveillance, 265, 266
    electronic card reader, 222
    ePassports, 224
    on the job, 222–224
    patrol sensors, 223
    personal devices, 223
    RFID tag, 264–265
    tamper-evident seals, 265
    video surveillance, 223
tenant evictions, 157
terrorism, 13, 225–226
threat
    credibility, 113
    specificity, 113
time-sensitive badges, 48
Toronto Gay Pride Parade, 195–196
tort, 144
traffic control
    accidents, 57–58
    apparel and equipment, 53–54
    authority over, 52
    emergency vehicles, 57
    enforcement of rules, 57
    hand signals, 54–56
    parking, 56–57
    private property and, 52
    traffic report, 75–77
trespass, 145
*Trespass to Property Act*, 57, 142, 207
    arrest rules under, 146–147
    definitions, 144–145
    prohibiting entry under, 145–146
    request to vacate premises, 147–148
tribunals, 128
tubular cylinder locks, 287–288
*Turner v Canadian Border Services Agency*, 191

# U

uniform requirements, 29, 165
use of force
    avoidance of, 207
    compliance techniques, 210
    consequences of, 213
    intermediate weapons, 210
    justification, 206
    lethal force, 210, 211
    nuclear power plants, 210
    policies, 206–208
    retail security, and, 211
    step-by-step process, 209, 211–213
    subject distress, 214–215

## V

vassal, 5
verbal communication, 164
victim statements, 79
video surveillance, 223
visitor control
vulnerabilities of ID cards, 47

## W

warded locks, 287
weapon emergency situations
    law enforcement arrival, 118–119
    security response, 117–118
    training requirements, 116–117
weapons, National Use of Force Framework, and, 215
WHMIS, see Workplace Hazardous Materials Information System (WHMIS)
Wiegand-effect card locks, 279
wi-fi enabled locks, 280
witness
    criminal trial, 126
    defined, 124
    evidence, 253
    statements, 79
workplace accident investigation
    checklist, 98
    domestic violence, 94
    pitfalls, 98
    procedures, 95–98
    purpose of, 93–94
    reporting requirements, 93
Workplace Hazardous Materials Information System (WHMIS), 86
    framework, 86–87
    GHS pictograms, 101–102
    hazardous materials classes, 100–102
    Safety Data Sheet (SDS), 103
    symbols, 101–102
workplace hazards
    administrative controls, 104
    classifications of, 98–99
    energy, 104
    engineering controls, 104
    personal protection equipment, 104–105
    work practices, 104
workplace health and safety representatives, 88

# Credits

## CHAPTER 1

Page 12 (Box): Sources: Trevor Sanders, "Rise of the Rent-A-Cop: Private Security in Canada, 1991-2001," *JustResearch* Issue No. 9 (2003). Research and Statistics Division, Department of Justice Canada. Retrieved from http://www.justice.gc.ca/eng/rp-pr/jr/jr09/jr09.pdf; Surge in private security raises concerns over rights. (2013, January 16). CBC.ca News. Retrieved from http://www.cbc.ca/news/canada/surge-in-private-security-raises-concerns-over-rights-1.1335730.

## CHAPTER 3

Page 54 (Figure 3.1): *Participant's Manual*, Manitoba Security Guard Training Program (2005), p. 13. Manitoba Justice, Copyright © 2005, Province of Manitoba. Used with permission.

Page 55 (Figure 3.2) *Participant's Manual*, Manitoba Security Guard Training Program (2005), p. 14. Manitoba Justice, Copyright © 2005, Province of Manitoba. Used with permission.

Page 56 (Figure 3.3) *Participant's Manual*, Manitoba Security Guard Training Program (2005), p. 15. Manitoba Justice, Copyright © 2005, Province of Manitoba. Used with permission.

## CHAPTER 5

Pages 101–102 (Figure 5.3): *OSH Answer Fact Sheets*, Canadian Centre for Occupational Health & Safety (CCOHS), 2015. Retrieved from http://www.ccohs.ca/oshanswers/chemicals/whmis_ghs/pictograms.html. Reproduced with the permission of CCOHS, 2017.

## CHAPTER 8

Page 146 (Photo): Pixabay.com

## CHAPTER 10

Page 189 (Figure 10.1): Source: "Countries of Canadian Permanent Residents in 2016." *The Canadian Magazine of Immigration*, April 23, 2017. Retrieved from: http://canadaimmigrants.com/canada-immigrants-by-source-country-2016/. Used with permission.

Page 190 (Figure 10.2): Adapted from "Supplementary Information 2017 Immigration Levels Plan." Retrieved from http://www.cic.gc.ca/english/department/media/notices/2016-10-31.asp. Immigration, Refugees and Citizenship Canada.

Page 196 (Figure 10.3): Day Owl/Shutterstock.com.

Page 198 (Figure 10.4): Ossie Michelin/Freelance Journalist and Photographer http://osmich.ca/.

Page 199 (Figure 10.5): Source: *Under suspicion: Research and consultation report on racial profiling in Ontario*, p. 20. Ontario Human Rights Commission, 2017, © Queen's Printer for Ontario, 2017. Used by permission.

Page 200 (Figure 10.6): Source: Under suspicion: Research and consultation report on racial profiling in Ontario, p. 26. Ontario Human Rights Commission, 2017, © Queen's Printer for Ontario, 2017. Used by permission.

## CHAPTER 11

Page 208 (Figure 11.1): Source: The Canadian Association of Chiefs of Police (CACP), *A National Use of Force Framework*, (November 2000). Used with permission.

## CHAPTER 12

Page 222 (Figure 12.1): Photo: Gmlykin/Shutterstock.com.

## CHAPTER 13

Page 238 (Figure 13.1): *Mobility Hub Guidelines*, "Crime Prevention through Environmental Design" (CPTED) (Figure 6.18) http://www.metrolinx.com/mobilityhubs/en/search/crimeprevention.aspx. © Copyright Metrolinx 2017. Courtesy of Metrolinx.

Page 244 (Figure 13.3): Photo: Security Audits (CPTED). Peel Regional Police. © Copyright 2015 Peel Regional Police. Retrieved from https://www.peelpolice.ca/en/crimeprevention/securityaudits.asp.

## CHAPTER 15

Page 262 (Figure 15.1): *Securing the Bottom Line, Canadian Retail Security Survey, 2012*, p. 8. PriceWaterhouseCoopers, LLP for the Retail Council of Canada. Retrieved from https://www.pwc.com/ca/en/retail-consumer/publications/pwc-security-survey-2012-10-29-en.pdf. © Copyright 2012 PriceWaterhouseCoopers, LLP, Ontario. Used with permission.

Page 264 (Figure 15.2): *Securing the Bottom Line, Canadian Retail Security Survey, 2012*, p. 6. PriceWaterhouseCoopers, LLP for the Retail Council of Canada. Retrieved from https://www.pwc.com/ca/en/retail-consumer/publications/pwc-security-survey-2012-10-29-en.pdf. © Copyright 2012 PriceWaterhouseCoopers, LLP, Ontario. Used with permission.

Page 265 (Figure 15.3): Photo: Roger Wissmann/Shutterstock.com.

Page 267 (Figure 15.4): Photo: Ales Veluscek/iStock.com.

## CHAPTER 16

Page 280 (Figure 16.1): Photo: Mikkel Williams/iStock.com.

Page 281 (Figure 16.2): Source: Adapted from David Ruggles, 2002.

Page 282 (Figure 16.3) Photo: Alexander Kirch/Shutterstock.com.